Ninja Girls

3

Hosana Tanaka

Translated and adapted by
Andria Cheng

Lettered by
North Market Street Graphics

D1269674

DEL
REY

Ballantine Books ★ New York

A Del Rey Manga/Kodansha Trade Paperback Original

Ninja Girls volume 3 copyright © 2007 Hosana Tanaka
English translation copyright © 2010 Hosana Tanaka

Published in the United States by Del Rey, an imprint of The Random House Publishing Group, a division of Random House, Inc., New York.

DEL REY is a registered trademark and the Del Rey colophon is a trademark of Random House, Inc.

Publication rights arranged through Kodansha Ltd.

First published in Japan in 2007 by Kodansha Ltd., Tokyo, as *Rappi Rangai*, volume 3.

ISBN 978-0-345-51244-4

Printed in the United States of America

www.delreymanga.com

9 8 7 6 5 4 3 2 1

Translator/adapter: Andria Cheng
Lettering: North Market Street Graphics

CONTENTS

HONORIFICS EXPLAINED

Throughout the Del Rey Manga books, you will find Japanese honorifics left intact in the translations. For those not familiar with how the Japanese use honorifics and, more important, how they differ from American honorifics, we present this brief overview.

Politeness has always been a critical facet of Japanese culture. Ever since the feudal era, when Japan was a highly stratified society, use of honorifics—which can be defined as polite speech that indicates relationship or status—has played an essential role in the Japanese language. When addressing someone in Japanese, an honorific usually takes the form of a suffix attached to one's name (example: "Asuna-san"), is used as a title at the end of one's name, or appears in place of the name itself (example: "Negi-sensei," or simply "Sensei!").

Honorifics can be expressions of respect or endearment. In the context of manga and anime, honorifics give insight into the nature of the relationship between characters. Many English translations leave out these important honorifics and therefore distort the feel of the original Japanese. Because Japanese honorifics contain nuances that English honorifics lack, it is our policy at Del Rey not to translate them. Here, instead, is a guide to some of the honorifics you may encounter in Del Rey Manga.

-*san*: This is the most common honorific and is equivalent to Mr., Miss, Ms., or Mrs. It is the all-purpose honorific and can be used in any situation where politeness is required.

-*sama*: This is one level higher than "-san" and is used to confer great respect.

-*dono*: This comes from the word "tono," which means "lord." It is an even higher level than "-sama" and confers utmost respect.

-*kun*: This suffix is used at the end of boys' names to express familiarity or endearment. It is also sometimes used by men among friends, or when addressing someone younger or of a lower station.

-chan: This is used to express endearment, mostly toward girls. It is also used for little boys, pets, and even among lovers. It gives a sense of childish cuteness.

Bozu: This is an informal way to refer to a boy, similar to the English terms "kid" and "squirt."

Sempai/
Senpai: This title suggests that the addressee is one's senior in a group or organization. It is most often used in a school setting, where underclassmen refer to their upperclassmen as "sempai." It can also be used in the workplace, such as when a newer employee addresses an employee who has seniority in the company.

Kohai: This is the opposite of "sempai" and is used toward underclassmen in school or newcomers in the workplace. It connotes that the addressee is of a lower station.

Sensei: Literally meaning "one who has come before," this title is used for teachers, doctors, or masters of any profession or art.

-[blank]: This is usually forgotten in these lists, but it is perhaps the most significant difference between Japanese and English. The lack of honorific means that the speaker has permission to address the person in a very intimate way. Usually, only family, spouses, or very close friends have this kind of permission. Known as *yobisute*, it can be gratifying when someone who has earned the intimacy starts to call one by one's name without an honorific. But when that intimacy hasn't been earned, it can be very insulting.

3

Ninja Girls

Hosana Tanaka

Ninja Girls
Volume 3

Contents

The Rebellion so far:

The only surviving member of the Katana family, Raizō, set off on a journey with the Katana shinobi:

Kagari, whose special technique is Shintaigō, Kisarabi, a clairvoyant sniper, and Himemaru, a shape-shifting rope-master. Raizō's life is thrown into chaos by these three beautiful yet dangerous shinobi. Their goal is to restore the Katana family.

Recently, they traveled to Sōraku to win over its princess, Hibari, but were caught up in internal strife. They managed to solve those problems, which brought Raizō and Hibari closer together. However, unaccustomed to happiness, Raizō fled! Disheartened by losing their once-in-a-lifetime opportunity, they move on to the next province...

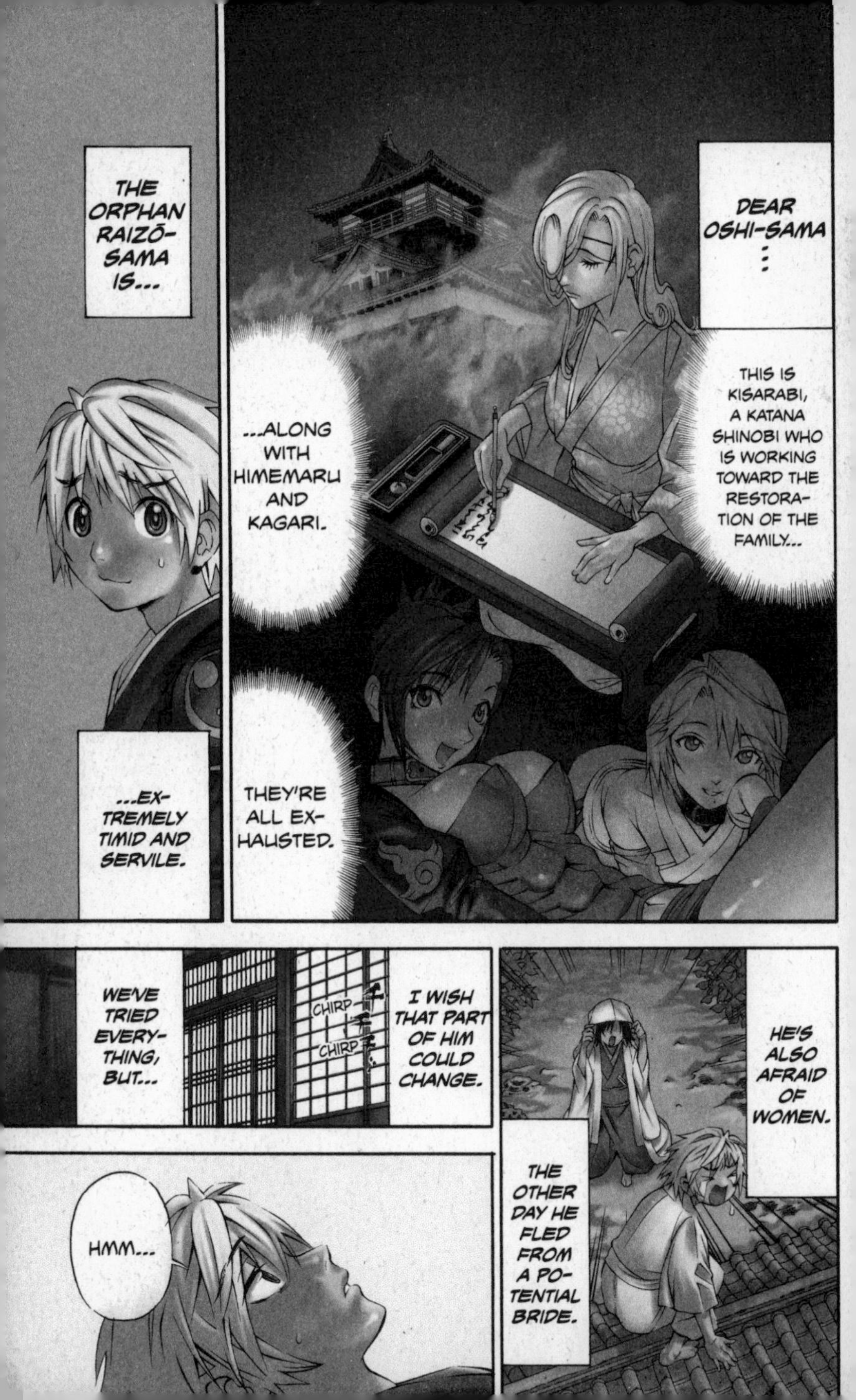
DEAR OSHI-SAMA
...
THIS IS KISARABI, A KATANA SHINOBI WHO IS WORKING TOWARD THE RESTORA-TION OF THE FAMILY...
...ALONG WITH HIMEMARU AND KAGARI.
THEY'RE ALL EX-HAUSTED.
THE ORPHAN RAIZŌ-SAMA IS...
...EX-TREMELY TIMID AND SERVILE.
HE'S ALSO AFRAID OF WOMEN.
THE OTHER DAY HE FLED FROM A PO-TENTIAL BRIDE.
I WISH THAT PART OF HIM COULD CHANGE.
CHIRP
CHIRP
WE'VE TRIED EVERY-THING, BUT...
HMM...

12 Onikiri Rebellion

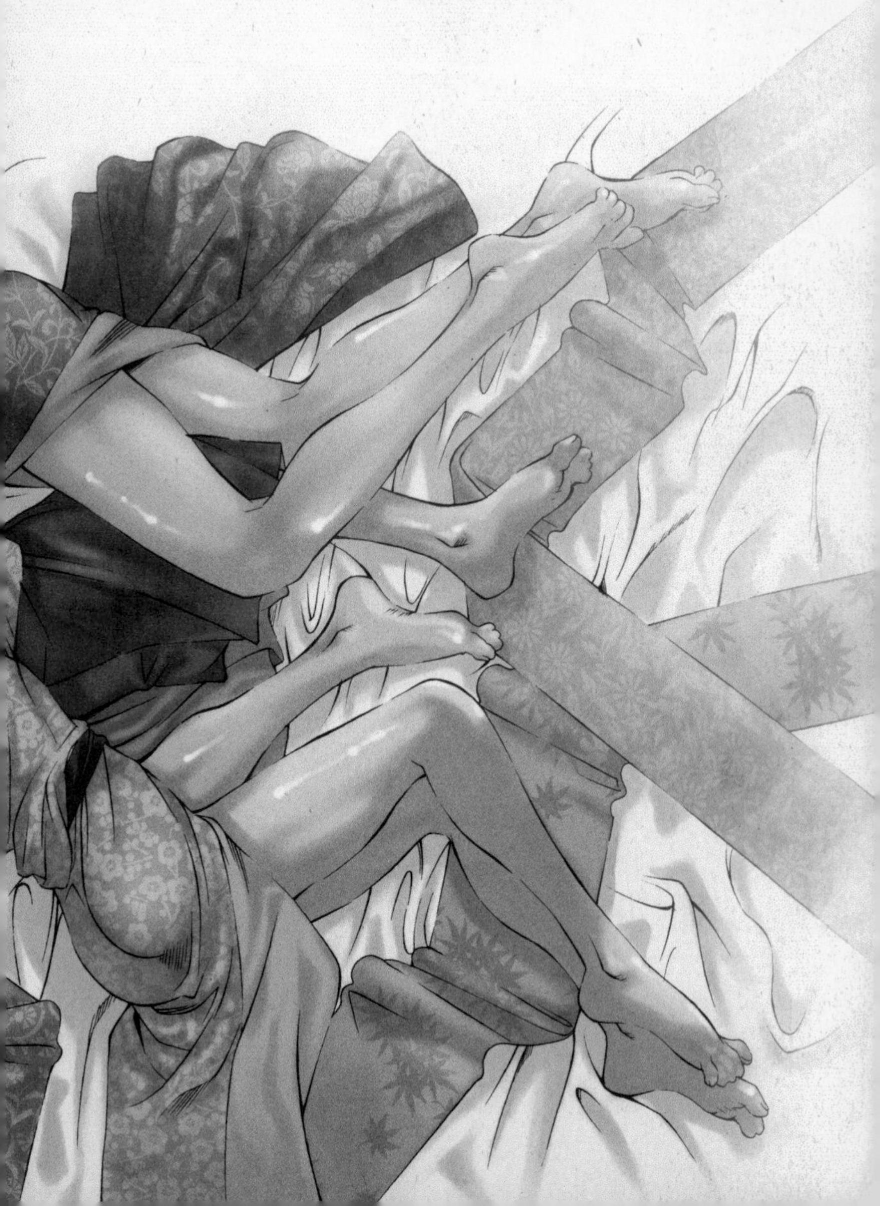

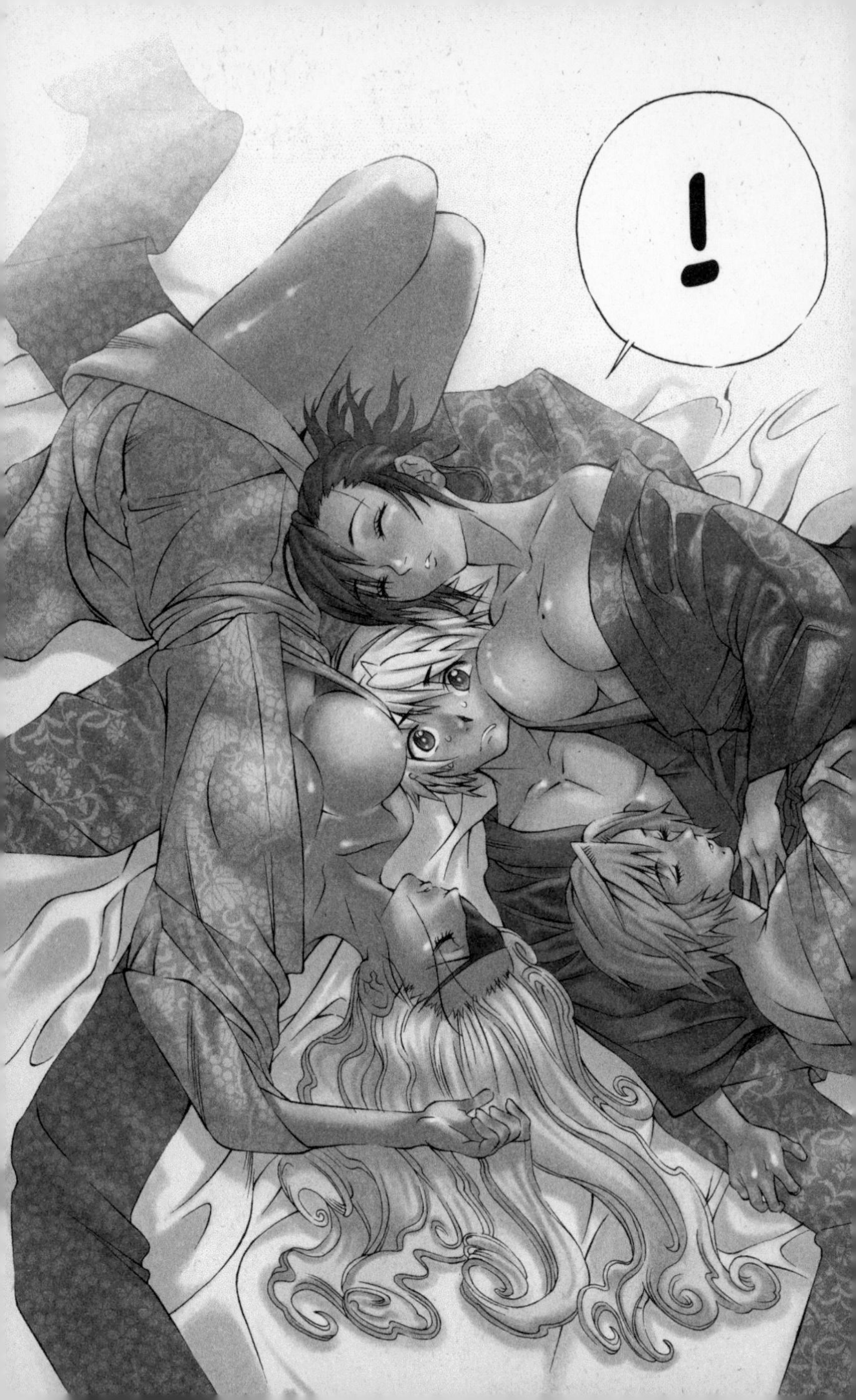
!

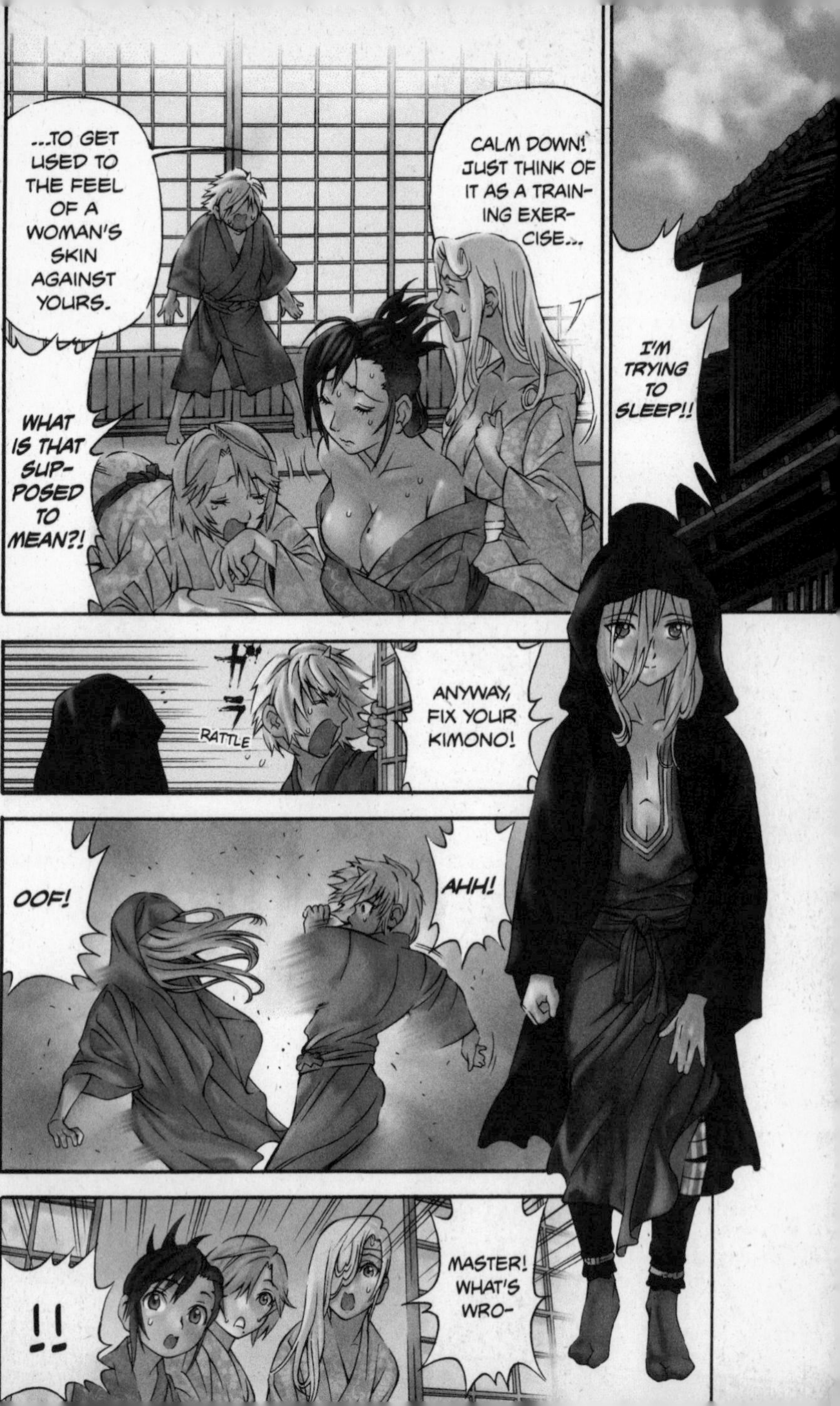
I'M TRYING TO SLEEP!!
CALM DOWN! JUST THINK OF IT AS A TRAINING EXERCISE...
...TO GET USED TO THE FEEL OF A WOMAN'S SKIN AGAINST YOURS.
WHAT IS THAT SUPPOSED TO MEAN?!
ANYWAY, FIX YOUR KIMONO!
RATTLE
AHH!
OOF!
MASTER! WHAT'S WRO-
!!

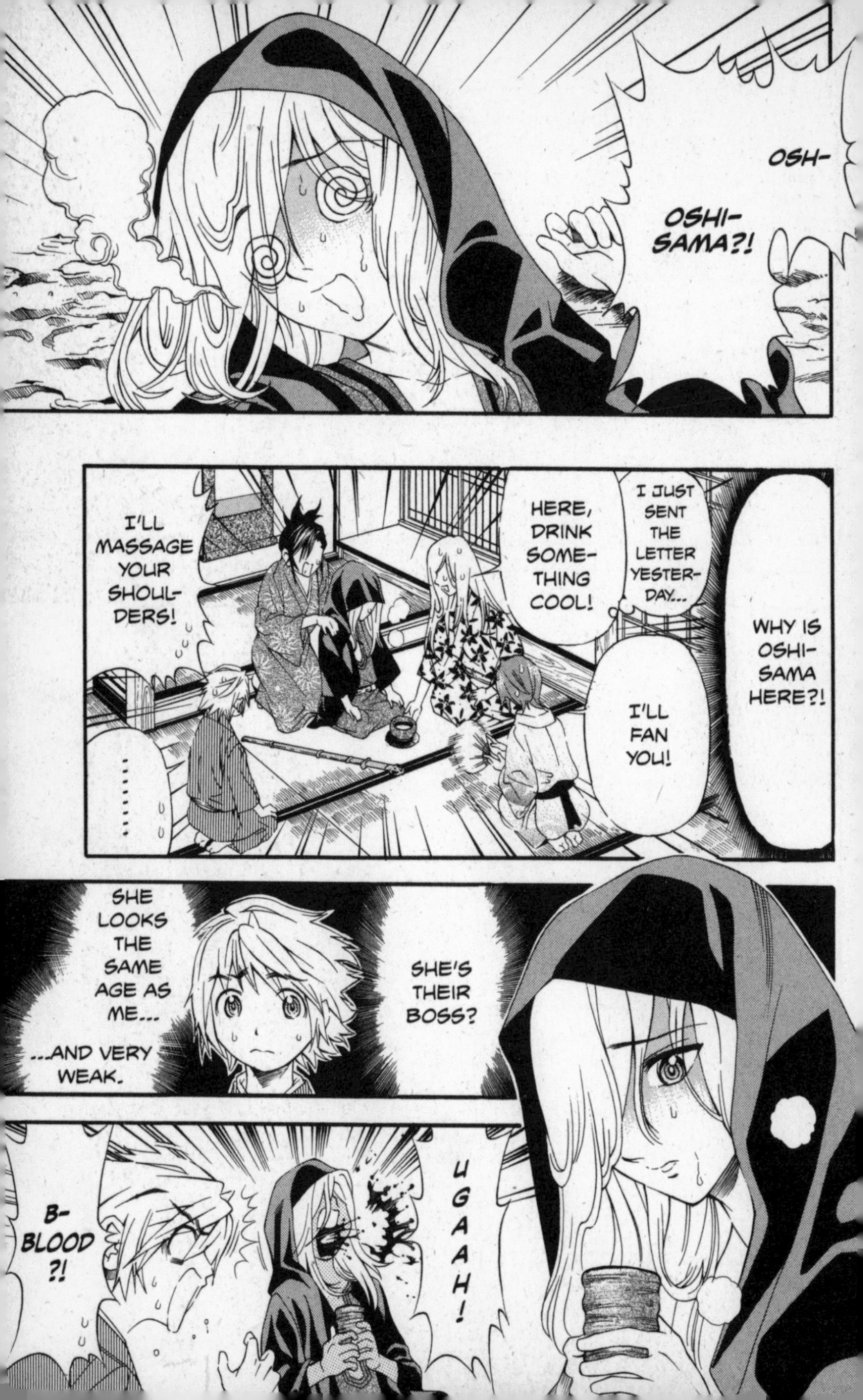
OSH-
OSHI-SAMA?!
WHY IS OSHI-SAMA HERE?!
I JUST SENT THE LETTER YESTERDAY...
HERE, DRINK SOMETHING COOL!
I'LL FAN YOU!
I'LL MASSAGE YOUR SHOULDERS!
......
SHE'S THEIR BOSS?
SHE LOOKS THE SAME AGE AS ME...
...AND VERY WEAK.
UGAAH!
B-BLOOD?!

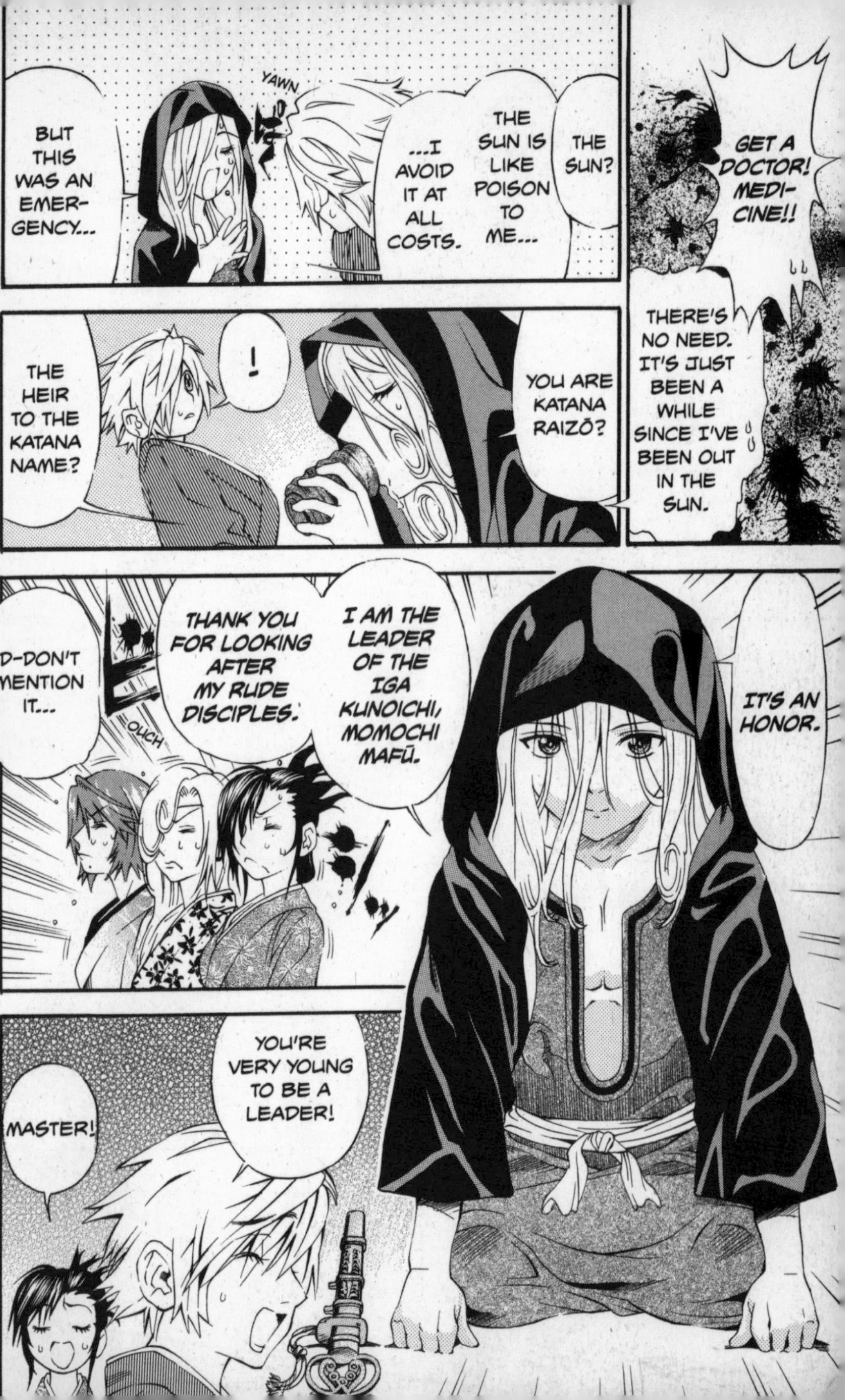
GET A DOCTOR! MEDICINE!!
THERE'S NO NEED. IT'S JUST BEEN A WHILE SINCE I'VE BEEN OUT IN THE SUN.
THE SUN?
THE SUN IS LIKE POISON TO ME...
...I AVOID IT AT ALL COSTS.
YAWN
BUT THIS WAS AN EMERGENCY...
YOU ARE KATANA RAIZŌ?
!
THE HEIR TO THE KATANA NAME?
IT'S AN HONOR.
I AM THE LEADER OF THE IGA KUNOICHI, MOMOCHI MAFŪ.
THANK YOU FOR LOOKING AFTER MY RUDE DISCIPLES.
D-DON'T MENTION IT...
OUCH
YOU'RE VERY YOUNG TO BE A LEADER!
MASTER!

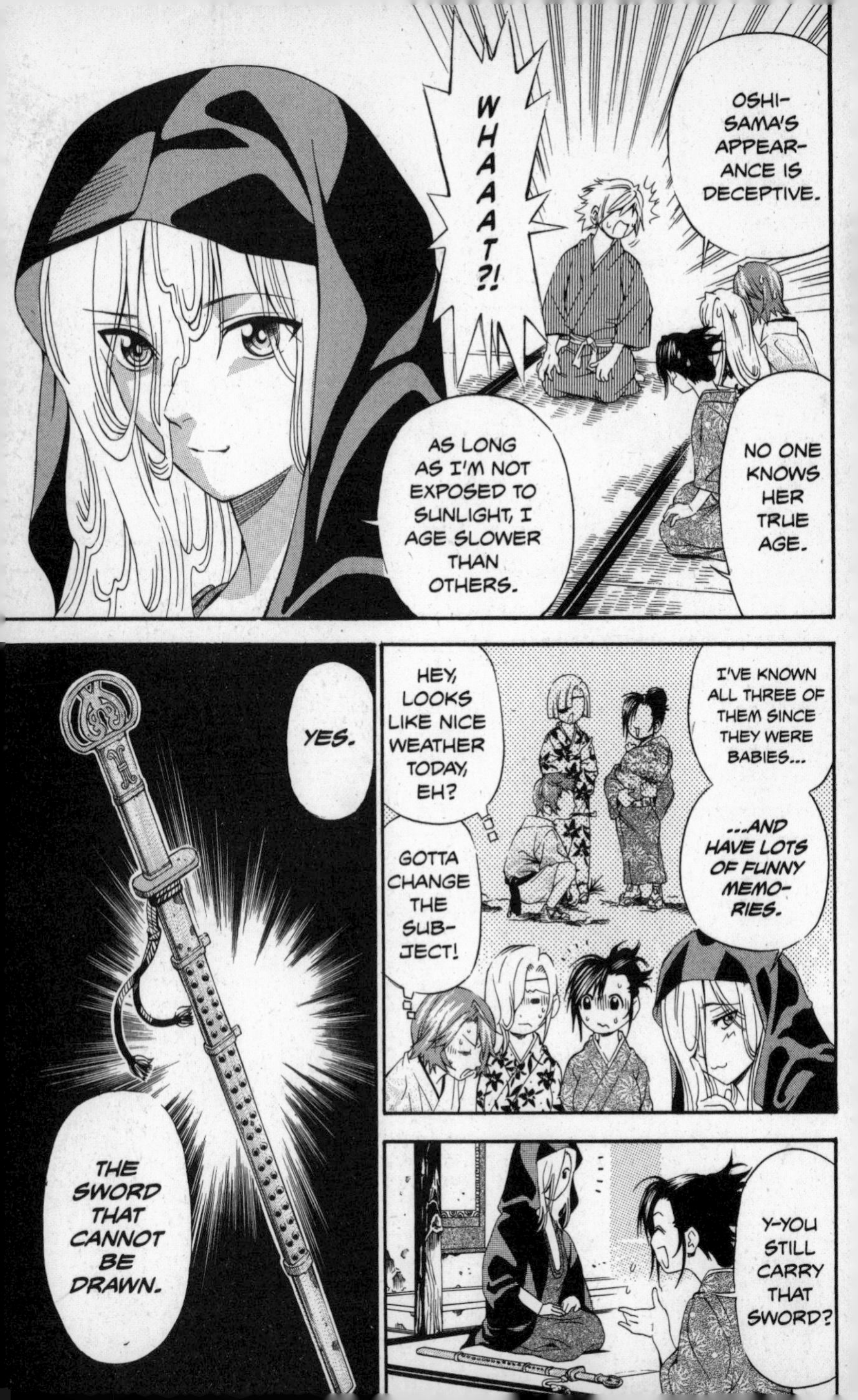
OSHI-SAMA'S APPEARANCE IS DECEPTIVE.
WHAAAAT?!
NO ONE KNOWS HER TRUE AGE.
AS LONG AS I'M NOT EXPOSED TO SUNLIGHT, I AGE SLOWER THAN OTHERS.
I'VE KNOWN ALL THREE OF THEM SINCE THEY WERE BABIES...
...AND HAVE LOTS OF FUNNY MEMORIES.
HEY, LOOKS LIKE NICE WEATHER TODAY, EH?
GOTTA CHANGE THE SUBJECT!
Y-YOU STILL CARRY THAT SWORD?
...
YES.
THE SWORD THAT CANNOT BE DRAWN.

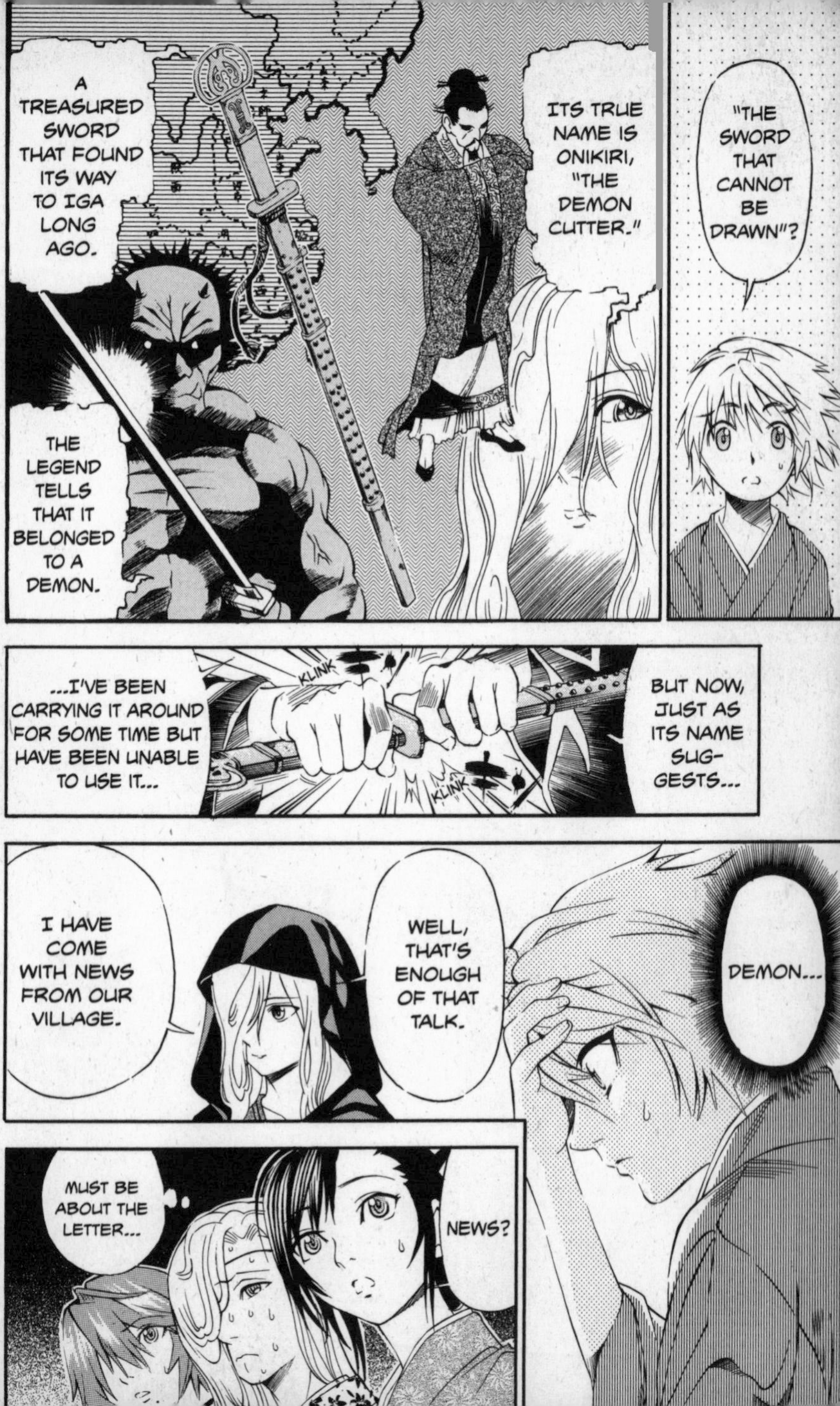
"THE SWORD THAT CANNOT BE DRAWN"?
ITS TRUE NAME IS ONIKIRI, "THE DEMON CUTTER."
A TREASURED SWORD THAT FOUND ITS WAY TO IGA LONG AGO.
THE LEGEND TELLS THAT IT BELONGED TO A DEMON.
BUT NOW, JUST AS ITS NAME SUG-GESTS...
KLINK
KLINK
...I'VE BEEN CARRYING IT AROUND FOR SOME TIME BUT HAVE BEEN UNABLE TO USE IT...
DEMON...
WELL, THAT'S ENOUGH OF THAT TALK.
I HAVE COME WITH NEWS FROM OUR VILLAGE.
NEWS?
MUST BE ABOUT THE LETTER...

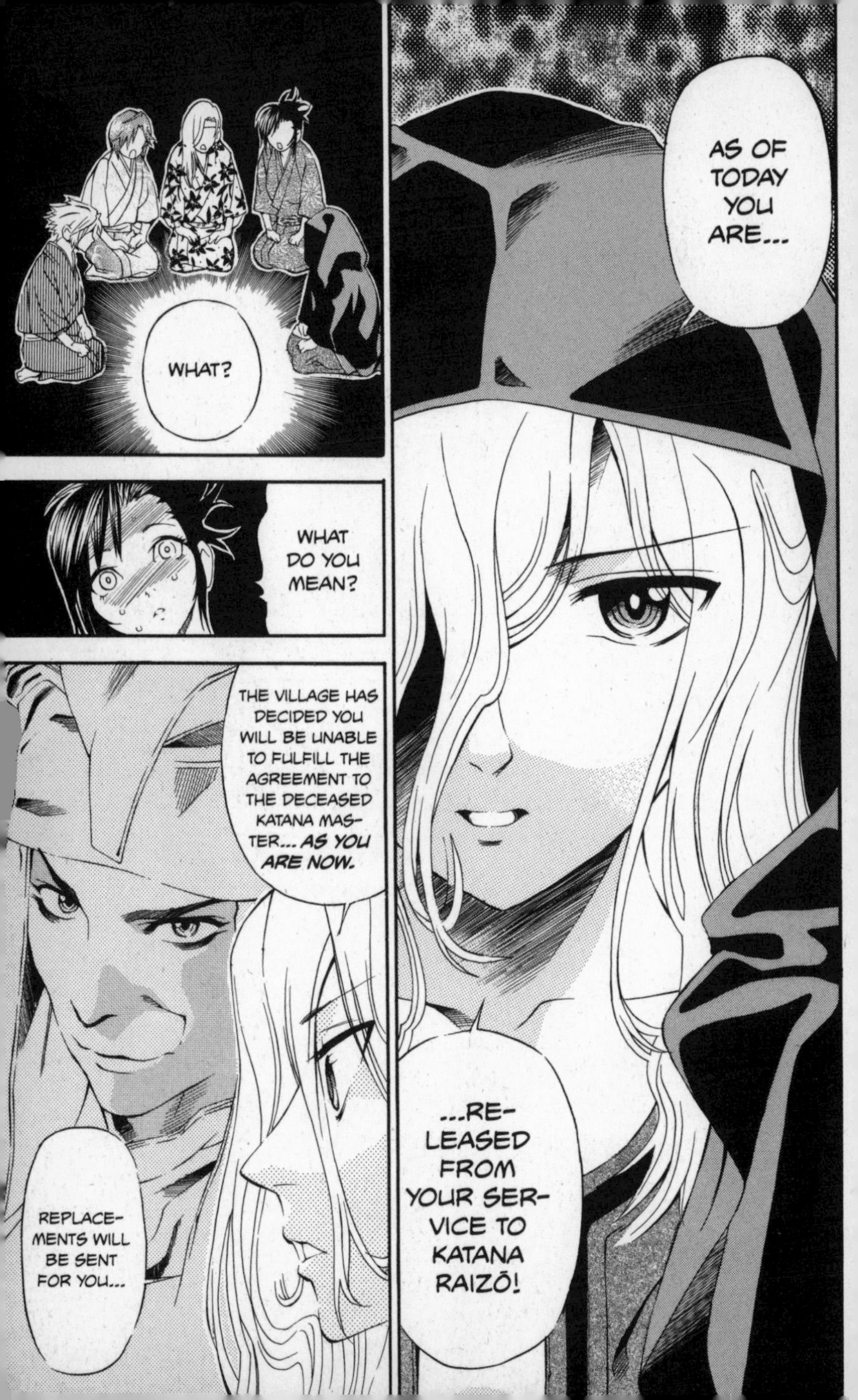
AS OF TODAY YOU ARE...
...RELEASED FROM YOUR SERVICE TO KATANA RAIZŌ!
WHAT?
WHAT DO YOU MEAN?
THE VILLAGE HAS DECIDED YOU WILL BE UNABLE TO FULFILL THE AGREEMENT TO THE DECEASED KATANA MASTER... AS YOU ARE NOW.
REPLACEMENTS WILL BE SENT FOR YOU...

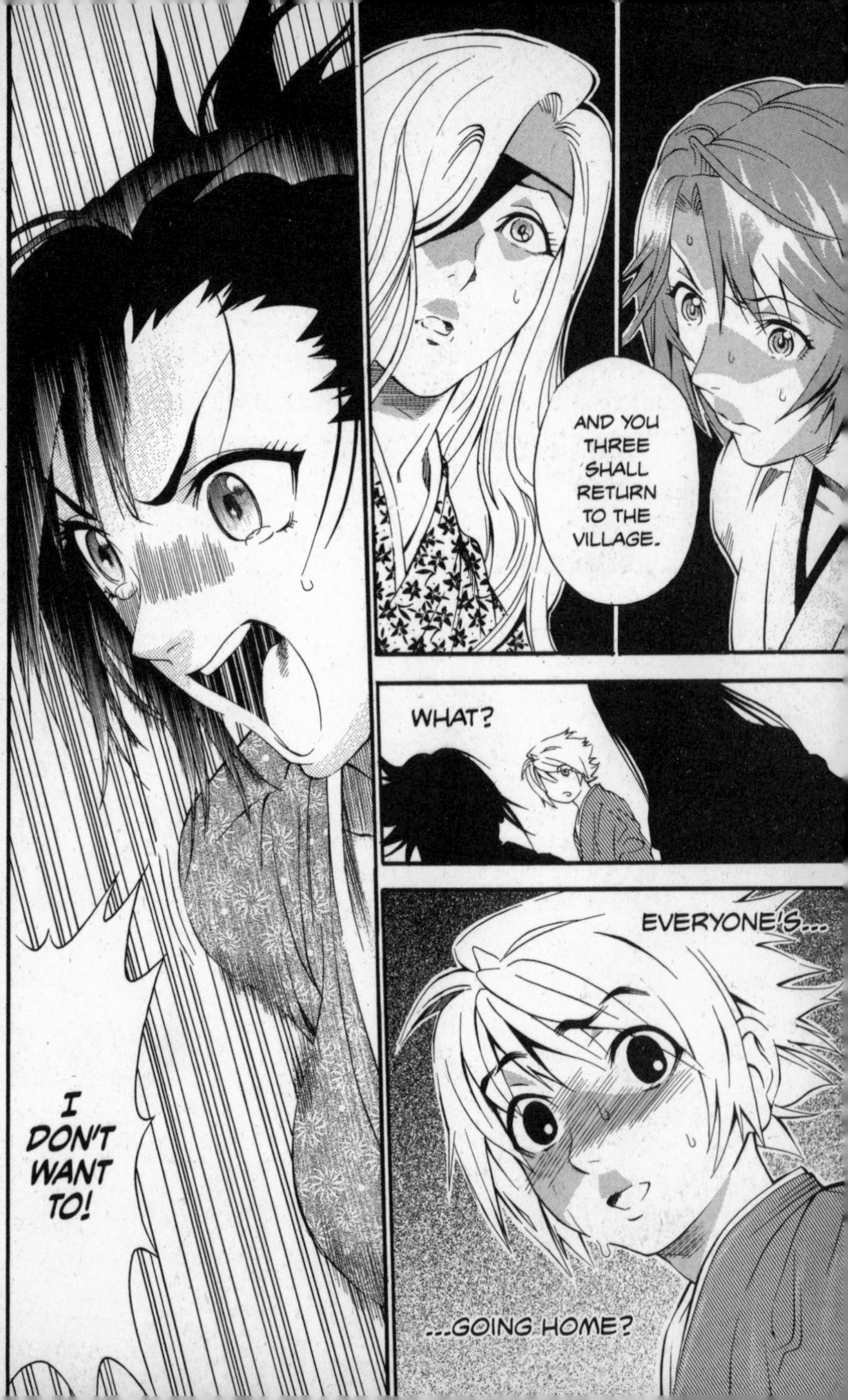
AND YOU THREE SHALL RETURN TO THE VILLAGE.
WHAT?
EVERYONE'S...
...GOING HOME?
I DON'T WANT TO!

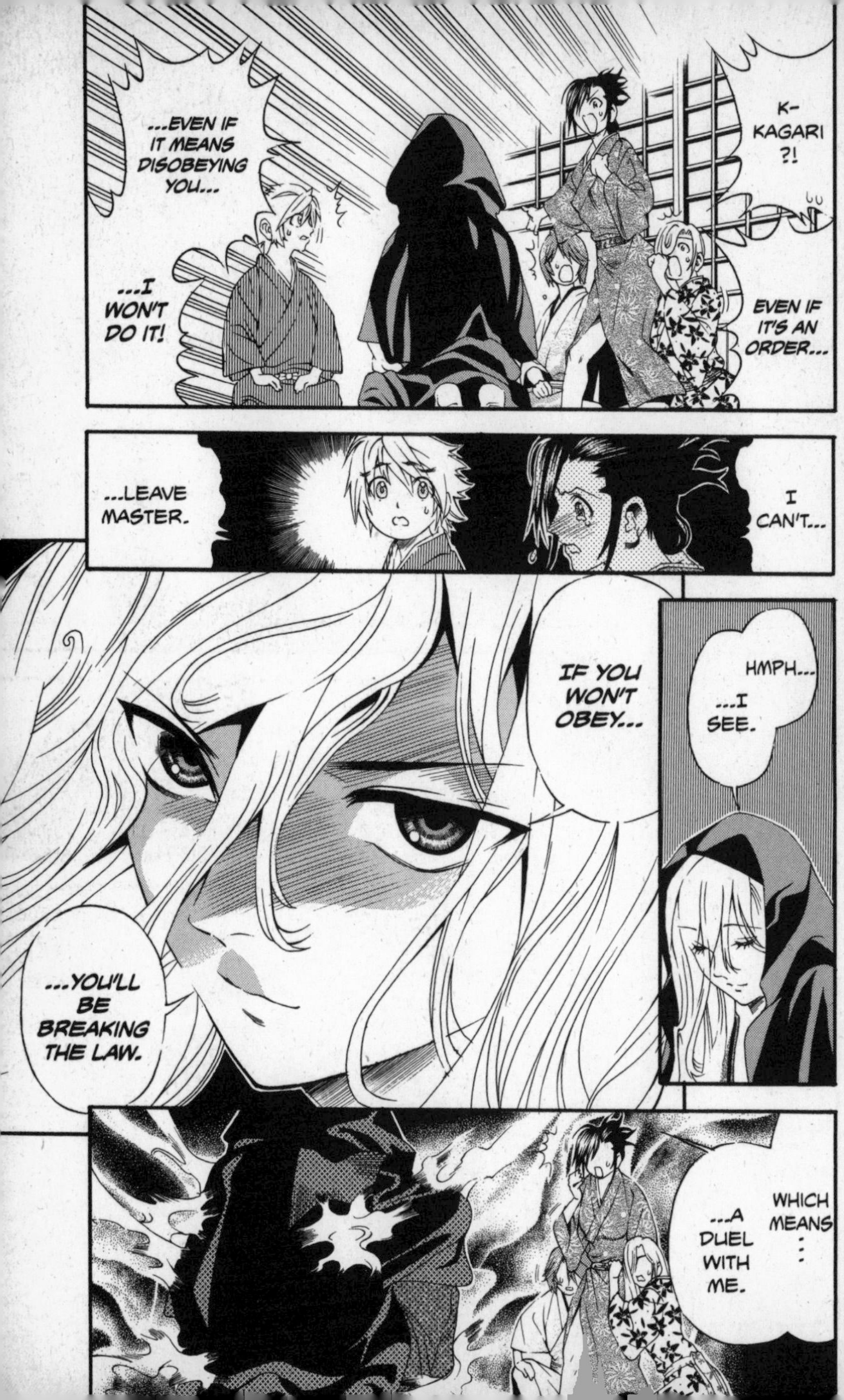
K-KAGARI ?!
EVEN IF IT'S AN ORDER...
...EVEN IF IT MEANS DISOBEYING YOU...
...I WON'T DO IT!
I CAN'T...
...LEAVE MASTER.
HMPH...
...I SEE.
IF YOU WON'T OBEY...
...YOU'LL BE BREAKING THE LAW.
WHICH MEANS...
...A DUEL WITH ME.

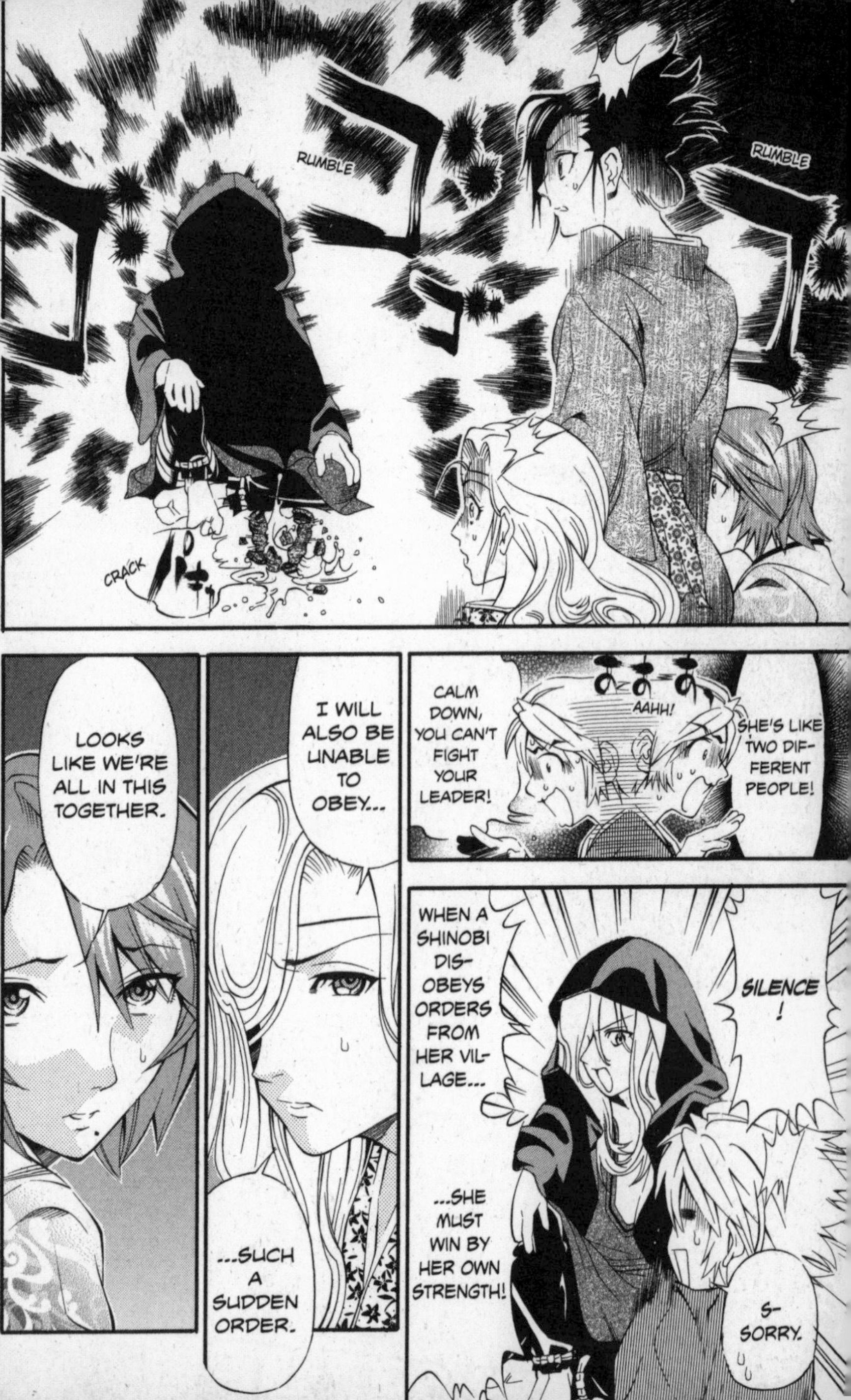
RUMBLE
RUMBLE
CRACK
SHE'S LIKE TWO DIFFERENT PEOPLE!
AAHH!
CALM DOWN, YOU CAN'T FIGHT YOUR LEADER!
SILENCE!
WHEN A SHINOBI DISOBEYS ORDERS FROM HER VILLAGE...
...SHE MUST WIN BY HER OWN STRENGTH!
S-SORRY.
I WILL ALSO BE UNABLE TO OBEY...
...SUCH A SUDDEN ORDER.
LOOKS LIKE WE'RE ALL IN THIS TOGETHER.

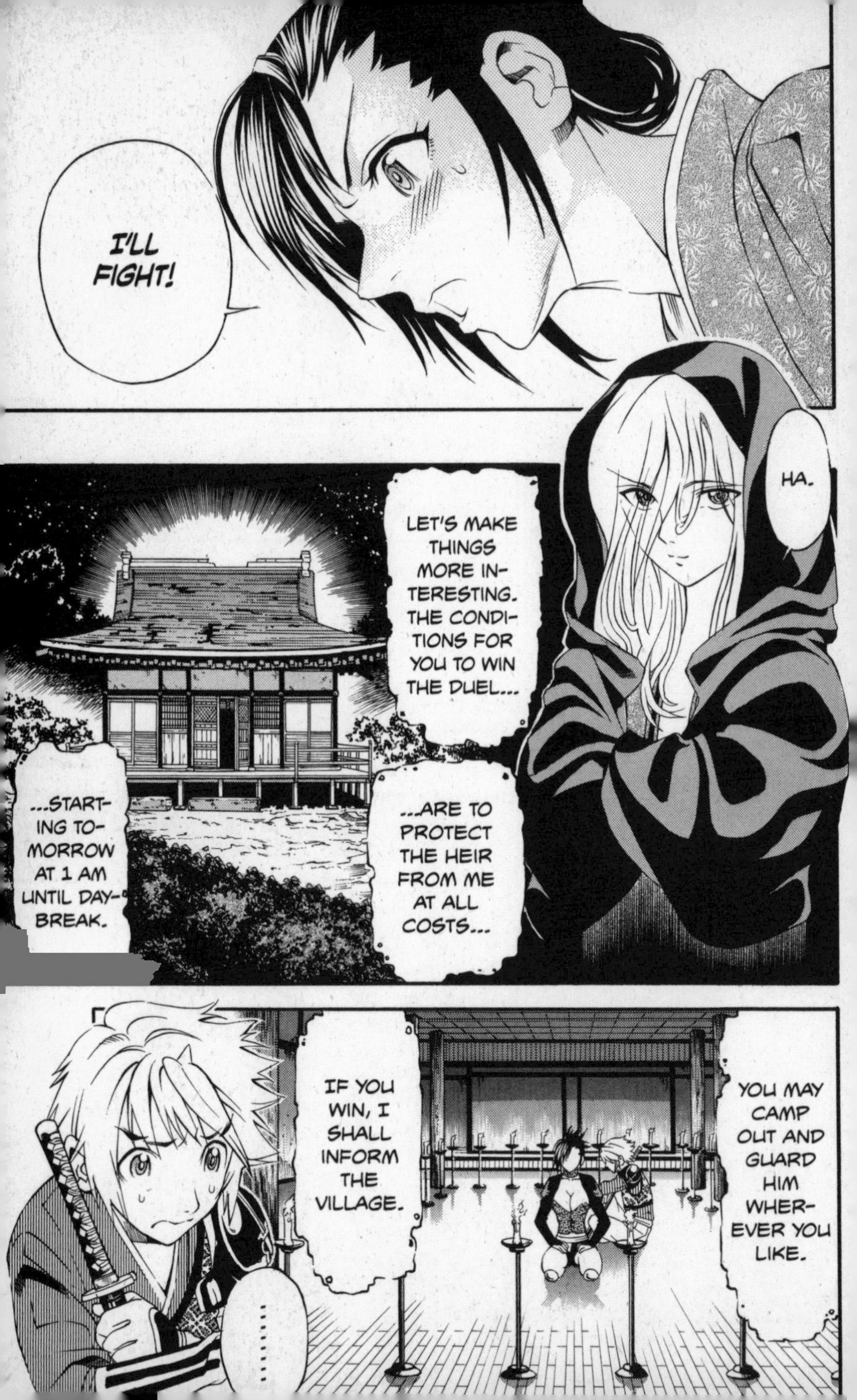
I'LL FIGHT!
HA.
LET'S MAKE THINGS MORE INTERESTING. THE CONDITIONS FOR YOU TO WIN THE DUEL...
...ARE TO PROTECT THE HEIR FROM ME AT ALL COSTS...
...STARTING TOMORROW AT 1 AM UNTIL DAYBREAK.
YOU MAY CAMP OUT AND GUARD HIM WHEREVER YOU LIKE.
IF YOU WIN, I SHALL INFORM THE VILLAGE.
......

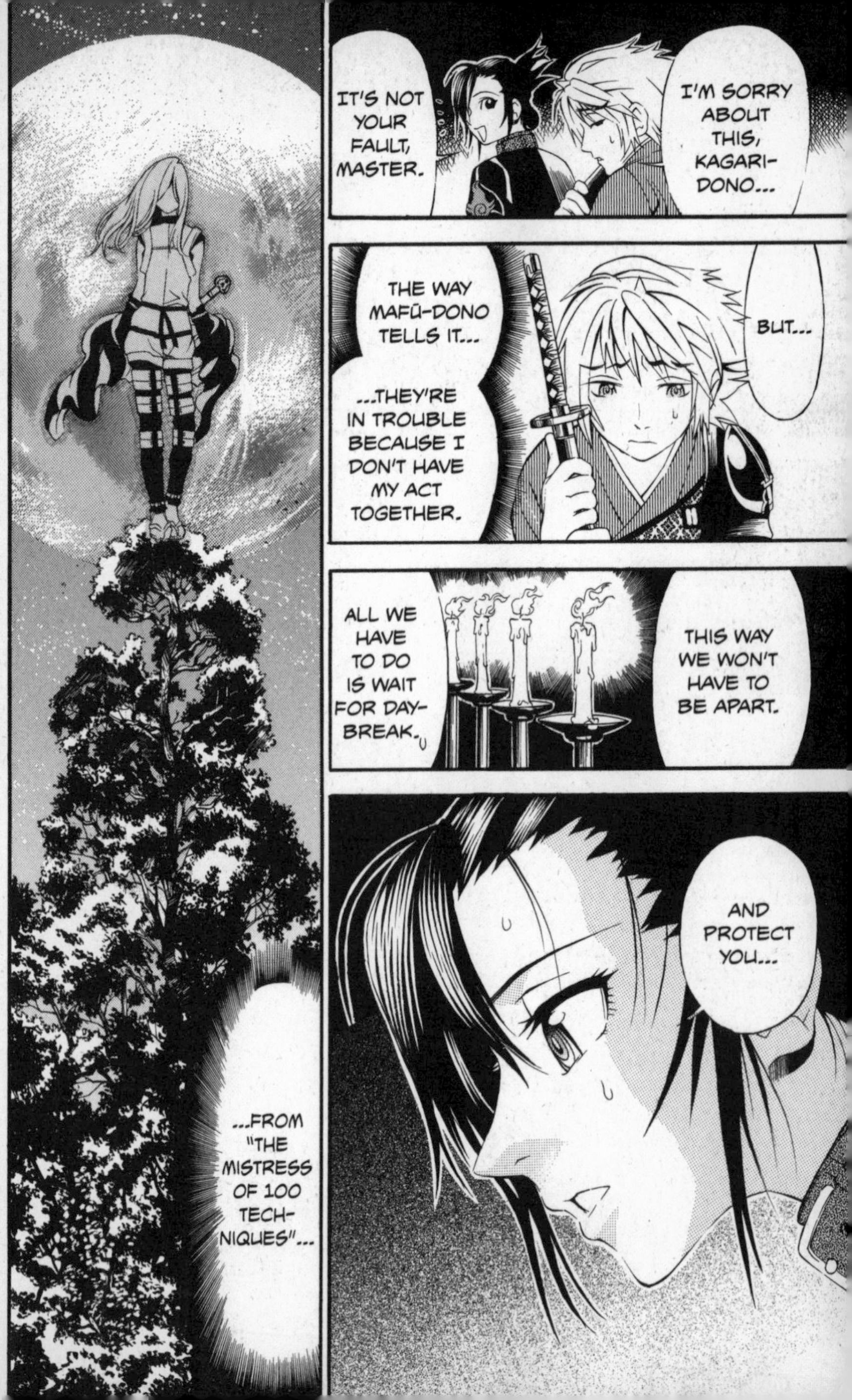
I'M SORRY ABOUT THIS, KAGARI-DONO...
IT'S NOT YOUR FAULT, MASTER.
BUT...
THE WAY MAFŪ-DONO TELLS IT...
...THEY'RE IN TROUBLE BECAUSE I DON'T HAVE MY ACT TOGETHER.
THIS WAY WE WON'T HAVE TO BE APART.
ALL WE HAVE TO DO IS WAIT FOR DAY-BREAK.
AND PROTECT YOU...
...FROM "THE MISTRESS OF 100 TECH-NIQUES"...

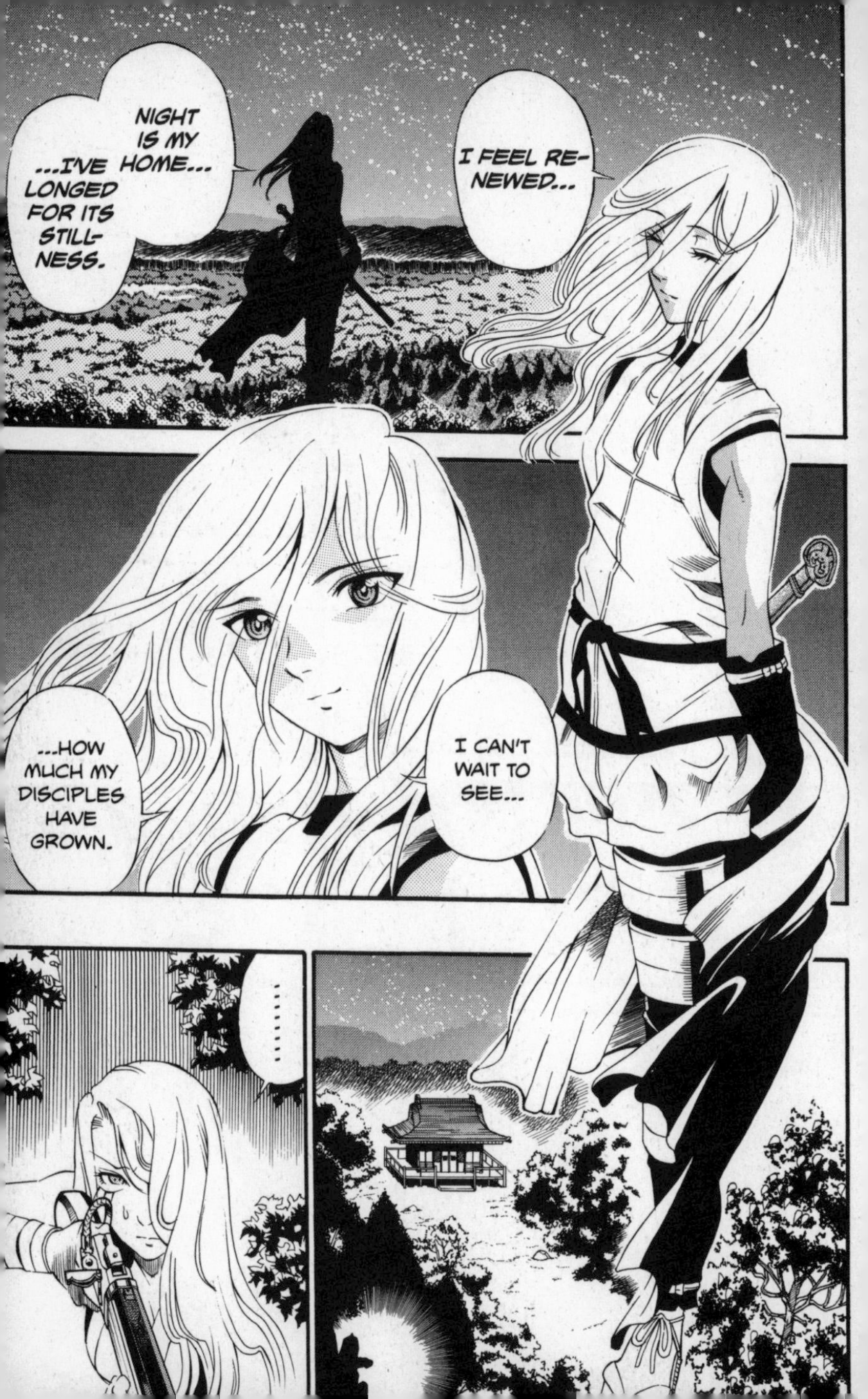
I FEEL RE-NEWED...
NIGHT IS MY HOME...
...I'VE LONGED FOR ITS STILL-NESS.
I CAN'T WAIT TO SEE...
...HOW MUCH MY DISCIPLES HAVE GROWN.
......

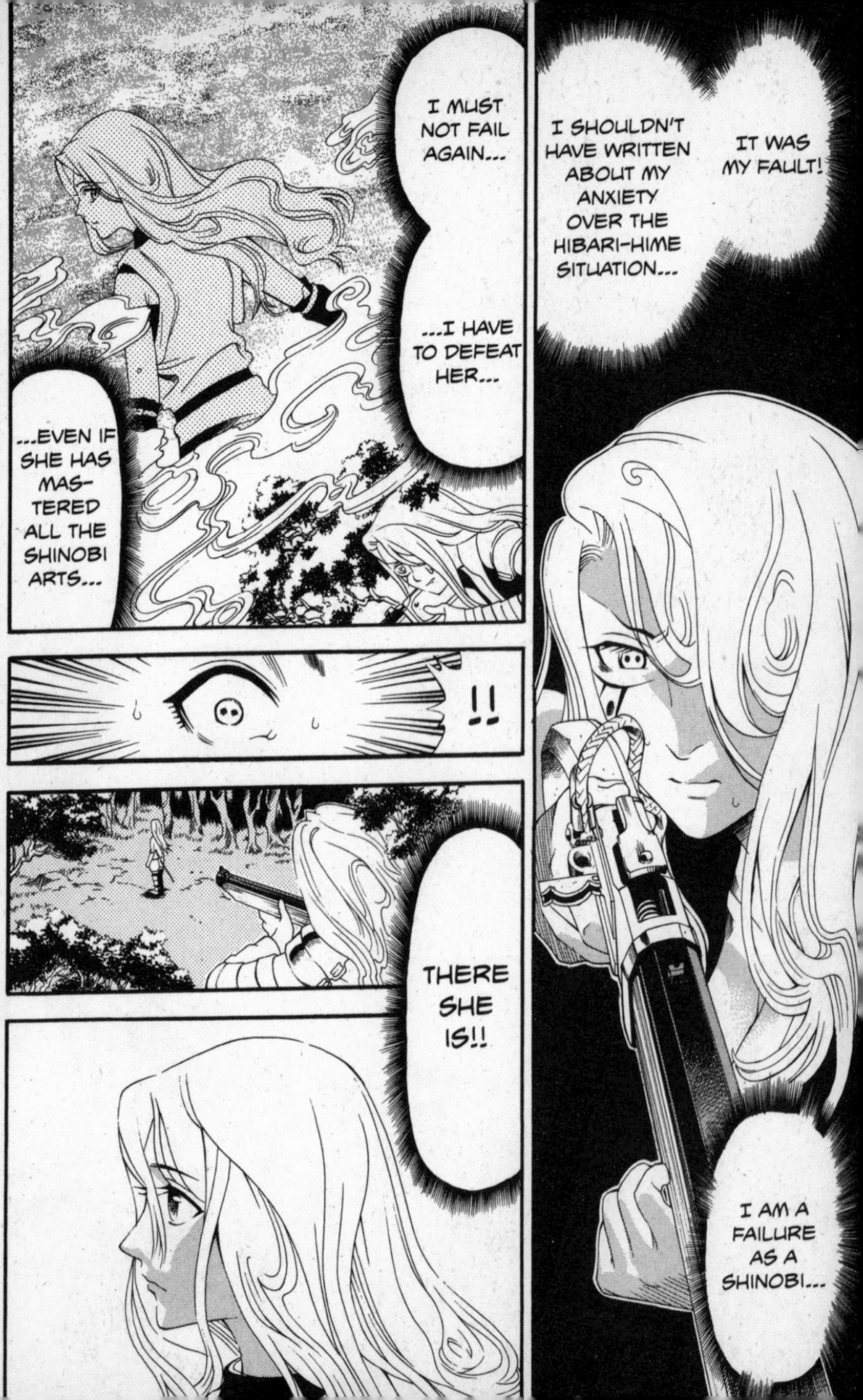
IT WAS MY FAULT!
I SHOULDN'T HAVE WRITTEN ABOUT MY ANXIETY OVER THE HIBARI-HIME SITUATION...
I AM A FAILURE AS A SHINOBI...
I MUST NOT FAIL AGAIN...
...I HAVE TO DEFEAT HER...
...EVEN IF SHE HAS MAS-TERED ALL THE SHINOBI ARTS...
!!
THERE SHE IS!!

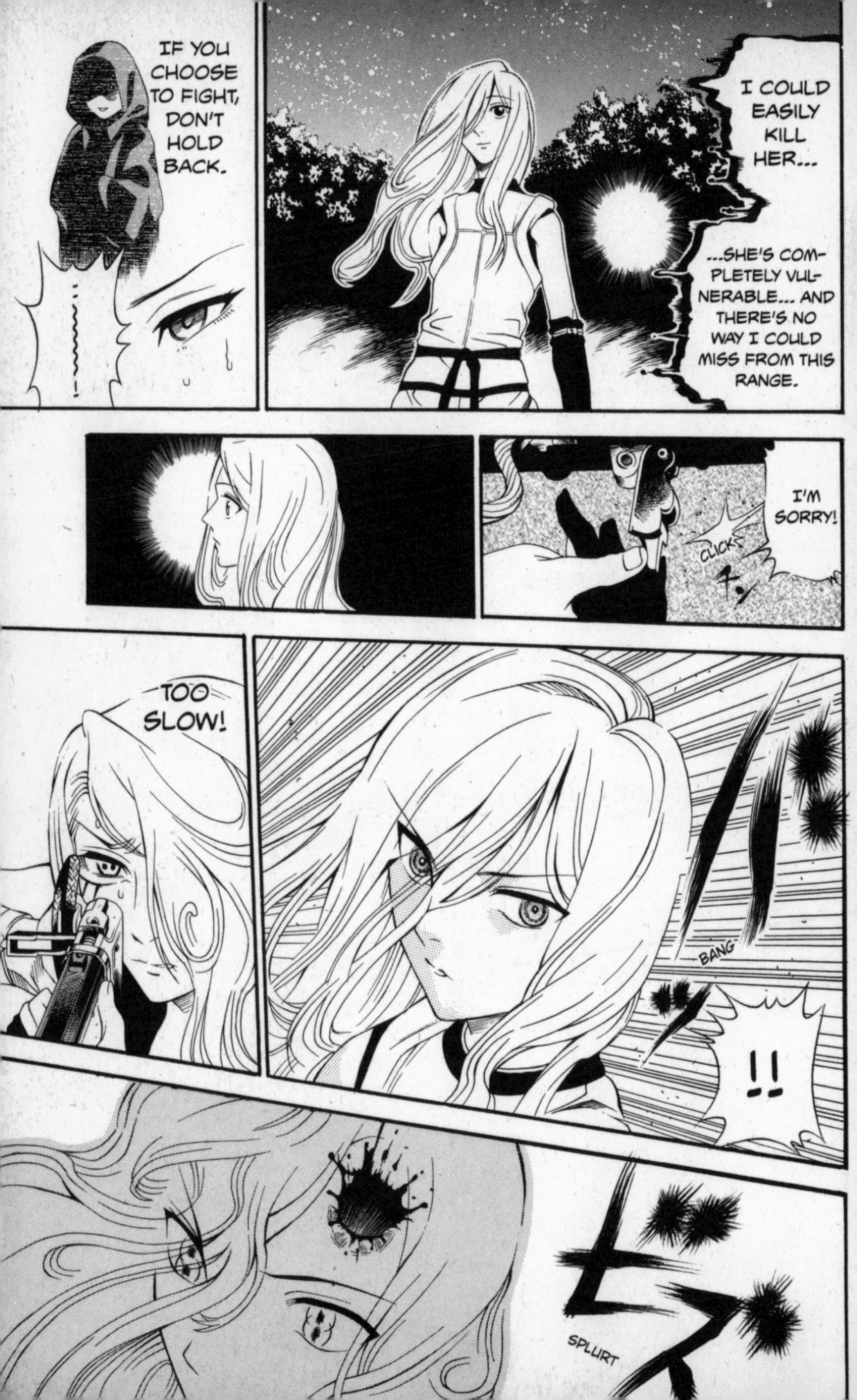
I COULD EASILY KILL HER...
...SHE'S COMPLETELY VULNERABLE... AND THERE'S NO WAY I COULD MISS FROM THIS RANGE.
IF YOU CHOOSE TO FIGHT, DON'T HOLD BACK.
...!
I'M SORRY!
CLICK
BANG
!!
TOO SLOW!
SPLURT

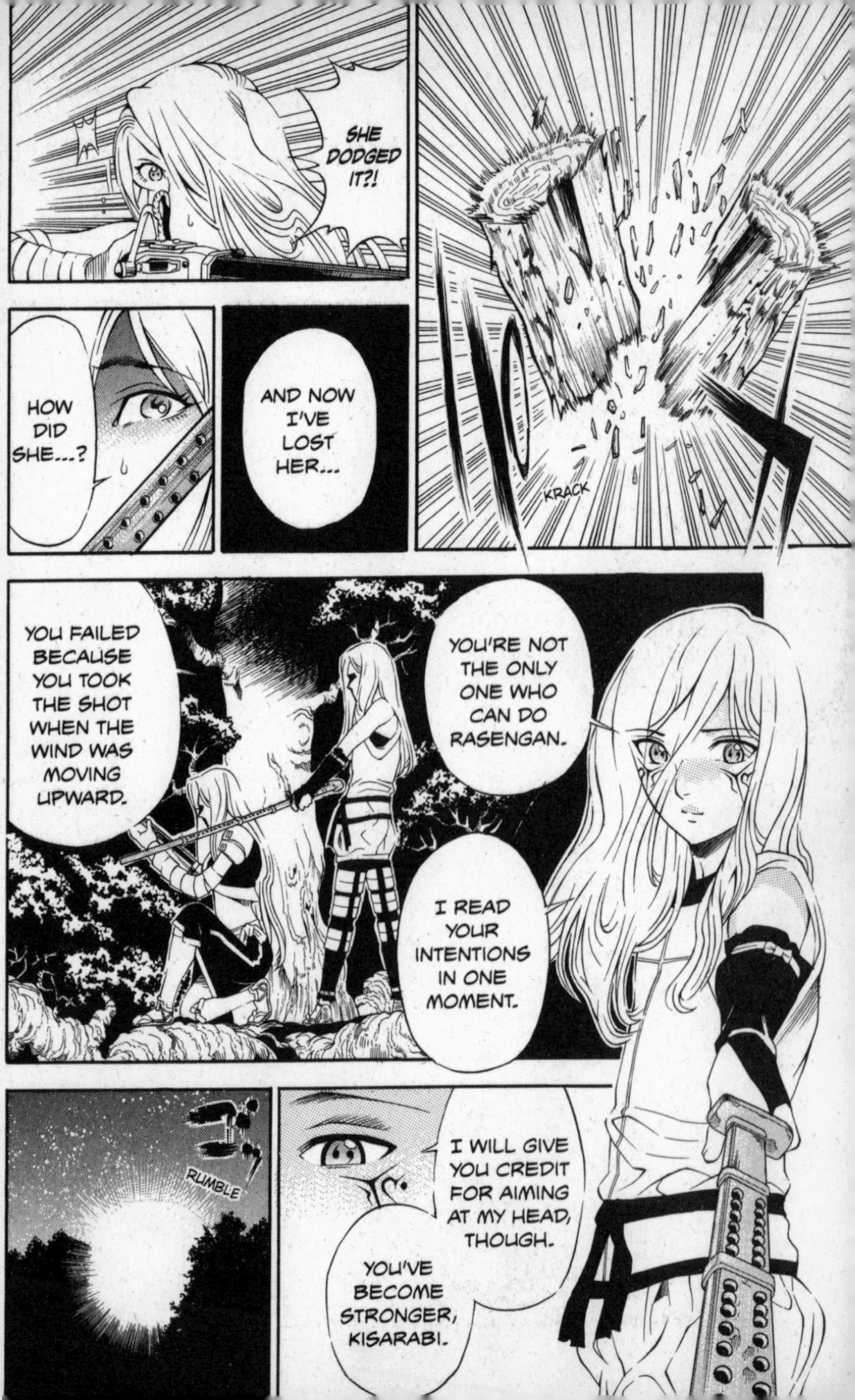
KRACK
SHE DODGED IT?!
AND NOW I'VE LOST HER...
HOW DID SHE...?
YOU'RE NOT THE ONLY ONE WHO CAN DO RASENGAN.
I READ YOUR INTENTIONS IN ONE MOMENT.
YOU FAILED BECAUSE YOU TOOK THE SHOT WHEN THE WIND WAS MOVING UPWARD.
I WILL GIVE YOU CREDIT FOR AIMING AT MY HEAD, THOUGH.
YOU'VE BECOME STRONGER, KISARABI.
RUMBLE

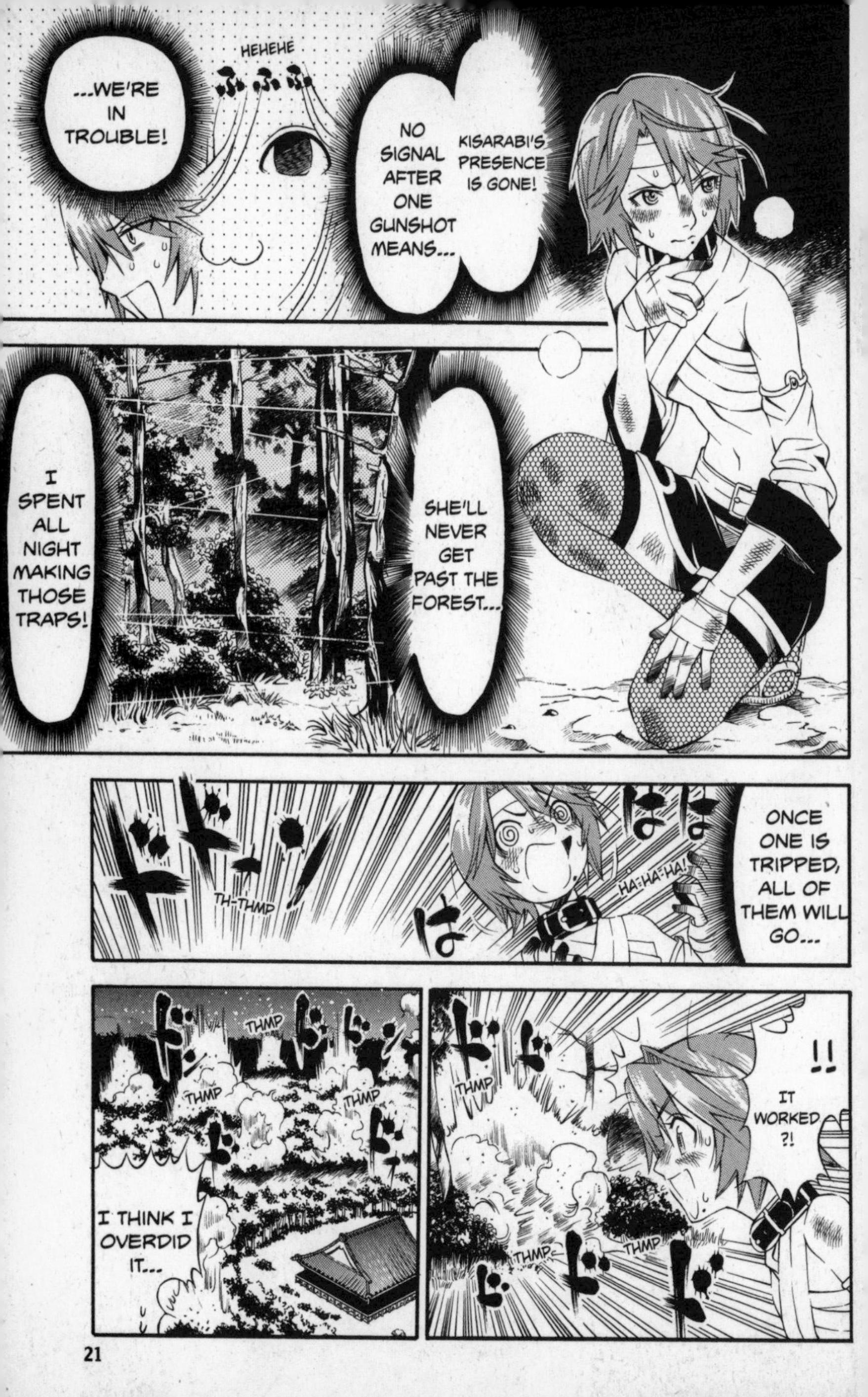
KISARABI'S PRESENCE IS GONE!
NO SIGNAL AFTER ONE GUNSHOT MEANS...
HEHEHE
...WE'RE IN TROUBLE!
SHE'LL NEVER GET PAST THE FOREST...
I SPENT ALL NIGHT MAKING THOSE TRAPS!
ONCE ONE IS TRIPPED, ALL OF THEM WILL GO...
HA-HA-HA!
TH-THMP
!!
IT WORKED ?!
THMP
THMP
THMP
THMP
THMP
THMP
I THINK I OVERDID IT...

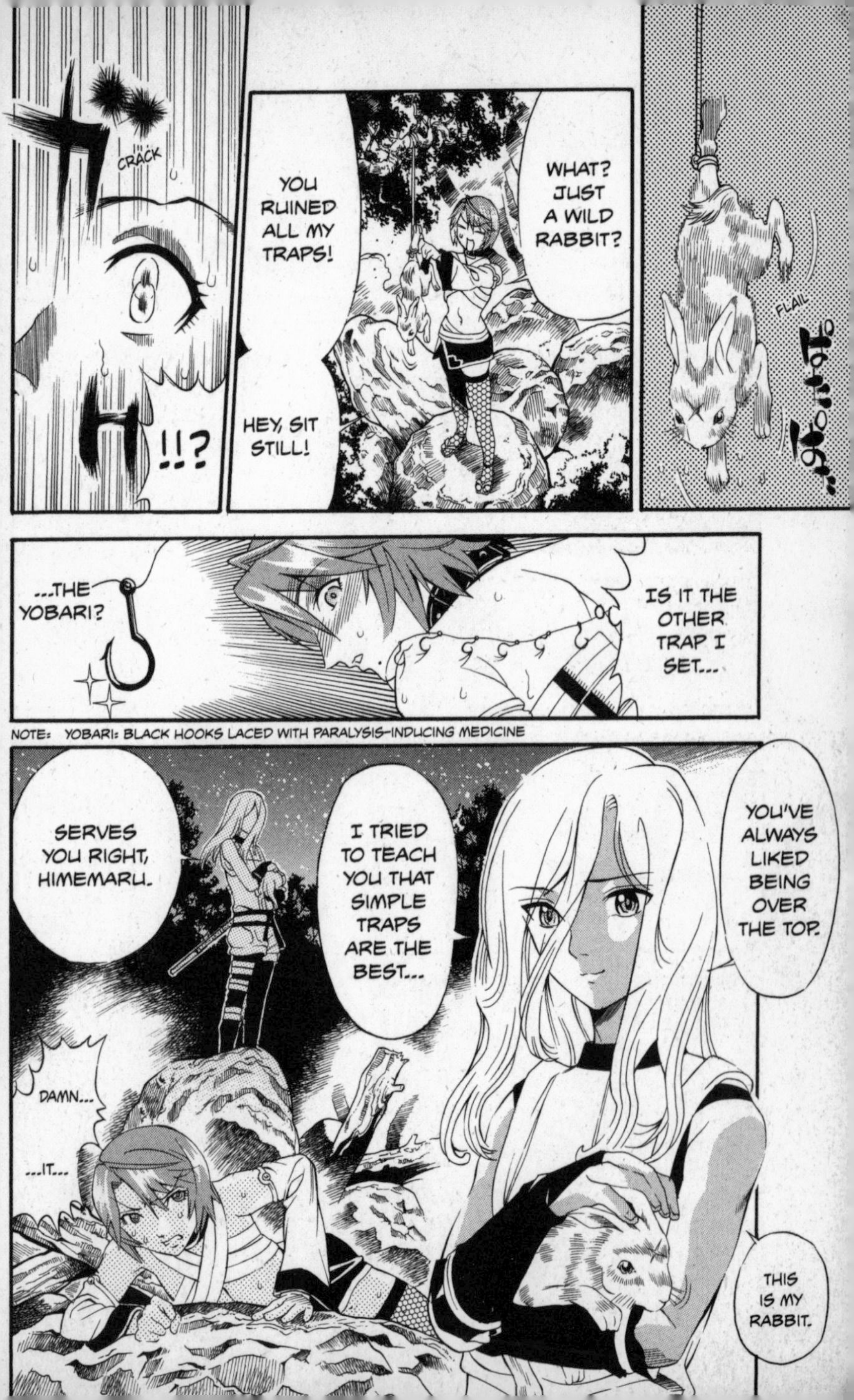
FLAIL
WHAT? JUST A WILD RABBIT?
YOU RUINED ALL MY TRAPS!
HEY, SIT STILL!
CRACK
!!?
IS IT THE OTHER TRAP I SET...
...THE YOBARI?
NOTE: YOBARI: BLACK HOOKS LACED WITH PARALYSIS-INDUCING MEDICINE
YOU'VE ALWAYS LIKED BEING OVER THE TOP.
I TRIED TO TEACH YOU THAT SIMPLE TRAPS ARE THE BEST...
SERVES YOU RIGHT, HIMEMARU.
THIS IS MY RABBIT.
DAMN...
...IT...

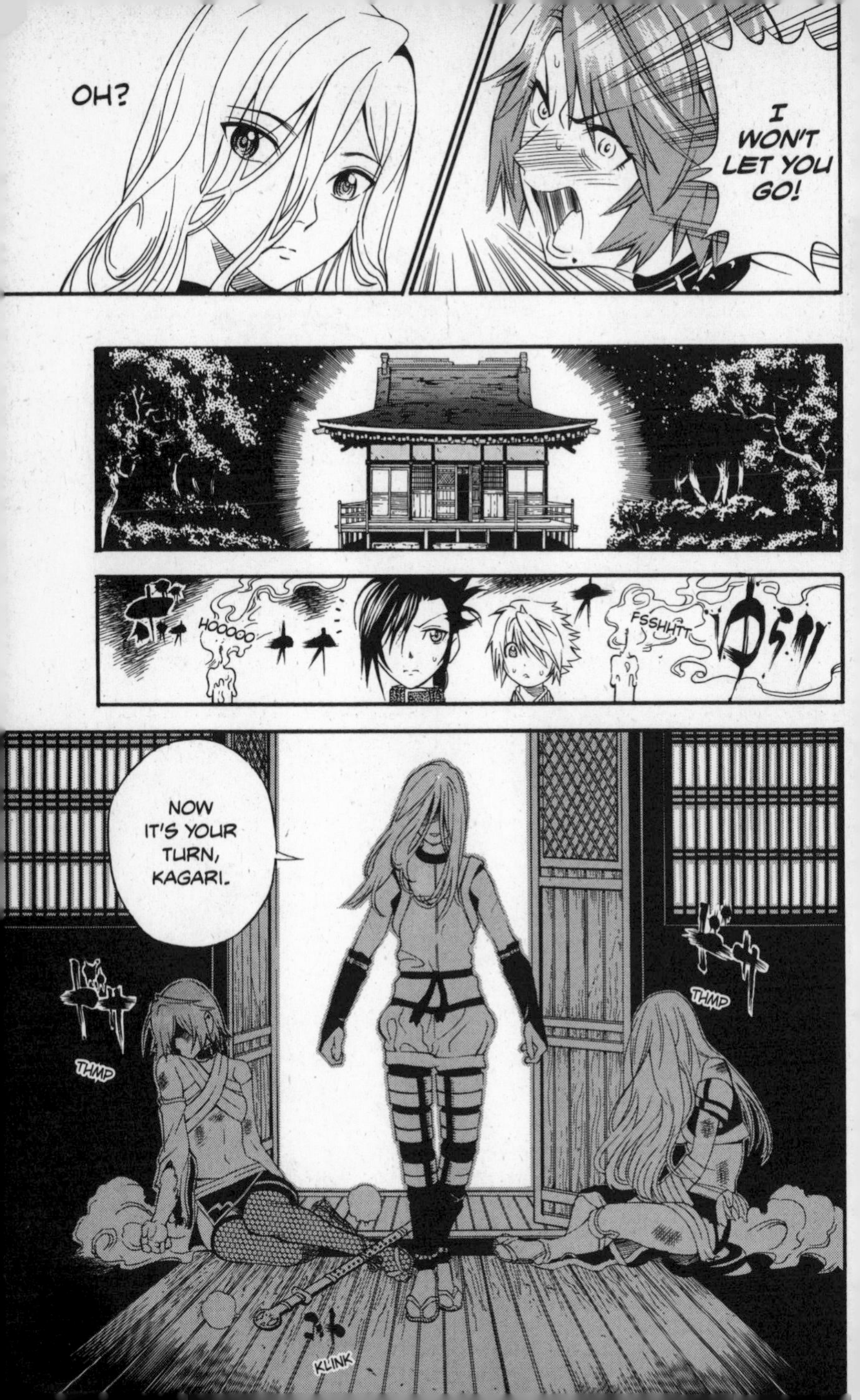
I WON'T LET YOU GO!
OH?
FSSHHTT
HOOOOO
NOW IT'S YOUR TURN, KAGARI.
THMP
THMP
KLINK

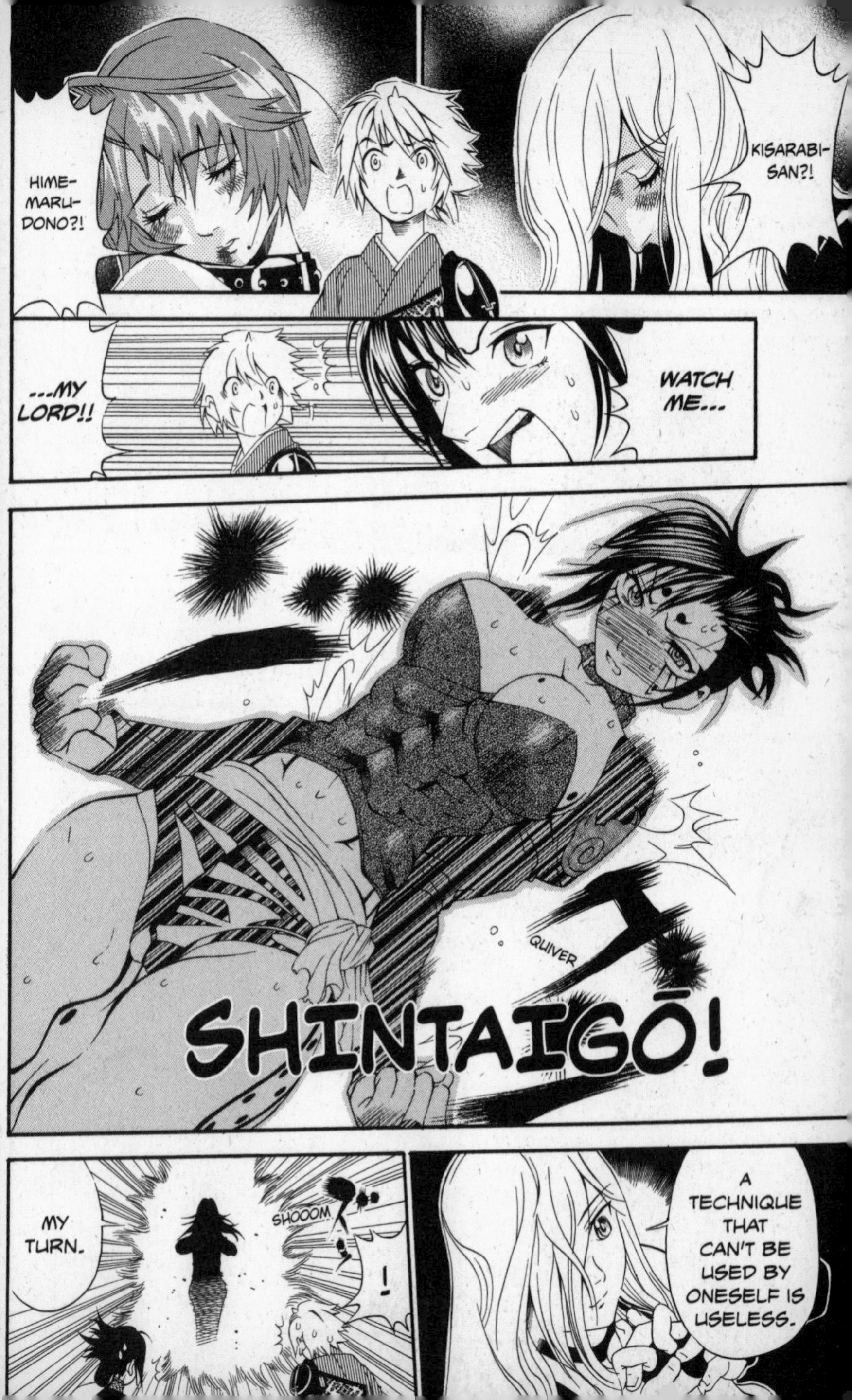
KISARABI-SAN?!
HIME-MARU-DONO?!
WATCH ME...
...MY LORD!!
QUIVER
SHINTAIGŌ!
A TECHNIQUE THAT CAN'T BE USED BY ONESELF IS USELESS.
SHOOOM
!
MY TURN.

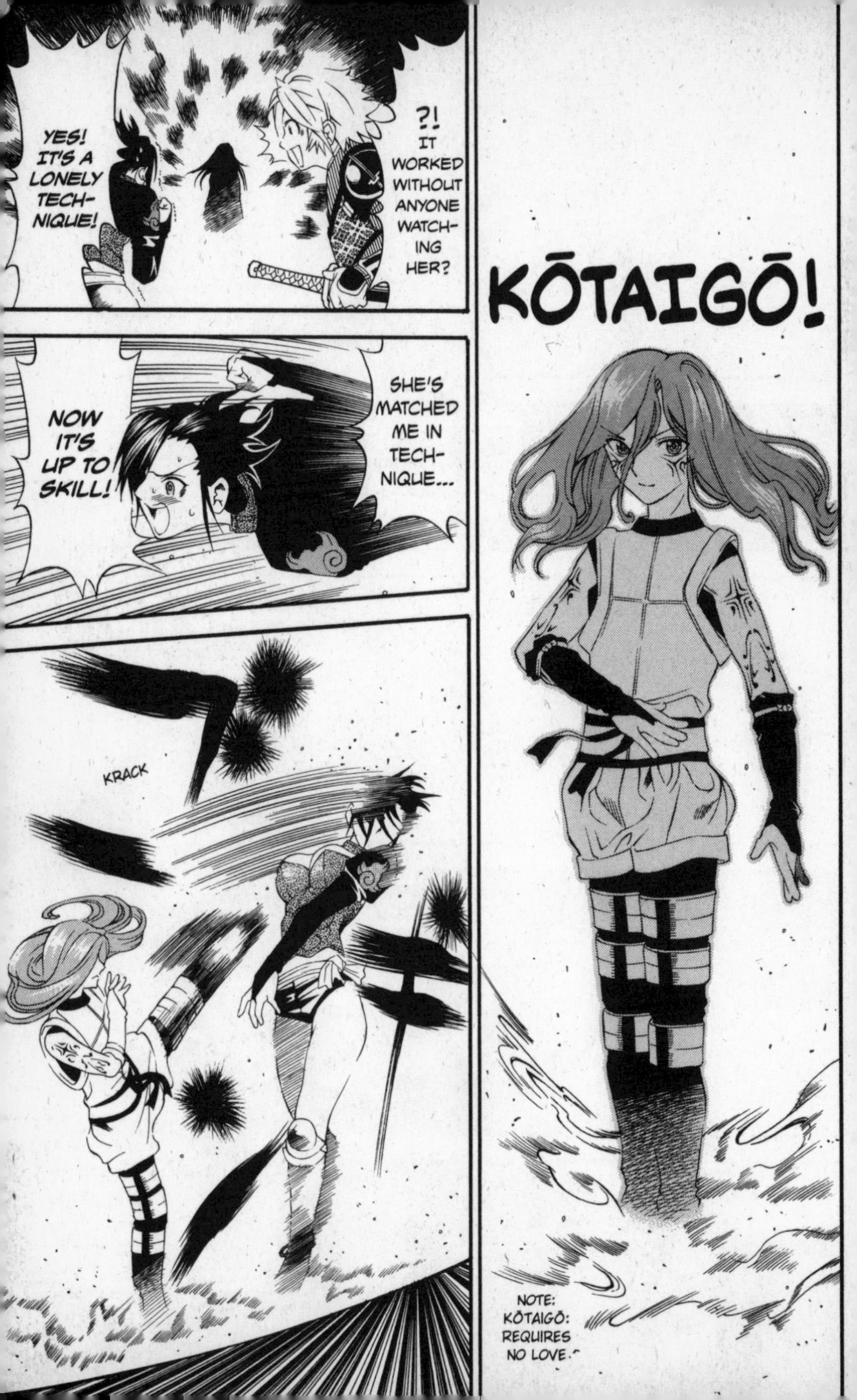
KŌTAIGŌ!
NOTE: KŌTAIGŌ: REQUIRES NO LOVE.
?! IT WORKED WITHOUT ANYONE WATCHING HER?
YES! IT'S A LONELY TECHNIQUE!
SHE'S MATCHED ME IN TECHNIQUE...
NOW IT'S UP TO SKILL!
KRACK

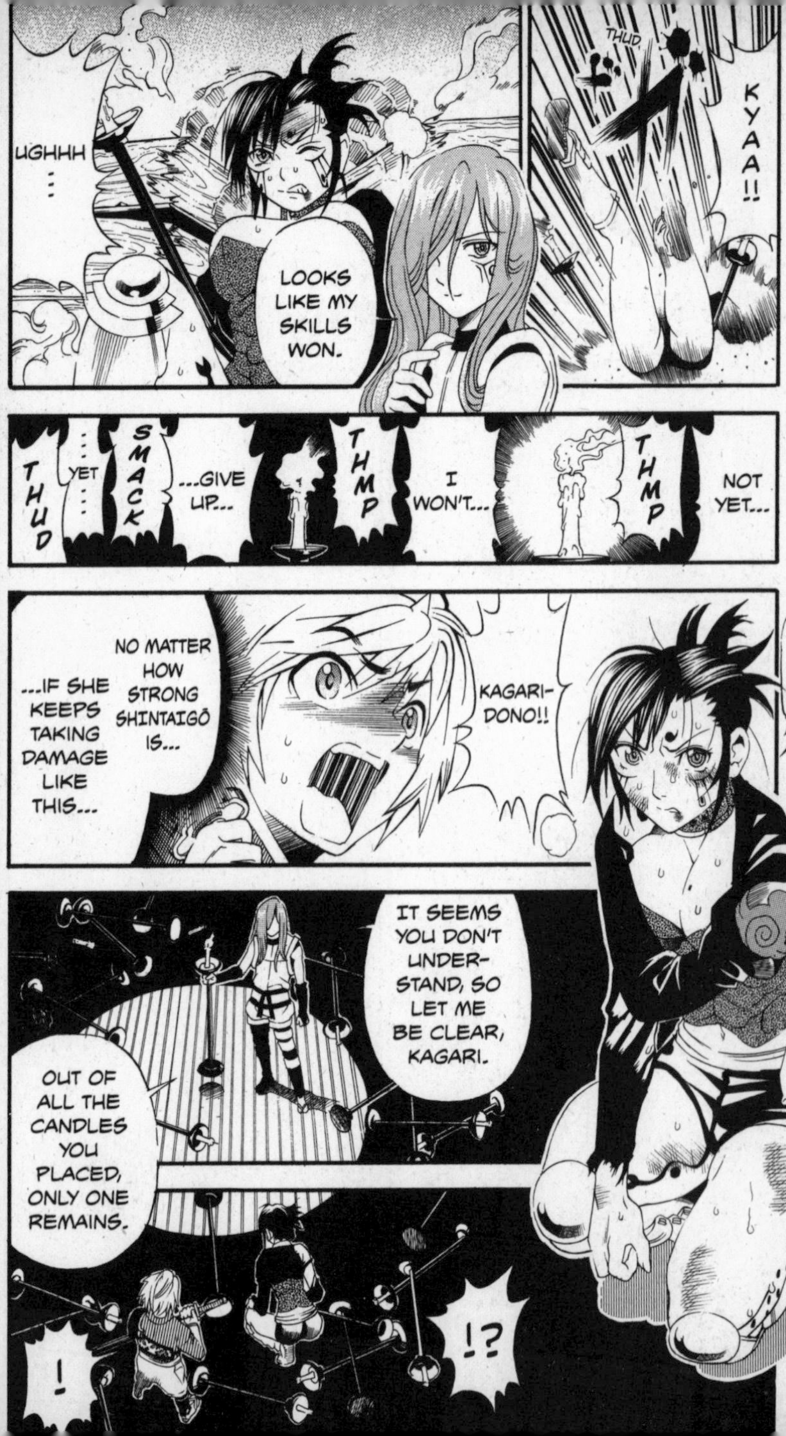
THUD
KYAA!!
LOOKS LIKE MY SKILLS WON.
UGHHH...
NOT YET...
THMP
I WON'T...
THMP
...GIVE UP...
SMACK
...YET...
THUD
UGHH...
KAGARI-DONO!!
NO MATTER HOW STRONG SHINTAIGŌ IS...
...IF SHE KEEPS TAKING DAMAGE LIKE THIS...
IT SEEMS YOU DON'T UNDER-STAND, SO LET ME BE CLEAR, KAGARI.
OUT OF ALL THE CANDLES YOU PLACED, ONLY ONE REMAINS.
!?
!

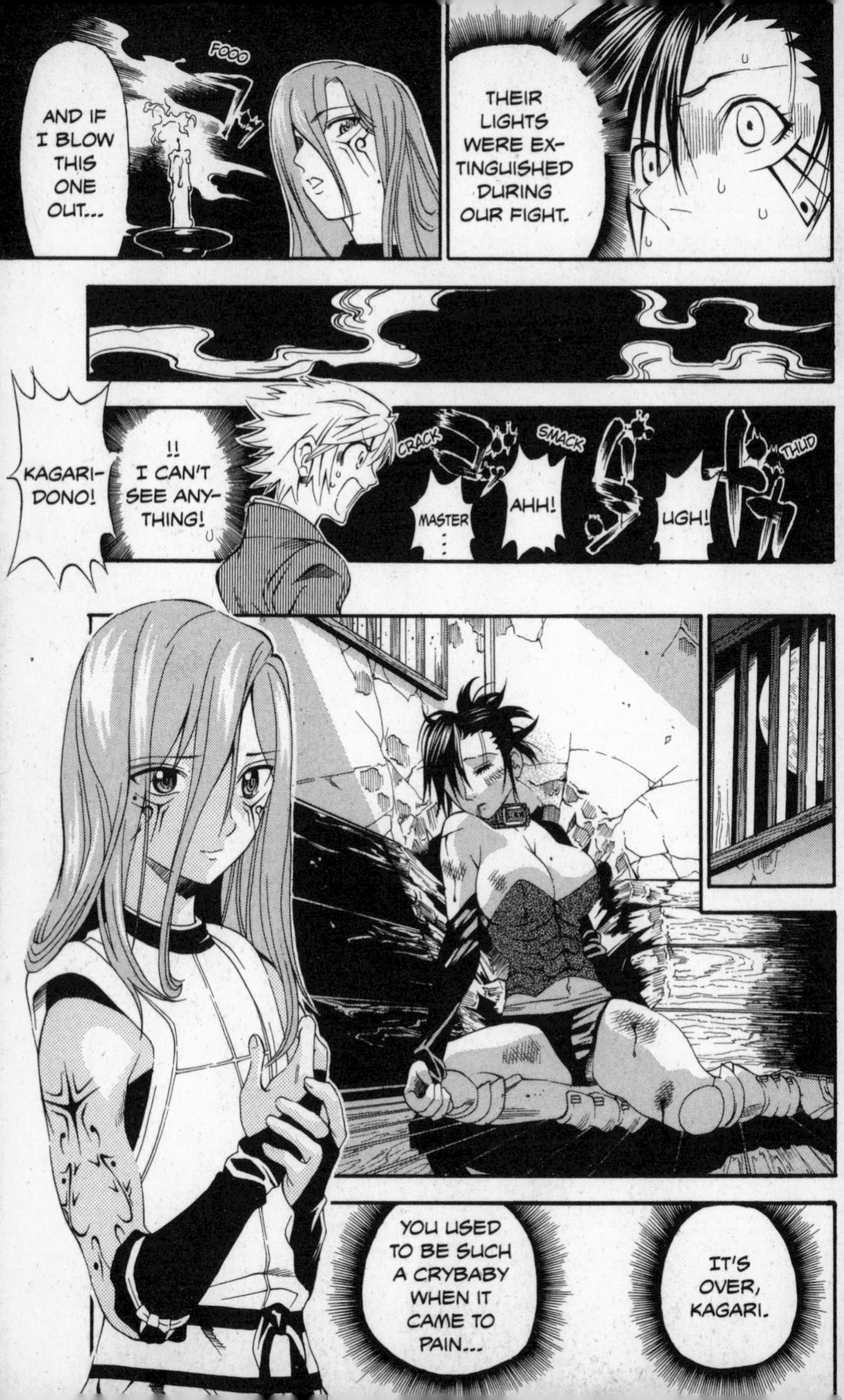
THEIR LIGHTS WERE EXTINGUISHED DURING OUR FIGHT.
FOOO
AND IF I BLOW THIS ONE OUT...
THUD
UGH!
SMACK
AHH!
CRACK
MASTER...
!! I CAN'T SEE ANYTHING!
KAGARI-DONO!
IT'S OVER, KAGARI.
YOU USED TO BE SUCH A CRYBABY WHEN IT CAME TO PAIN...

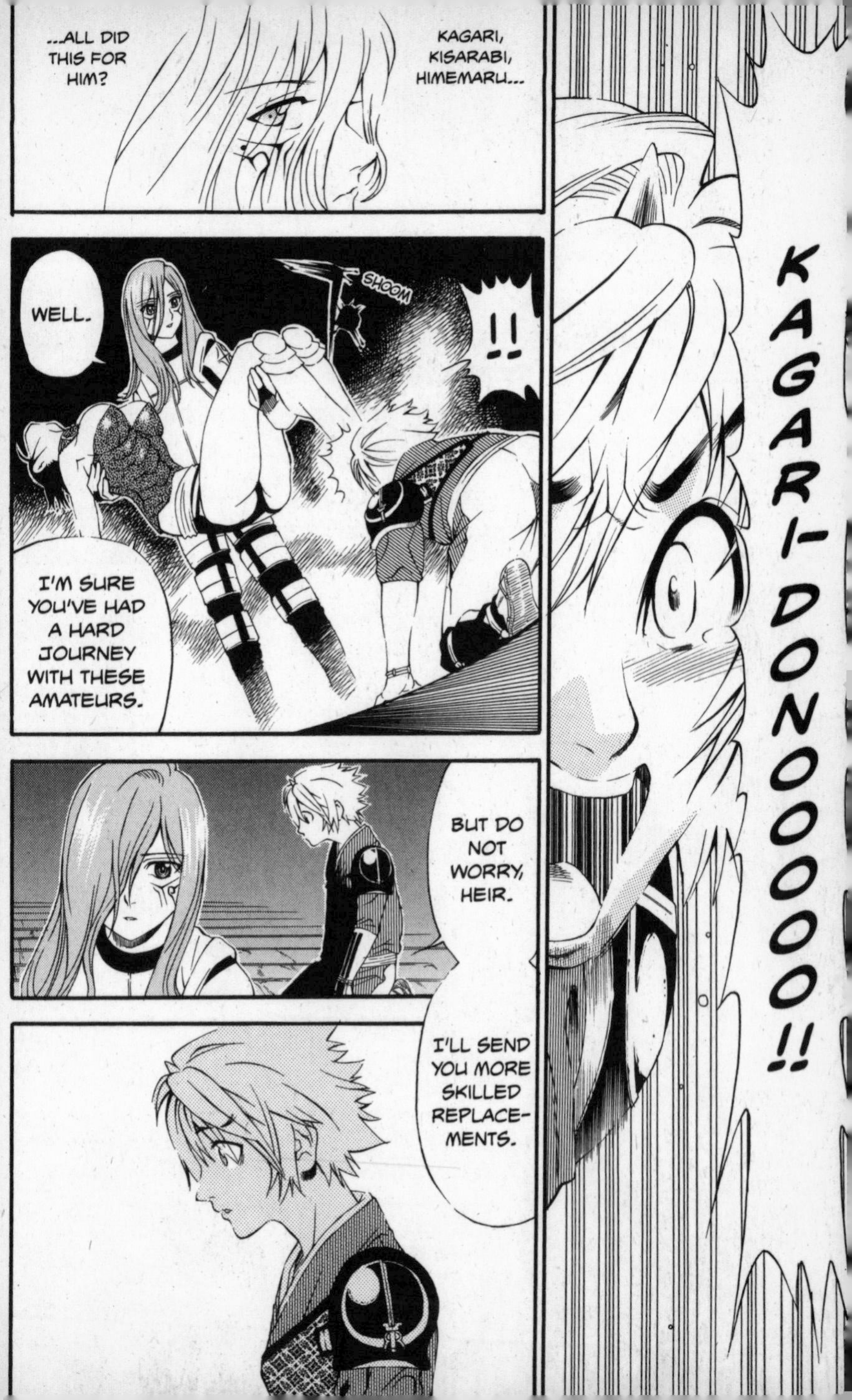
KAGARI-DONOOOOOO!!
KAGARI, KISARABI, HIMEMARU...
...ALL DID THIS FOR HIM?
!!
SHOOM
WELL.
I'M SURE YOU'VE HAD A HARD JOURNEY WITH THESE AMATEURS.
BUT DO NOT WORRY, HEIR.
I'LL SEND YOU MORE SKILLED REPLACE-MENTS.

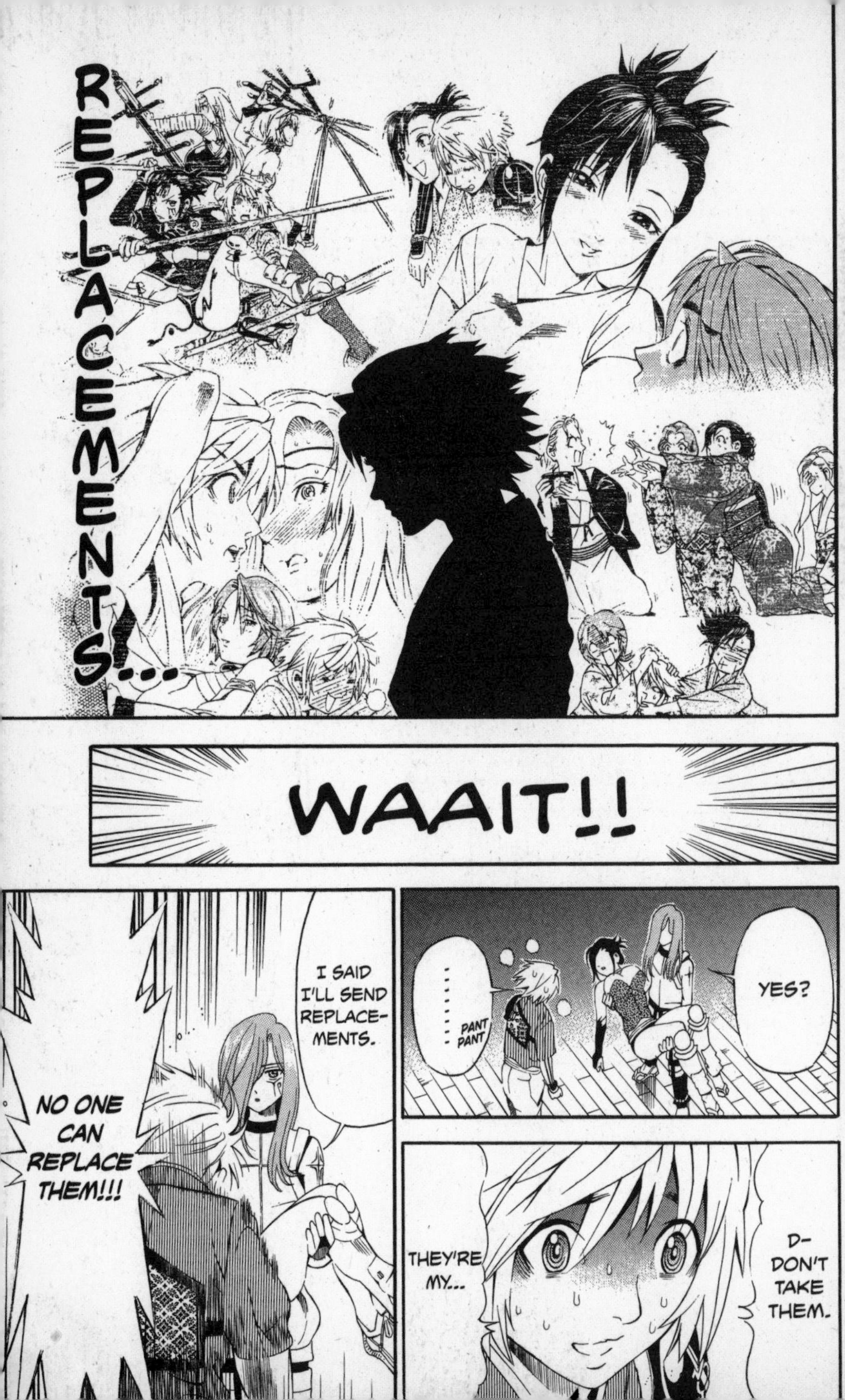
REPLACEMENTS....
WAAIT!!
YES?
......
PANT PANT
D- DON'T TAKE THEM.
THEY'RE MY...
I SAID I'LL SEND REPLACE-MENTS.
NO ONE CAN REPLACE THEM!!!

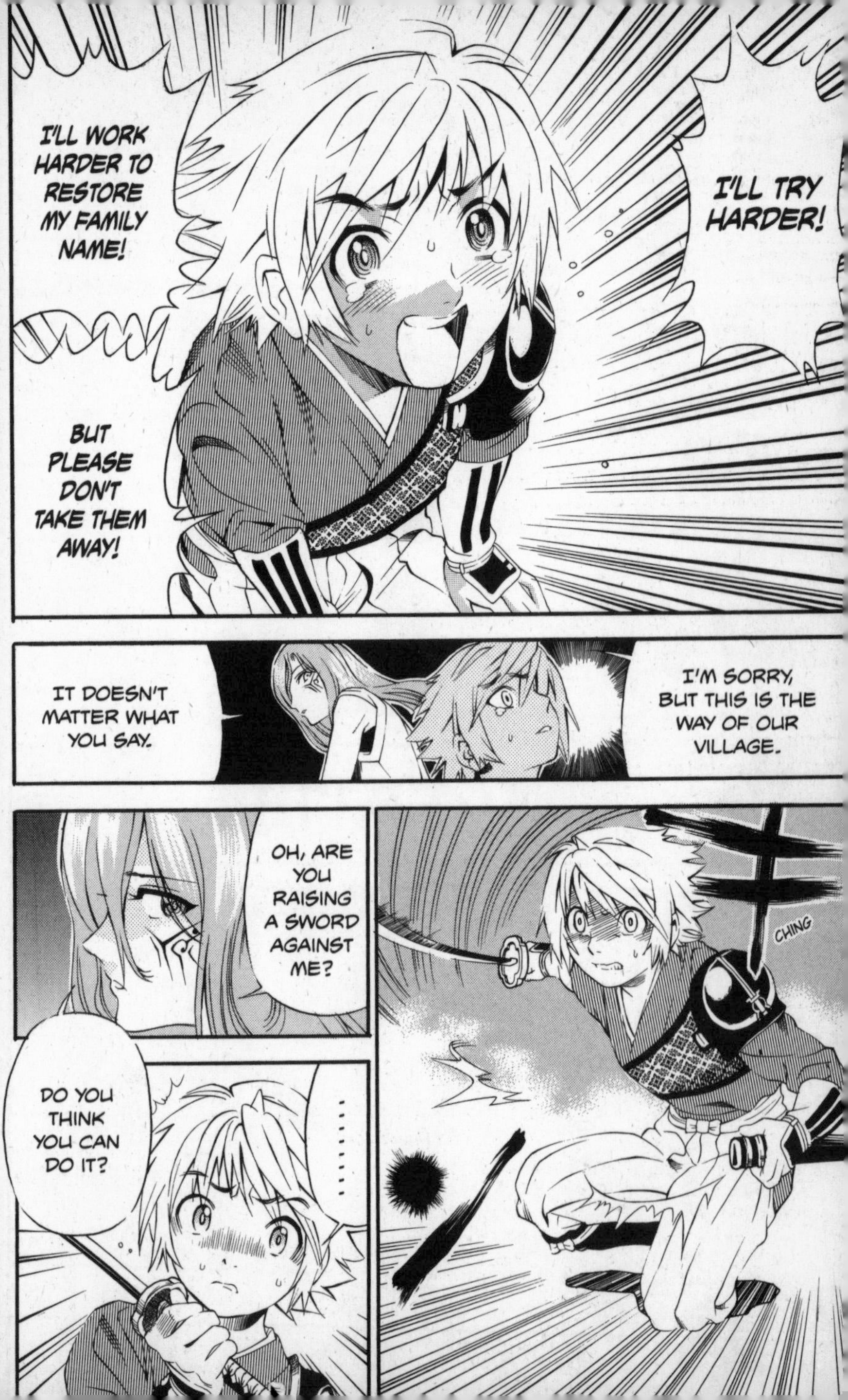
I'LL TRY HARDER!
I'LL WORK HARDER TO RESTORE MY FAMILY NAME!
BUT PLEASE DON'T TAKE THEM AWAY!
I'M SORRY, BUT THIS IS THE WAY OF OUR VILLAGE.
IT DOESN'T MATTER WHAT YOU SAY.
CHING
OH, ARE YOU RAISING A SWORD AGAINST ME?
DO YOU THINK YOU CAN DO IT?
......

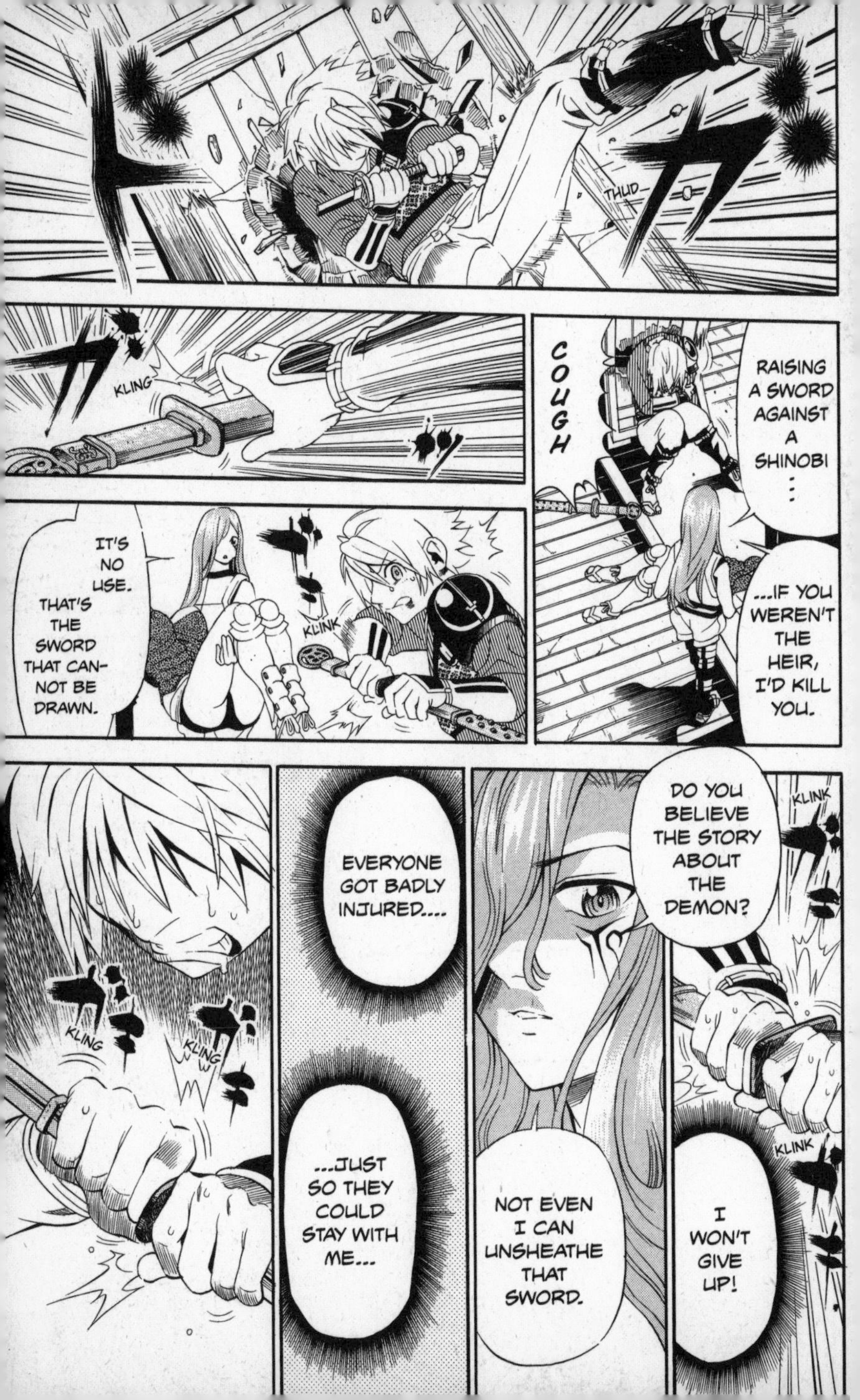
THUD
COUGH
RAISING A SWORD AGAINST A SHINOBI...
...IF YOU WEREN'T THE HEIR, I'D KILL YOU.
KLING
IT'S NO USE. THAT'S THE SWORD THAT CAN-NOT BE DRAWN.
KLINK
DO YOU BELIEVE THE STORY ABOUT THE DEMON?
KLINK
NOT EVEN I CAN UNSHEATHE THAT SWORD.
KLINK
I WON'T GIVE UP!
EVERYONE GOT BADLY INJURED....
...JUST SO THEY COULD STAY WITH ME...
KLING
KLING

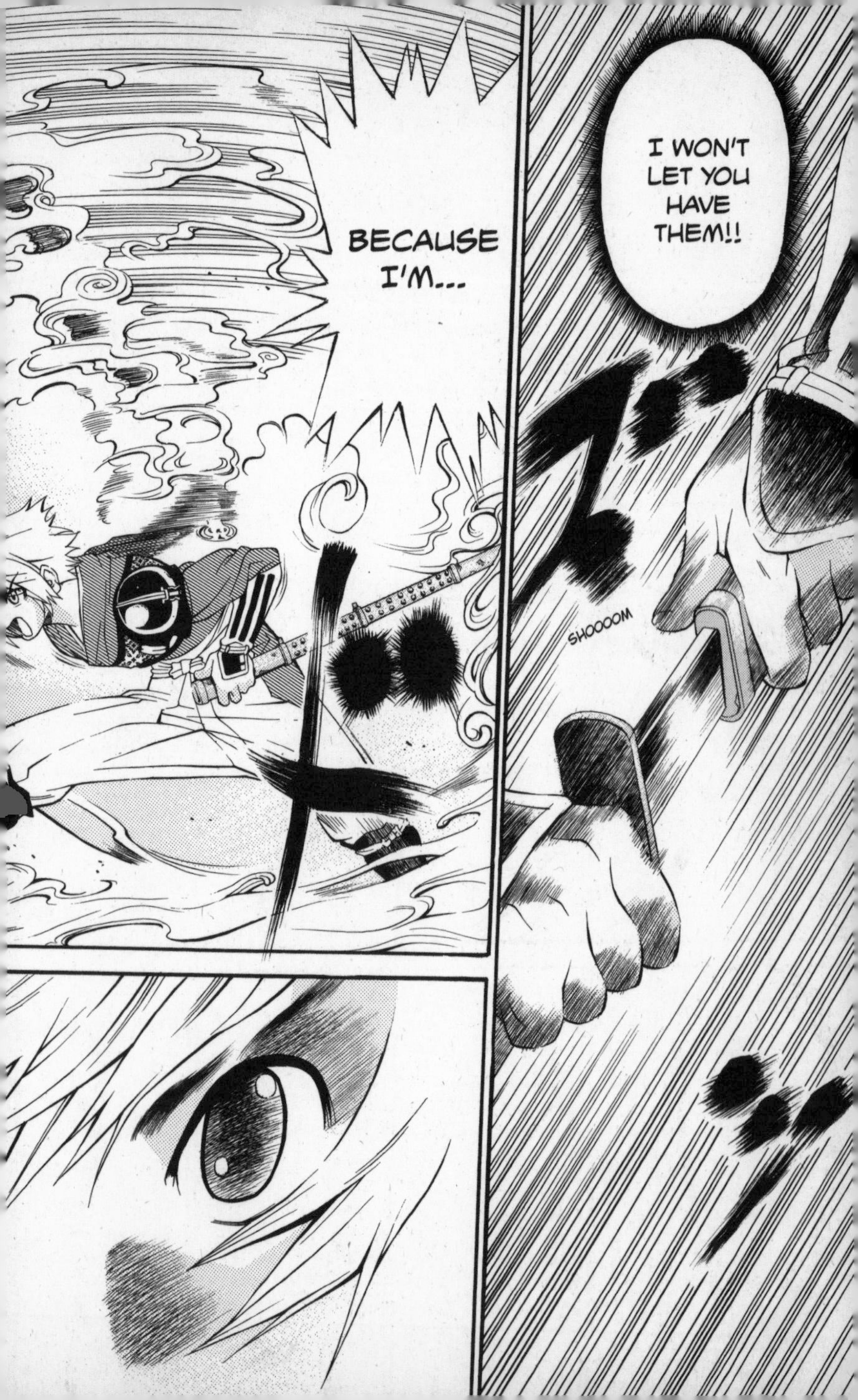
I WON'T LET YOU HAVE THEM!!
SHOOOOM
BECAUSE I'M...

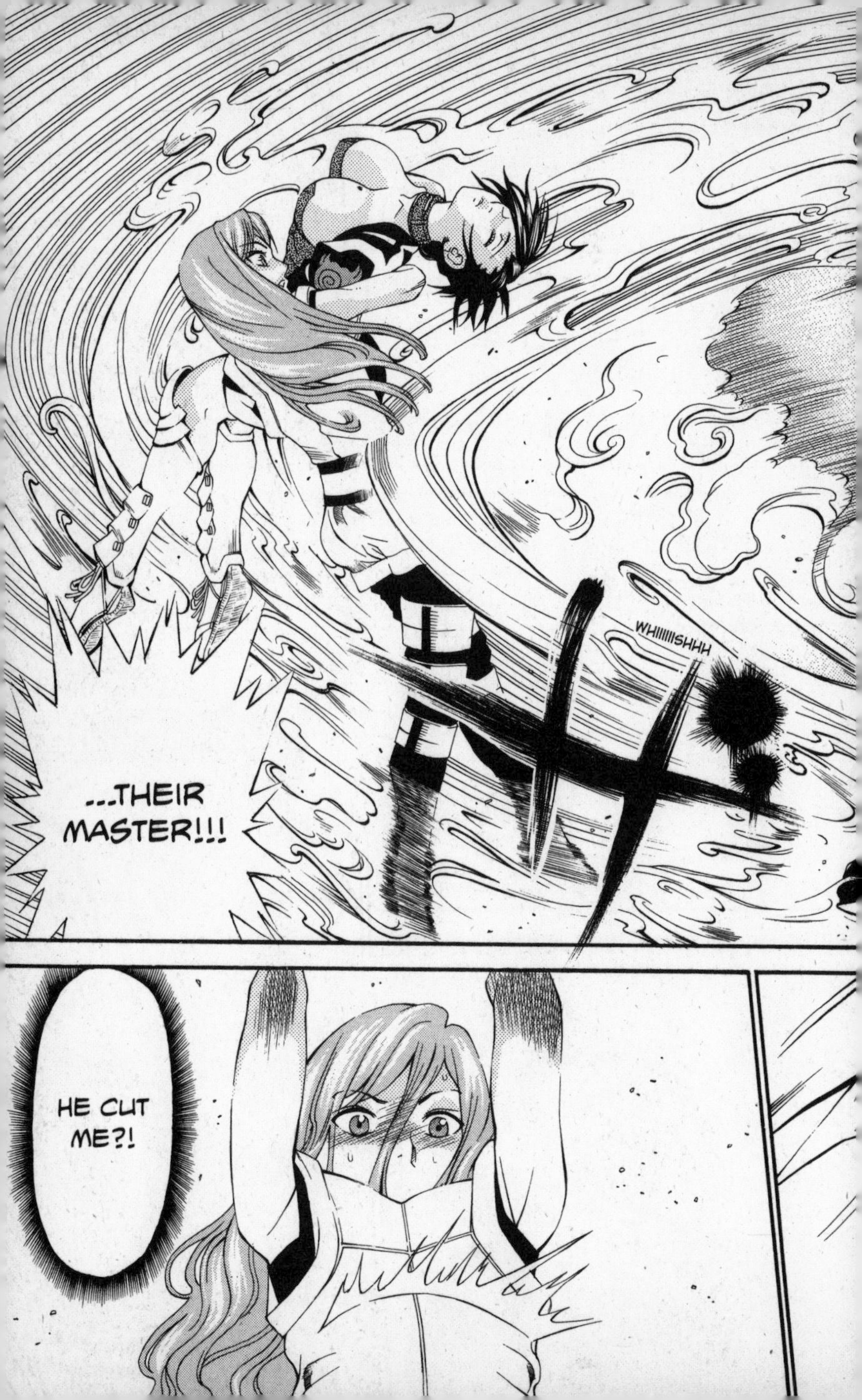
WHIIIIISHHH
...THEIR MASTER!!!
HE CUT ME?!

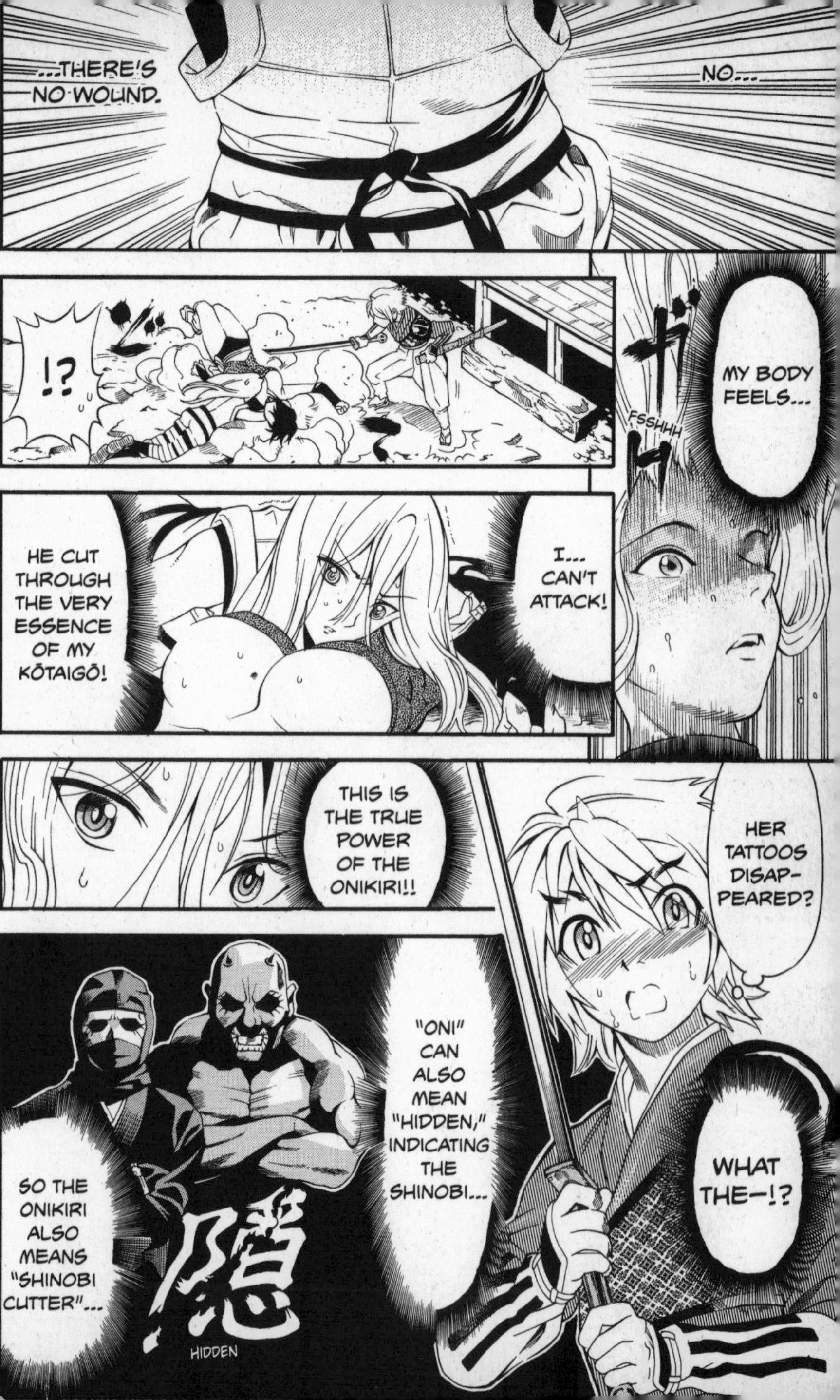
NO...
...THERE'S NO WOUND.
MY BODY FEELS...
FSSHHH
!?
I... CAN'T ATTACK!
HE CUT THROUGH THE VERY ESSENCE OF MY KŌTAIGŌ!
HER TATTOOS DISAP-PEARED?
WHAT THE—!?
THIS IS THE TRUE POWER OF THE ONIKIRI!!
"ONI" CAN ALSO MEAN "HIDDEN," INDICATING THE SHINOBI...
SO THE ONIKIRI ALSO MEANS "SHINOBI CUTTER"...
隠
HIDDEN

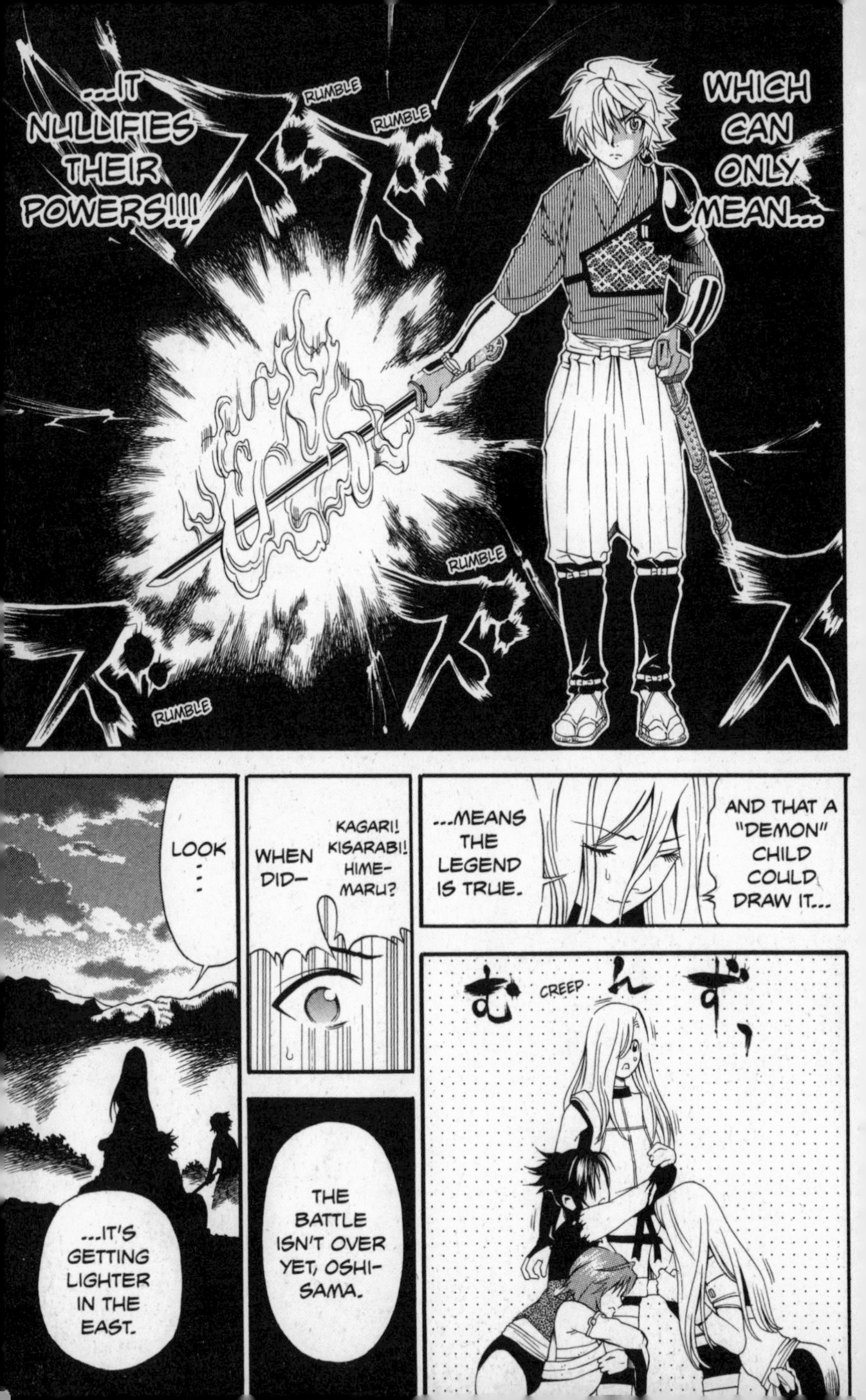
WHICH CAN ONLY MEAN...
RUMBLE
RUMBLE
...IT NULLIFIES THEIR POWERS!!!
RUMBLE
RUMBLE
AND THAT A "DEMON" CHILD COULD DRAW IT...
...MEANS THE LEGEND IS TRUE.
むんず
CREEP
KAGARI! KISARABI! HIME-MARU?
WHEN DID—
THE BATTLE ISN'T OVER YET, OSHI-SAMA.
LOOK...
...IT'S GETTING LIGHTER IN THE EAST.

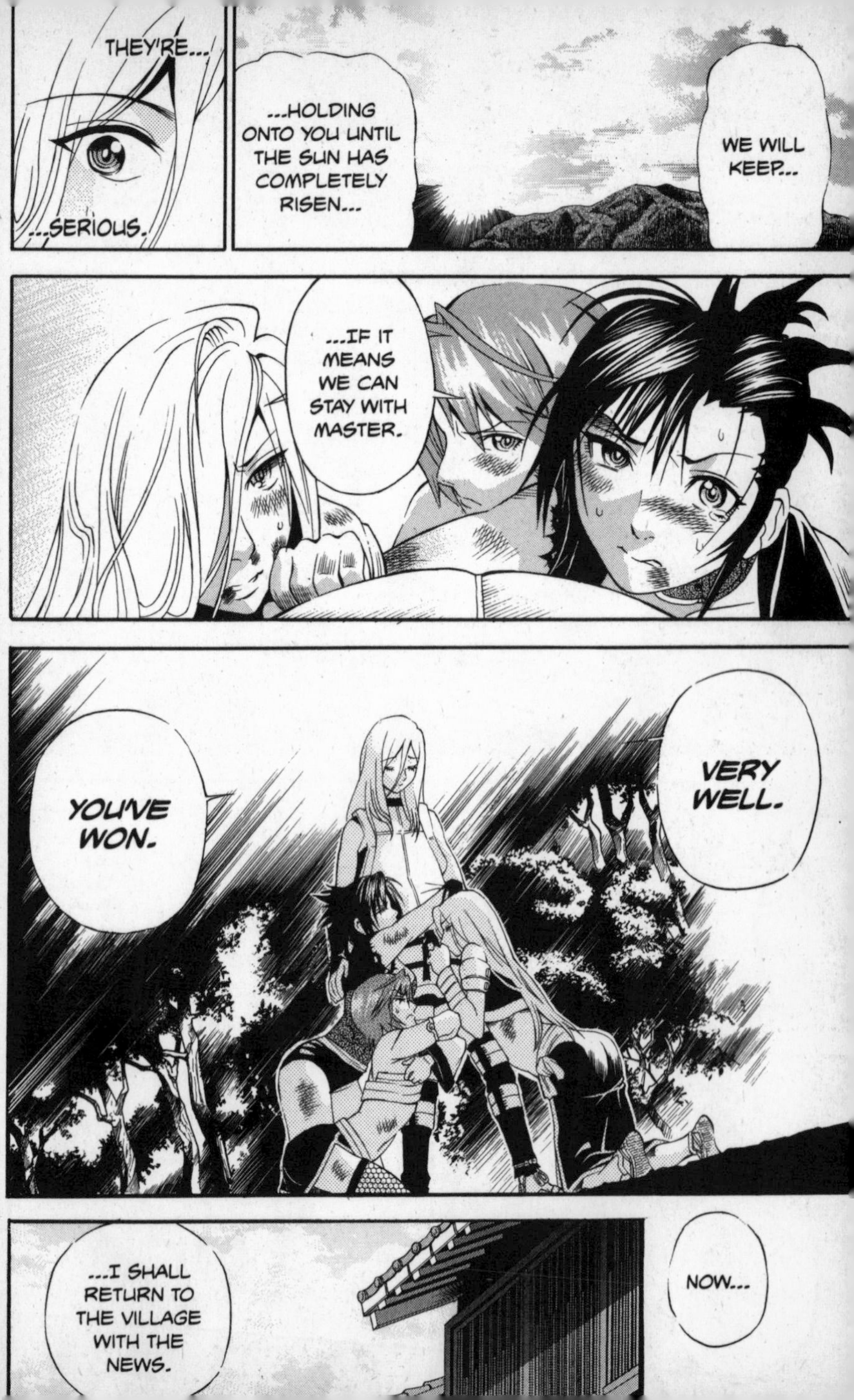
WE WILL KEEP...
...HOLDING ONTO YOU UNTIL THE SUN HAS COMPLETELY RISEN...
THEY'RE...
...SERIOUS.
...IF IT MEANS WE CAN STAY WITH MASTER.
VERY WELL.
YOU'VE WON.
NOW...
...I SHALL RETURN TO THE VILLAGE WITH THE NEWS.

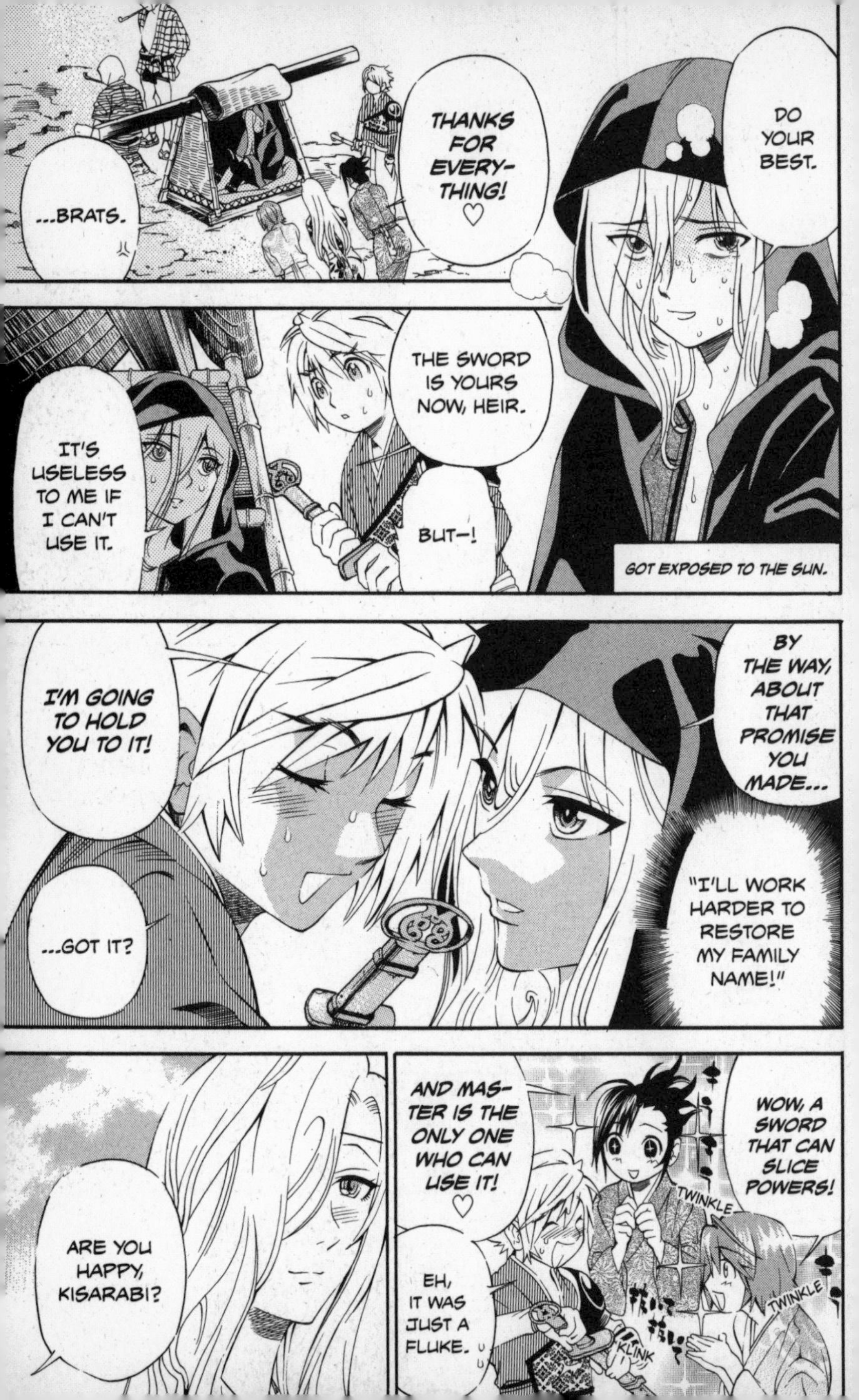

DO YOUR BEST.
GOT EXPOSED TO THE SUN.
THANKS FOR EVERY-THING! ♡
...BRATS.
THE SWORD IS YOURS NOW, HEIR.
IT'S USELESS TO ME IF I CAN'T USE IT.
BUT—!
BY THE WAY, ABOUT THAT PROMISE YOU MADE...
"I'LL WORK HARDER TO RESTORE MY FAMILY NAME!"
I'M GOING TO HOLD YOU TO IT!
...GOT IT?
WOW, A SWORD THAT CAN SLICE POWERS!
TWINKLE
AND MAS-TER IS THE ONLY ONE WHO CAN USE IT! ♡
TWINKLE
EH, IT WAS JUST A FLUKE.
KLINK
ARE YOU HAPPY, KISARABI?

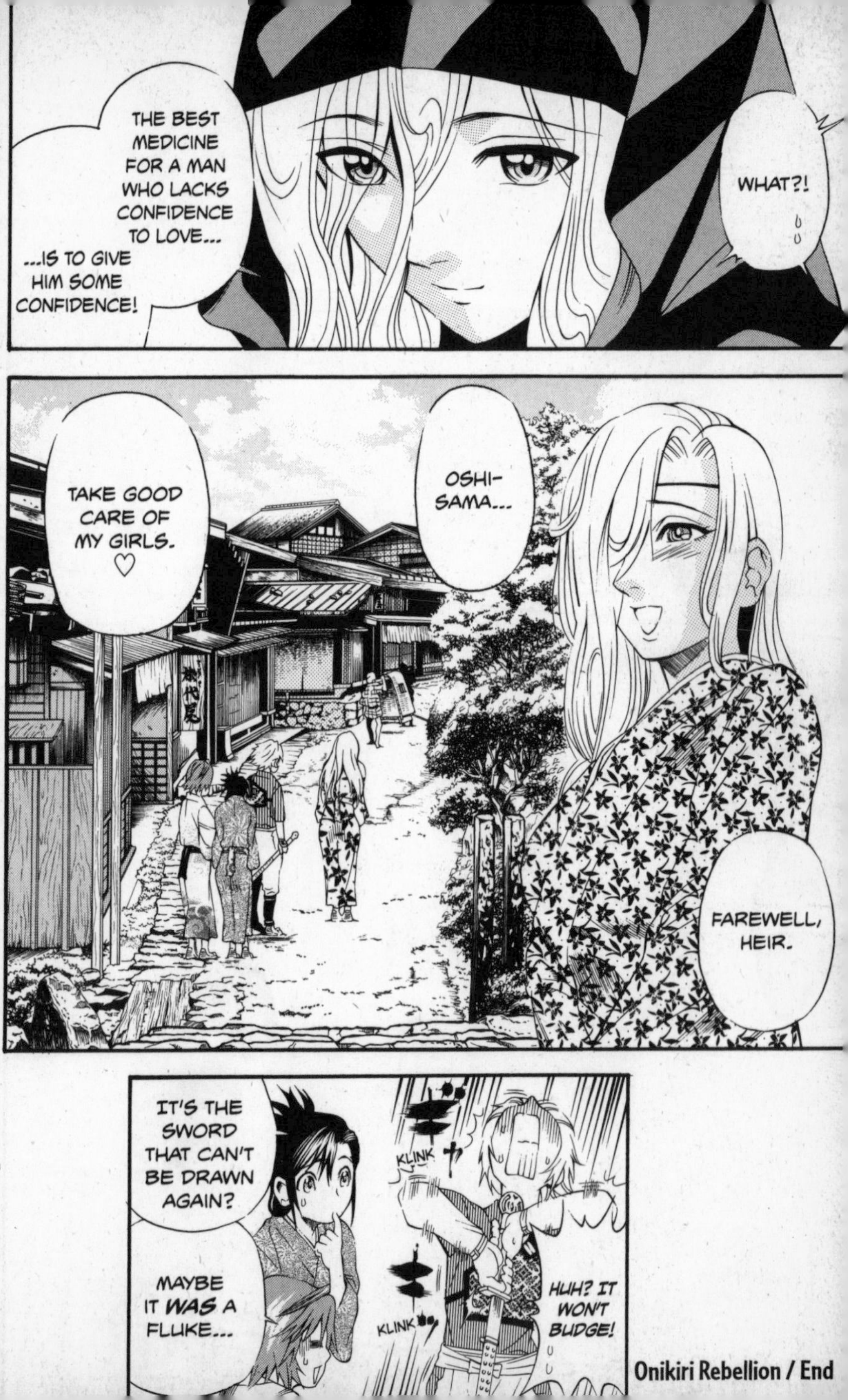
WHAT?!
THE BEST MEDICINE FOR A MAN WHO LACKS CONFIDENCE TO LOVE...
...IS TO GIVE HIM SOME CONFIDENCE!
OSHI-SAMA...
FAREWELL, HEIR.
TAKE GOOD CARE OF MY GIRLS. ♡
KLINK
HUH? IT WON'T BUDGE!
KLINK
IT'S THE SWORD THAT CAN'T BE DRAWN AGAIN?
MAYBE IT *WAS* A FLUKE...

Onikiri Rebellion / End

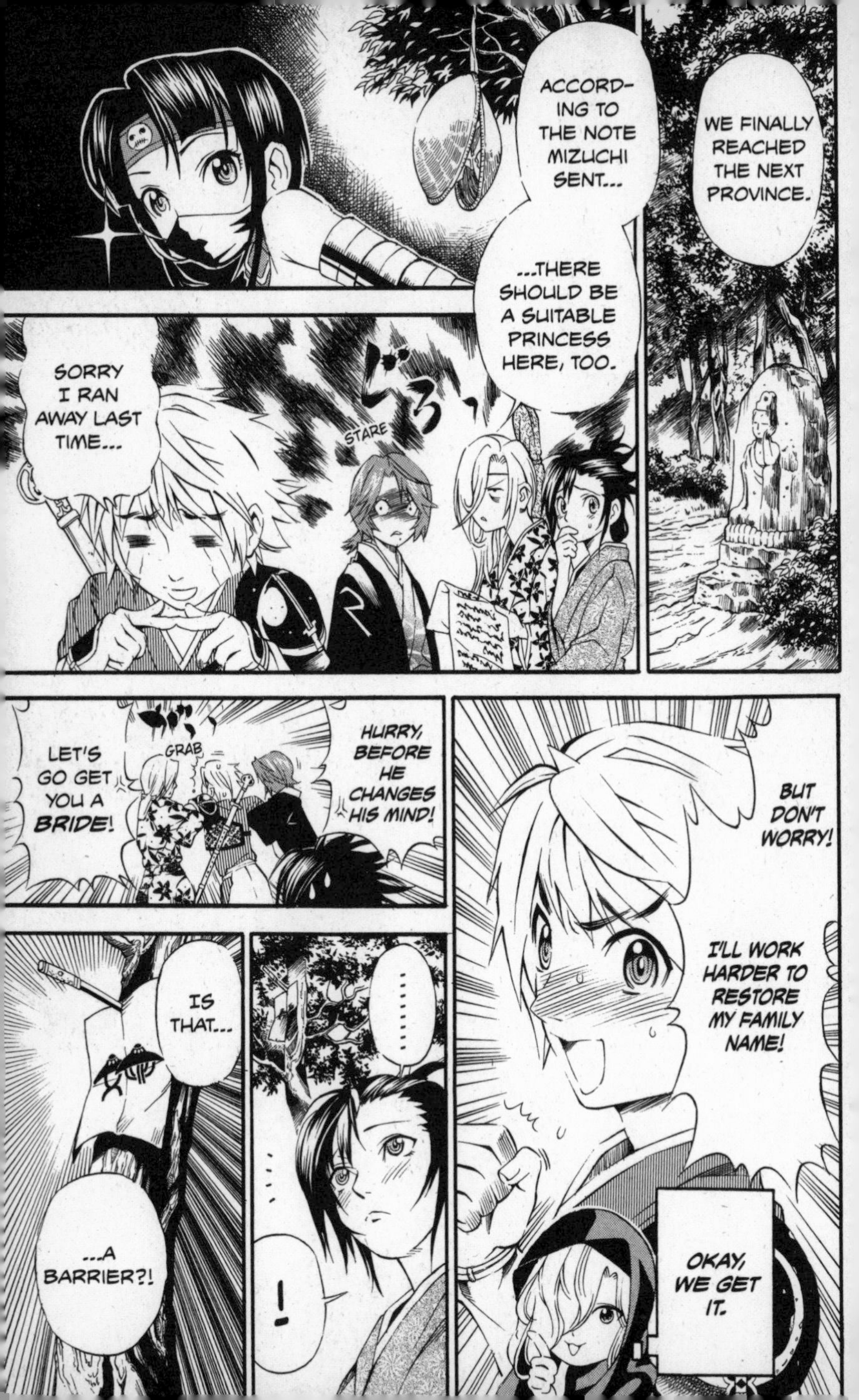
WE FINALLY REACHED THE NEXT PROVINCE.
ACCORDING TO THE NOTE MIZUCHI SENT...
...THERE SHOULD BE A SUITABLE PRINCESS HERE, TOO.
STARE
SORRY I RAN AWAY LAST TIME...
BUT DON'T WORRY!
I'LL WORK HARDER TO RESTORE MY FAMILY NAME!
OKAY, WE GET IT.
HURRY, BEFORE HE CHANGES HIS MIND!
GRAB
LET'S GO GET YOU A BRIDE!
......
...
!
IS THAT...
...A BARRIER?!

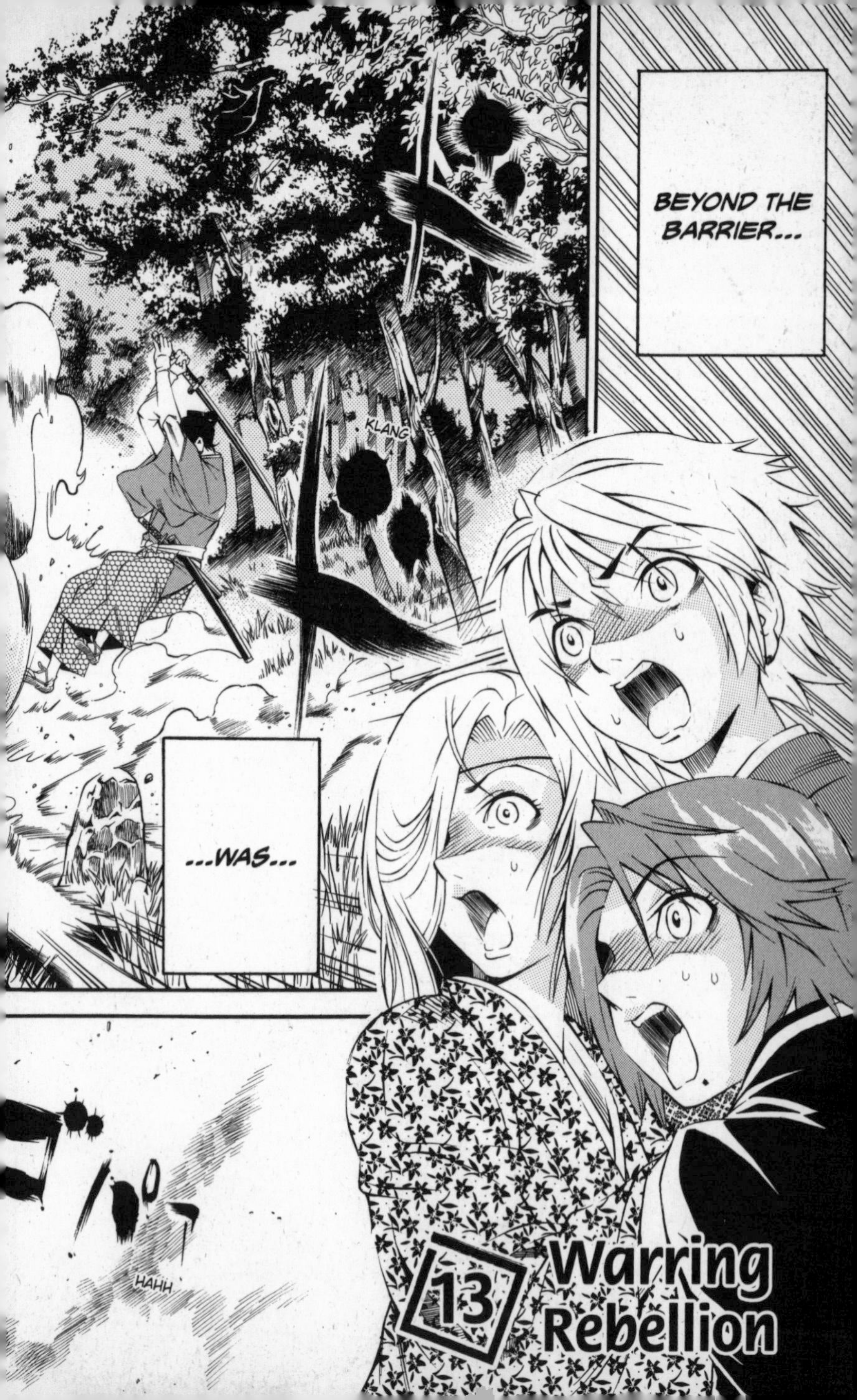
BEYOND THE BARRIER...
KLANG
KLANG
...WAS...
HAHH
13
Warring Rebellion

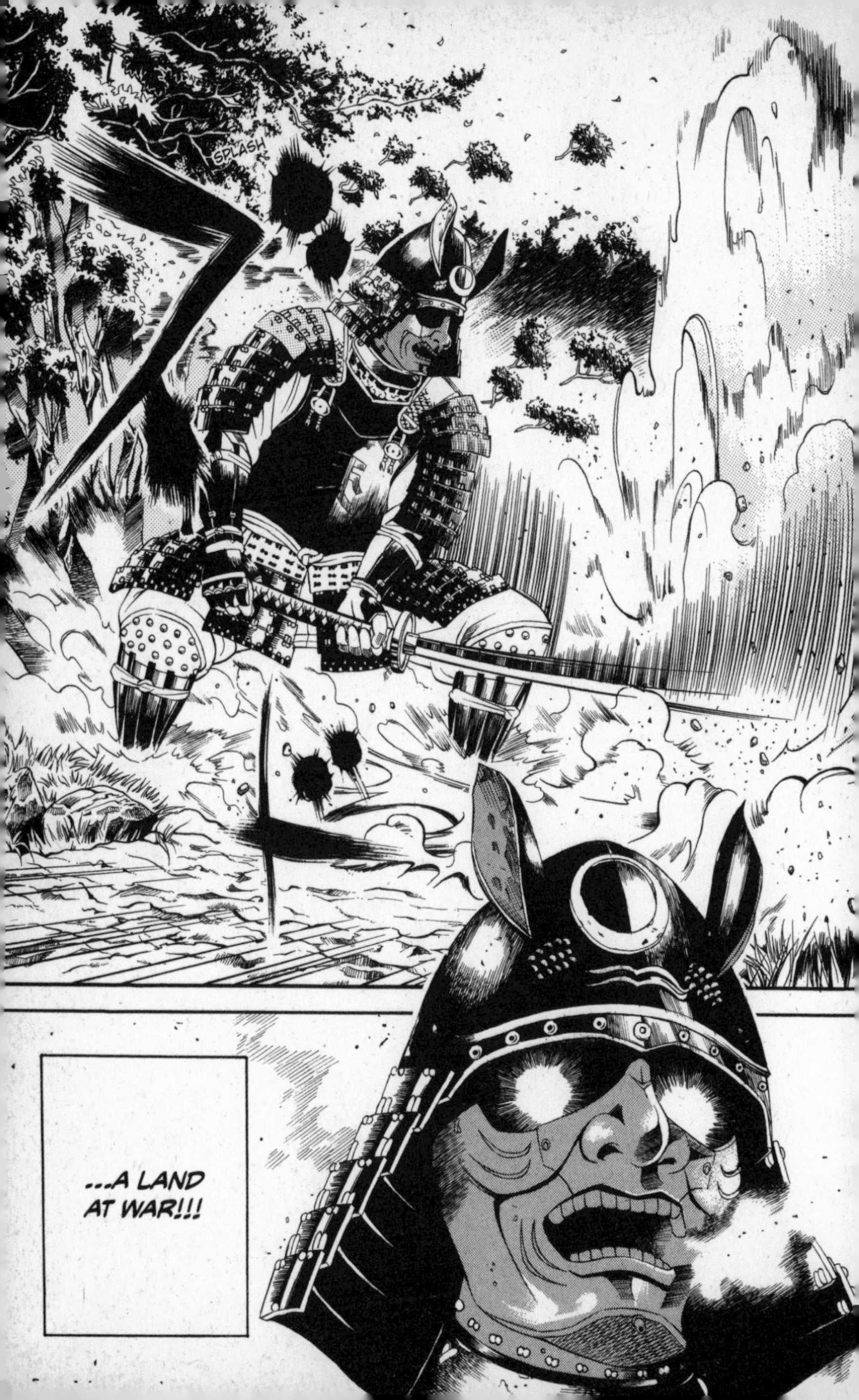
SPLASH
...A LAND
AT WAR!!!

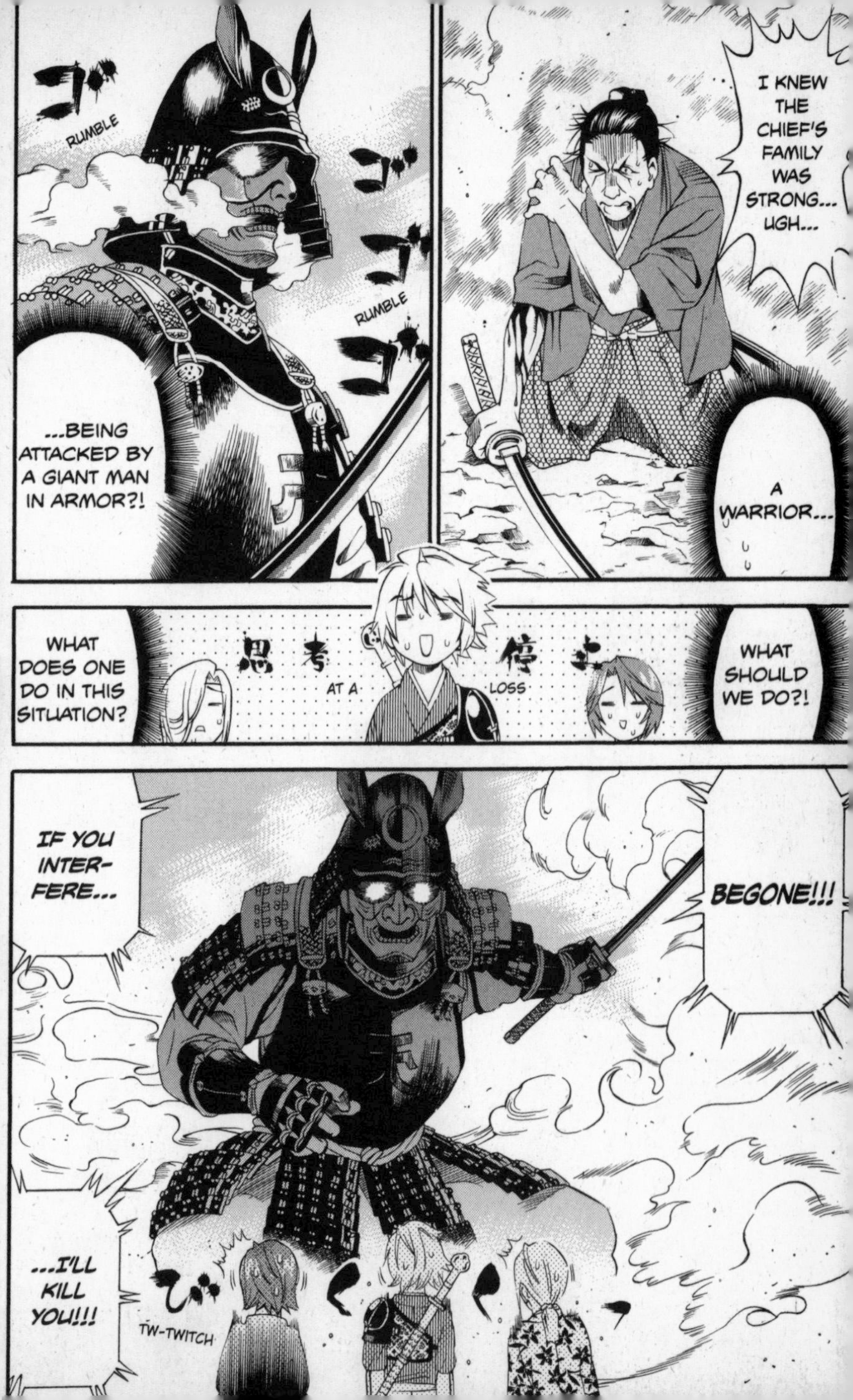
I KNEW THE CHIEF'S FAMILY WAS STRONG... UGH...
A WARRIOR...
RUMBLE
RUMBLE
...BEING ATTACKED BY A GIANT MAN IN ARMOR?!
WHAT SHOULD WE DO?!
思考停止
AT A LOSS
WHAT DOES ONE DO IN THIS SITUATION?
BEGONE!!!
IF YOU INTERFERE...
...I'LL KILL YOU!!!
TW-TWITCH

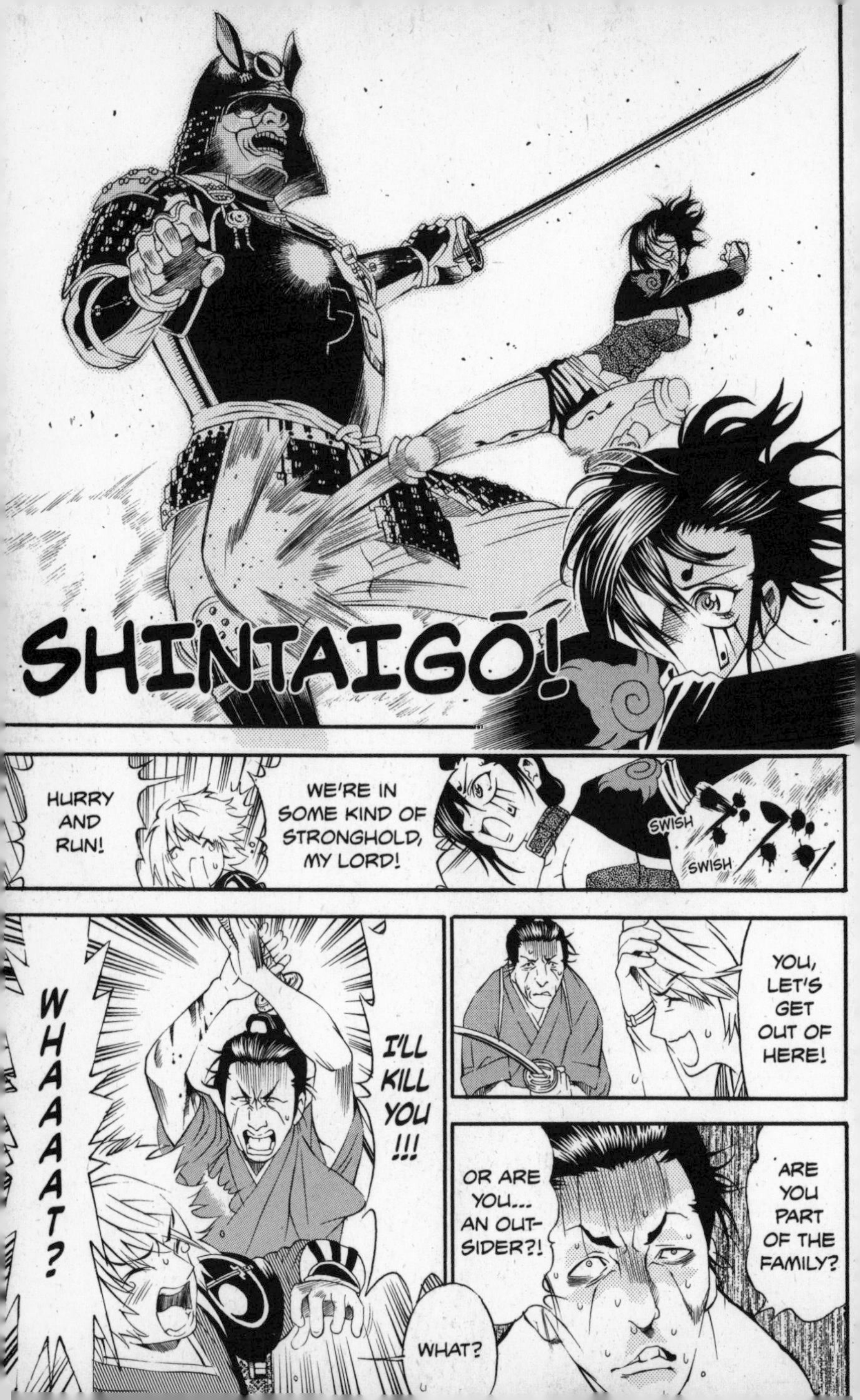
SHINTAIGŌ!
SWISH
SWISH
WE'RE IN SOME KIND OF STRONGHOLD, MY LORD!
HURRY AND RUN!
YOU, LET'S GET OUT OF HERE!
ARE YOU PART OF THE FAMILY?
OR ARE YOU... AN OUT-SIDER?!
WHAT?
I'LL KILL YOU!!!
WHAAAAAT?

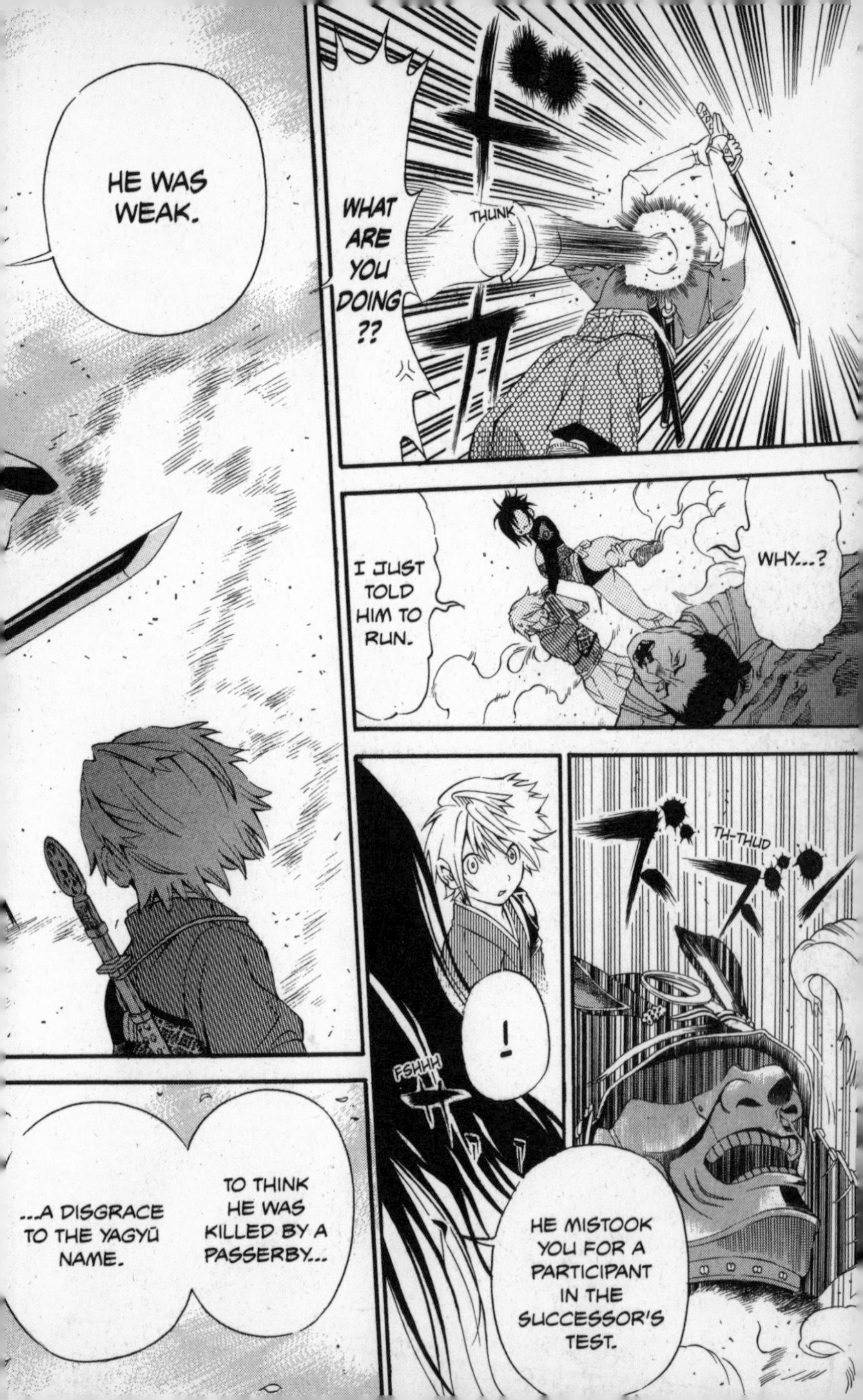
WHAT ARE YOU DOING??
THUNK
WHY...?
I JUST TOLD HIM TO RUN.
TH-THUD
!
FSHHH
HE MISTOOK YOU FOR A PARTICIPANT IN THE SUCCESSOR'S TEST.
HE WAS WEAK.
TO THINK HE WAS KILLED BY A PASSERBY...
...A DISGRACE TO THE YAGYŪ NAME.

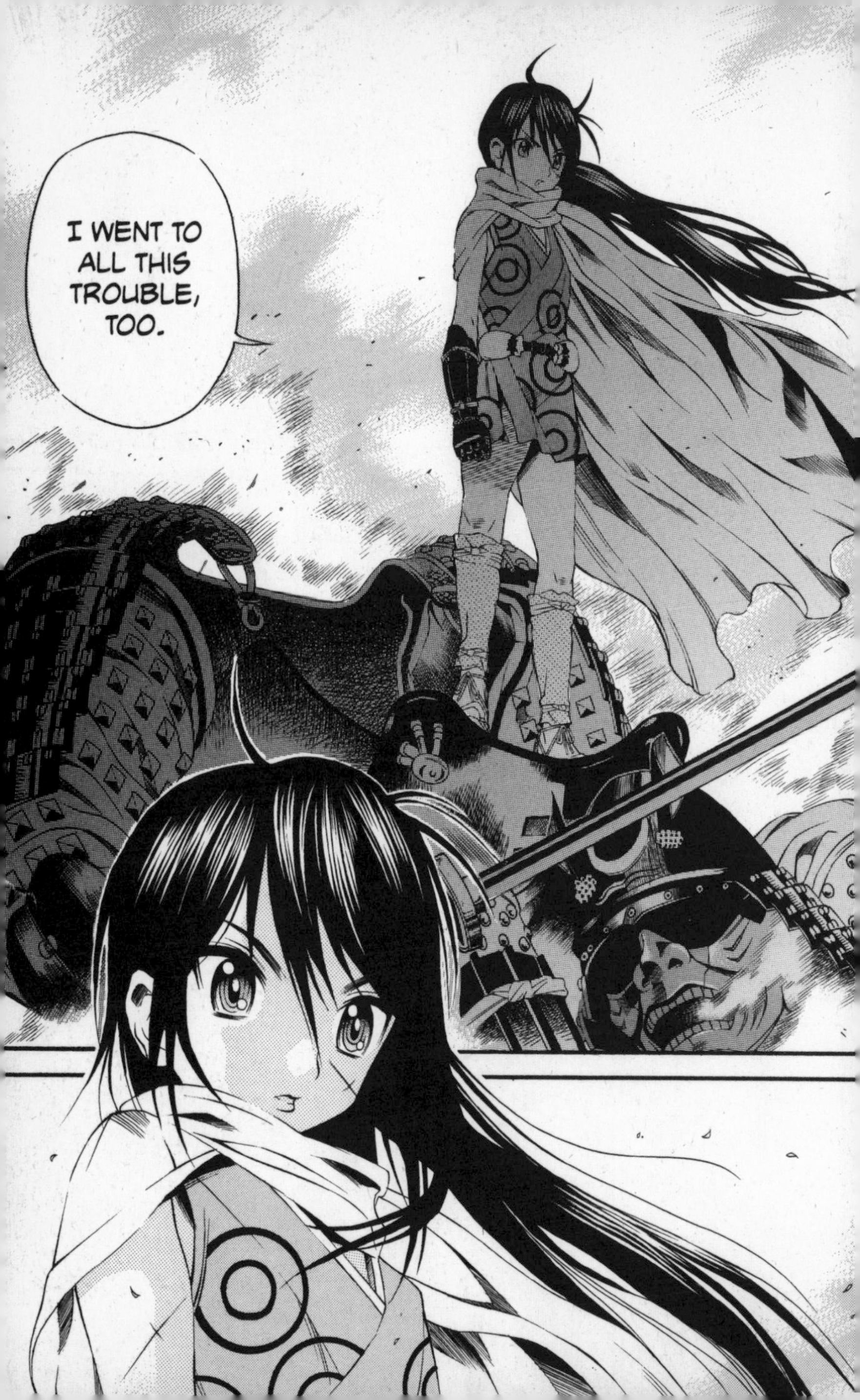
I WENT TO ALL THIS TROUBLE, TOO.

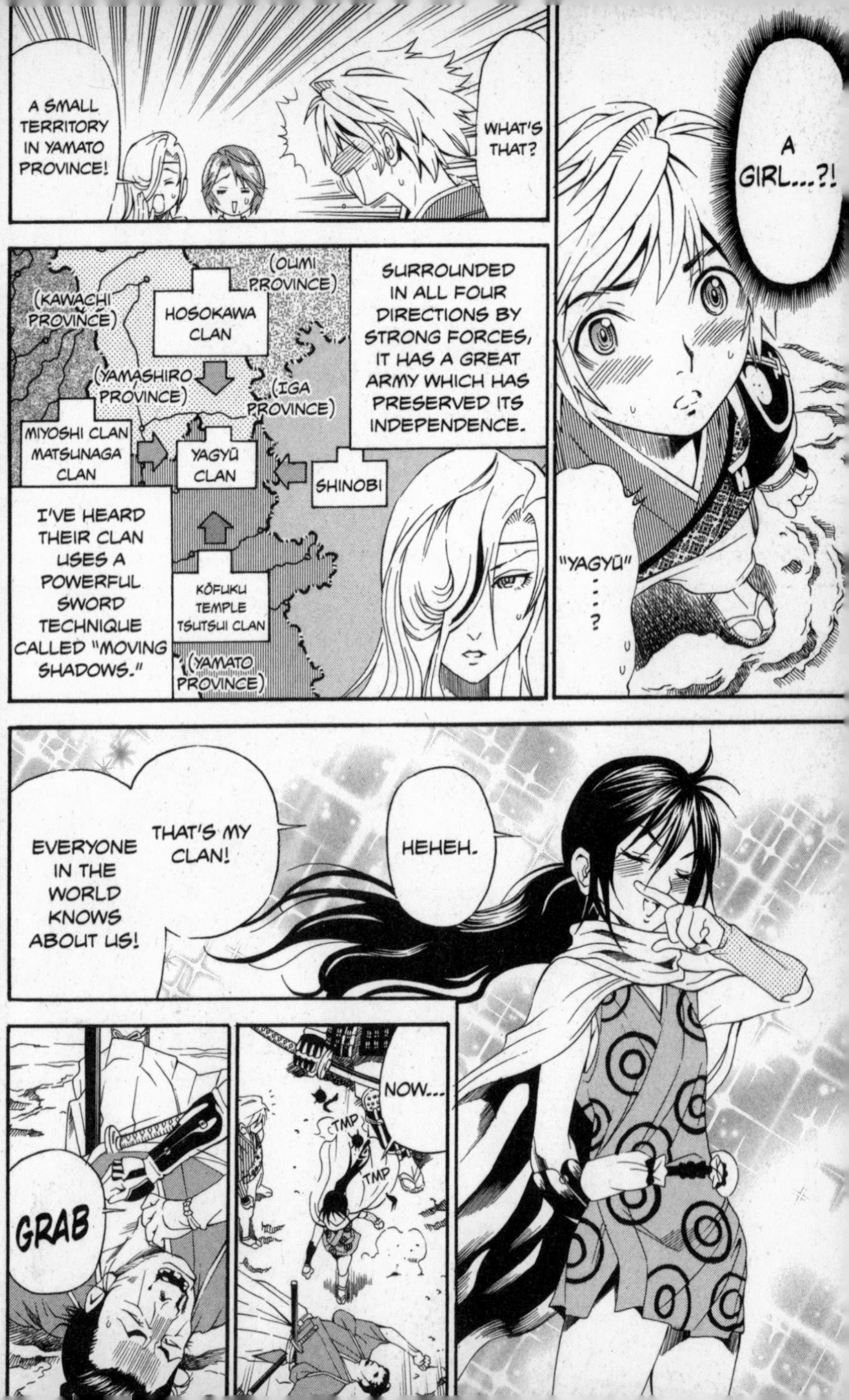
A GIRL...?!
"YAGYŪ"...?
WHAT'S THAT?
A SMALL TERRITORY IN YAMATO PROVINCE!
SURROUNDED IN ALL FOUR DIRECTIONS BY STRONG FORCES, IT HAS A GREAT ARMY WHICH HAS PRESERVED ITS INDEPENDENCE.
(OUMI PROVINCE)
HOSOKAWA CLAN
(KAWACHI PROVINCE)
(YAMASHIRO PROVINCE)
(IGA PROVINCE)
MIYOSHI CLAN MATSUNAGA CLAN
YAGYŪ CLAN
SHINOBI
KŌFUKU TEMPLE TSUTSUI CLAN
(YAMATO PROVINCE)
I'VE HEARD THEIR CLAN USES A POWERFUL SWORD TECHNIQUE CALLED "MOVING SHADOWS."
HEHEH.
THAT'S MY CLAN!
EVERYONE IN THE WORLD KNOWS ABOUT US!
NOW...
TMP
TMP
GRAB

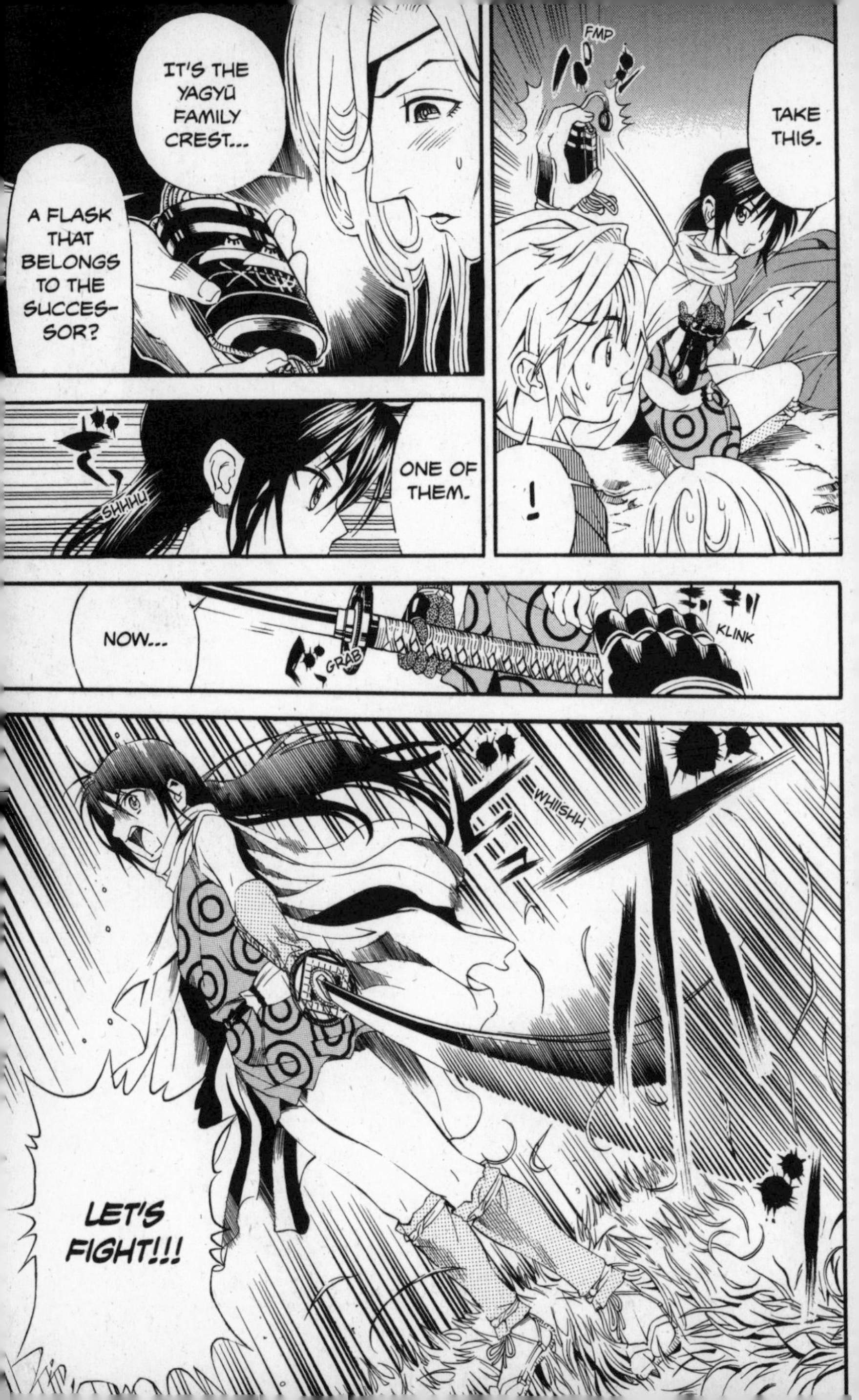
FMP
TAKE THIS.
!
IT'S THE YAGYŪ FAMILY CREST...
A FLASK THAT BELONGS TO THE SUCCES-SOR?
ONE OF THEM.
SHHHU
KLINK
GRAB
NOW...
WHIISHH
LET'S FIGHT!!!

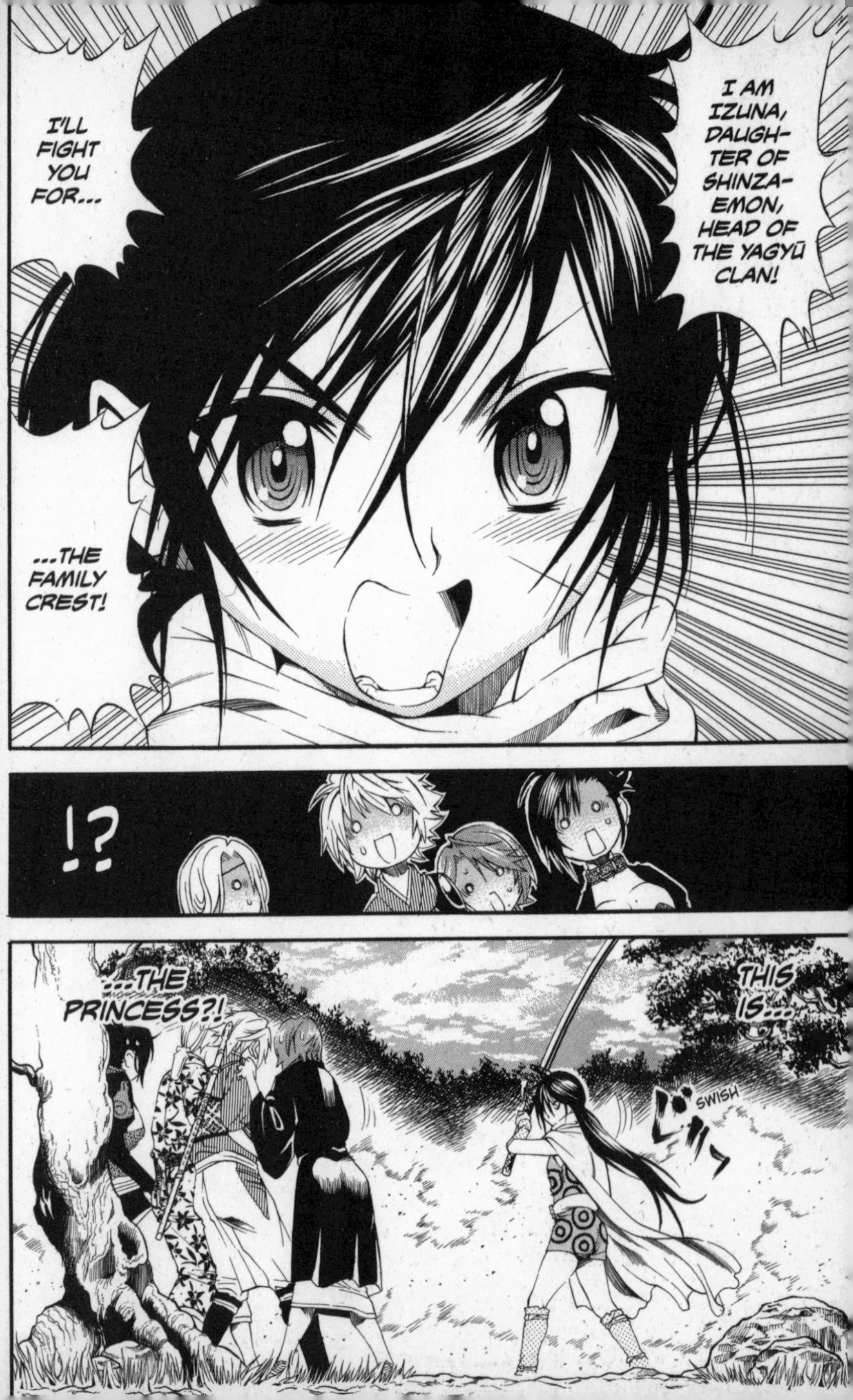
I AM IZUNA, DAUGHTER OF SHINZAEMON, HEAD OF THE YAGYŪ CLAN!
I'LL FIGHT YOU FOR...
...THE FAMILY CREST!
!?
THIS IS...
SWISH
...THE PRINCESS?!

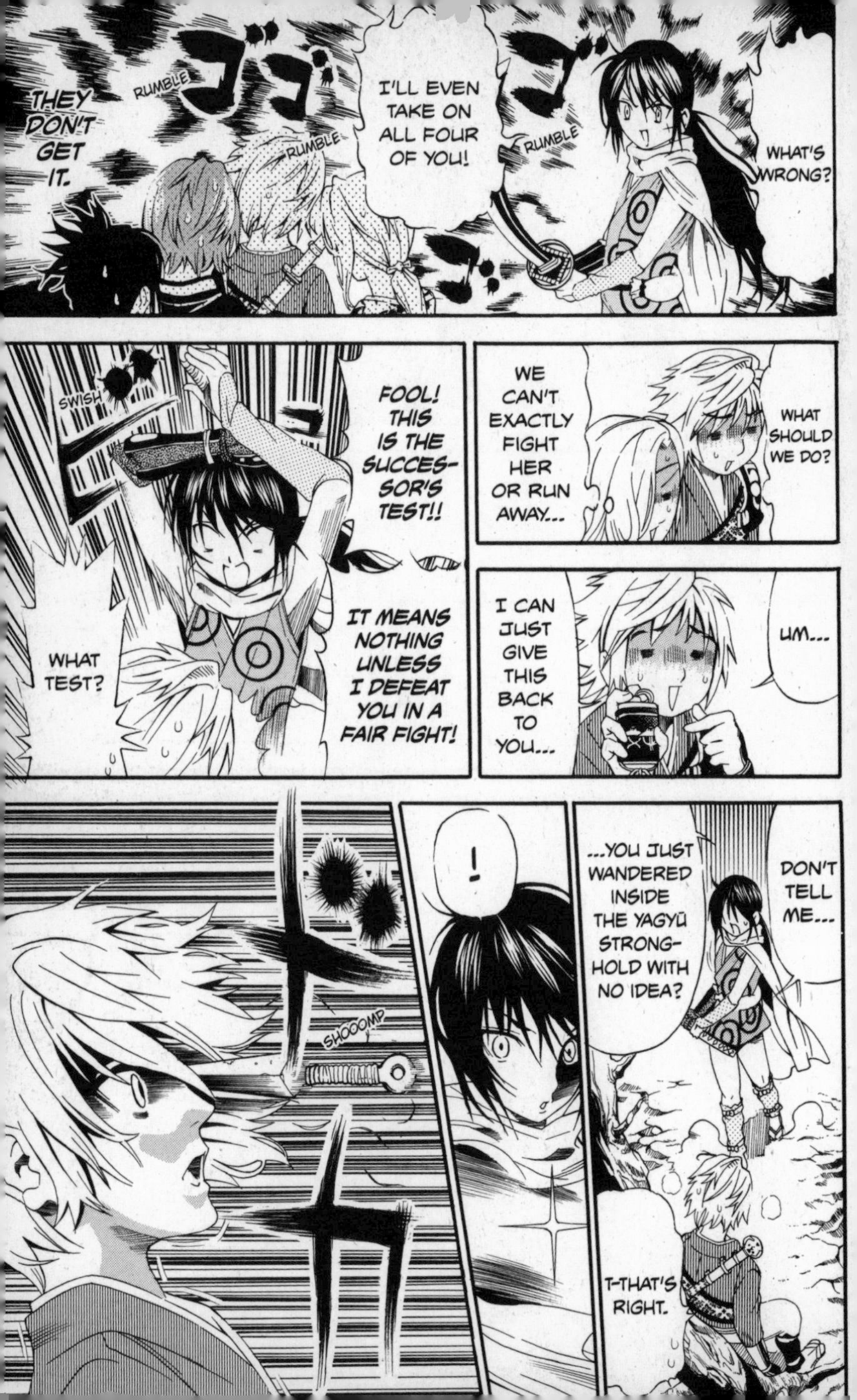
WHAT'S WRONG?
RUMBLE
I'LL EVEN TAKE ON ALL FOUR OF YOU!
RUMBLE
RUMBLE
THEY DON'T GET IT.
WHAT SHOULD WE DO?
WE CAN'T EXACTLY FIGHT HER OR RUN AWAY...
UM...
I CAN JUST GIVE THIS BACK TO YOU...
FOOL! THIS IS THE SUCCES-SOR'S TEST!!
IT MEANS NOTHING UNLESS I DEFEAT YOU IN A FAIR FIGHT!
SWISH
WHAT TEST?
DON'T TELL ME...
...YOU JUST WANDERED INSIDE THE YAGYŪ STRONG-HOLD WITH NO IDEA?
T-THAT'S RIGHT.
!
SHOOOMP

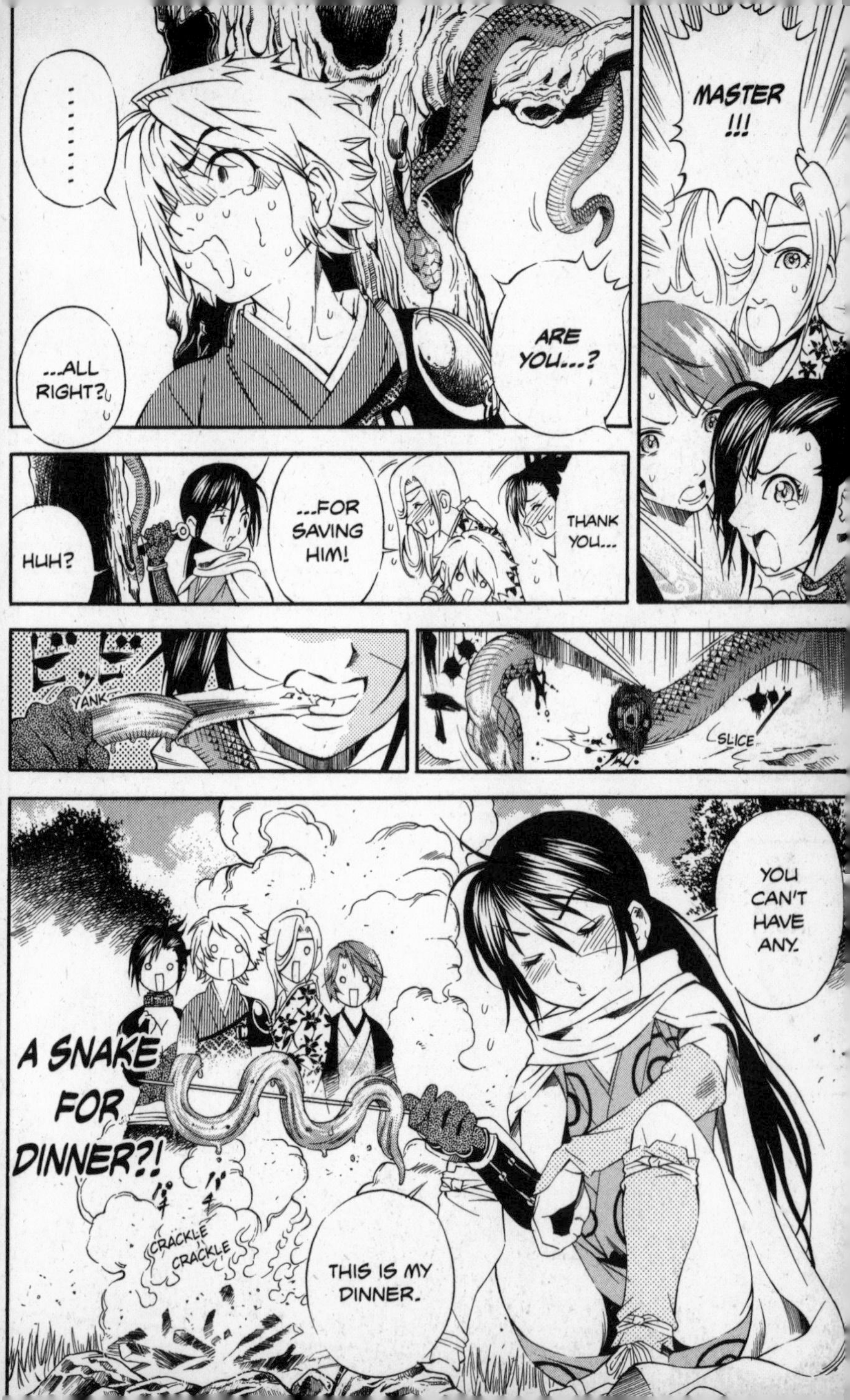
MASTER !!!
ARE YOU...?
...ALL RIGHT?
......
THANK YOU...
...FOR SAVING HIM!
HUH?
SLICE
YANK
YOU CAN'T HAVE ANY.
A SNAKE FOR DINNER?!
CRACKLE CRACKLE
THIS IS MY DINNER.

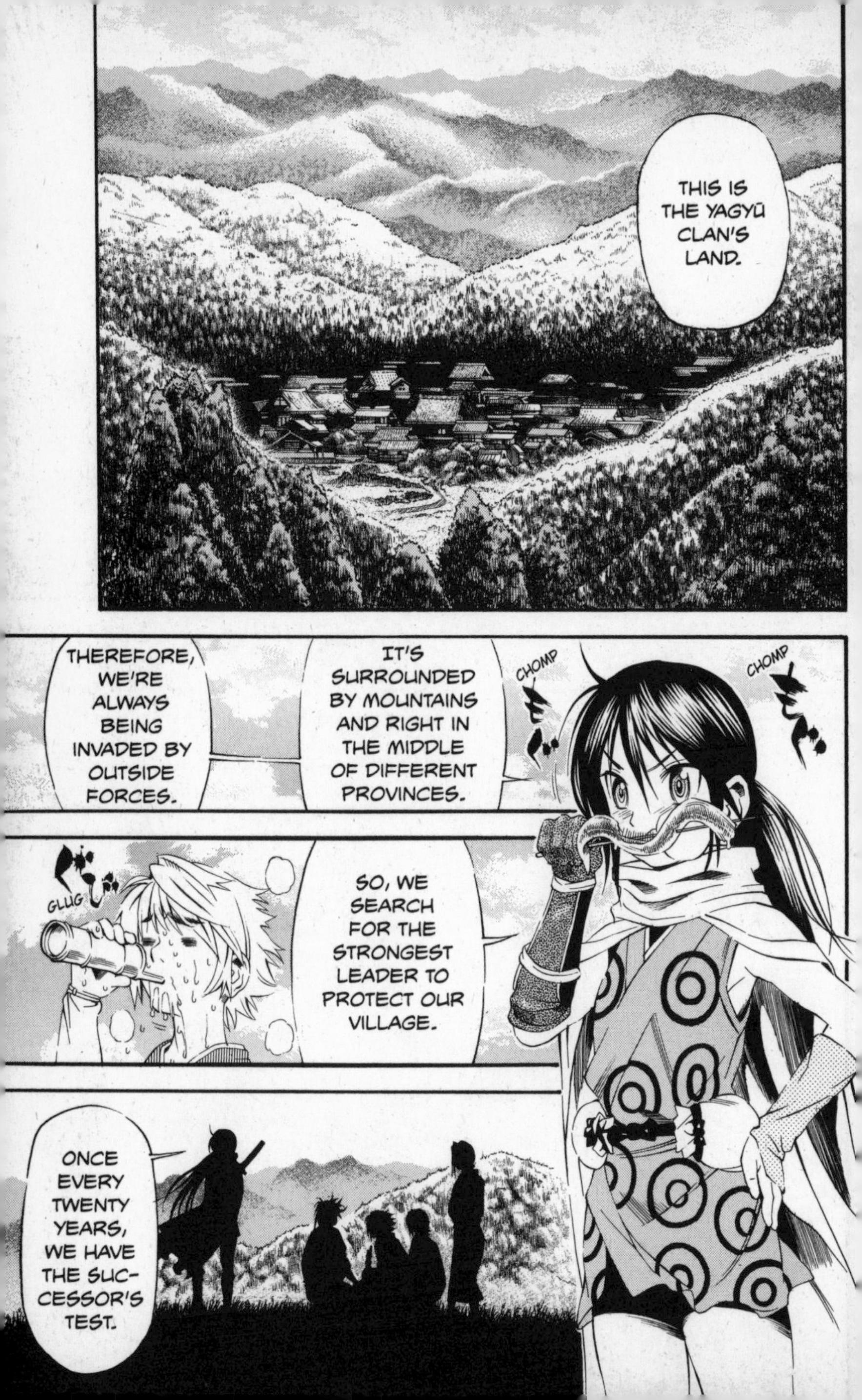
THIS IS THE YAGYŪ CLAN'S LAND.
CHOMP
CHOMP
IT'S SURROUNDED BY MOUNTAINS AND RIGHT IN THE MIDDLE OF DIFFERENT PROVINCES.
THEREFORE, WE'RE ALWAYS BEING INVADED BY OUTSIDE FORCES.
SO, WE SEARCH FOR THE STRONGEST LEADER TO PROTECT OUR VILLAGE.
GLUG
ONCE EVERY TWENTY YEARS, WE HAVE THE SUC-CESSOR'S TEST.

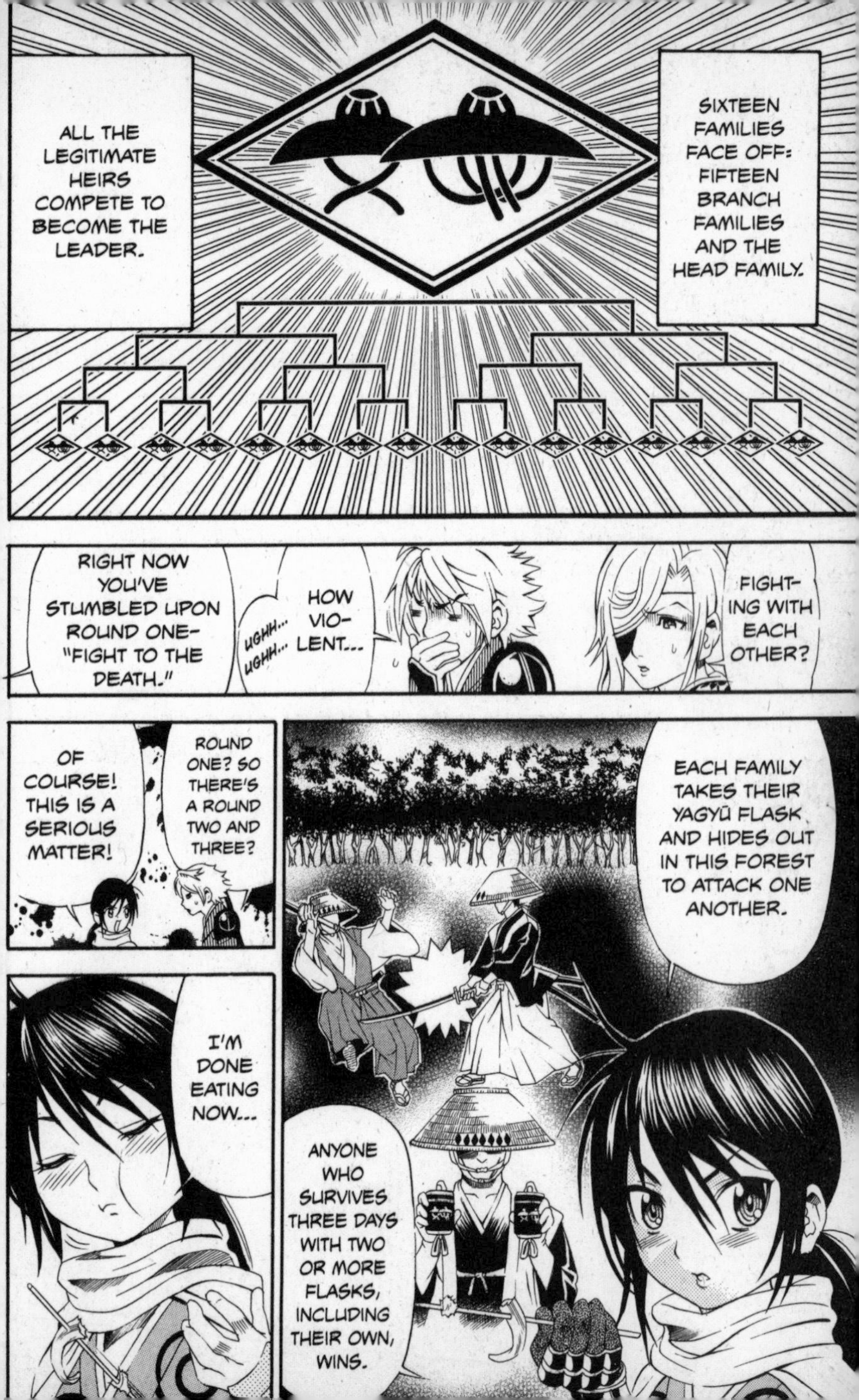
SIXTEEN FAMILIES FACE OFF: FIFTEEN BRANCH FAMILIES AND THE HEAD FAMILY.
ALL THE LEGITIMATE HEIRS COMPETE TO BECOME THE LEADER.
FIGHTING WITH EACH OTHER?
HOW VIOLENT...
UGHH... UGHH...
RIGHT NOW YOU'VE STUMBLED UPON ROUND ONE—"FIGHT TO THE DEATH."
EACH FAMILY TAKES THEIR YAGYŪ FLASK AND HIDES OUT IN THIS FOREST TO ATTACK ONE ANOTHER.
ANYONE WHO SURVIVES THREE DAYS WITH TWO OR MORE FLASKS, INCLUDING THEIR OWN, WINS.
ROUND ONE? SO THERE'S A ROUND TWO AND THREE?
OF COURSE! THIS IS A SERIOUS MATTER!
I'M DONE EATING NOW...

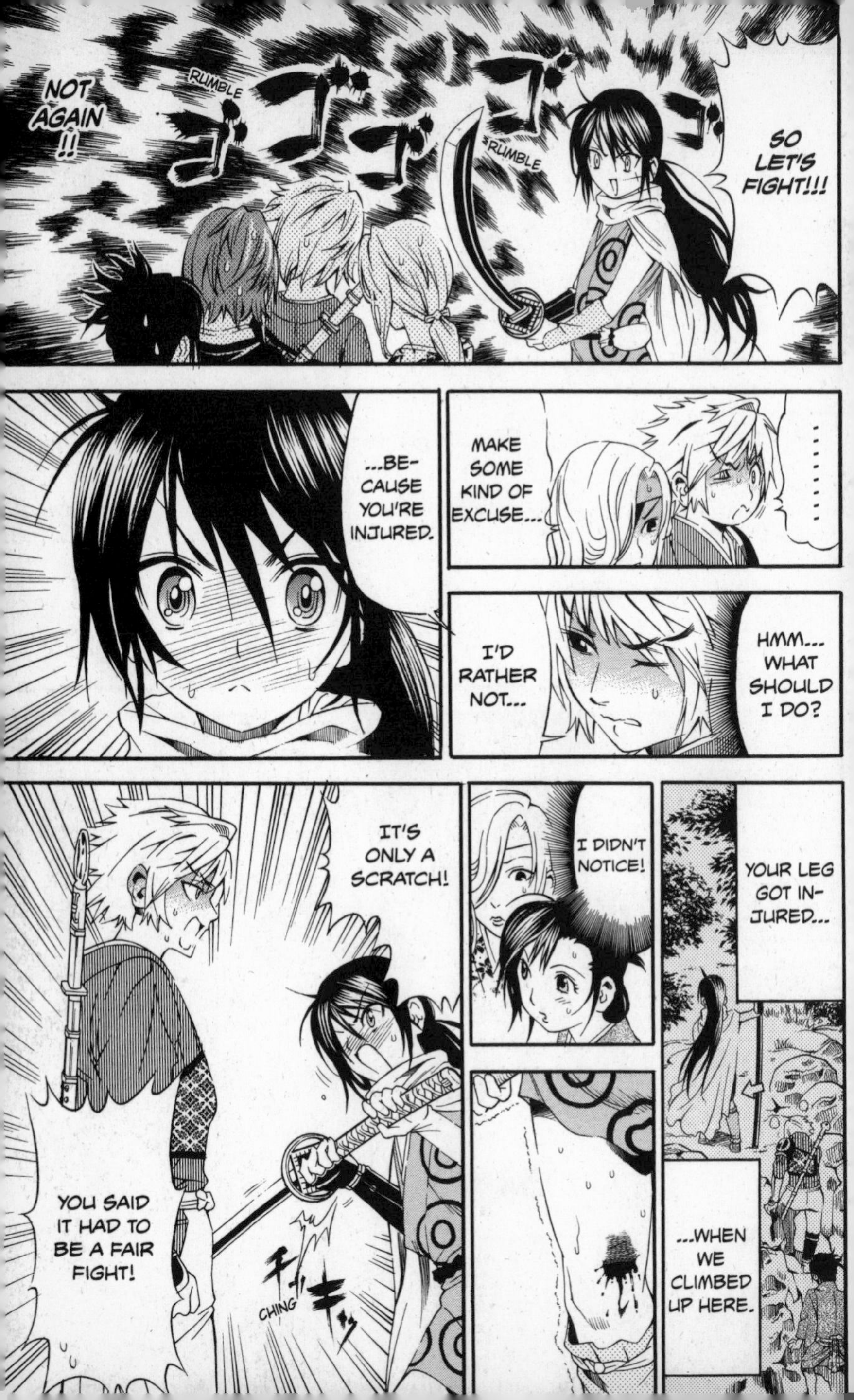
SO LET'S FIGHT!!!
RUMBLE
RUMBLE
NOT AGAIN!!
......
MAKE SOME KIND OF EXCUSE...
HMM... WHAT SHOULD I DO?
I'D RATHER NOT...
...BE-CAUSE YOU'RE INJURED.
YOUR LEG GOT IN-JURED...
...WHEN WE CLIMBED UP HERE.
I DIDN'T NOTICE!
IT'S ONLY A SCRATCH!
CHING
YOU SAID IT HAD TO BE A FAIR FIGHT!

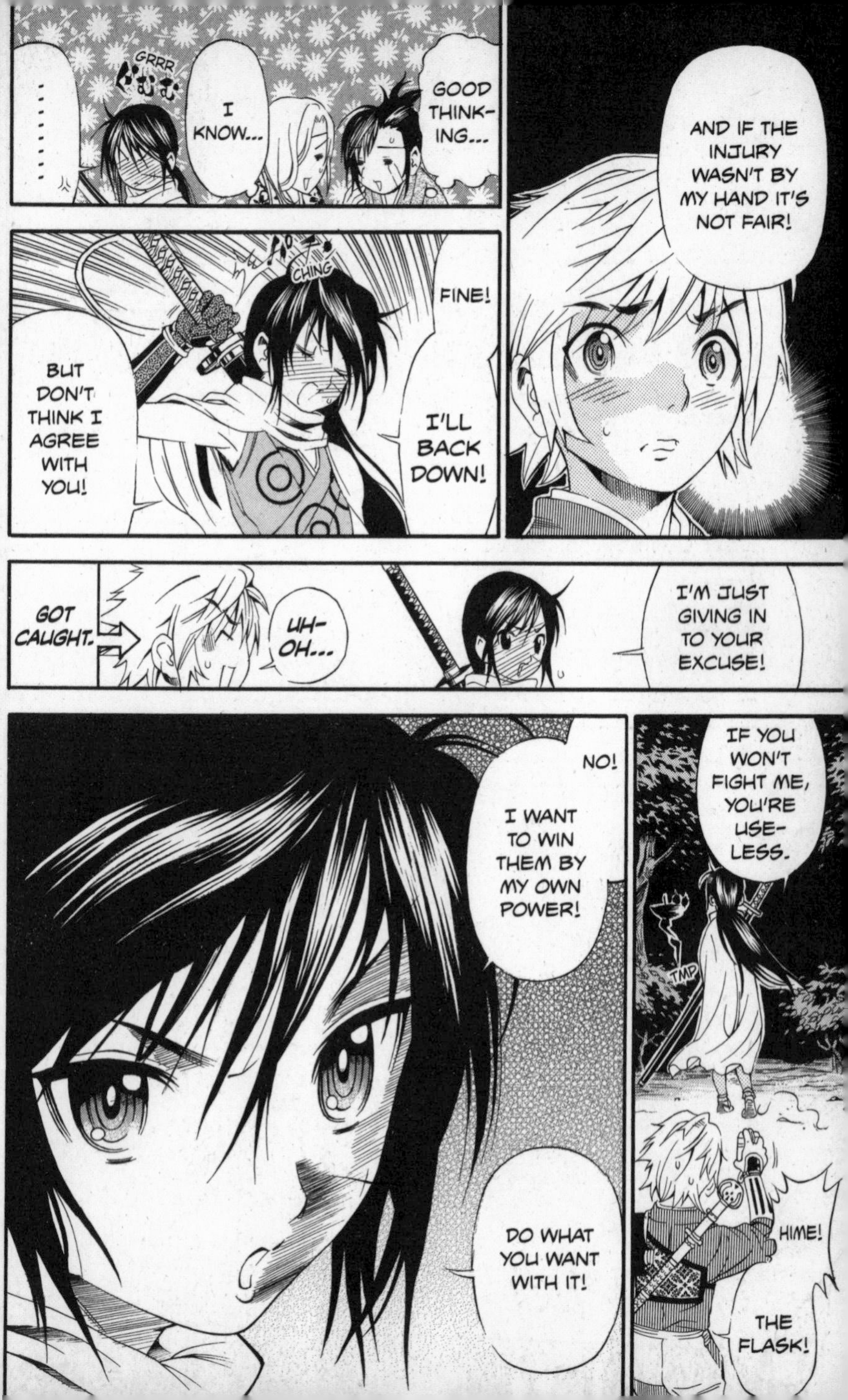
AND IF THE INJURY WASN'T BY MY HAND IT'S NOT FAIR!
GOOD THINK-ING...
I KNOW...
GRRR
....
CHING
FINE!
I'LL BACK DOWN!
BUT DON'T THINK I AGREE WITH YOU!
I'M JUST GIVING IN TO YOUR EXCUSE!
UH-OH...
GOT CAUGHT.
IF YOU WON'T FIGHT ME, YOU'RE USE-LESS.
TMP
HIME!
THE FLASK!
NO!
I WANT TO WIN THEM BY MY OWN POWER!
DO WHAT YOU WANT WITH IT!

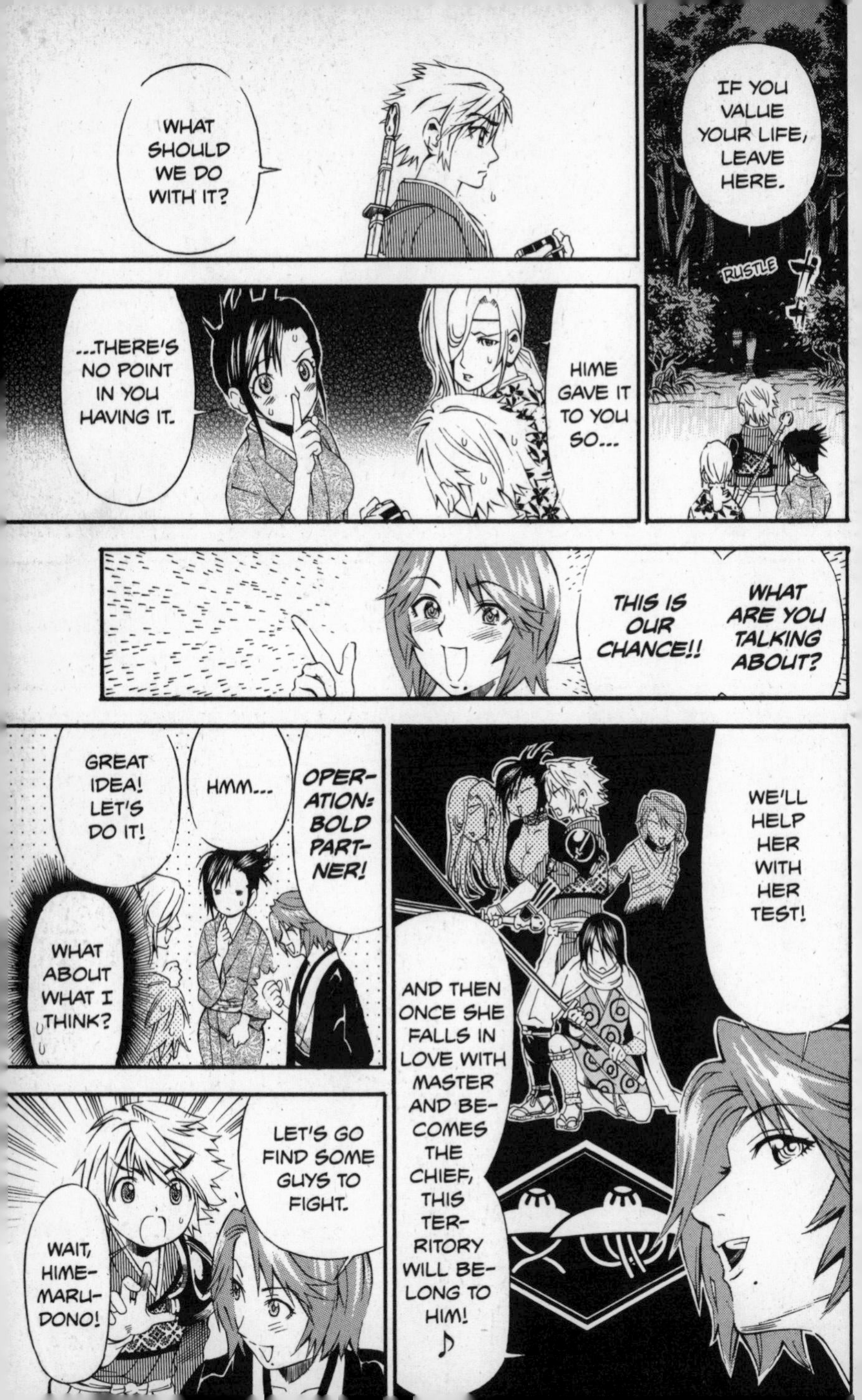
IF YOU VALUE YOUR LIFE, LEAVE HERE.
RUSTLE
WHAT SHOULD WE DO WITH IT?
HIME GAVE IT TO YOU SO...
...THERE'S NO POINT IN YOU HAVING IT.
WHAT ARE YOU TALKING ABOUT?
THIS IS OUR CHANCE!!
WE'LL HELP HER WITH HER TEST!
AND THEN ONCE SHE FALLS IN LOVE WITH MASTER AND BECOMES THE CHIEF, THIS TERRITORY WILL BELONG TO HIM! ♪
OPERATION: BOLD PARTNER!
HMM...
GREAT IDEA! LET'S DO IT!
WHAT ABOUT WHAT I THINK?
LET'S GO FIND SOME GUYS TO FIGHT.
WAIT, HIMEMARU-DONO!

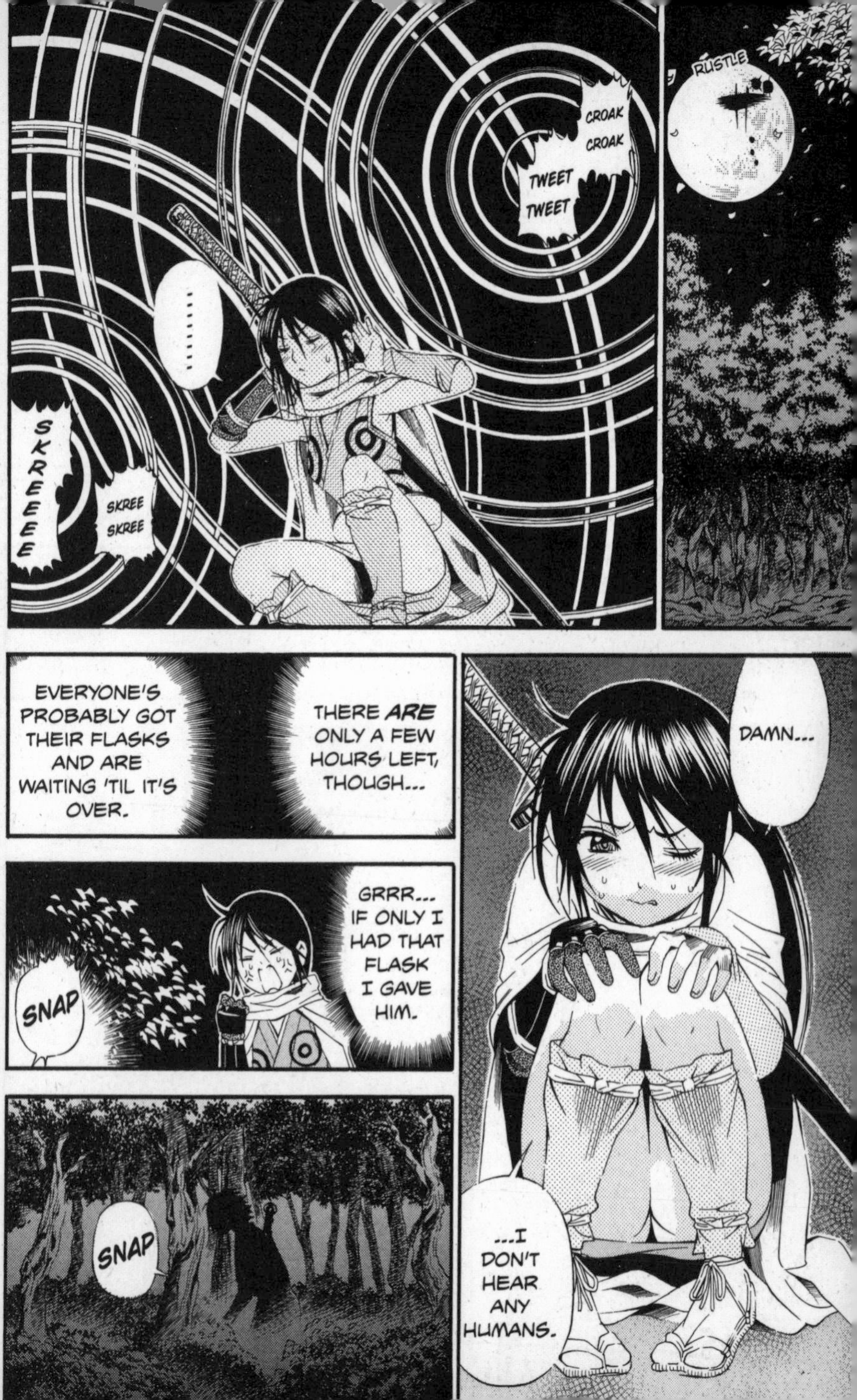
RUSTLE
CROAK CROAK
TWEET TWEET
......
SKREEEEE
SKREE SKREE
DAMN...
...I DON'T HEAR ANY HUMANS.
THERE *ARE* ONLY A FEW HOURS LEFT, THOUGH...
EVERYONE'S PROBABLY GOT THEIR FLASKS AND ARE WAITING 'TIL IT'S OVER.
GRRR... IF ONLY I HAD THAT FLASK I GAVE HIM.
SNAP
SNAP

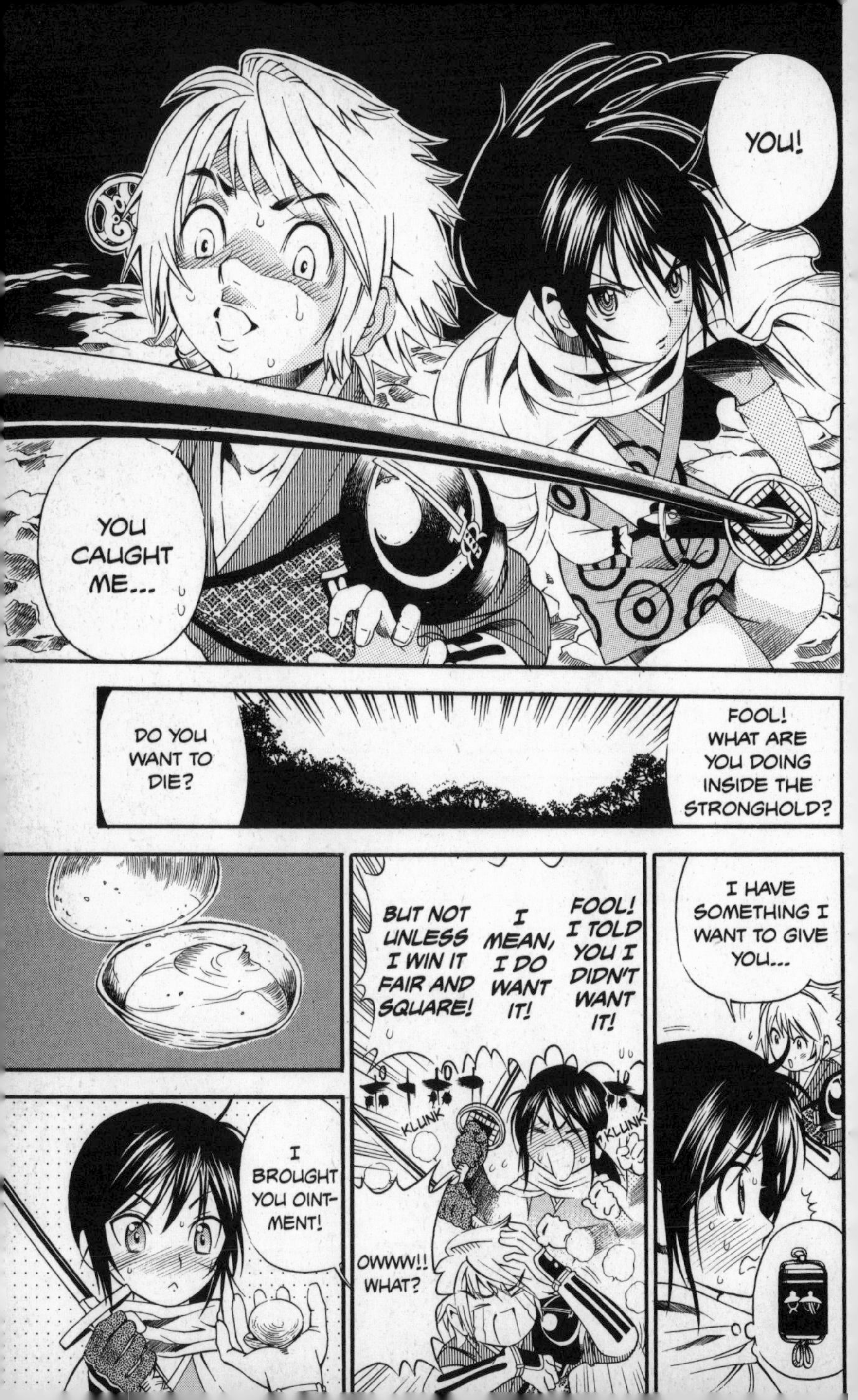
YOU!
YOU CAUGHT ME...
FOOL! WHAT ARE YOU DOING INSIDE THE STRONGHOLD?
DO YOU WANT TO DIE?
I HAVE SOMETHING I WANT TO GIVE YOU...
I BROUGHT YOU OINT-MENT!
FOOL! I TOLD YOU I DIDN'T WANT IT!
I MEAN, I DO WANT IT!
BUT NOT UNLESS I WIN IT FAIR AND SQUARE!
KLUNK
KLUNK
OWWW!! WHAT?

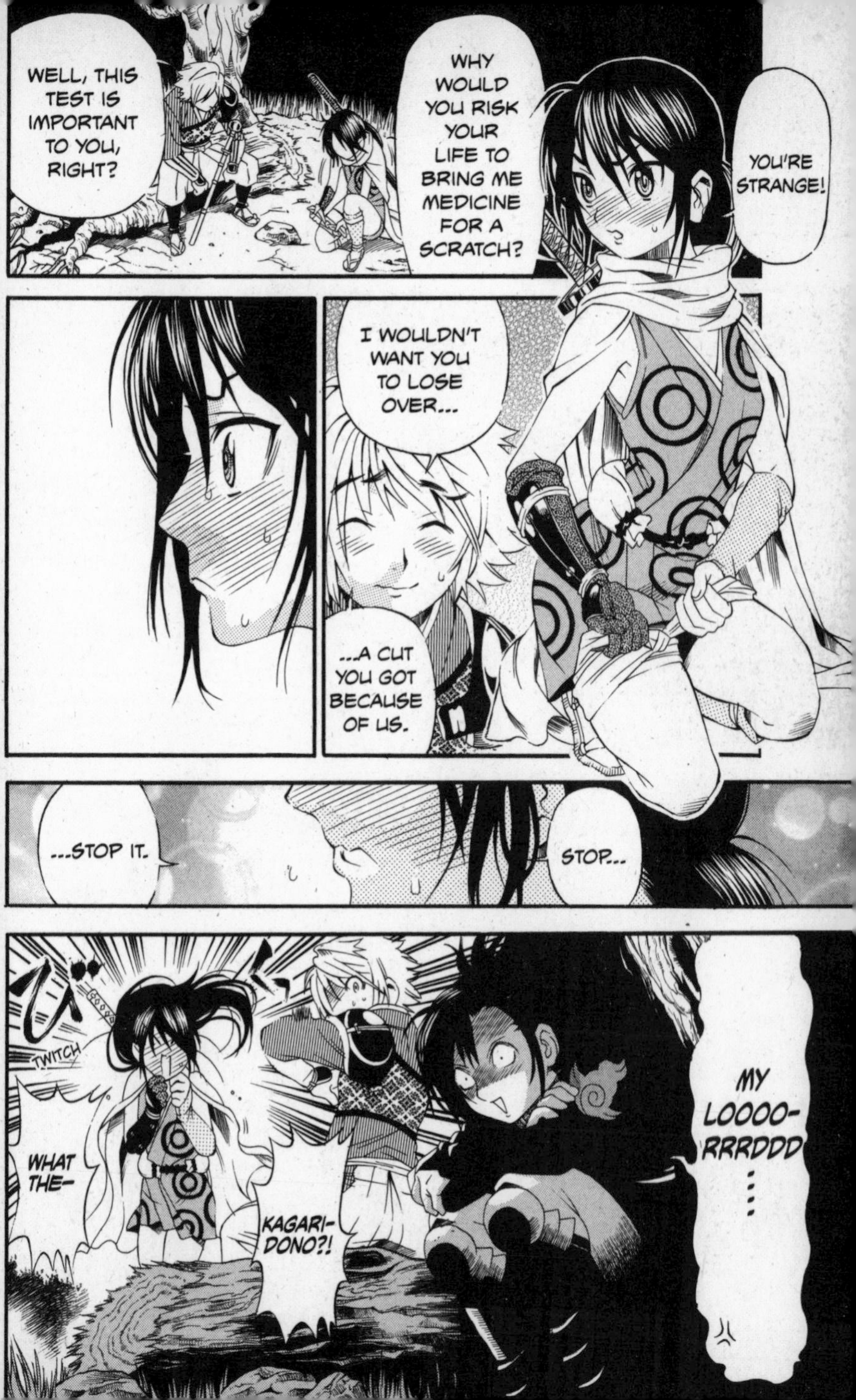
YOU'RE STRANGE!
WHY WOULD YOU RISK YOUR LIFE TO BRING ME MEDICINE FOR A SCRATCH?
WELL, THIS TEST IS IMPORTANT TO YOU, RIGHT?
I WOULDN'T WANT YOU TO LOSE OVER...
...A CUT YOU GOT BECAUSE OF US.
STOP...
...STOP IT.
MY LOOOO-RRRDDD ....
KAGARI-DONO?!
TWITCH
WHAT THE-

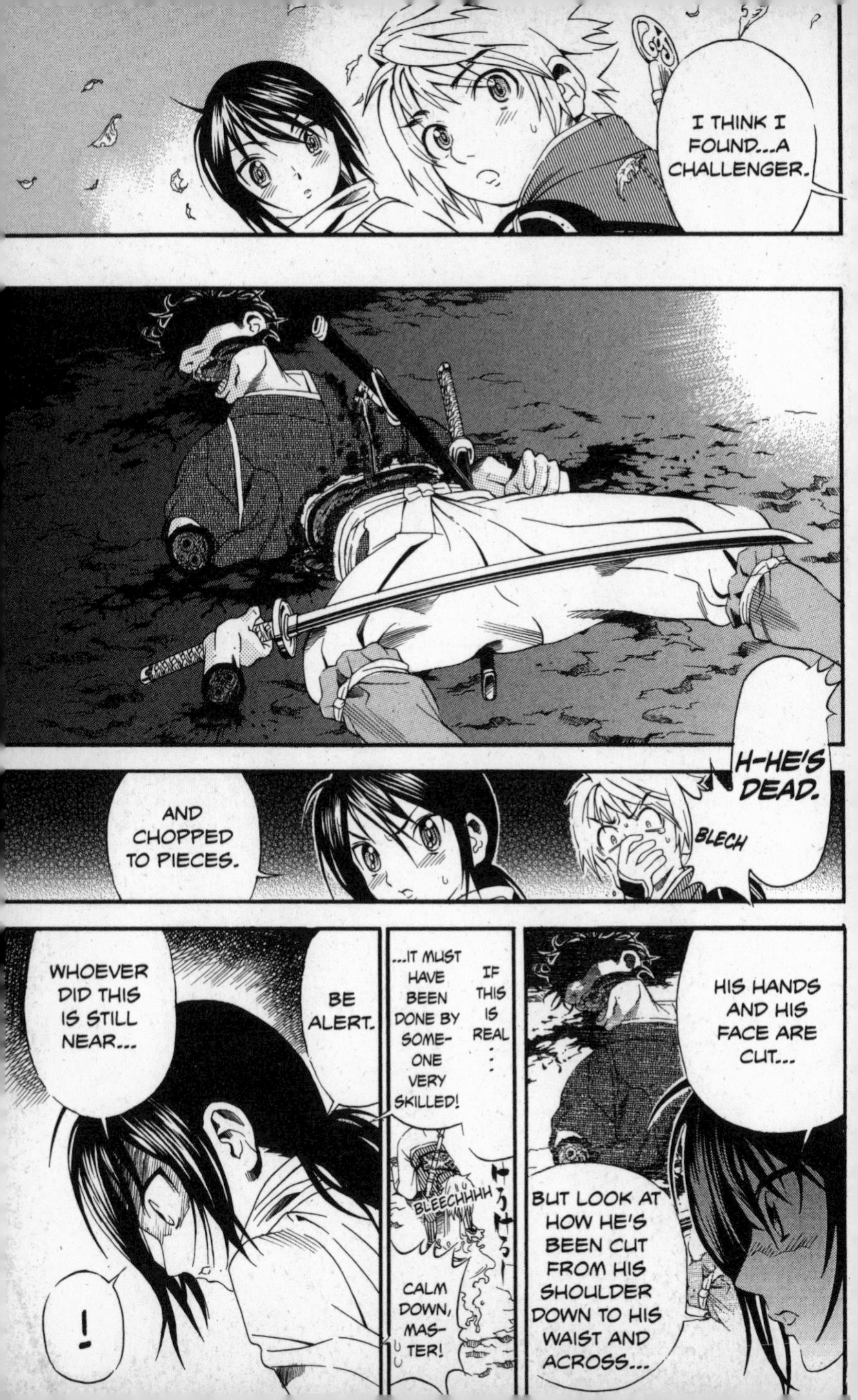
I THINK I FOUND...A CHALLENGER.
H-HE'S DEAD.
BLECH
AND CHOPPED TO PIECES.
HIS HANDS AND HIS FACE ARE CUT...
BUT LOOK AT HOW HE'S BEEN CUT FROM HIS SHOULDER DOWN TO HIS WAIST AND ACROSS...
IF THIS IS REAL...
...IT MUST HAVE BEEN DONE BY SOME-ONE VERY SKILLED!
BLEECHHHH
CALM DOWN, MAS-TER!
BE ALERT.
WHOEVER DID THIS IS STILL NEAR...
!

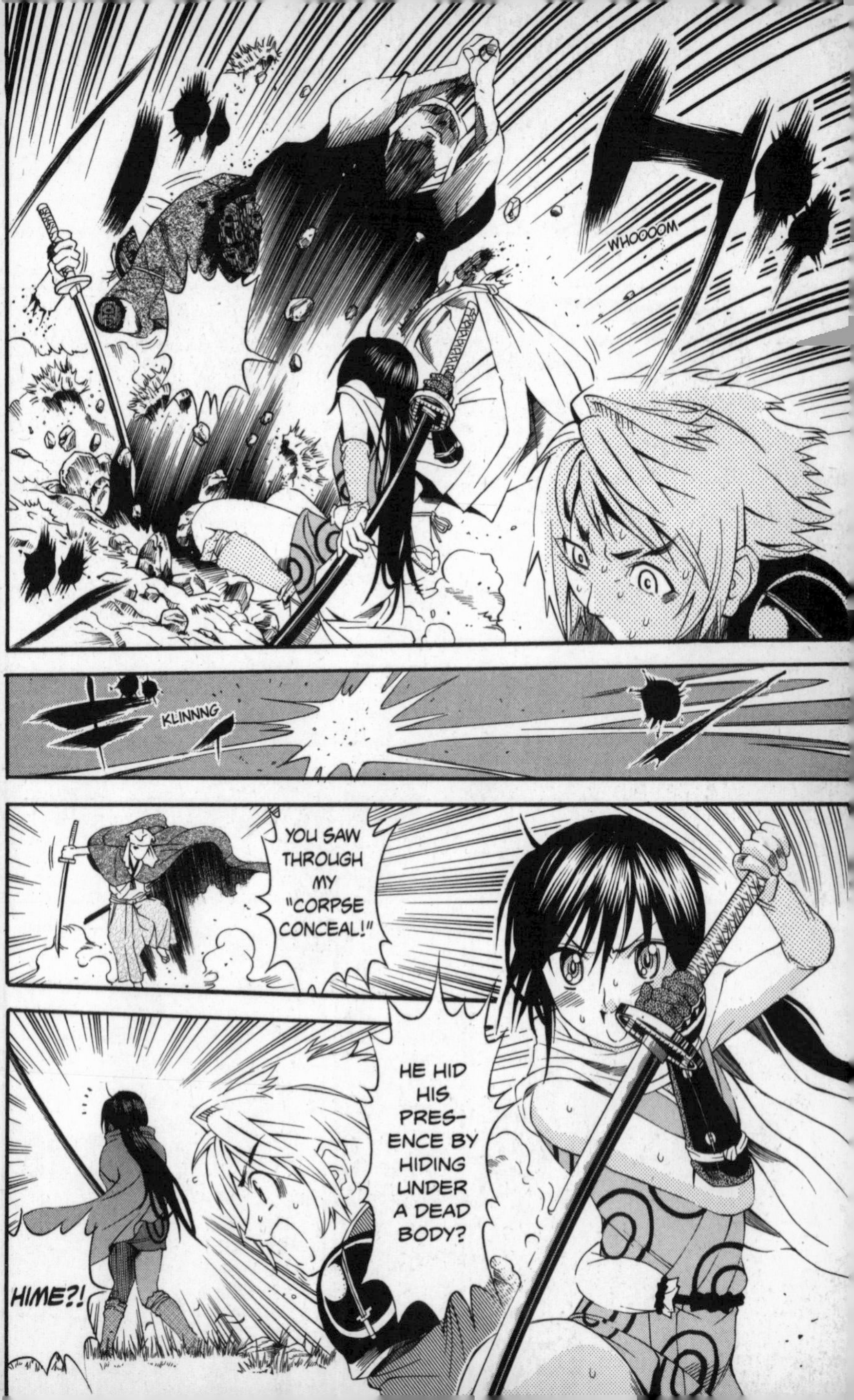
WHOOOOM
KLINNNG
YOU SAW THROUGH MY "CORPSE CONCEAL!"
HE HID HIS PRES-ENCE BY HIDING UNDER A DEAD BODY?
...
HIME?!

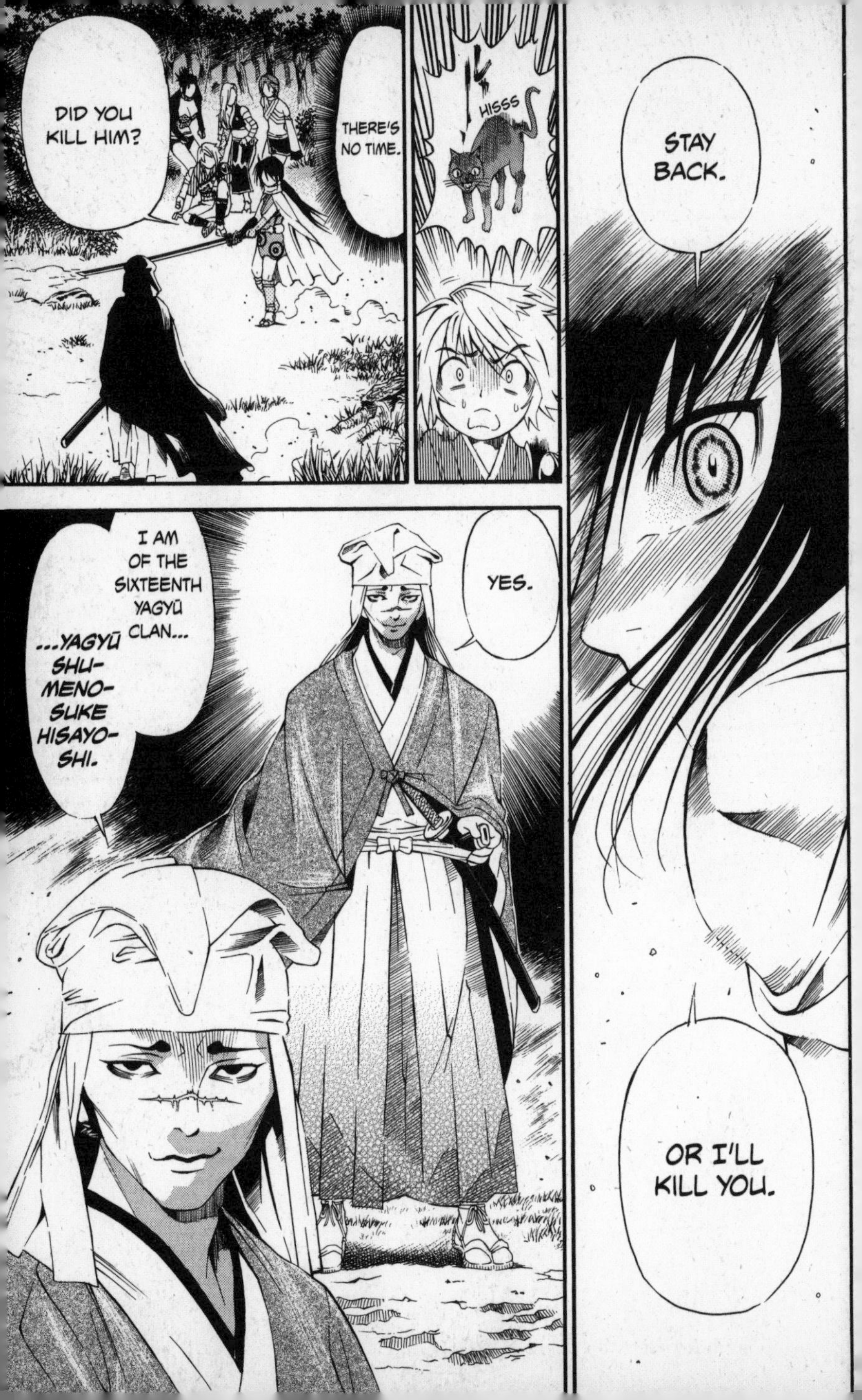
STAY BACK.
OR I'LL KILL YOU.
HISSS
THERE'S NO TIME.
DID YOU KILL HIM?
YES.
I AM OF THE SIXTEENTH YAGYŪ CLAN...
...YAGYŪ SHUMENOSUKE HISAYOSHI.

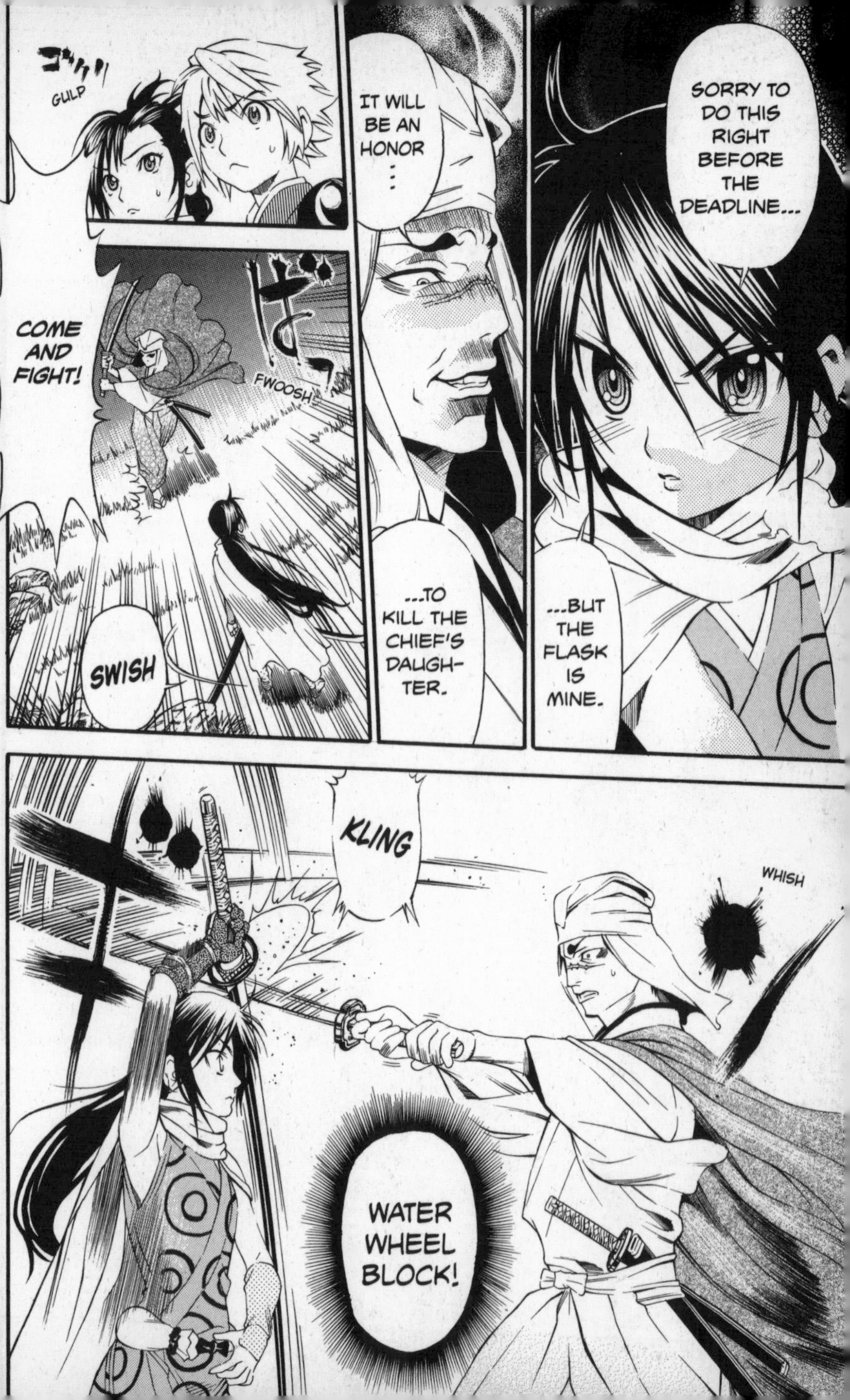
SORRY TO DO THIS RIGHT BEFORE THE DEADLINE...
...BUT THE FLASK IS MINE.
IT WILL BE AN HONOR ...
...TO KILL THE CHIEF'S DAUGH-TER.
GULP
COME AND FIGHT!
FWOOSH
SWISH
KLING
WHISH
WATER WHEEL BLOCK!

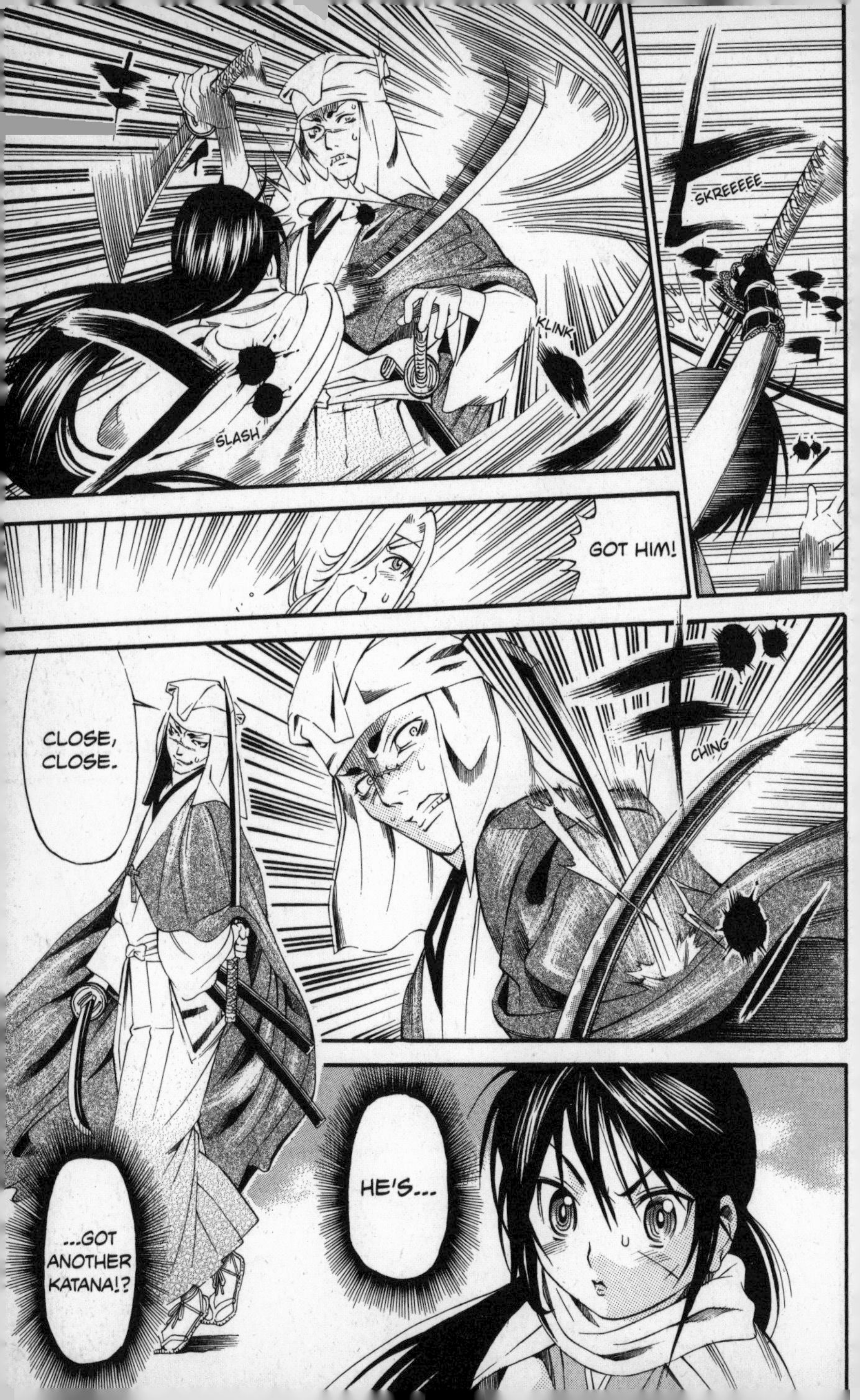
SKREEEEE
KLINK
SLASH
GOT HIM!
CHING
CLOSE, CLOSE.
HE'S...
...GOT ANOTHER KATANA!?

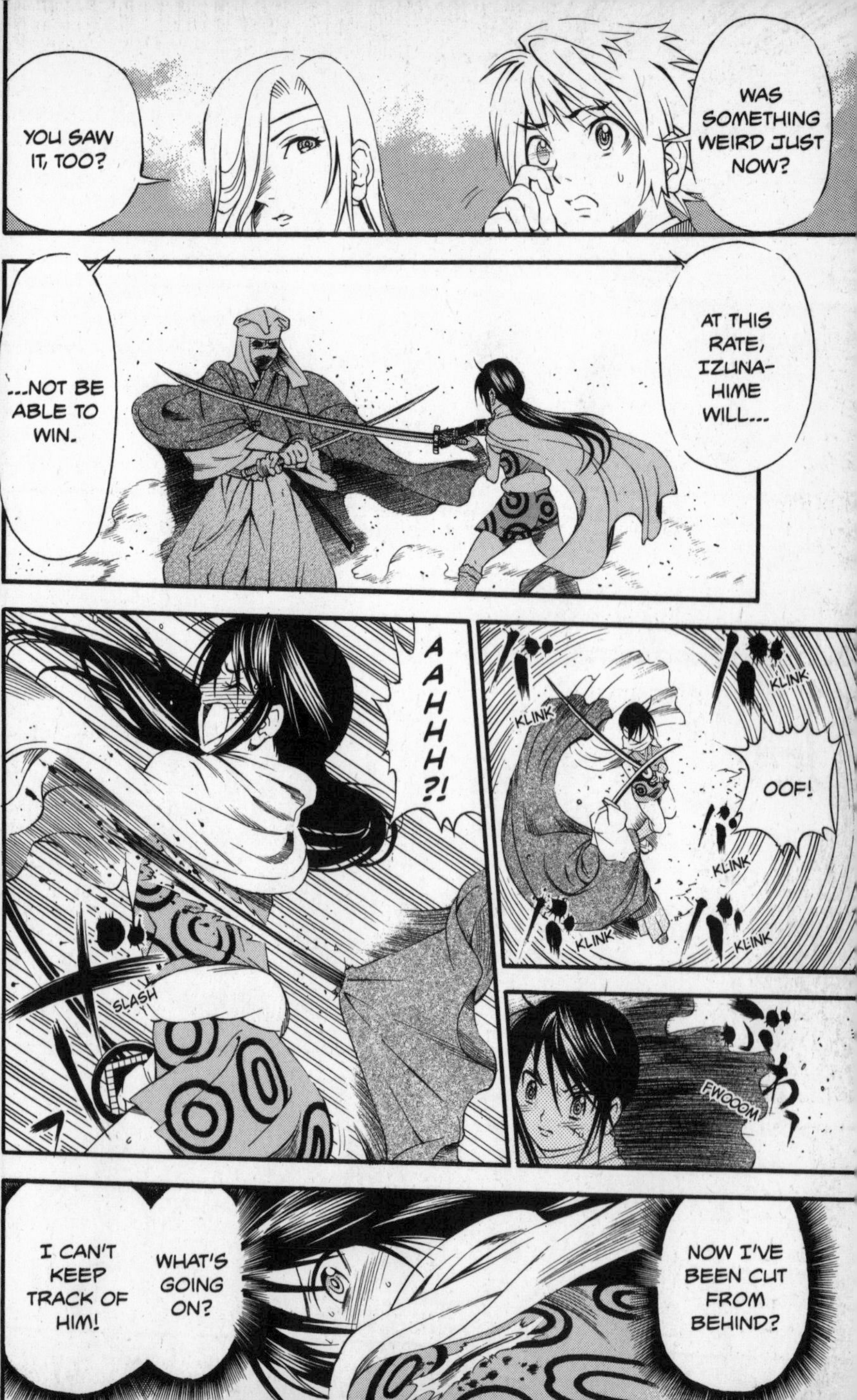
WAS SOMETHING WEIRD JUST NOW?
YOU SAW IT, TOO?
AT THIS RATE, IZUNA-HIME WILL...
...NOT BE ABLE TO WIN.
KLINK
KLINK
OOF!
KLINK
KLINK
KLINK
AAHHHH?!
SLASH
FWOOOM
NOW I'VE BEEN CUT FROM BEHIND?
WHAT'S GOING ON?
I CAN'T KEEP TRACK OF HIM!

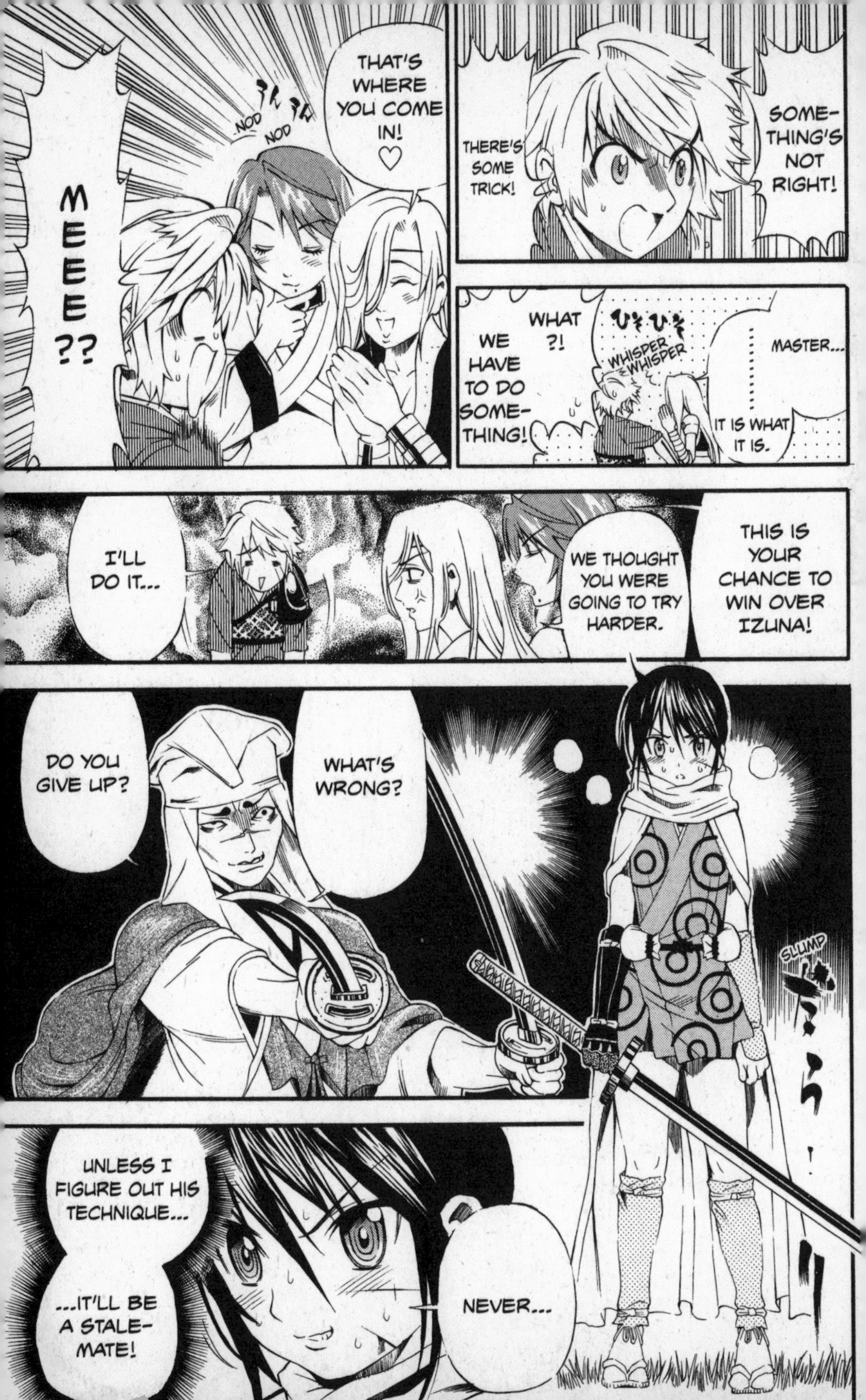

SOME-THING'S NOT RIGHT!
THERE'S SOME TRICK!
MASTER...
IT IS WHAT IT IS.
WHISPER WHISPER
WHAT ?!
WE HAVE TO DO SOME-THING!
THAT'S WHERE YOU COME IN! ♡
NOD NOD
MEEE ??
THIS IS YOUR CHANCE TO WIN OVER IZUNA!
WE THOUGHT YOU WERE GOING TO TRY HARDER.
I'LL DO IT...
SLUMP
WHAT'S WRONG?
DO YOU GIVE UP?
NEVER...
UNLESS I FIGURE OUT HIS TECHNIQUE...
...IT'LL BE A STALE-MATE!

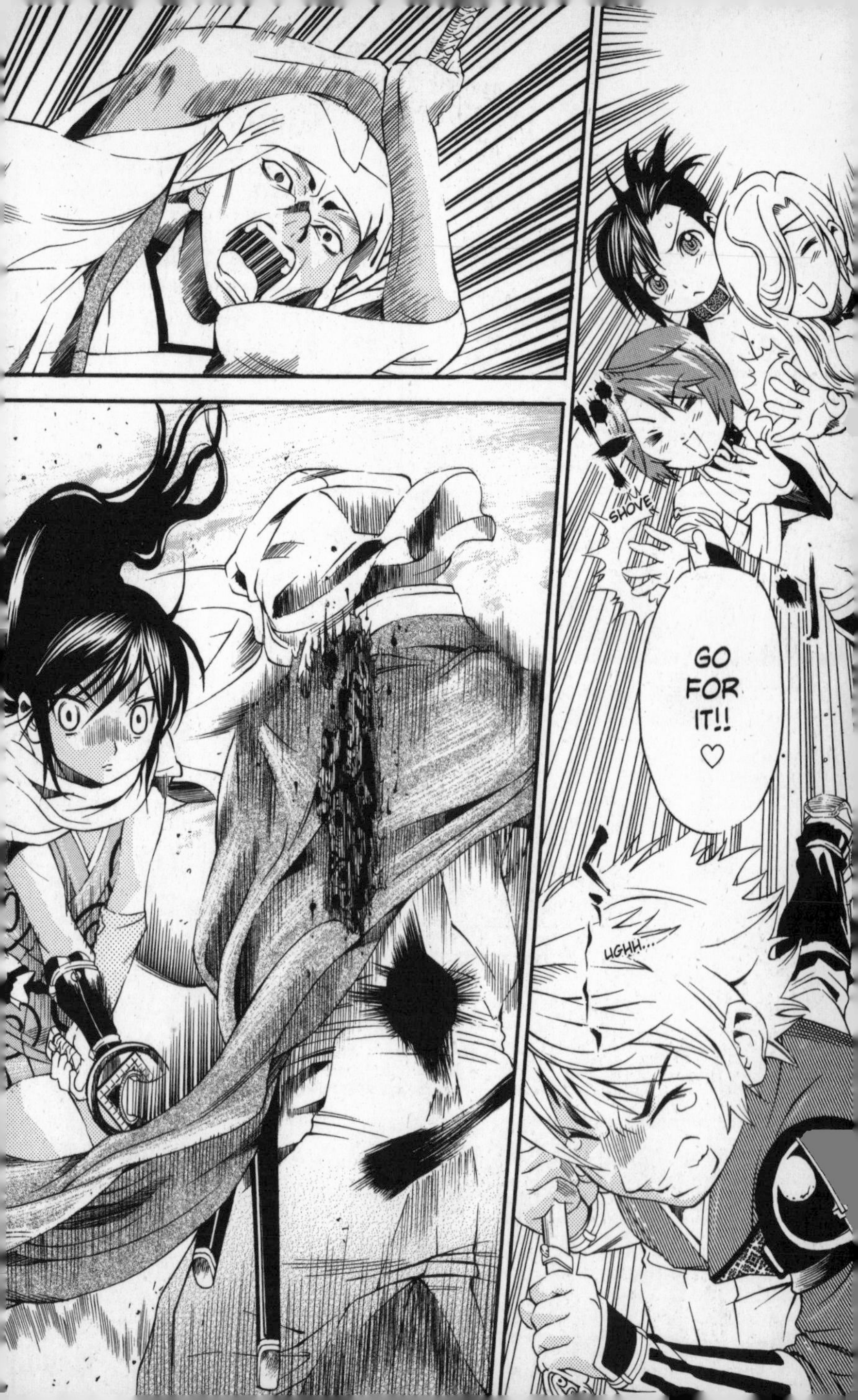
SHOVE
GO FOR IT!! ♥
UGHH...

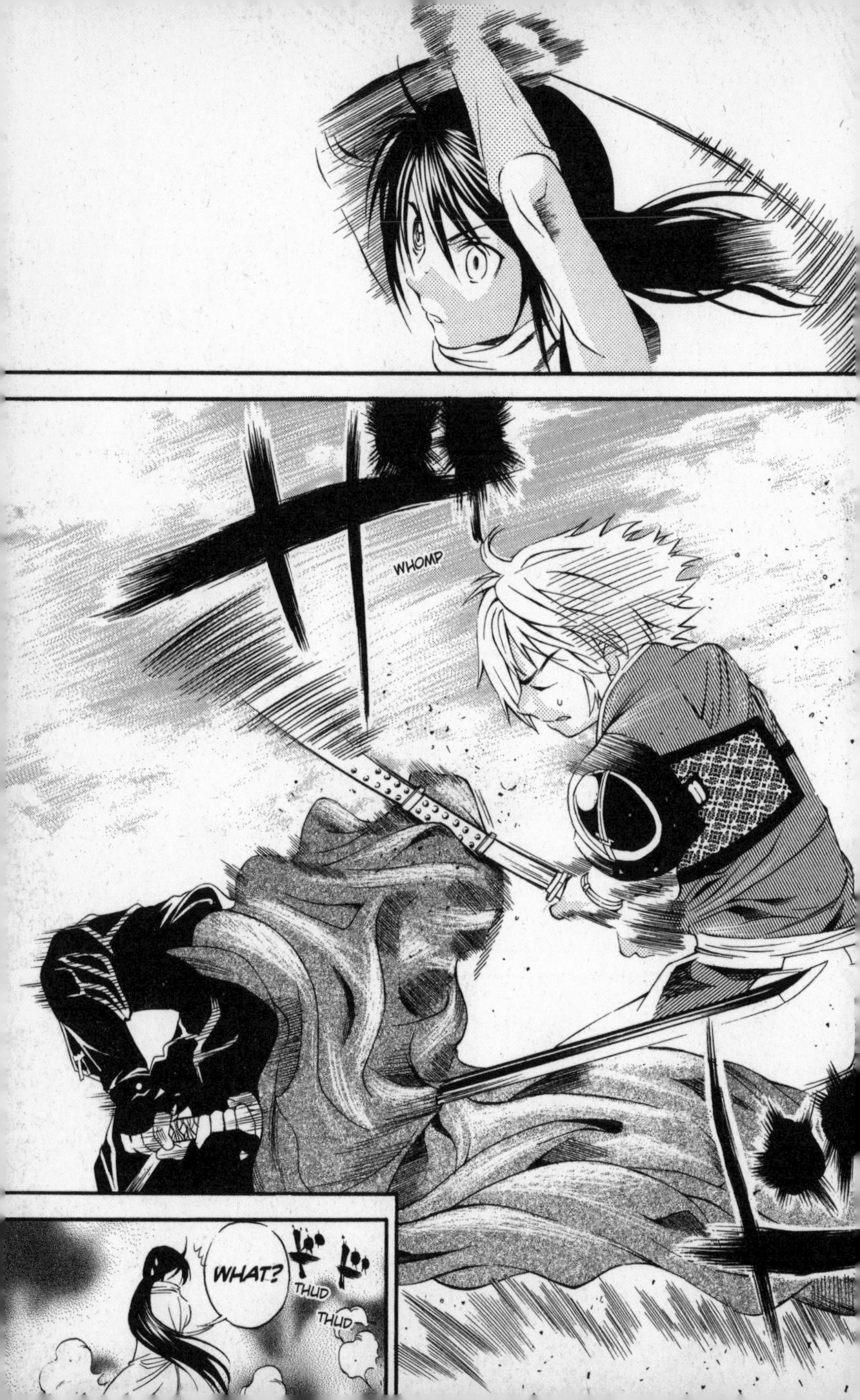
WHOMP
WHAT?
THUD
THUD

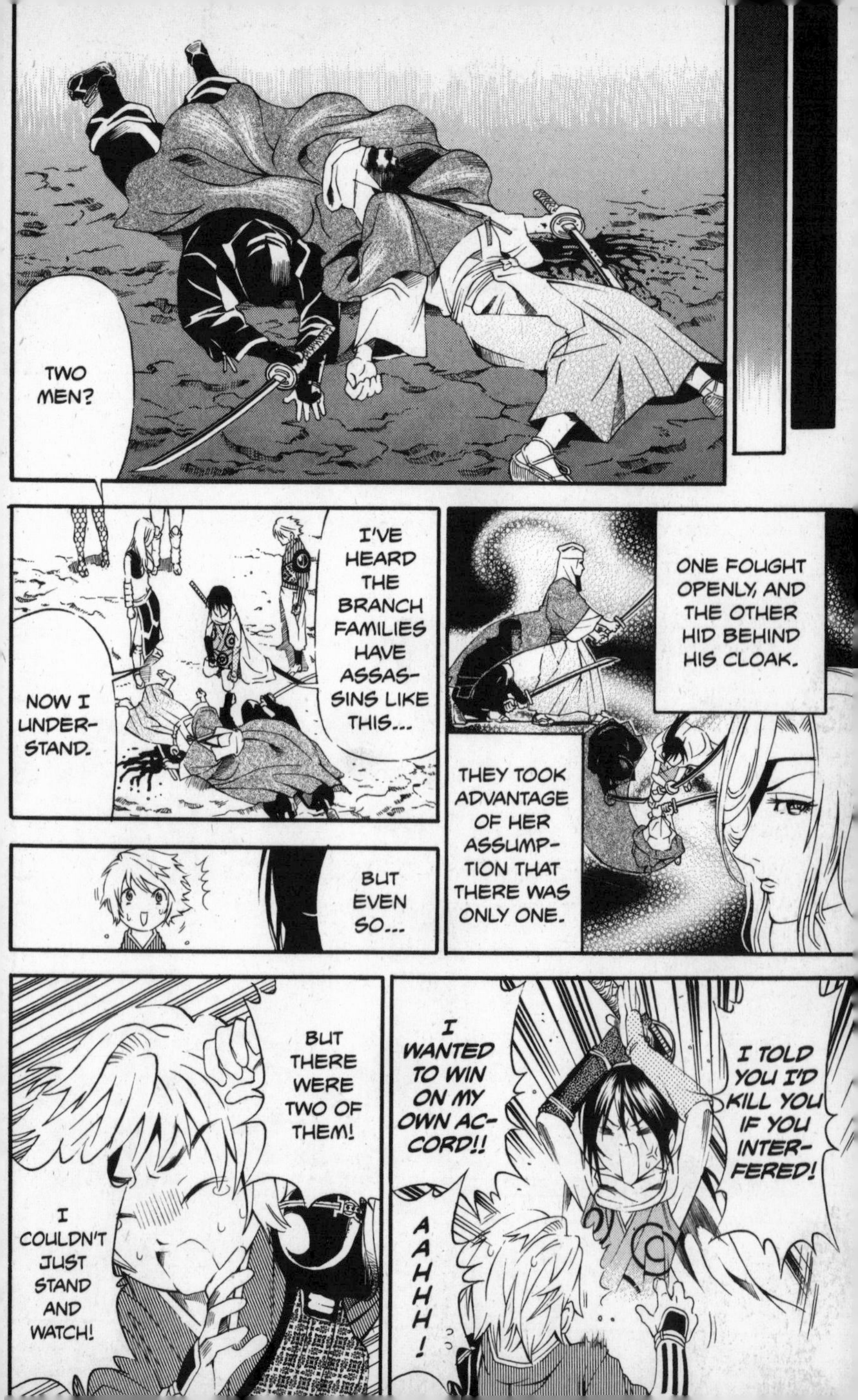
TWO MEN?
ONE FOUGHT OPENLY, AND THE OTHER HID BEHIND HIS CLOAK.
THEY TOOK ADVANTAGE OF HER ASSUMPTION THAT THERE WAS ONLY ONE.
I'VE HEARD THE BRANCH FAMILIES HAVE ASSASSINS LIKE THIS...
NOW I UNDERSTAND.
BUT EVEN SO...
I TOLD YOU I'D KILL YOU IF YOU INTERFERED!
I WANTED TO WIN ON MY OWN ACCORD!!
AAHHH!
BUT THERE WERE TWO OF THEM!
I COULDN'T JUST STAND AND WATCH!

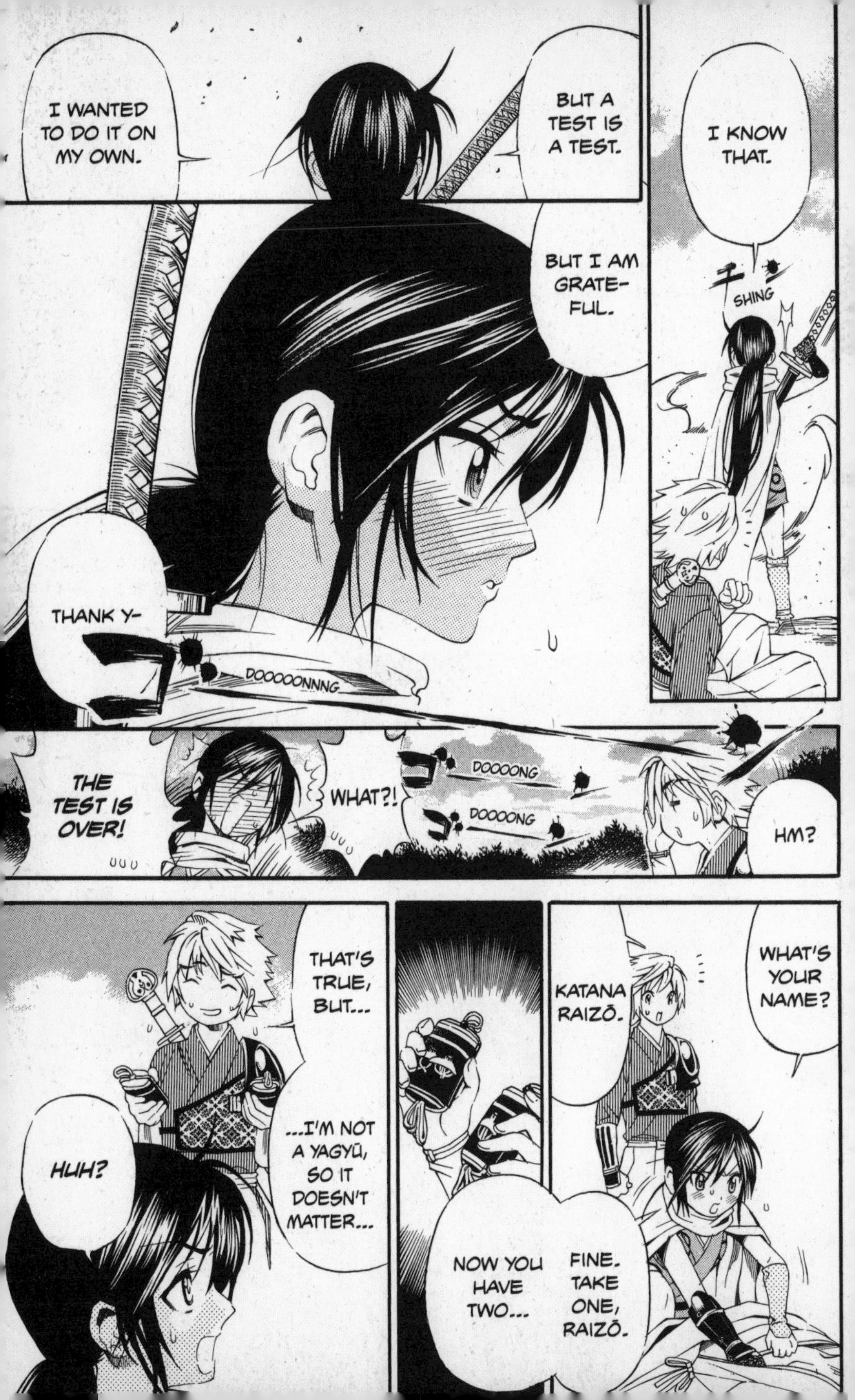
I KNOW THAT.
SHING
BUT A TEST IS A TEST.
I WANTED TO DO IT ON MY OWN.
BUT I AM GRATEFUL.
THANK Y-
DOOOOONNNG
HM?
DOOOONG
DOOOONG
WHAT?!
THE TEST IS OVER!
WHAT'S YOUR NAME?
KATANA RAIZŌ.
FINE. TAKE ONE, RAIZŌ.
NOW YOU HAVE TWO...
THAT'S TRUE, BUT...
...I'M NOT A YAGYŪ, SO IT DOESN'T MATTER...
HUH?

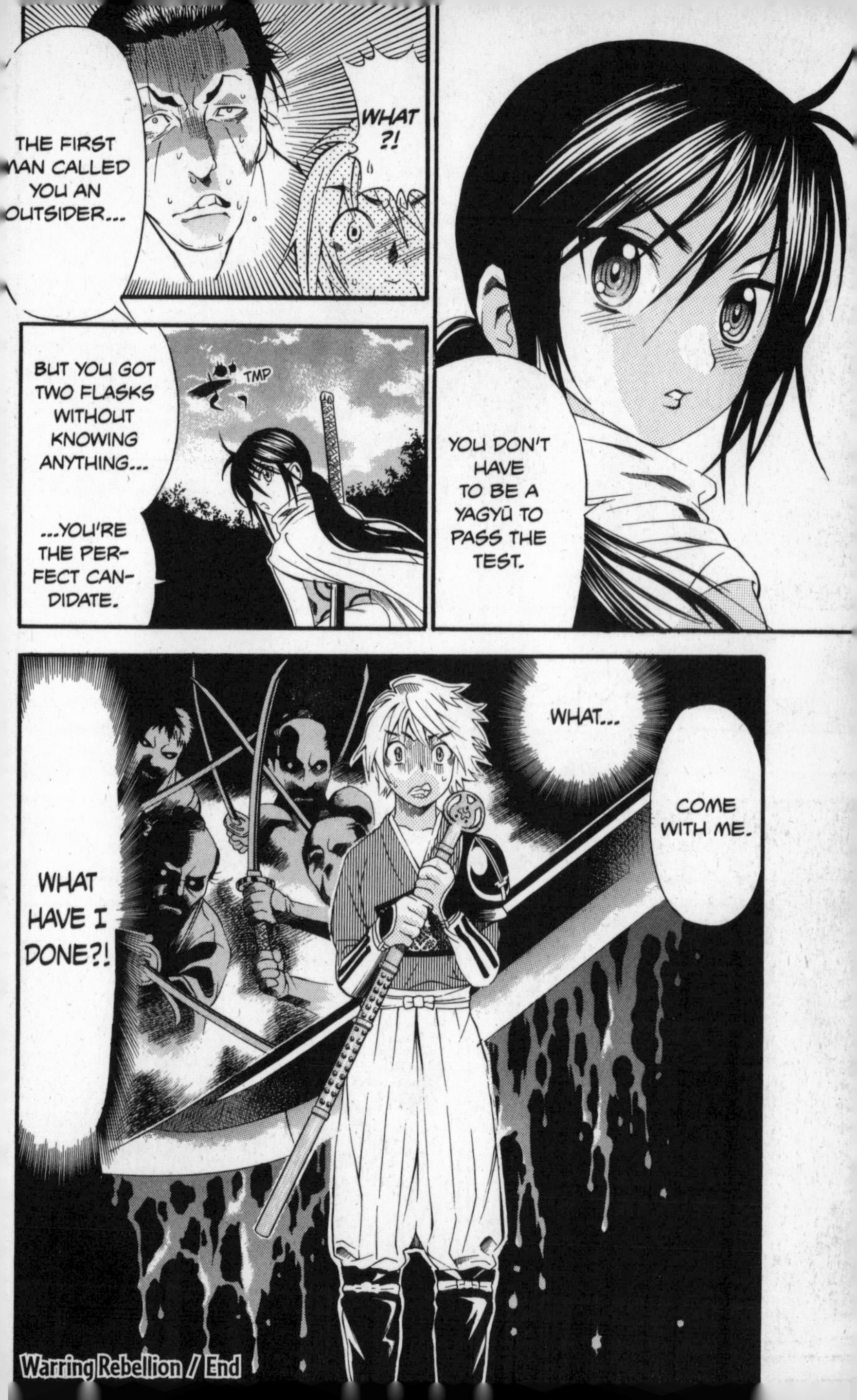
YOU DON'T HAVE TO BE A YAGYŪ TO PASS THE TEST.
WHAT ?!
THE FIRST MAN CALLED YOU AN OUTSIDER...
TMP
BUT YOU GOT TWO FLASKS WITHOUT KNOWING ANYTHING...
...YOU'RE THE PER-FECT CAN-DIDATE.
WHAT...
COME WITH ME.
WHAT HAVE I DONE?!
Warring Rebellion / End

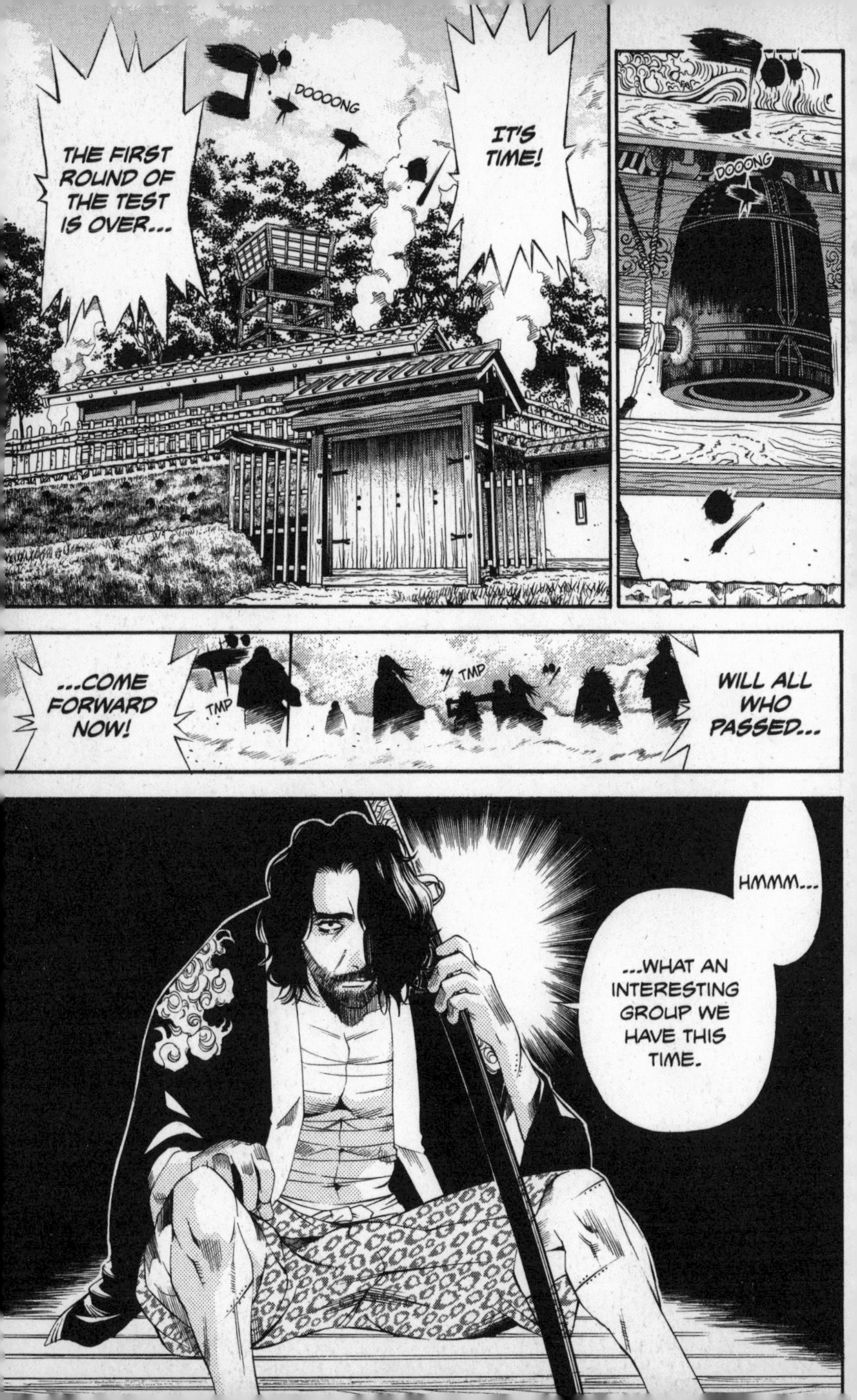
DOOONG
DOOOONG
IT'S TIME!
THE FIRST ROUND OF THE TEST IS OVER...
WILL ALL WHO PASSED...
TMP
TMP
...COME FORWARD NOW!
HMMM...
...WHAT AN INTERESTING GROUP WE HAVE THIS TIME.

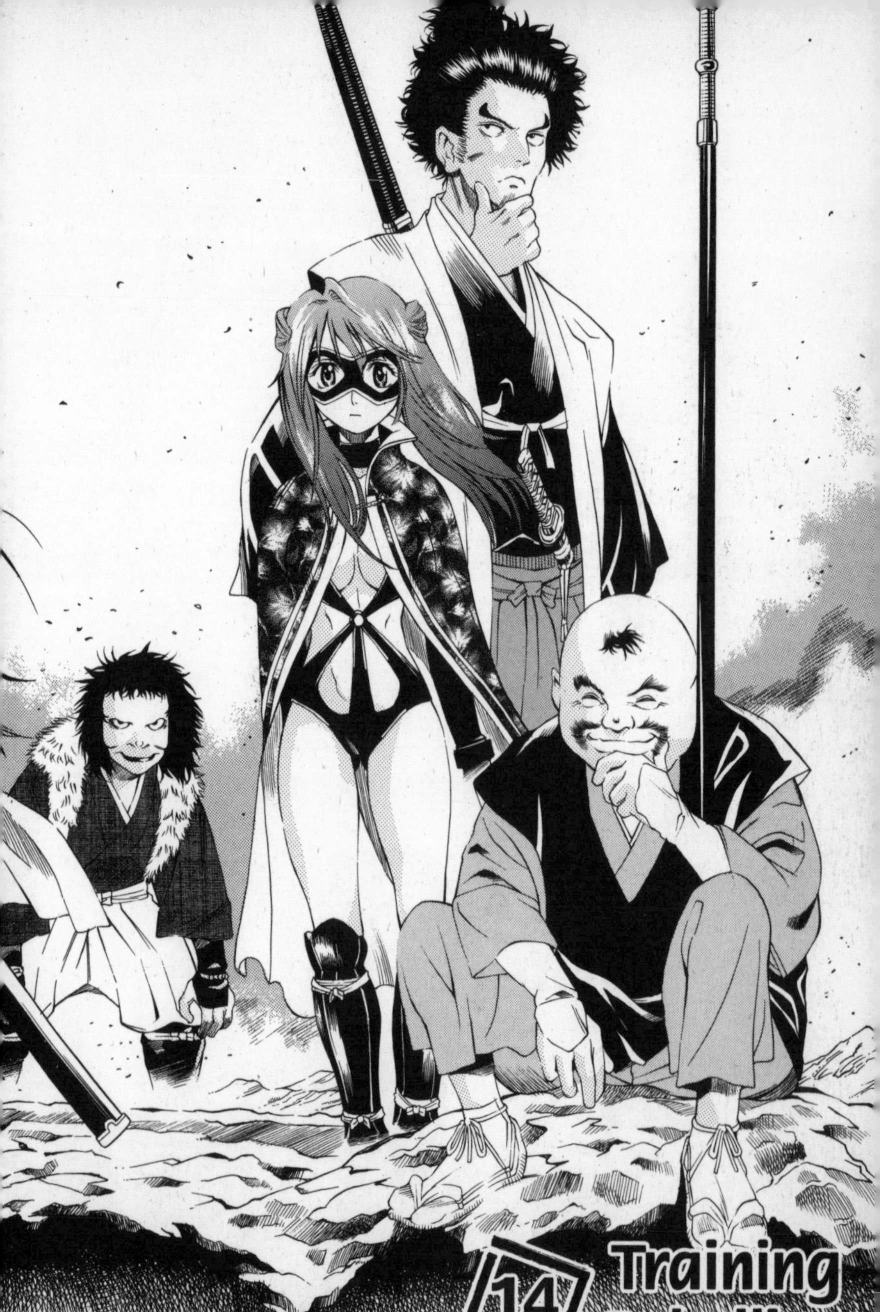
14
Training

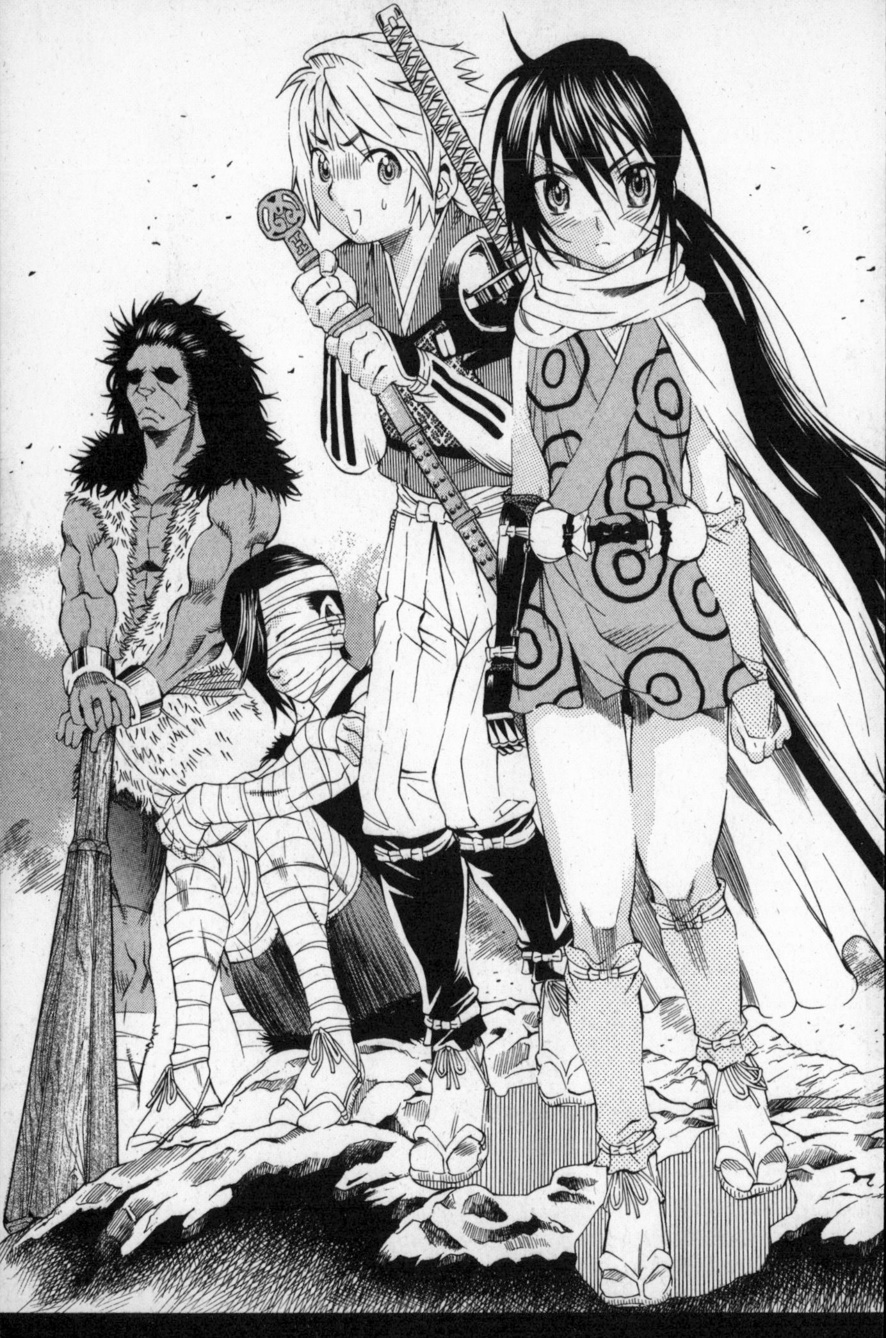

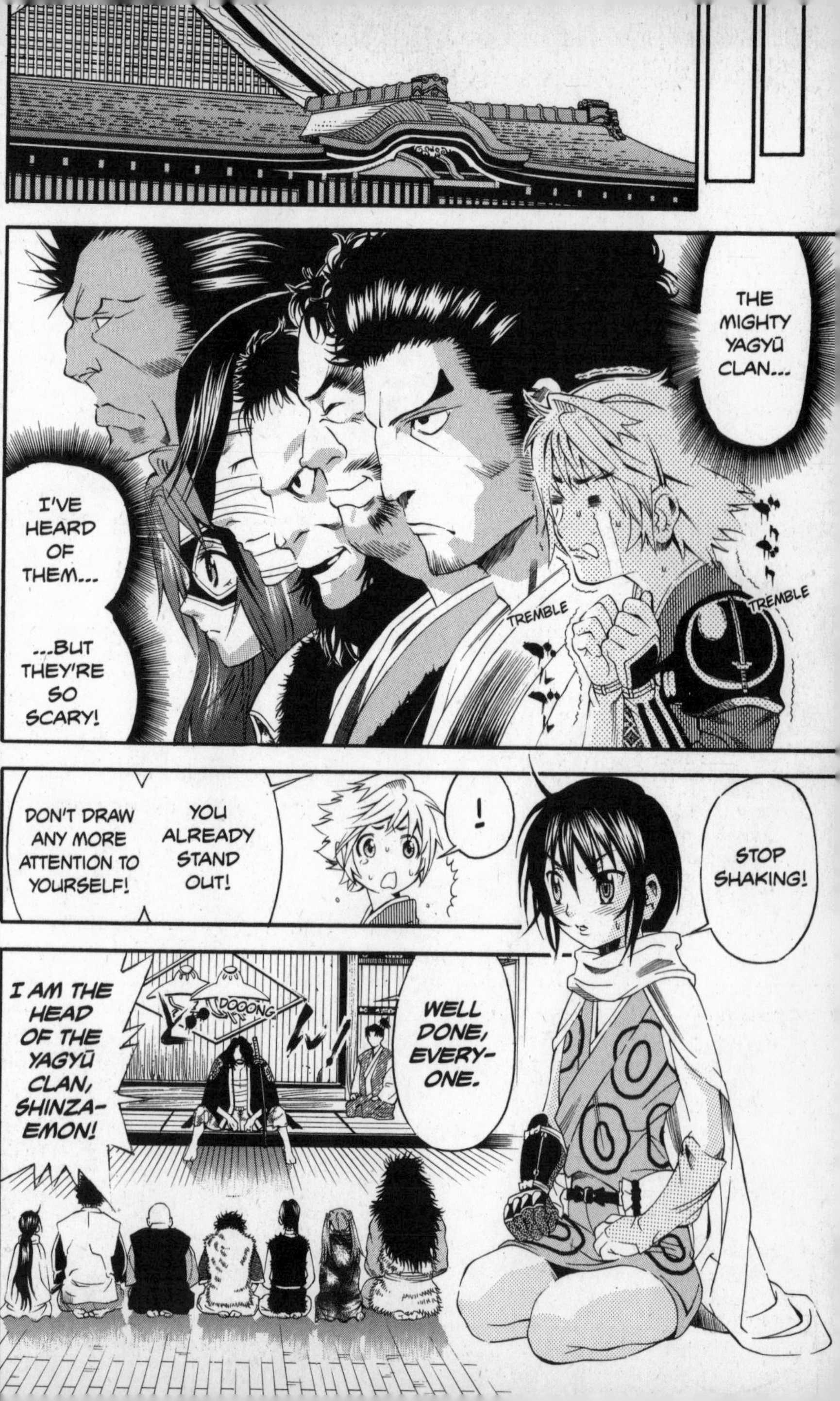
THE MIGHTY YAGYŪ CLAN...
TREMBLE
TREMBLE
I'VE HEARD OF THEM...
...BUT THEY'RE SO SCARY!
STOP SHAKING!
!
YOU ALREADY STAND OUT!
DON'T DRAW ANY MORE ATTENTION TO YOURSELF!
DOOONG
WELL DONE, EVERYONE.
I AM THE HEAD OF THE YAGYŪ CLAN, SHINZAEMON!

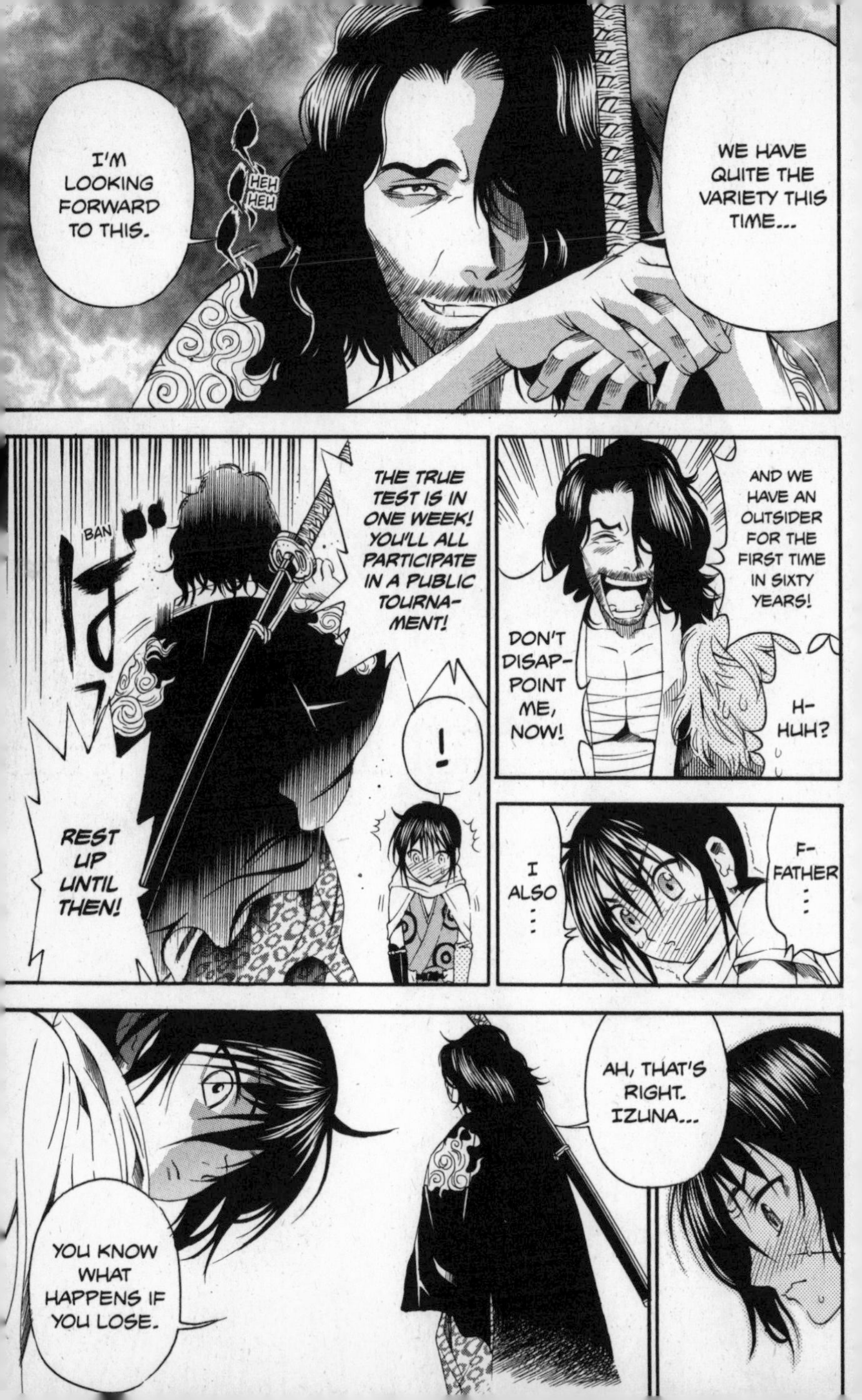
WE HAVE QUITE THE VARIETY THIS TIME...
HEH HEH
I'M LOOKING FORWARD TO THIS.
AND WE HAVE AN OUTSIDER FOR THE FIRST TIME IN SIXTY YEARS!
DON'T DISAP-POINT ME, NOW!
H-HUH?
F-FATHER...
I ALSO...
THE TRUE TEST IS IN ONE WEEK! YOU'LL ALL PARTICIPATE IN A PUBLIC TOURNA-MENT!
BAN
!
REST UP UNTIL THEN!
AH, THAT'S RIGHT. IZUNA...
YOU KNOW WHAT HAPPENS IF YOU LOSE.

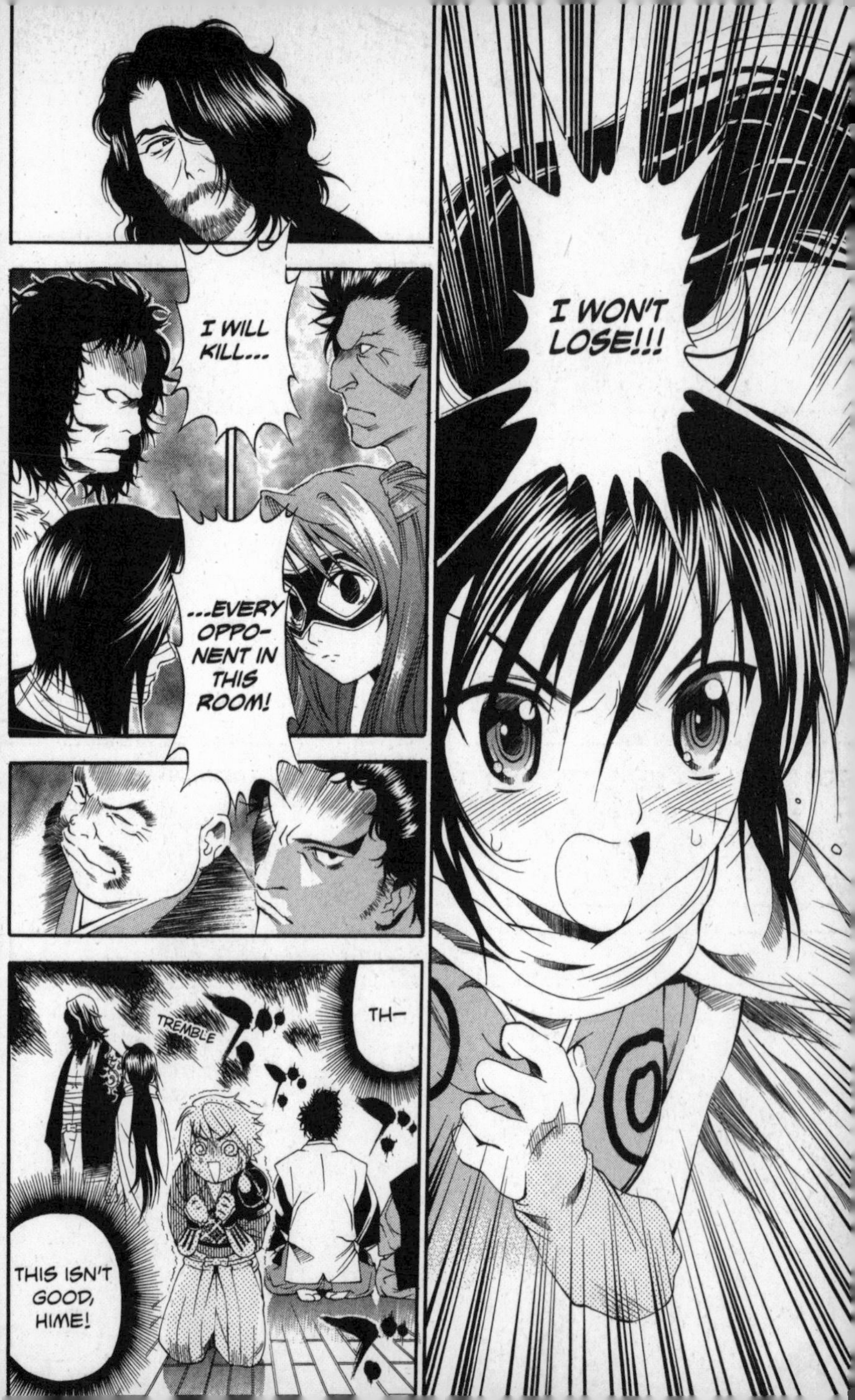

I WON'T LOSE!!!
I WILL KILL...
...EVERY OPPONENT IN THIS ROOM!
TH-
TREMBLE
THIS ISN'T GOOD, HIME!

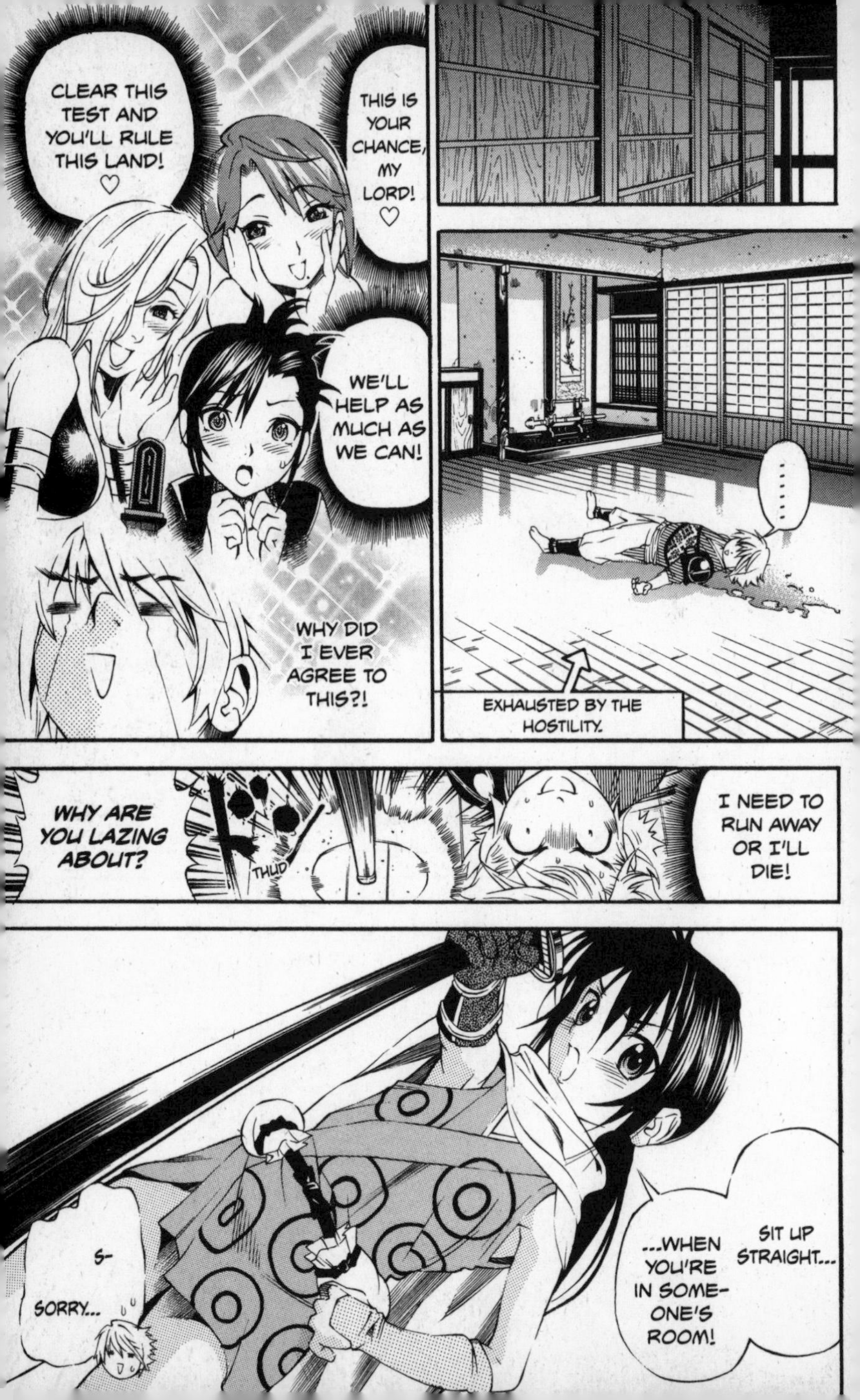
......
EXHAUSTED BY THE HOSTILITY.
THIS IS YOUR CHANCE, MY LORD! ♡
CLEAR THIS TEST AND YOU'LL RULE THIS LAND! ♡
WE'LL HELP AS MUCH AS WE CAN!
WHY DID I EVER AGREE TO THIS?!
I NEED TO RUN AWAY OR I'LL DIE!
THUD
WHY ARE YOU LAZING ABOUT?
SIT UP STRAIGHT...
...WHEN YOU'RE IN SOME-ONE'S ROOM!
S- SORRY...

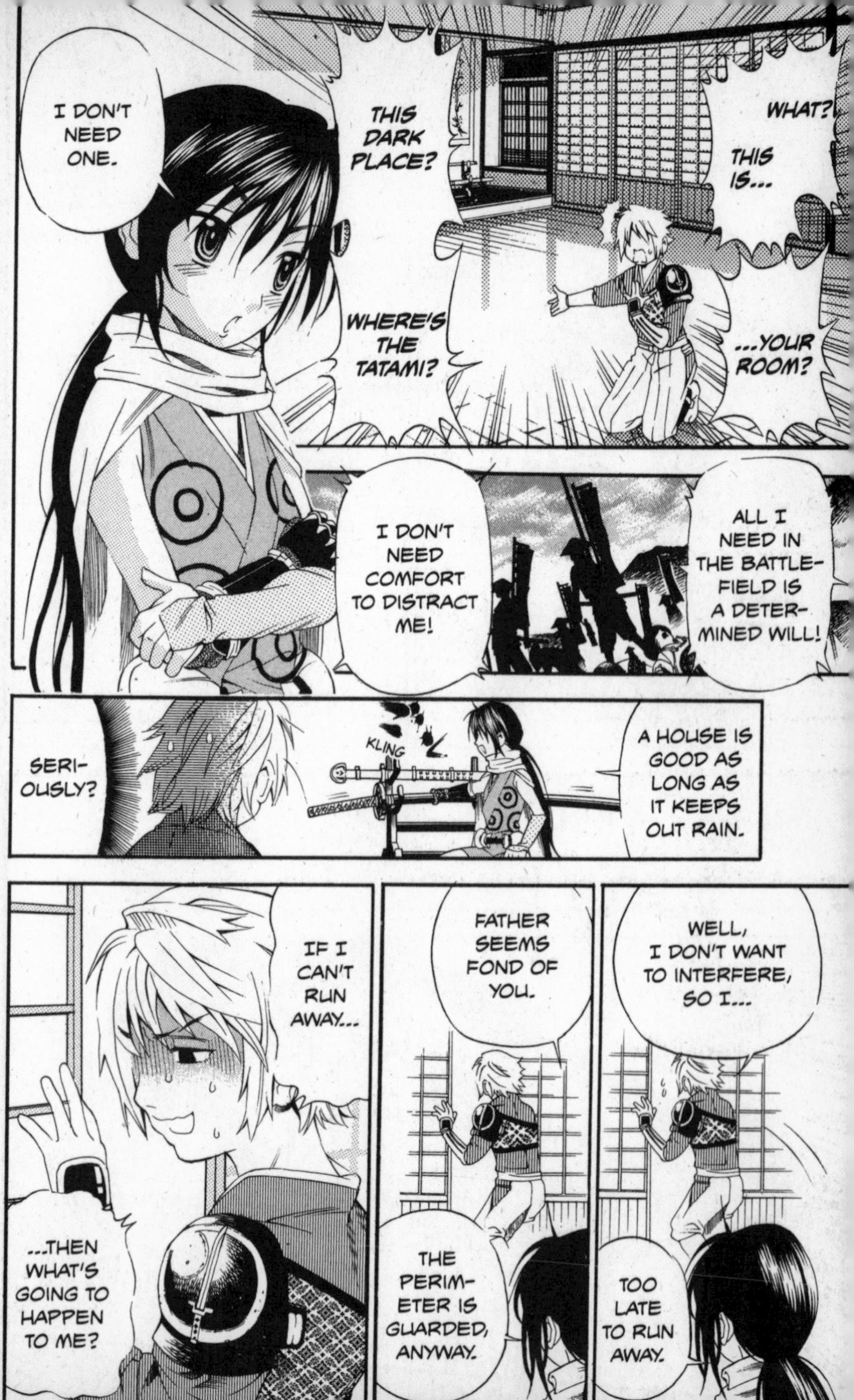
WHAT?
THIS IS...
...YOUR ROOM?
THIS DARK PLACE?
WHERE'S THE TATAMI?
ALL I NEED IN THE BATTLE-FIELD IS A DETER-MINED WILL!
I DON'T NEED COMFORT TO DISTRACT ME!
I DON'T NEED ONE.
A HOUSE IS GOOD AS LONG AS IT KEEPS OUT RAIN.
KLING
SERI-OUSLY?
WELL, I DON'T WANT TO INTERFERE, SO I...
TOO LATE TO RUN AWAY.
FATHER SEEMS FOND OF YOU.
THE PERIM-ETER IS GUARDED, ANYWAY.
IF I CAN'T RUN AWAY...
...THEN WHAT'S GOING TO HAPPEN TO ME?

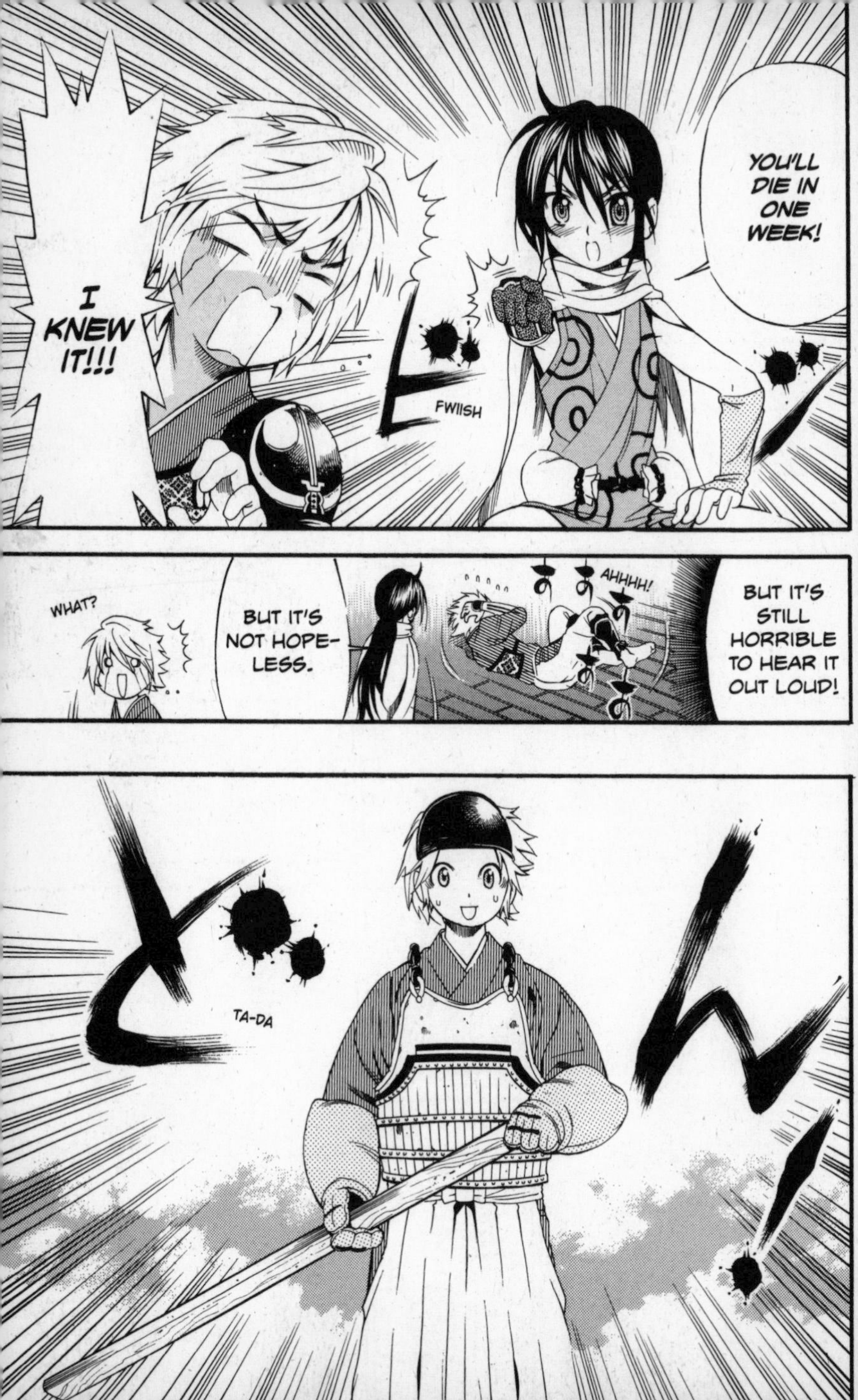
YOU'LL DIE IN ONE WEEK!
FWIISH
I KNEW IT!!!
BUT IT'S STILL HORRIBLE TO HEAR IT OUT LOUD!
AHHHH!
BUT IT'S NOT HOPE-LESS.
WHAT?
TA-DA

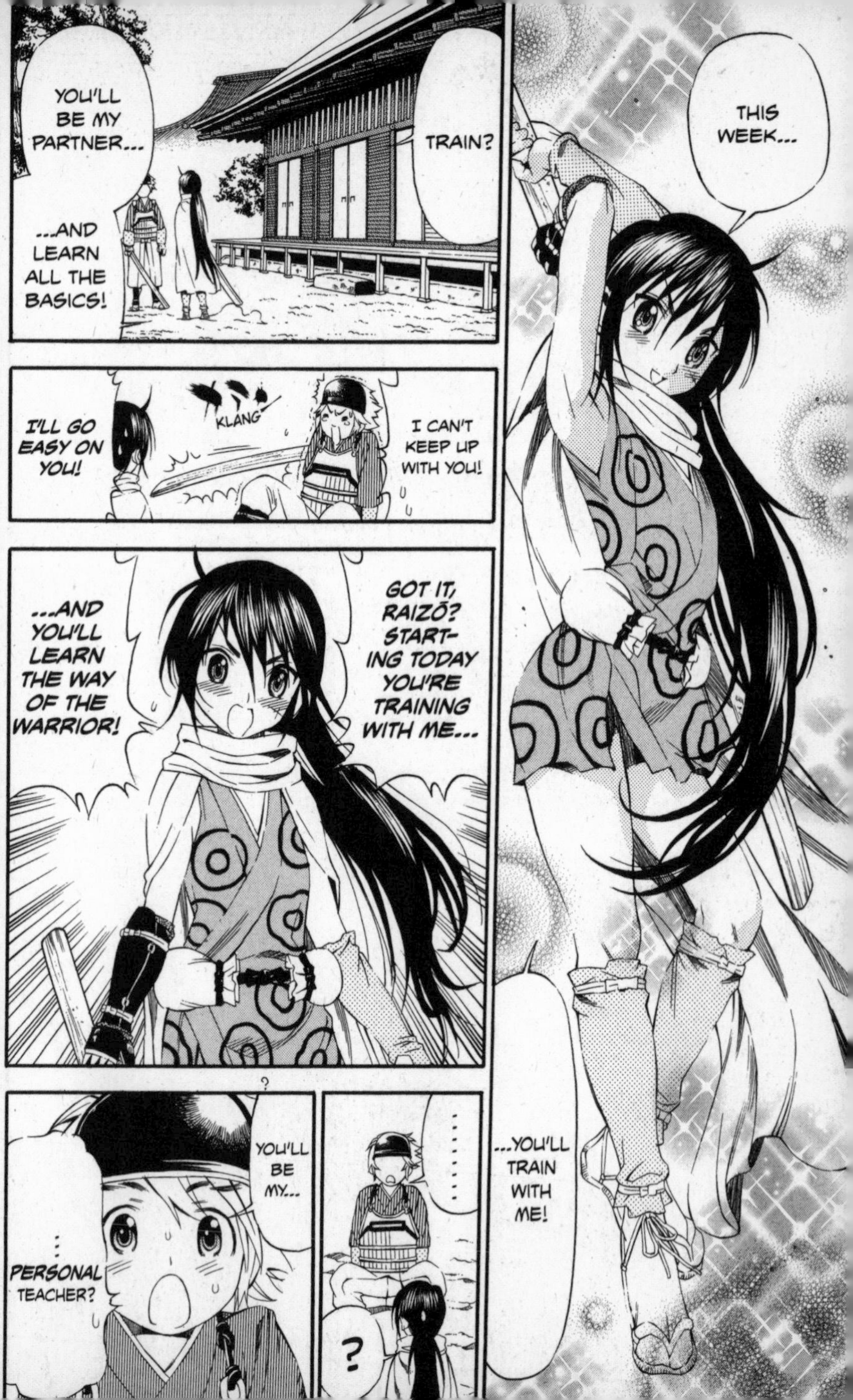
THIS WEEK...
...YOU'LL TRAIN WITH ME!
TRAIN?
YOU'LL BE MY PARTNER...
...AND LEARN ALL THE BASICS!
I CAN'T KEEP UP WITH YOU!
KLANG
I'LL GO EASY ON YOU!
GOT IT, RAIZŌ? STARTING TODAY YOU'RE TRAINING WITH ME...
...AND YOU'LL LEARN THE WAY OF THE WARRIOR!
......
YOU'LL BE MY...
?
?
...PERSONAL TEACHER?

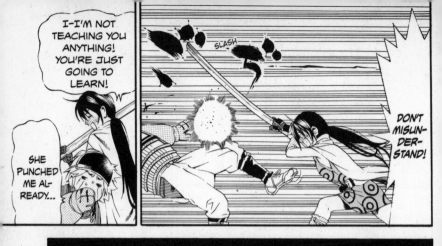

SLASH
DON'T MISUN-DER-STAND!
I-I'M NOT TEACHING YOU ANYTHING! YOU'RE JUST GOING TO LEARN!
SHE PUNCHED ME AL-READY...
SPECIAL TRAINING BEGINS
#1: SANGAKUEN-NO-TACHI
KLUNK
WHAT HAP-PENED TO GOING EASY ON ME?
NO! YOU DIDN'T TAKE THE BLOW COR-RECTLY!

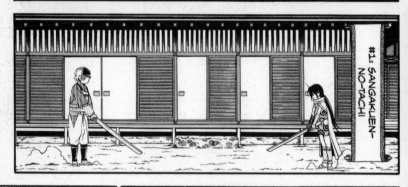

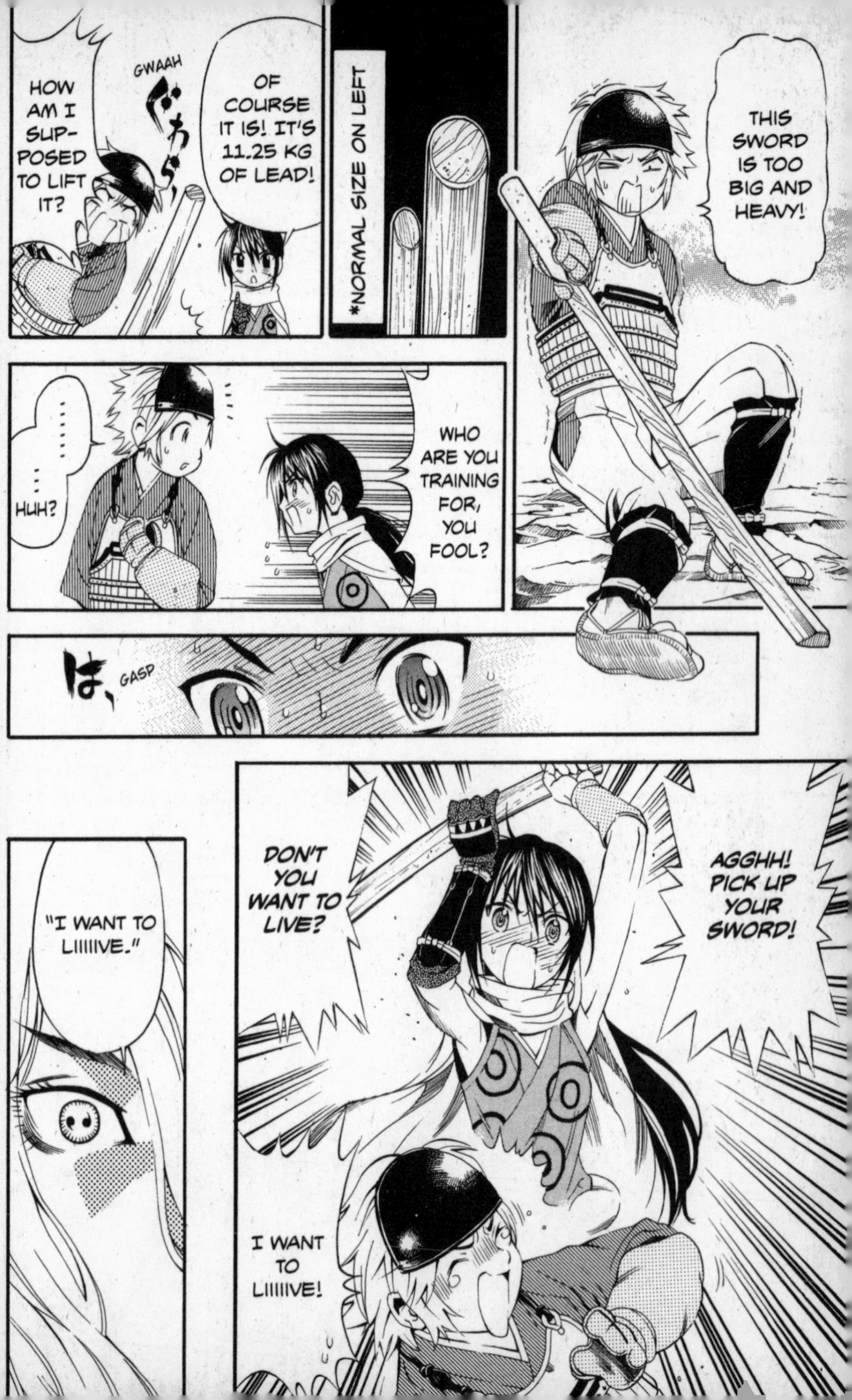
THIS SWORD IS TOO BIG AND HEAVY!
*NORMAL SIZE ON LEFT
OF COURSE IT IS! IT'S 11.25 KG OF LEAD!
GWAAH
HOW AM I SUP-POSED TO LIFT IT?
WHO ARE YOU TRAINING FOR, YOU FOOL?
......
......HUH?
は、
GASP
AGGHH! PICK UP YOUR SWORD!
DON'T YOU WANT TO LIVE?
I WANT TO LIIIIIVE!
"I WANT TO LIIIIIVE."

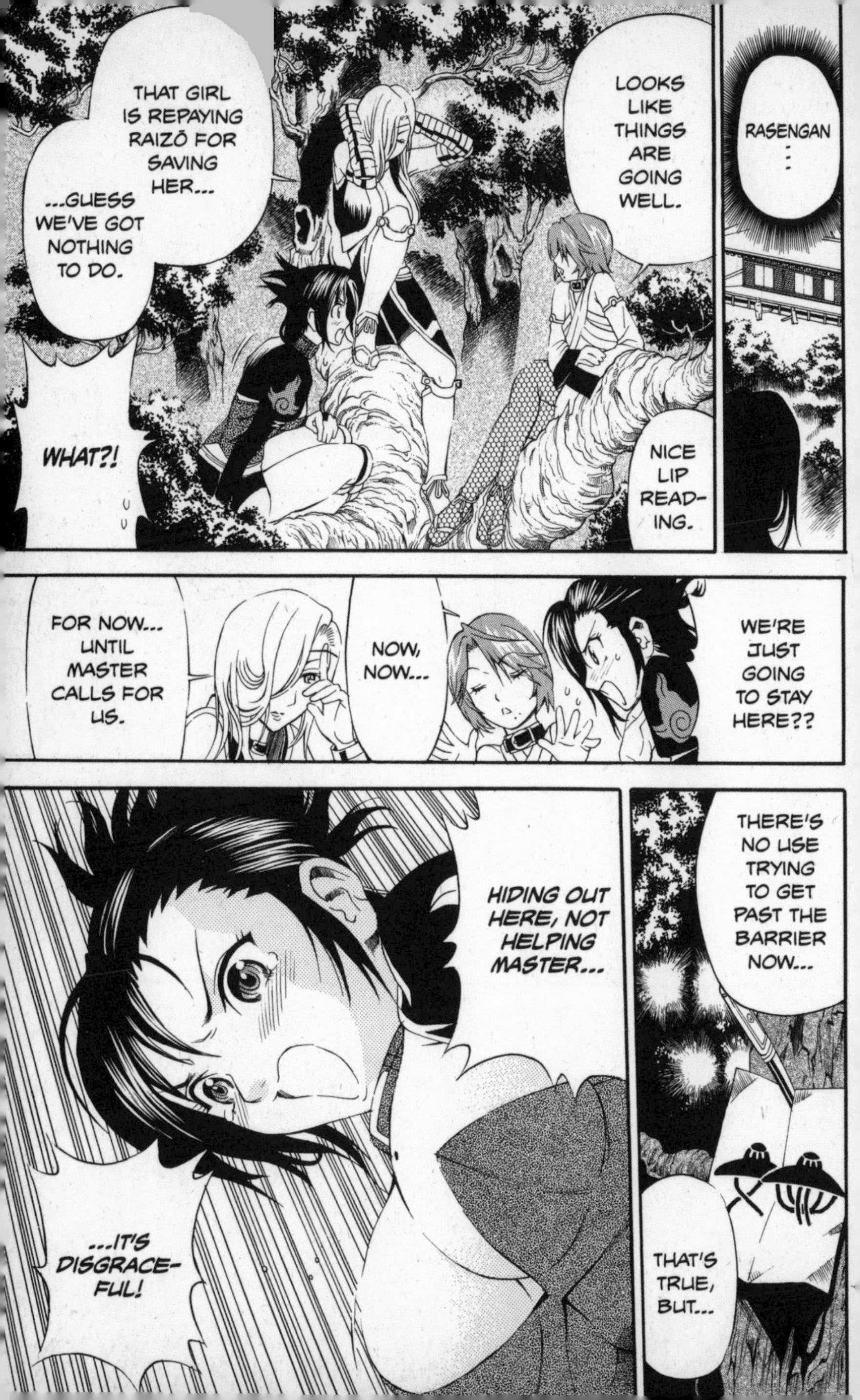
RASENGAN...
LOOKS LIKE THINGS ARE GOING WELL.
NICE LIP READING.
THAT GIRL IS REPAYING RAIZŌ FOR SAVING HER...
...GUESS WE'VE GOT NOTHING TO DO.
WHAT?!
WE'RE JUST GOING TO STAY HERE??
NOW, NOW...
FOR NOW... UNTIL MASTER CALLS FOR US.
THERE'S NO USE TRYING TO GET PAST THE BARRIER NOW...
THAT'S TRUE, BUT...
HIDING OUT HERE, NOT HELPING MASTER...
...IT'S DISGRACEFUL!

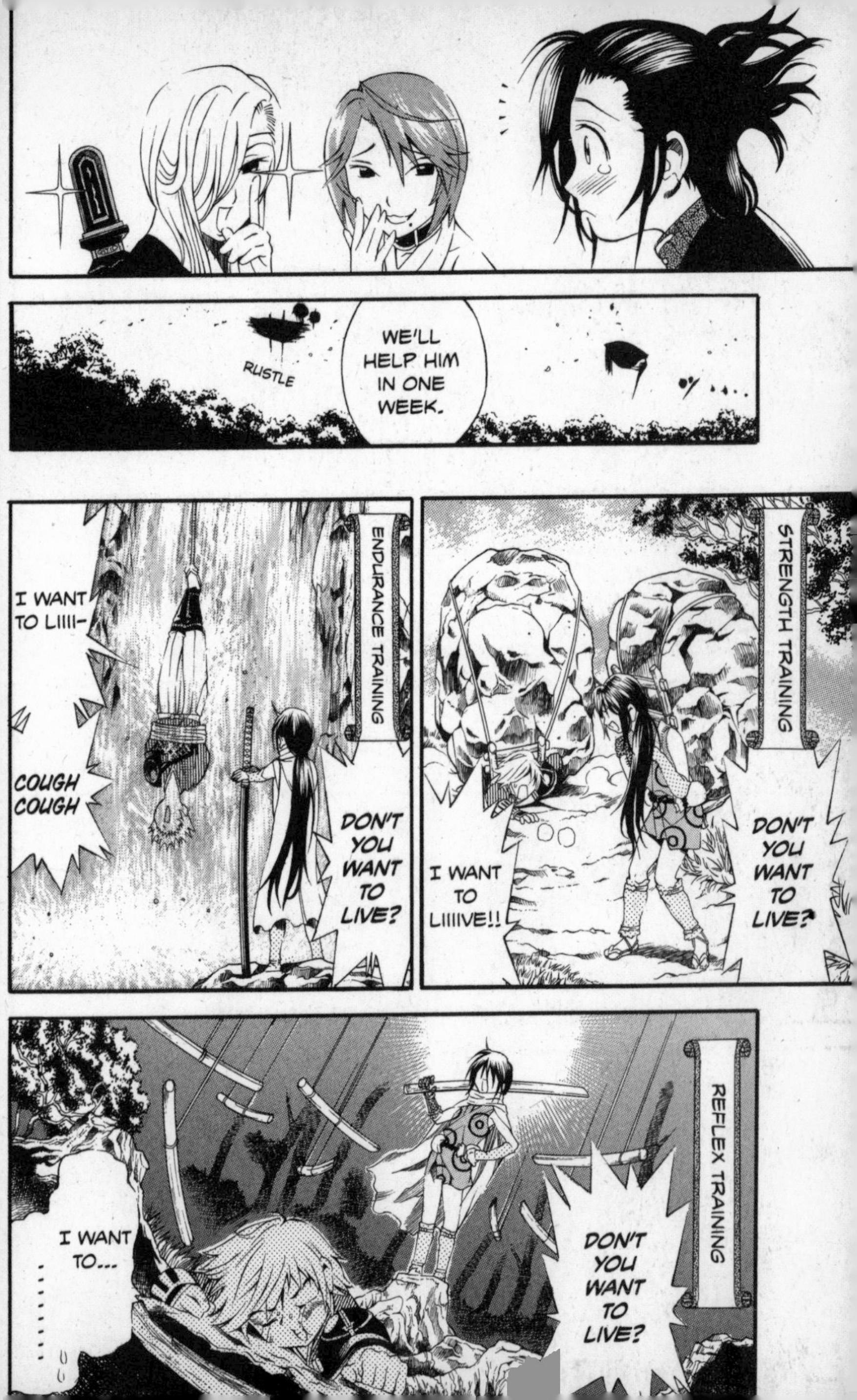
RUSTLE
WE'LL HELP HIM IN ONE WEEK.
STRENGTH TRAINING
DON'T YOU WANT TO LIVE?
I WANT TO LIIIIVE!!
ENDURANCE TRAINING
DON'T YOU WANT TO LIVE?
I WANT TO LIIII-
COUGH COUGH
REFLEX TRAINING
DON'T YOU WANT TO LIVE?
I WANT TO...

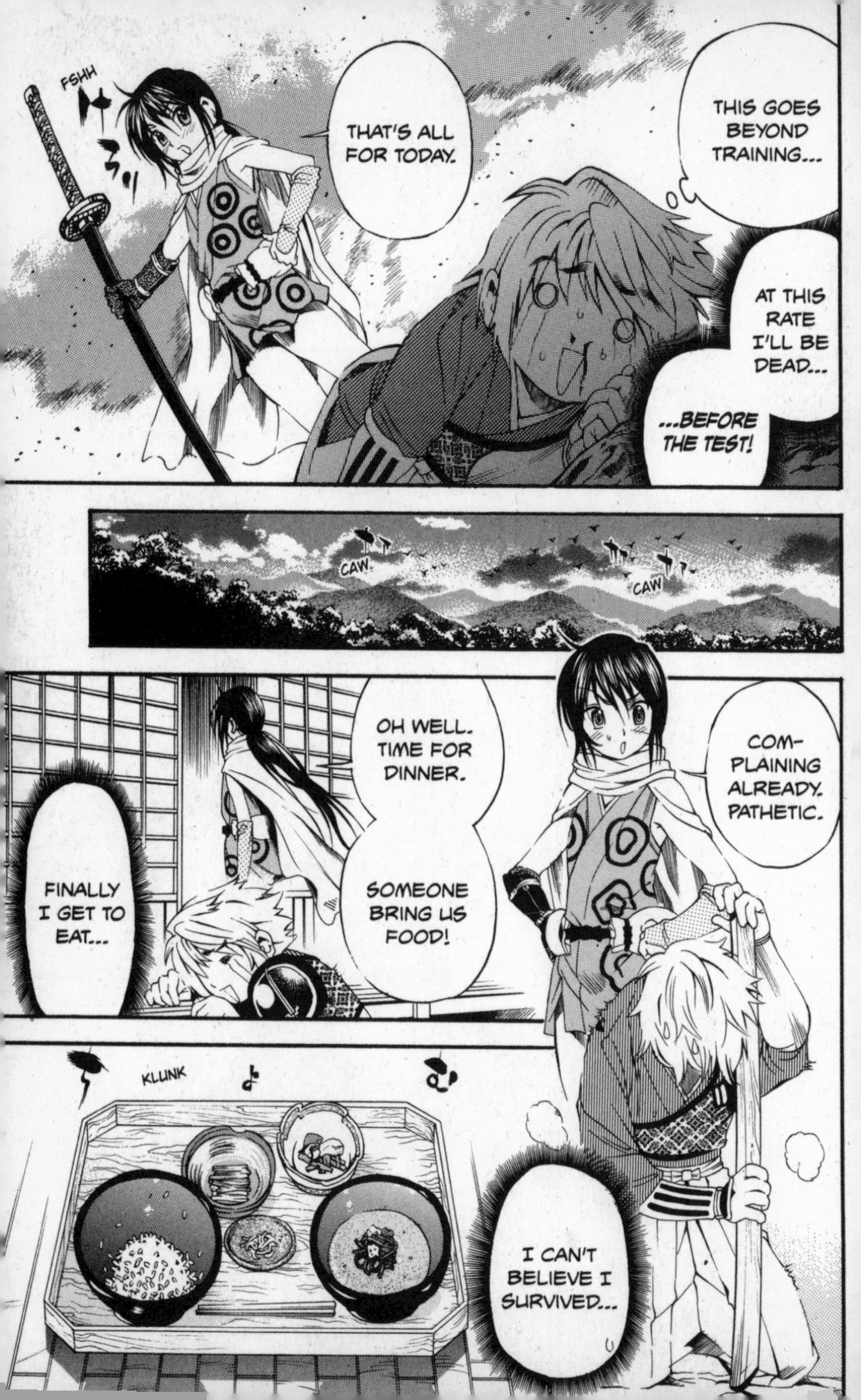
THIS GOES BEYOND TRAINING...
AT THIS RATE I'LL BE DEAD...
...BEFORE THE TEST!
THAT'S ALL FOR TODAY.
FSHH
CAW
CAW
COM-PLAINING ALREADY. PATHETIC.
I CAN'T BELIEVE I SURVIVED...
OH WELL. TIME FOR DINNER.
SOMEONE BRING US FOOD!
FINALLY I GET TO EAT...
KLUNK

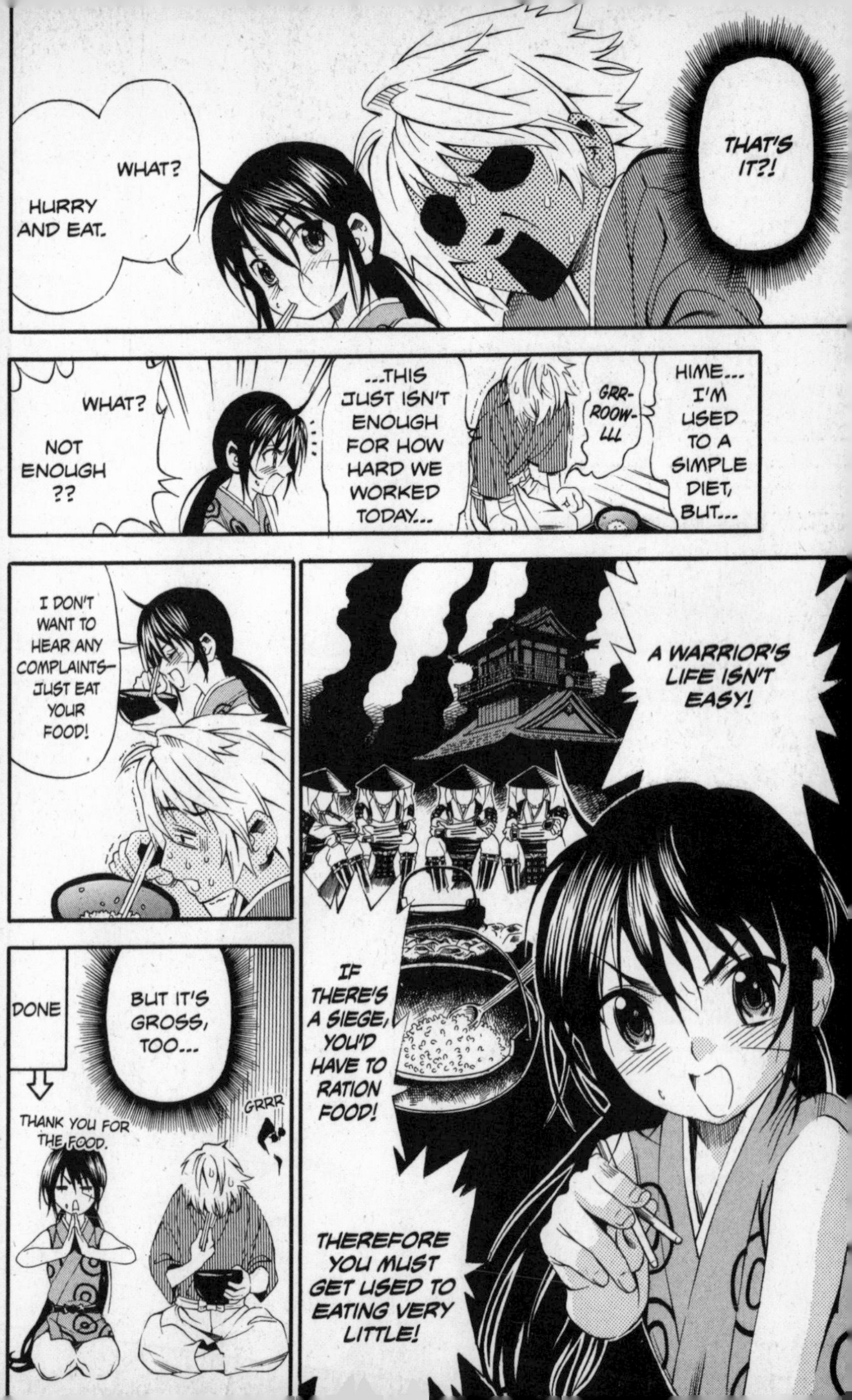
THAT'S IT?!
WHAT?
HURRY AND EAT.
HIME... I'M USED TO A SIMPLE DIET, BUT...
GRR-ROOW-LLL
...THIS JUST ISN'T ENOUGH FOR HOW HARD WE WORKED TODAY...
WHAT?
NOT ENOUGH ??
A WARRIOR'S LIFE ISN'T EASY!
IF THERE'S A SIEGE, YOU'D HAVE TO RATION FOOD!
THEREFORE YOU MUST GET USED TO EATING VERY LITTLE!
I DON'T WANT TO HEAR ANY COMPLAINTS—JUST EAT YOUR FOOD!
BUT IT'S GROSS, TOO...
DONE
THANK YOU FOR THE FOOD.
GRRR

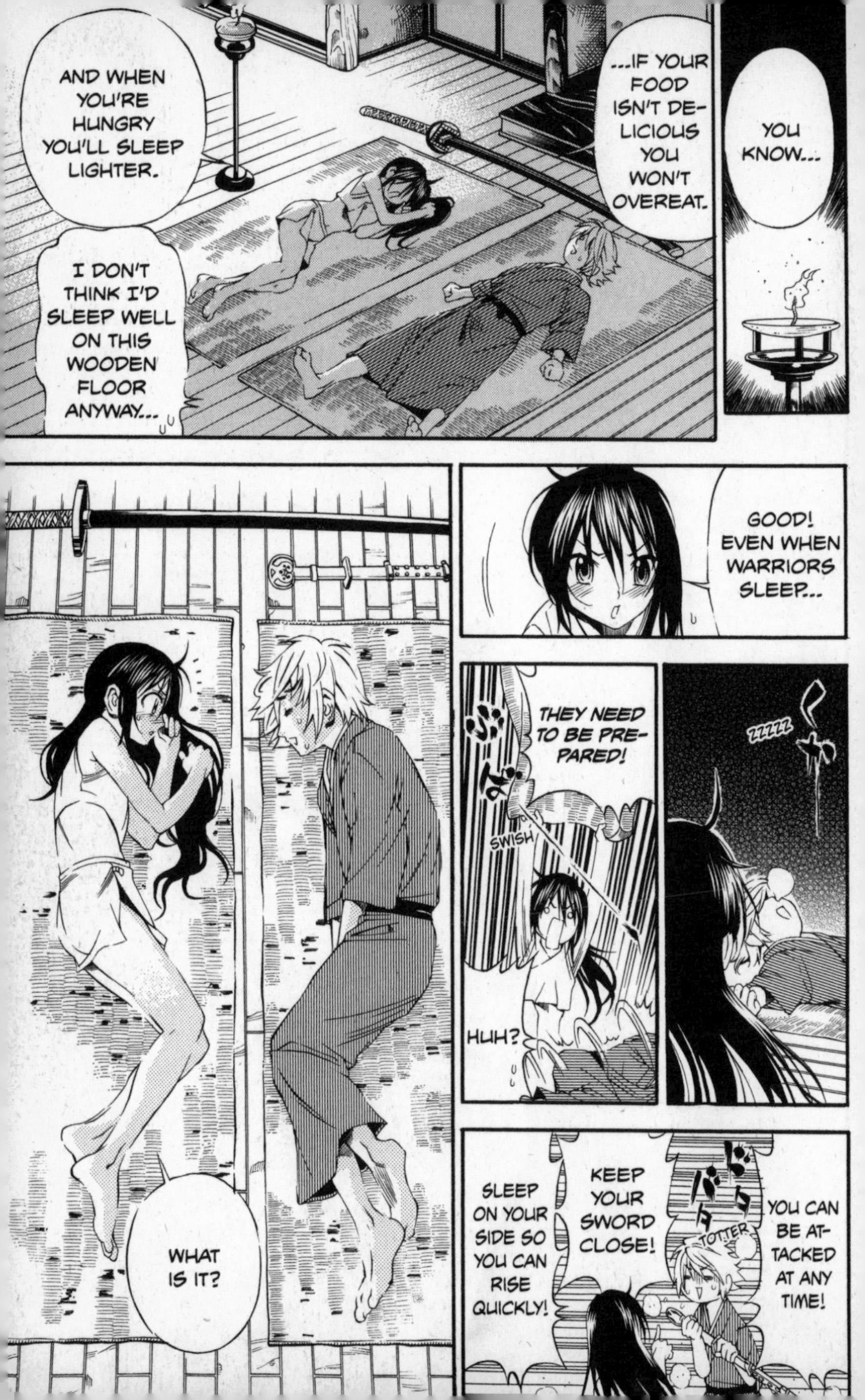
YOU KNOW...
...IF YOUR FOOD ISN'T DE-LICIOUS YOU WON'T OVEREAT.
AND WHEN YOU'RE HUNGRY YOU'LL SLEEP LIGHTER.
I DON'T THINK I'D SLEEP WELL ON THIS WOODEN FLOOR ANYWAY...
GOOD! EVEN WHEN WARRIORS SLEEP...
ZZZZZ
THEY NEED TO BE PRE-PARED!
SWISH
HUH?
YOU CAN BE AT-TACKED AT ANY TIME!
TOTTER
KEEP YOUR SWORD CLOSE!
SLEEP ON YOUR SIDE SO YOU CAN RISE QUICKLY!
WHAT IS IT?

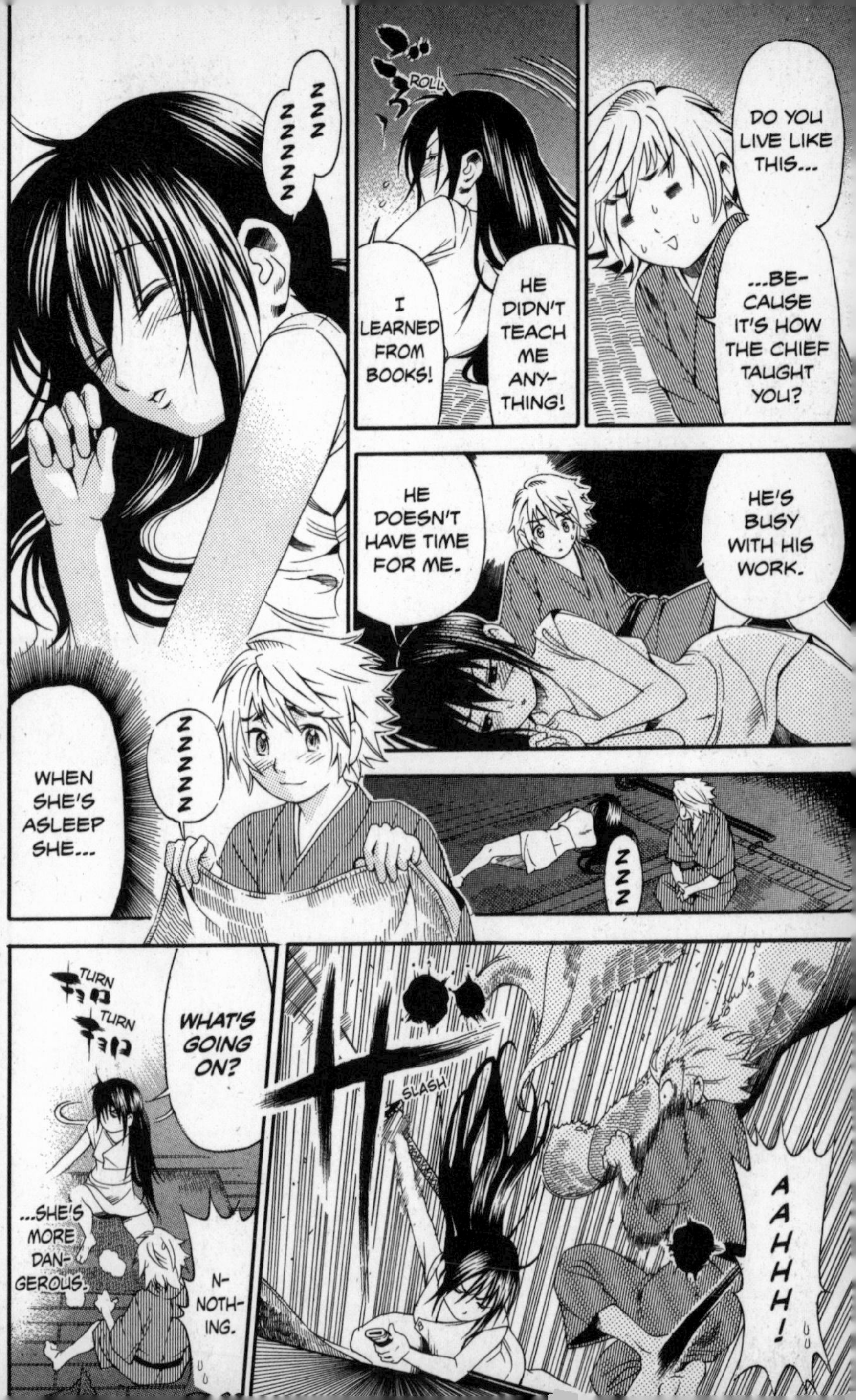
DO YOU LIVE LIKE THIS...
...BE-CAUSE IT'S HOW THE CHIEF TAUGHT YOU?
ROLL
HE DIDN'T TEACH ME ANY-THING!
I LEARNED FROM BOOKS!
HE'S BUSY WITH HIS WORK.
HE DOESN'T HAVE TIME FOR ME.
ZZZ
ZZZ ZZZZZ
ZZZZZ
WHEN SHE'S ASLEEP SHE...
SLASH
AAHHH!
WHAT'S GOING ON?
TURN
TURN
N-NOTH-ING.
...SHE'S MORE DAN-GEROUS.

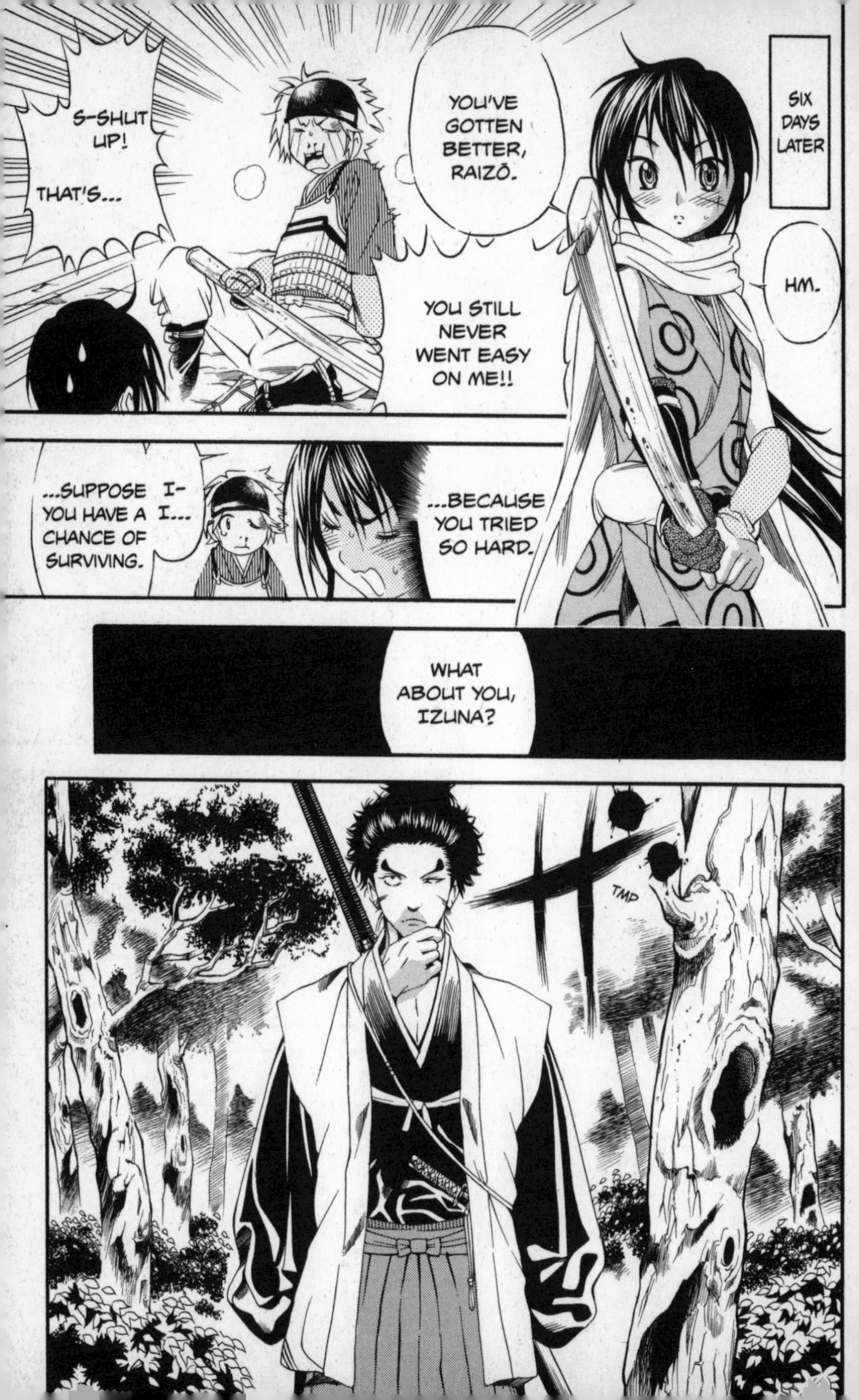
SIX DAYS LATER
HM.
YOU'VE GOTTEN BETTER, RAIZŌ.
S-SHUT UP!
THAT'S...
YOU STILL NEVER WENT EASY ON ME!!
...BECAUSE YOU TRIED SO HARD.
I- I...
...SUPPOSE YOU HAVE A CHANCE OF SURVIVING.
WHAT ABOUT YOU, IZUNA?
TMP

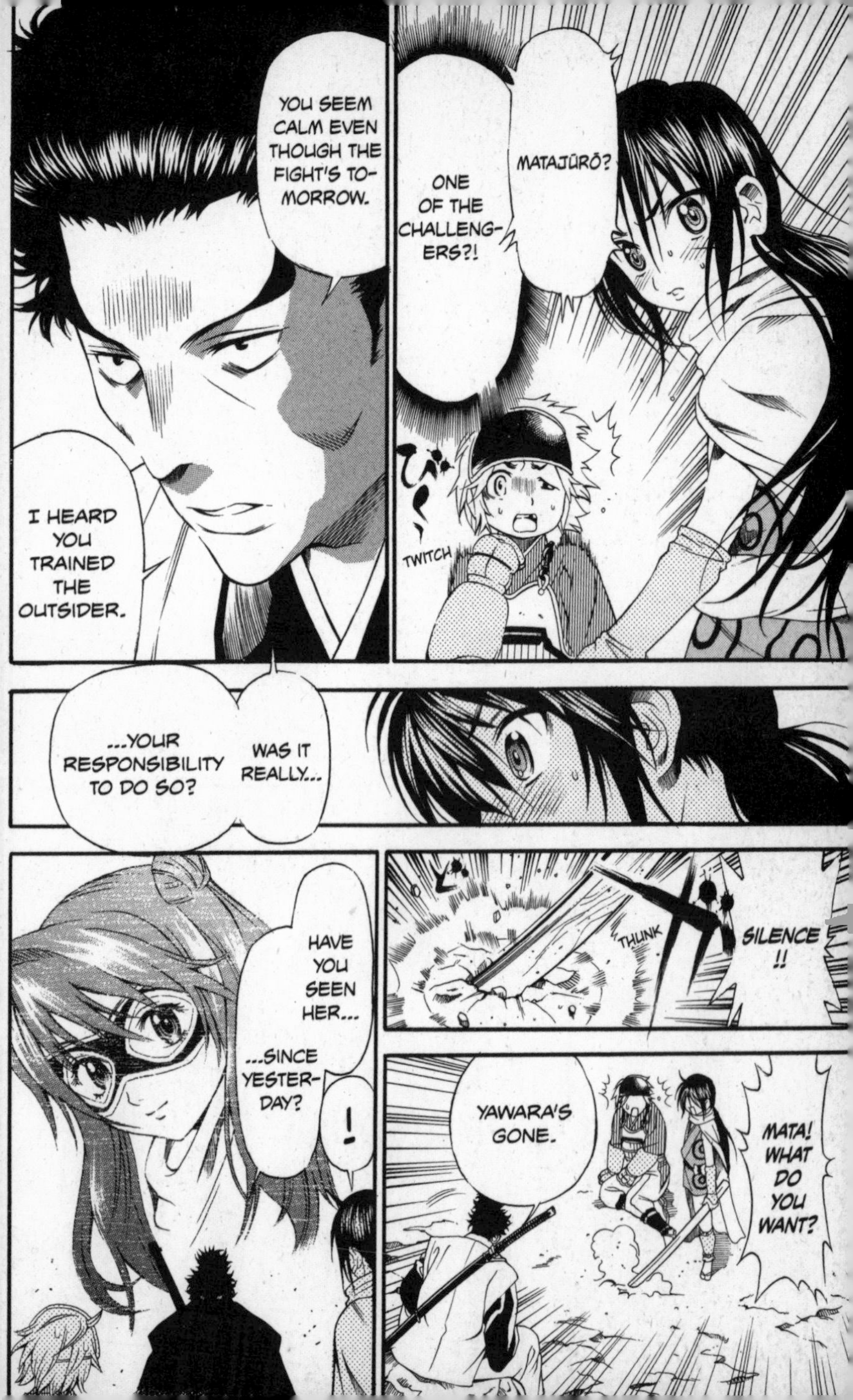
MATAJŪRŌ?
ONE OF THE CHALLENGERS?!
TWITCH
YOU SEEM CALM EVEN THOUGH THE FIGHT'S TOMORROW.
I HEARD YOU TRAINED THE OUTSIDER.
WAS IT REALLY...
...YOUR RESPONSIBILITY TO DO SO?
SILENCE!!
THUNK
MATA! WHAT DO YOU WANT?
YAWARA'S GONE.
HAVE YOU SEEN HER...
...SINCE YESTERDAY?
!

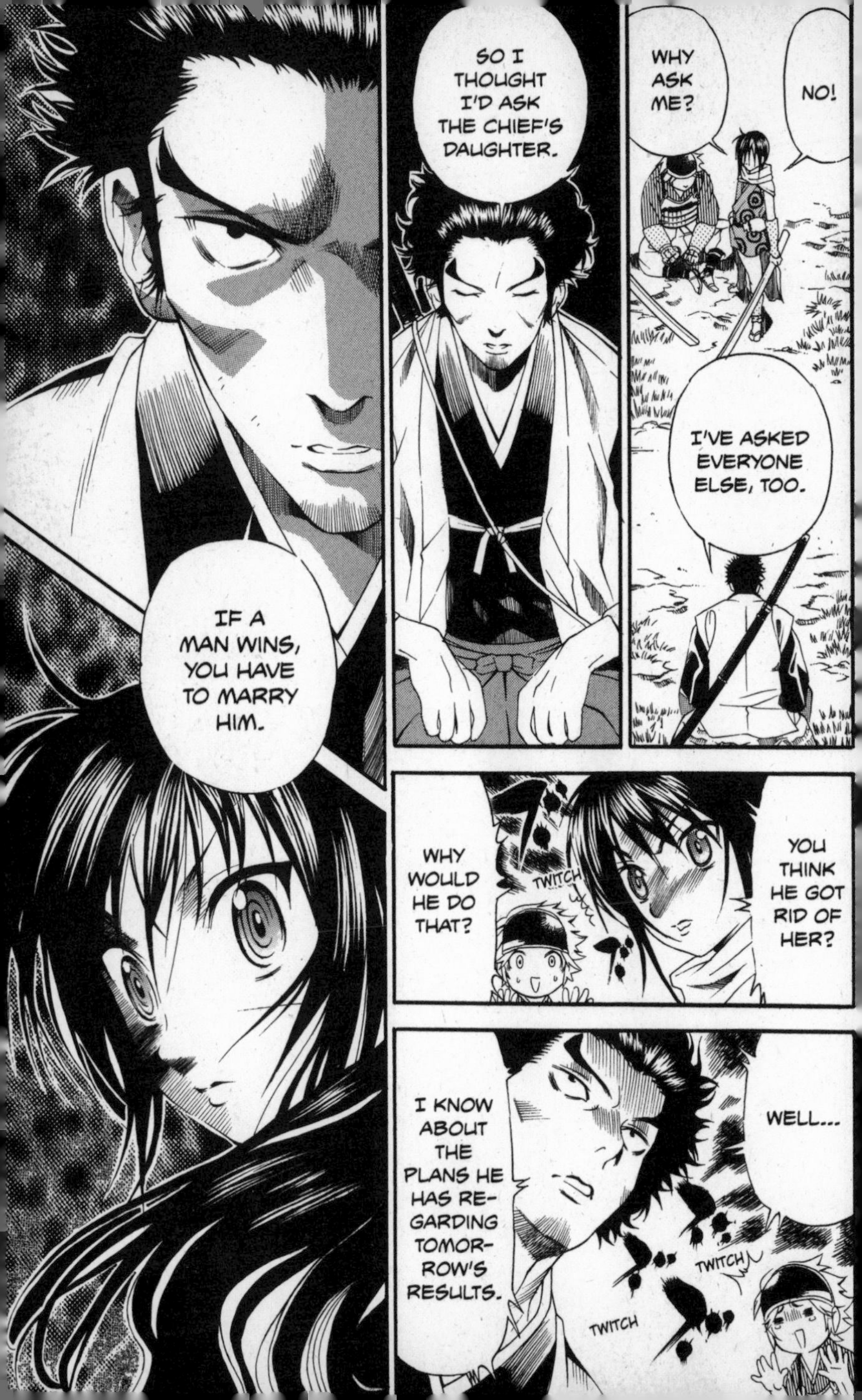
NO!
WHY ASK ME?
I'VE ASKED EVERYONE ELSE, TOO.
SO I THOUGHT I'D ASK THE CHIEF'S DAUGHTER.
YOU THINK HE GOT RID OF HER?
TWITCH
WHY WOULD HE DO THAT?
WELL...
I KNOW ABOUT THE PLANS HE HAS RE-GARDING TOMOR-ROW'S RESULTS.
TWITCH
TWITCH
IF A MAN WINS, YOU HAVE TO MARRY HIM.

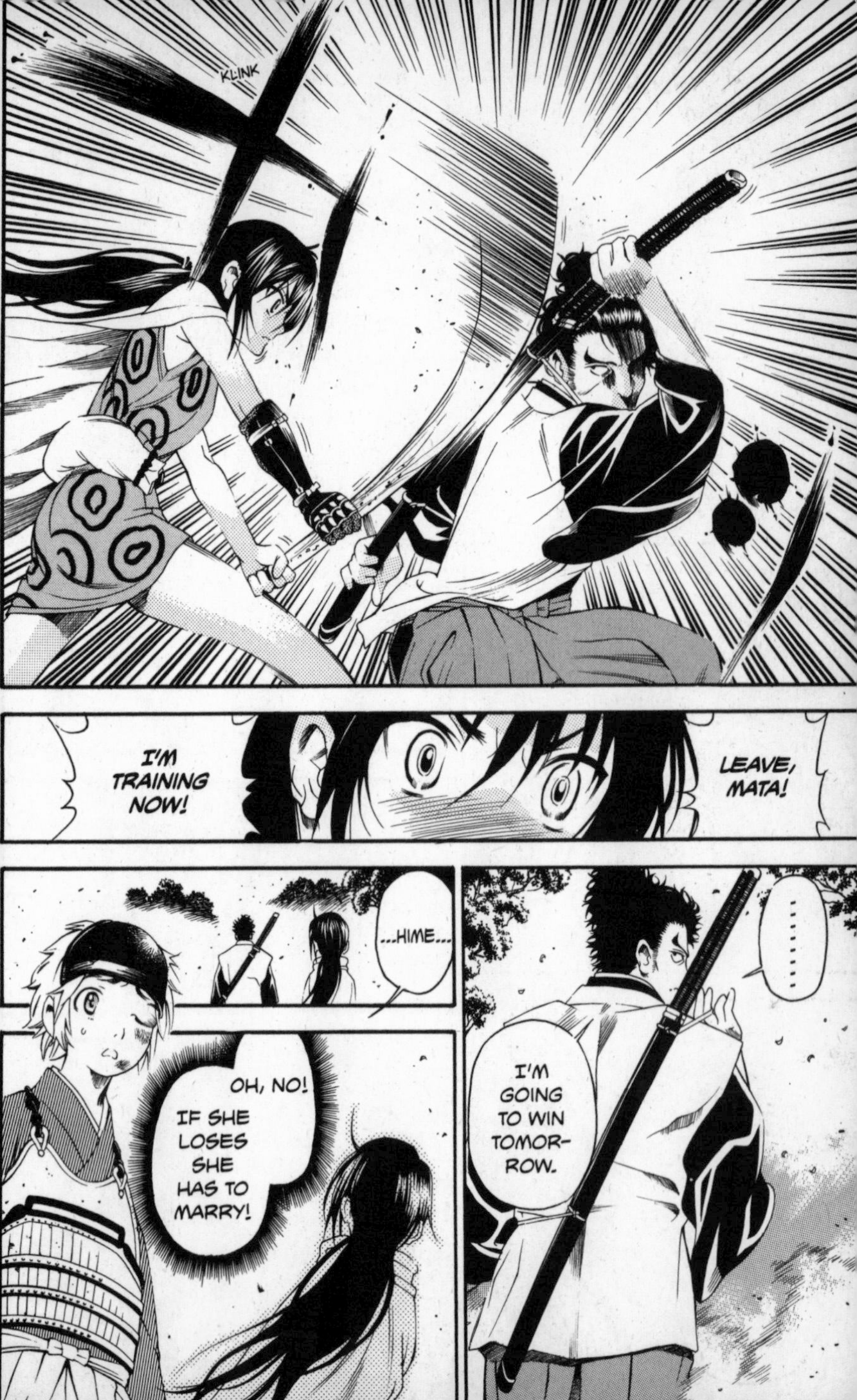
KLINK
LEAVE, MATA!
I'M TRAINING NOW!
......
I'M GOING TO WIN TOMORROW.
...HIME...
OH, NO!
IF SHE LOSES SHE HAS TO MARRY!

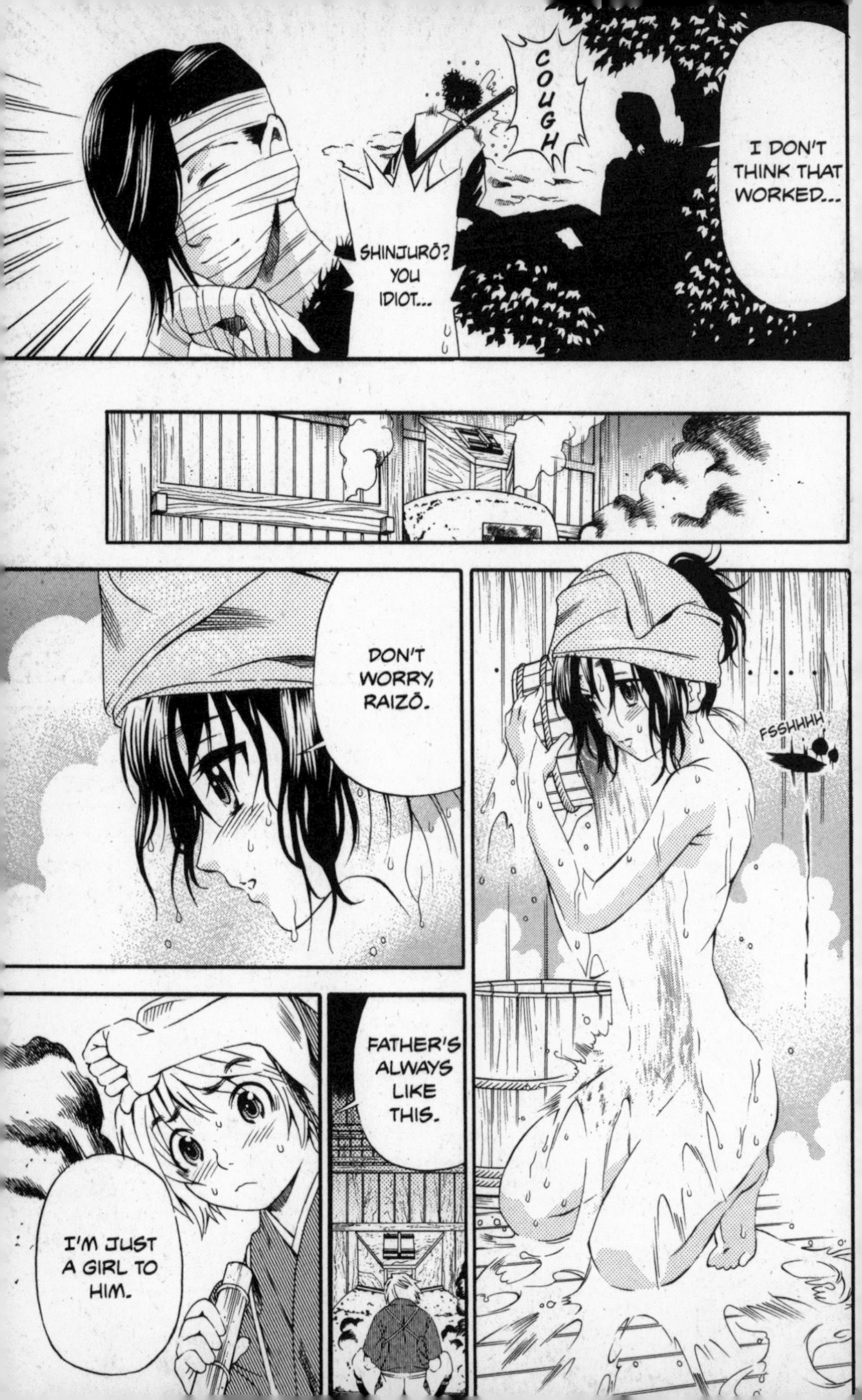
I DON'T THINK THAT WORKED...
COUGH
SHINJURŌ? YOU IDIOT...
FSSHHHH
DON'T WORRY, RAIZŌ.
FATHER'S ALWAYS LIKE THIS.
I'M JUST A GIRL TO HIM.

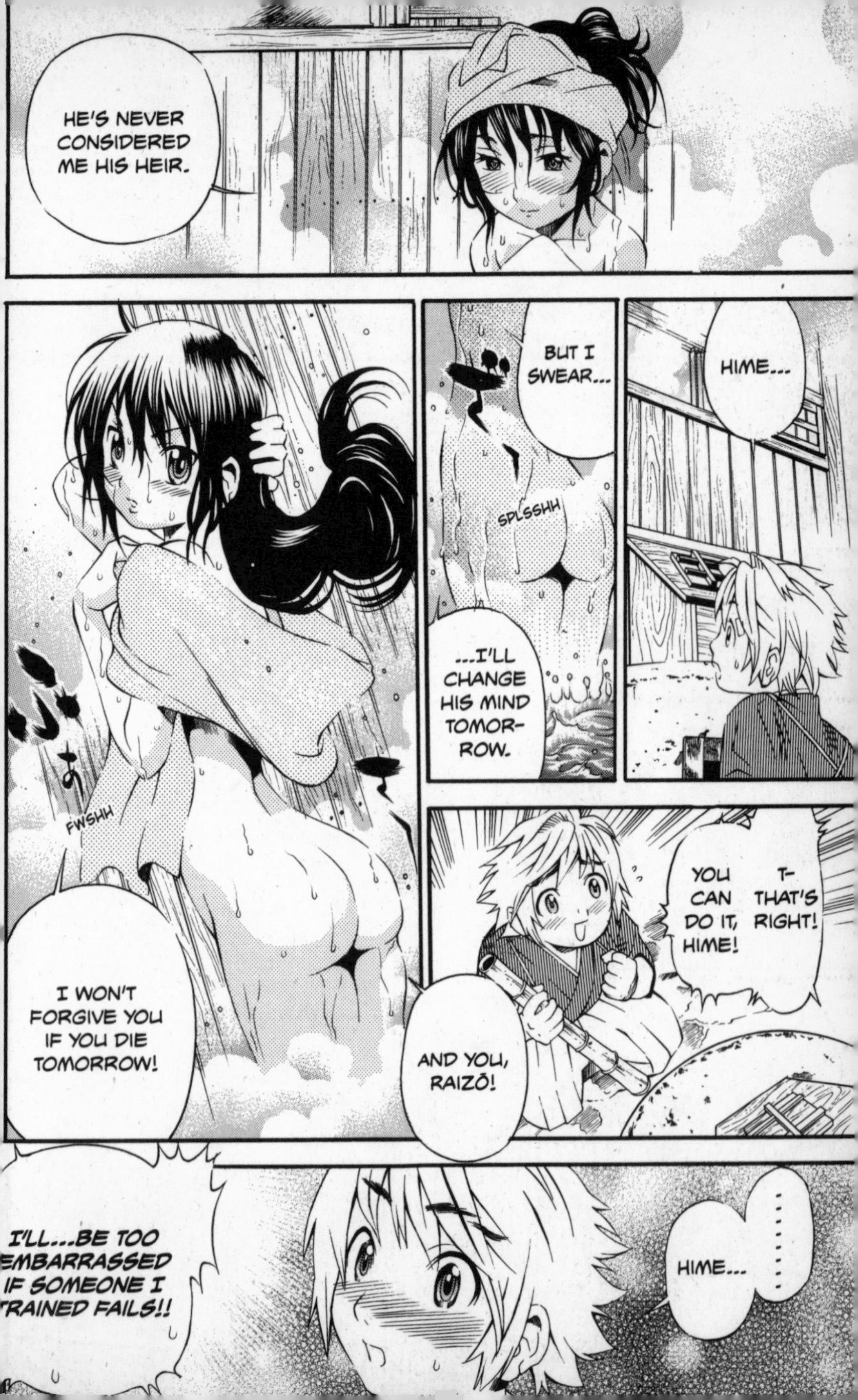
HE'S NEVER CONSIDERED ME HIS HEIR.
HIME...
BUT I SWEAR...
SPLSSHH
...I'LL CHANGE HIS MIND TOMOR-ROW.
T-THAT'S RIGHT!
YOU CAN DO IT, HIME!
AND YOU, RAIZŌ!
FWSHH
I WON'T FORGIVE YOU IF YOU DIE TOMORROW!
......
HIME...
I'LL...BE TOO EMBARRASSED IF SOMEONE I TRAINED FAILS!!

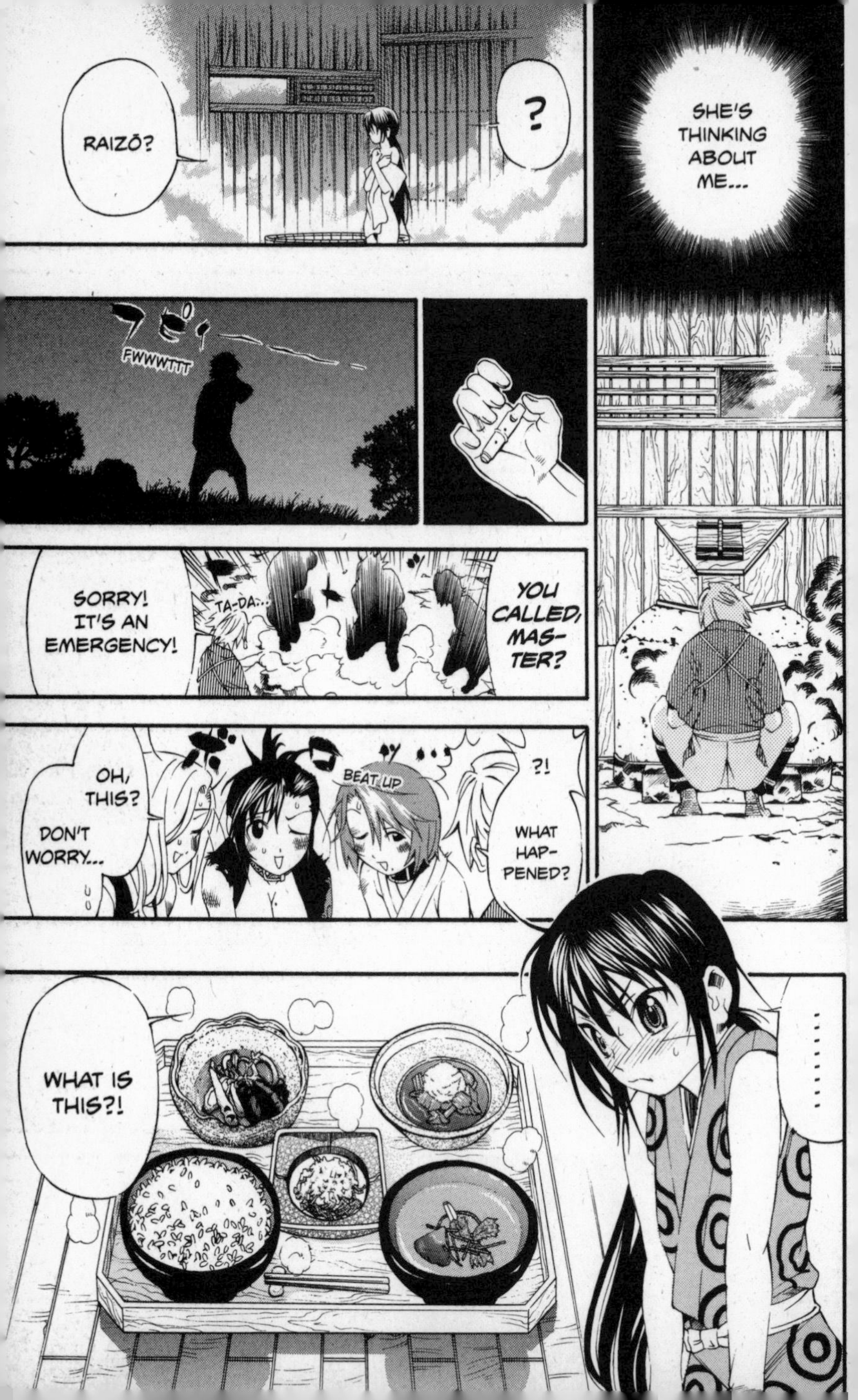
SHE'S THINKING ABOUT ME...
?
RAIZŌ?
FWWWTTT
YOU CALLED, MASTER?
TA-DA...
SORRY! IT'S AN EMERGENCY!
?!
WHAT HAPPENED?
BEAT UP
OH, THIS?
DON'T WORRY...
......
WHAT IS THIS?!

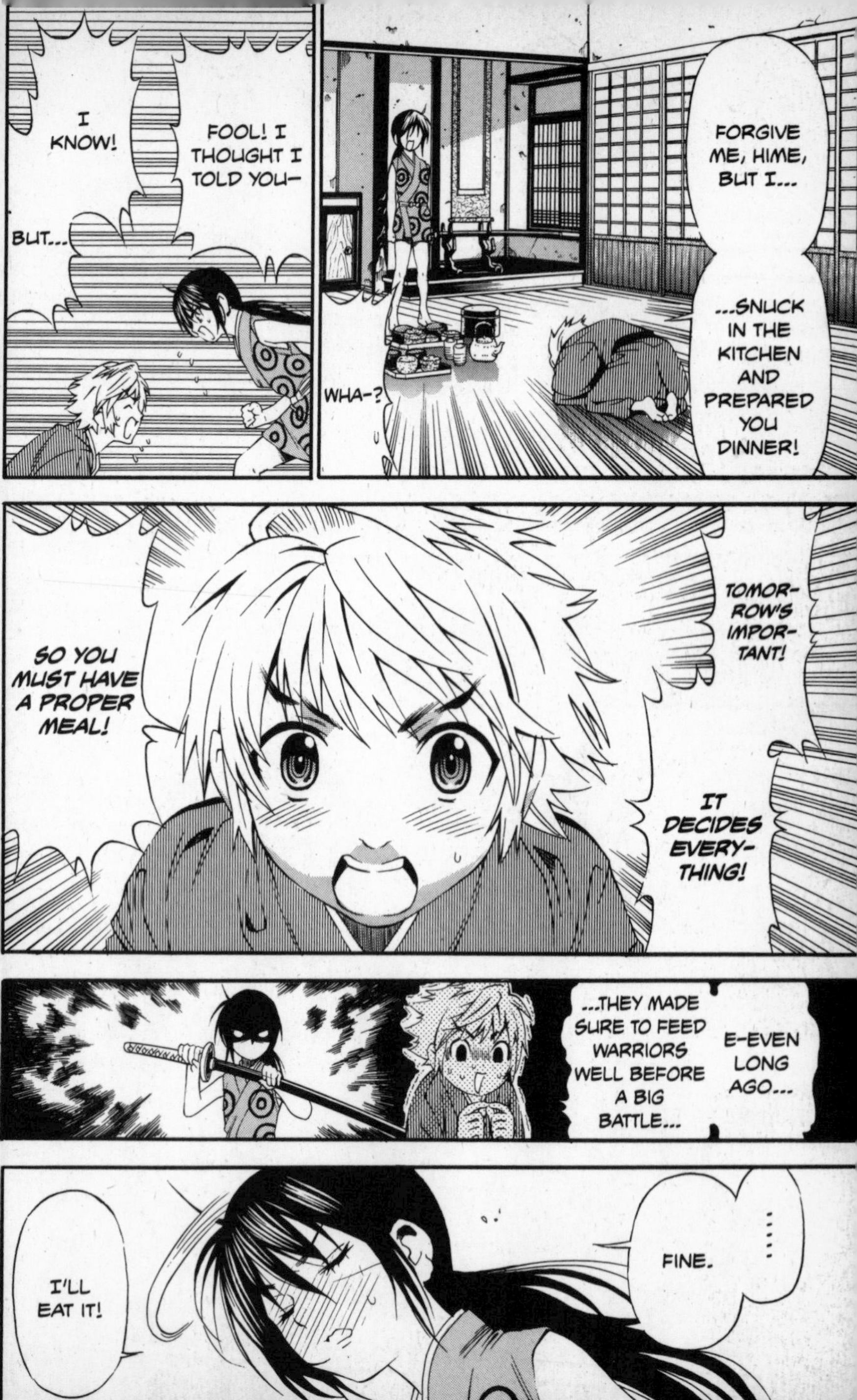
FORGIVE ME, HIME, BUT I...
...SNUCK IN THE KITCHEN AND PREPARED YOU DINNER!
WHA-?
FOOL! I THOUGHT I TOLD YOU—
I KNOW!
BUT...
TOMORROW'S IMPORTANT!
IT DECIDES EVERYTHING!
SO YOU MUST HAVE A PROPER MEAL!
E-EVEN LONG AGO...
...THEY MADE SURE TO FEED WARRIORS WELL BEFORE A BIG BATTLE...
......
FINE.
I'LL EAT IT!

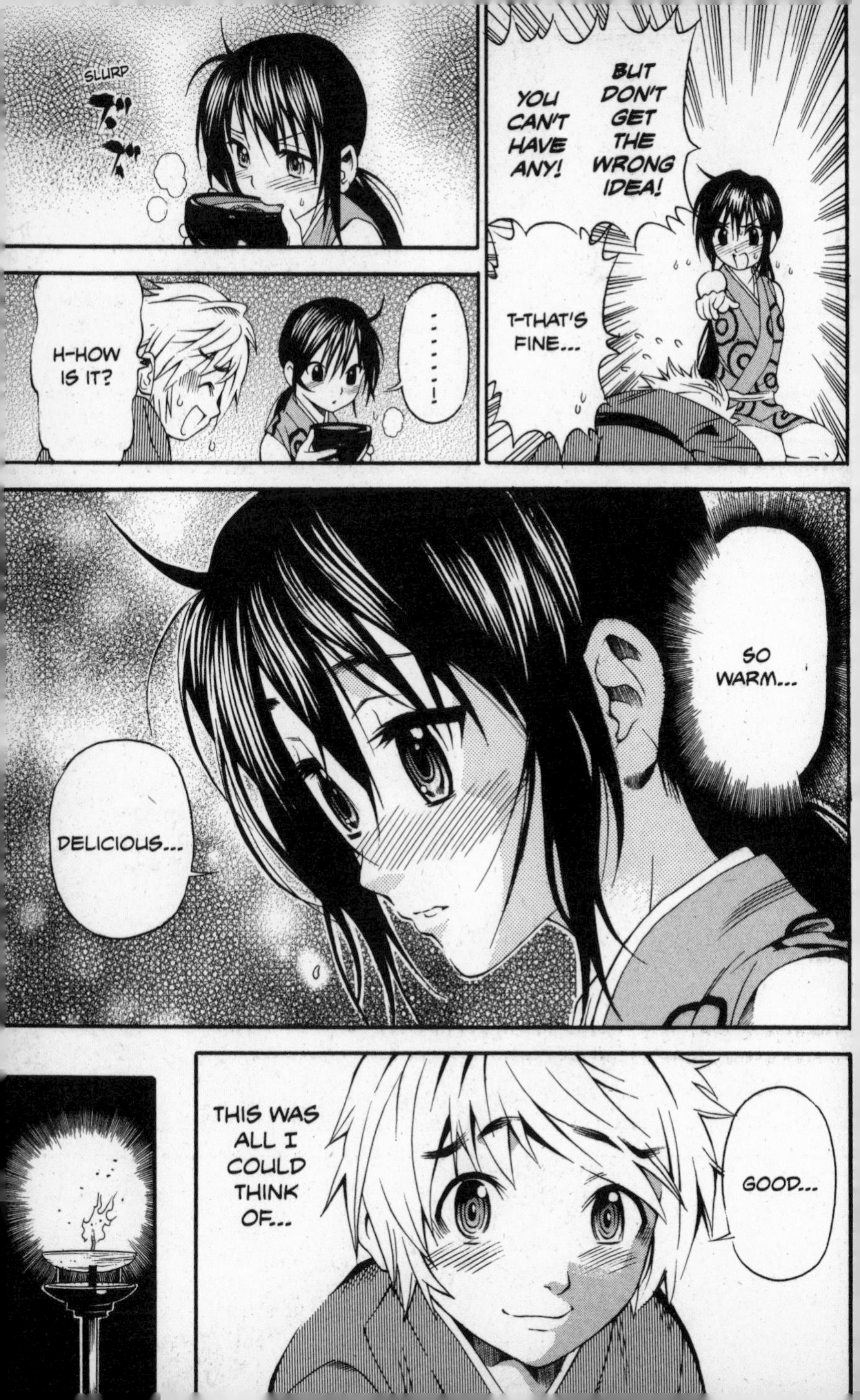
BUT DON'T GET THE WRONG IDEA!
YOU CAN'T HAVE ANY!
T-THAT'S FINE...
SLURP
......!
H-HOW IS IT?
SO WARM...
DELICIOUS...
GOOD...
THIS WAS ALL I COULD THINK OF...

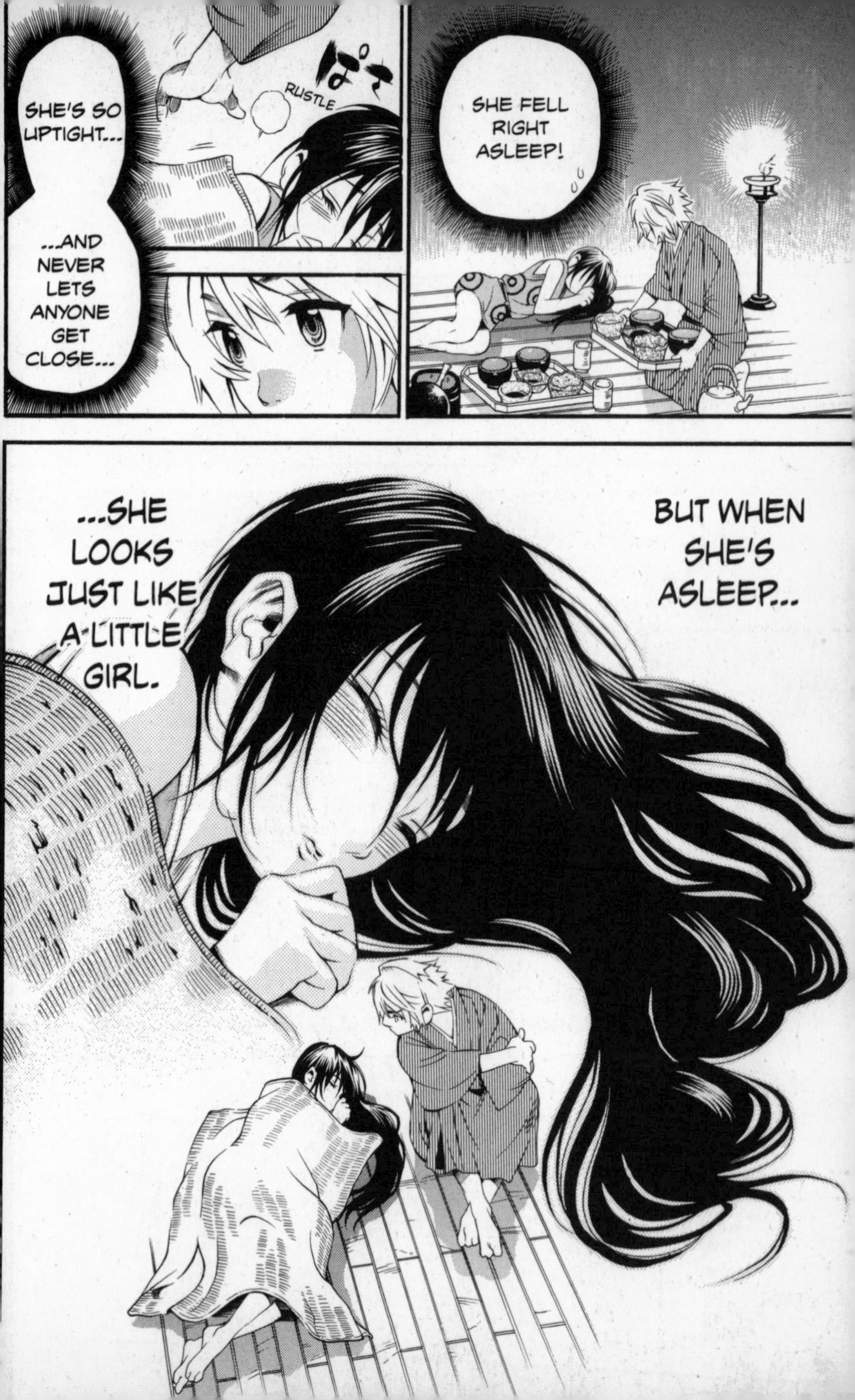
SHE FELL RIGHT ASLEEP!
ぱさ
RUSTLE
SHE'S SO UPTIGHT...
...AND NEVER LETS ANYONE GET CLOSE...
BUT WHEN SHE'S ASLEEP...
...SHE LOOKS JUST LIKE A LITTLE GIRL.

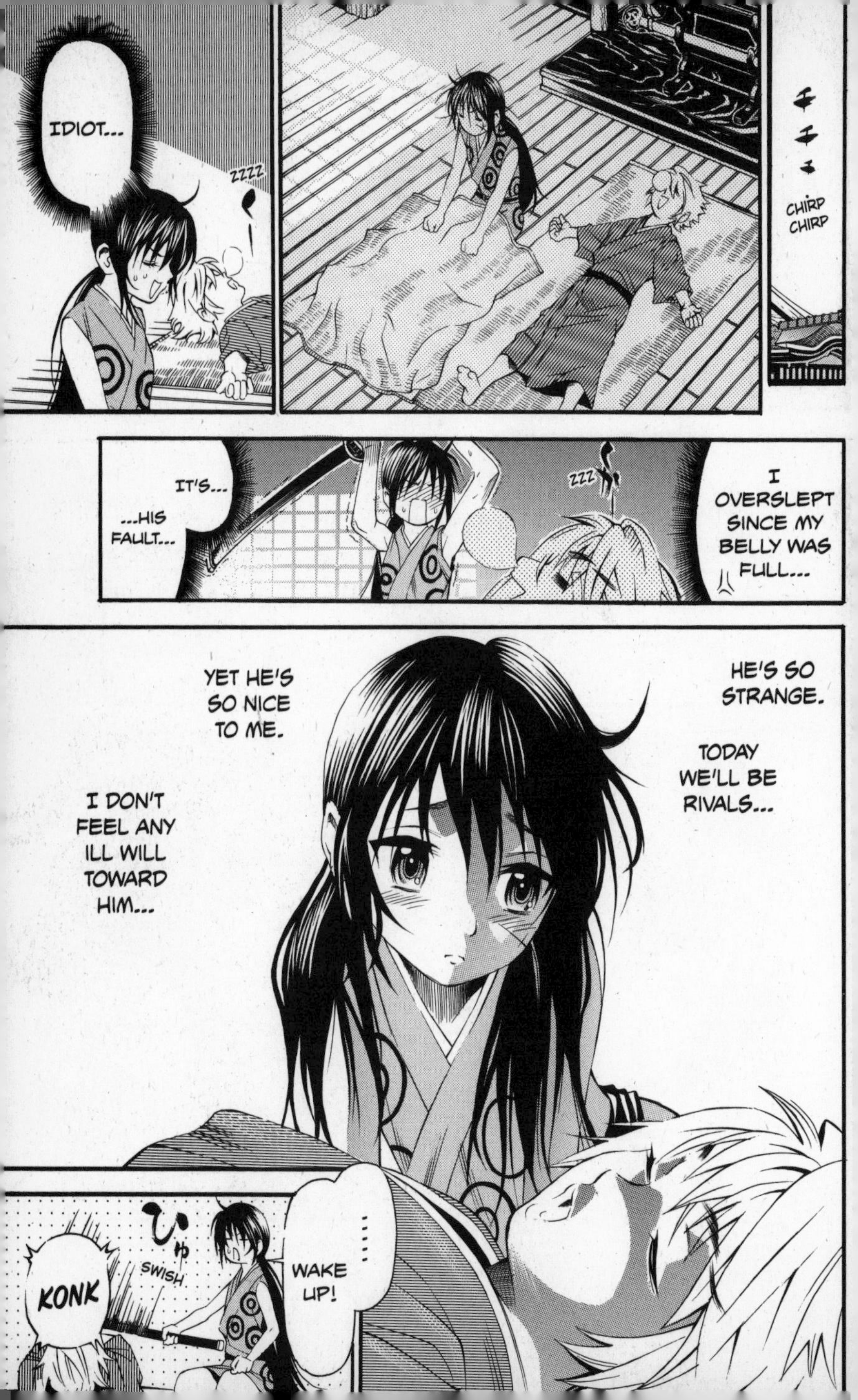
チチチ
CHIRP CHIRP
IDIOT...
ZZZZ
I OVERSLEPT SINCE MY BELLY WAS FULL...
ZZZ
IT'S...
...HIS FAULT...
HE'S SO STRANGE.
TODAY WE'LL BE RIVALS...
YET HE'S SO NICE TO ME.
I DON'T FEEL ANY ILL WILL TOWARD HIM...
.....
WAKE UP!
ひゅ
SWISH
KONK

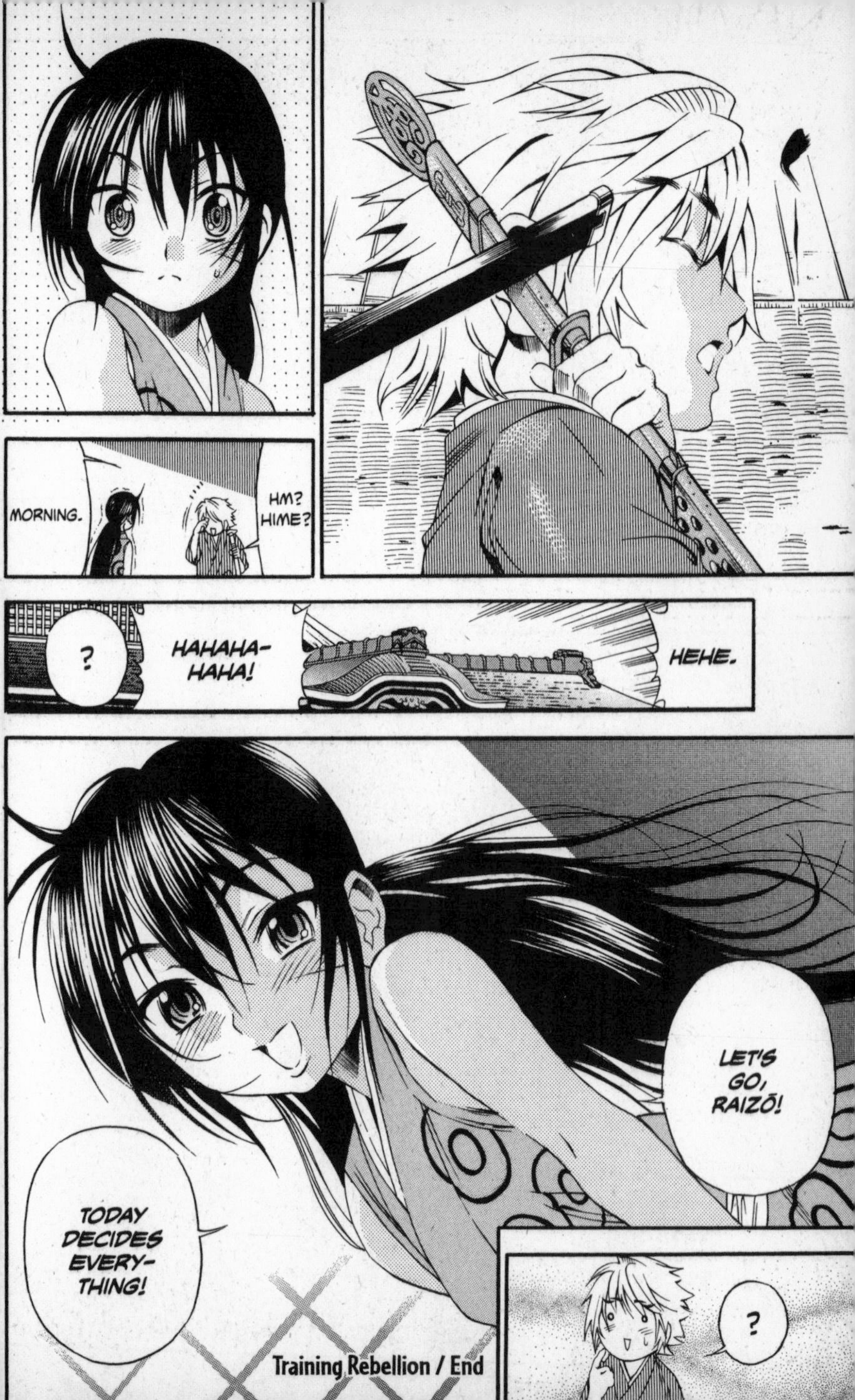
HM? HIME?
MORNING.
HEHE.
HAHAHA-HAHA!
?
LET'S GO, RAIZŌ!
TODAY DECIDES EVERY-THING!
?

Training Rebellion / End

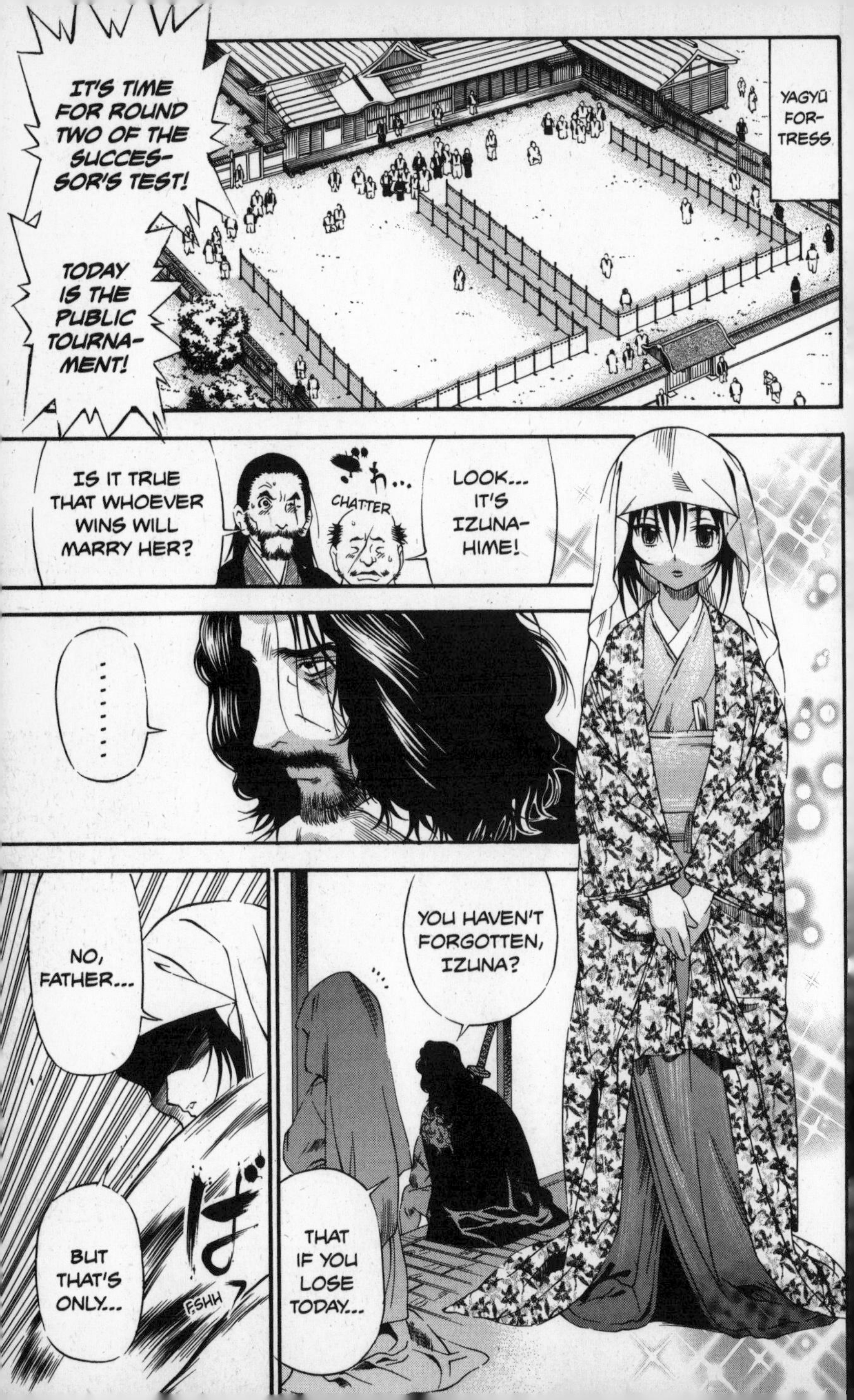
YAGYŪ FOR-TRESS
IT'S TIME FOR ROUND TWO OF THE SUCCES-SOR'S TEST!
TODAY IS THE PUBLIC TOURNA-MENT!
LOOK... IT'S IZUNA-HIME!
ざわ...
CHATTER
IS IT TRUE THAT WHOEVER WINS WILL MARRY HER?
......
YOU HAVEN'T FORGOTTEN, IZUNA?
...
THAT IF YOU LOSE TODAY...
NO, FATHER...
F.SHH
BUT THAT'S ONLY...

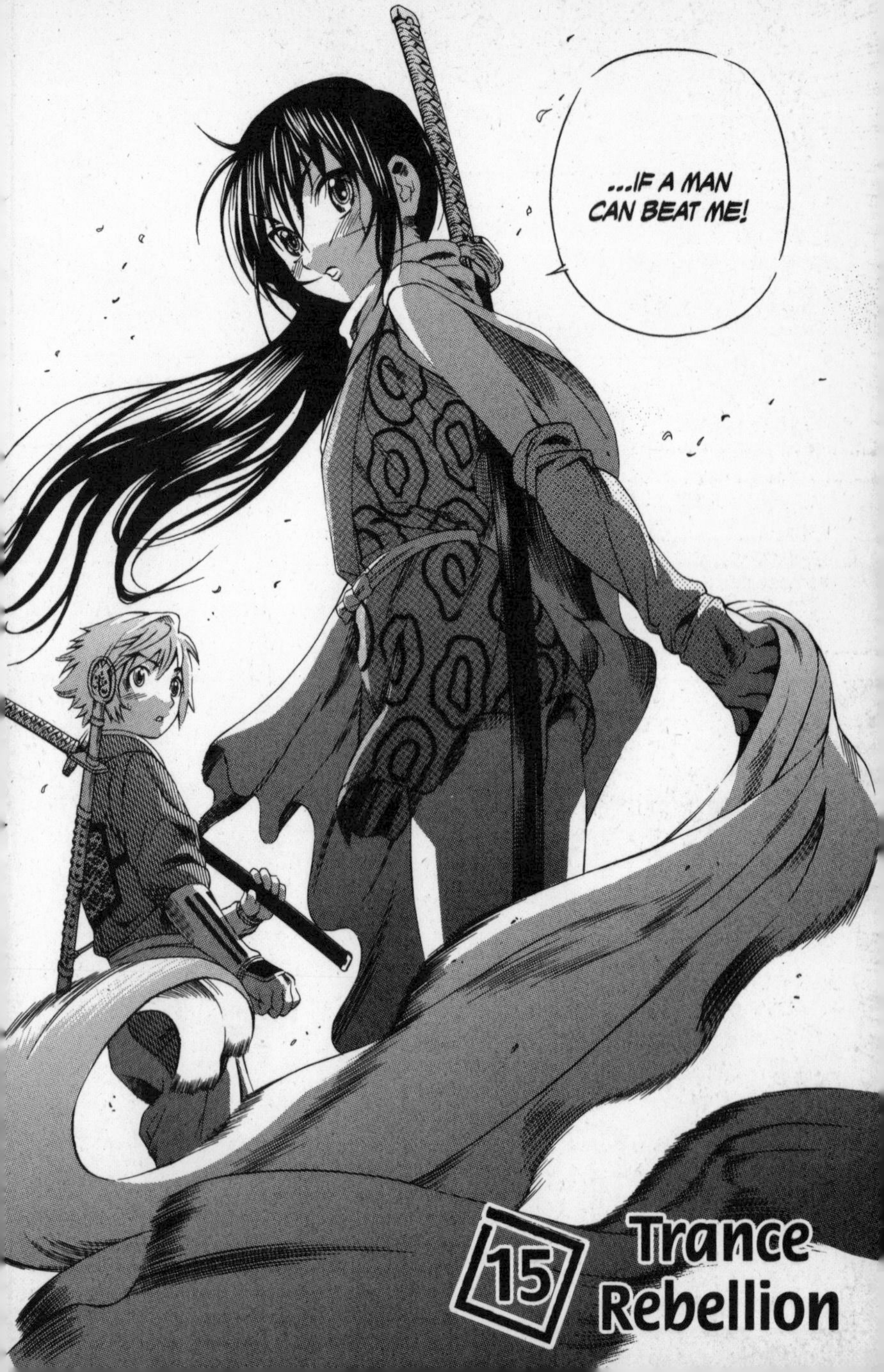

15 Trance Rebellion

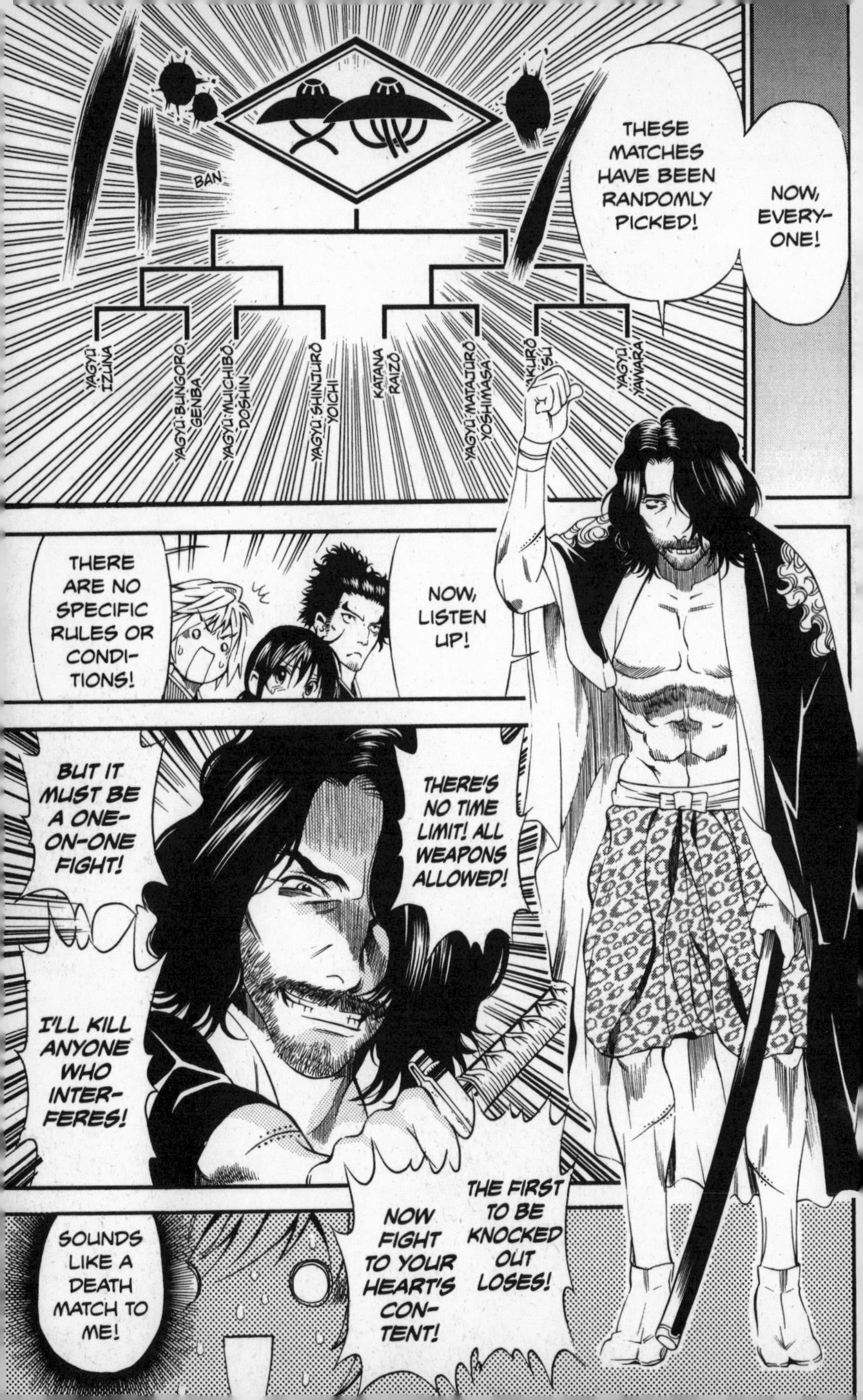
NOW, EVERYONE!
THESE MATCHES HAVE BEEN RANDOMLY PICKED!
BAN
YAGYŪ YAWARA
YAGYŪ MATAJURŌ YOSHIMASA
KATANA RAIZŌ
YAGYŪ SHINJURŌ YOICHI
YAGYŪ MUICHIBŌ DOSHIN
YAGYŪ BUNGORO GENBA
YAGYŪ IZUNA
NOW, LISTEN UP!
THERE ARE NO SPECIFIC RULES OR CONDITIONS!
THERE'S NO TIME LIMIT! ALL WEAPONS ALLOWED!
BUT IT MUST BE A ONE-ON-ONE FIGHT!
I'LL KILL ANYONE WHO INTERFERES!
THE FIRST TO BE KNOCKED OUT LOSES!
NOW FIGHT TO YOUR HEART'S CONTENT!
SOUNDS LIKE A DEATH MATCH TO ME!

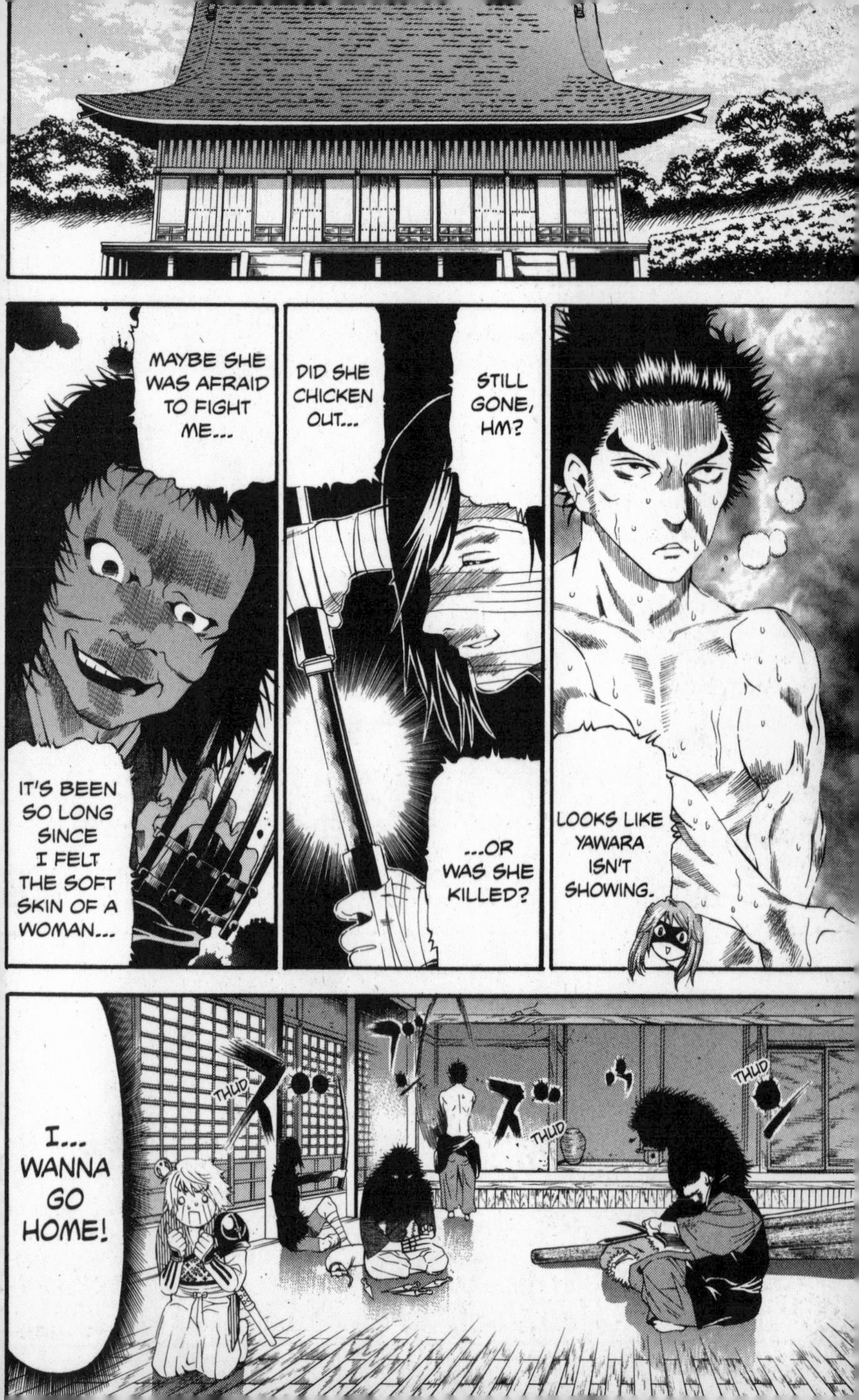
STILL GONE, HM?
LOOKS LIKE YAWARA ISN'T SHOWING.
DID SHE CHICKEN OUT...
...OR WAS SHE KILLED?
MAYBE SHE WAS AFRAID TO FIGHT ME...
IT'S BEEN SO LONG SINCE I FELT THE SOFT SKIN OF A WOMAN...
THUD
THUD
THUD
I... WANNA GO HOME!

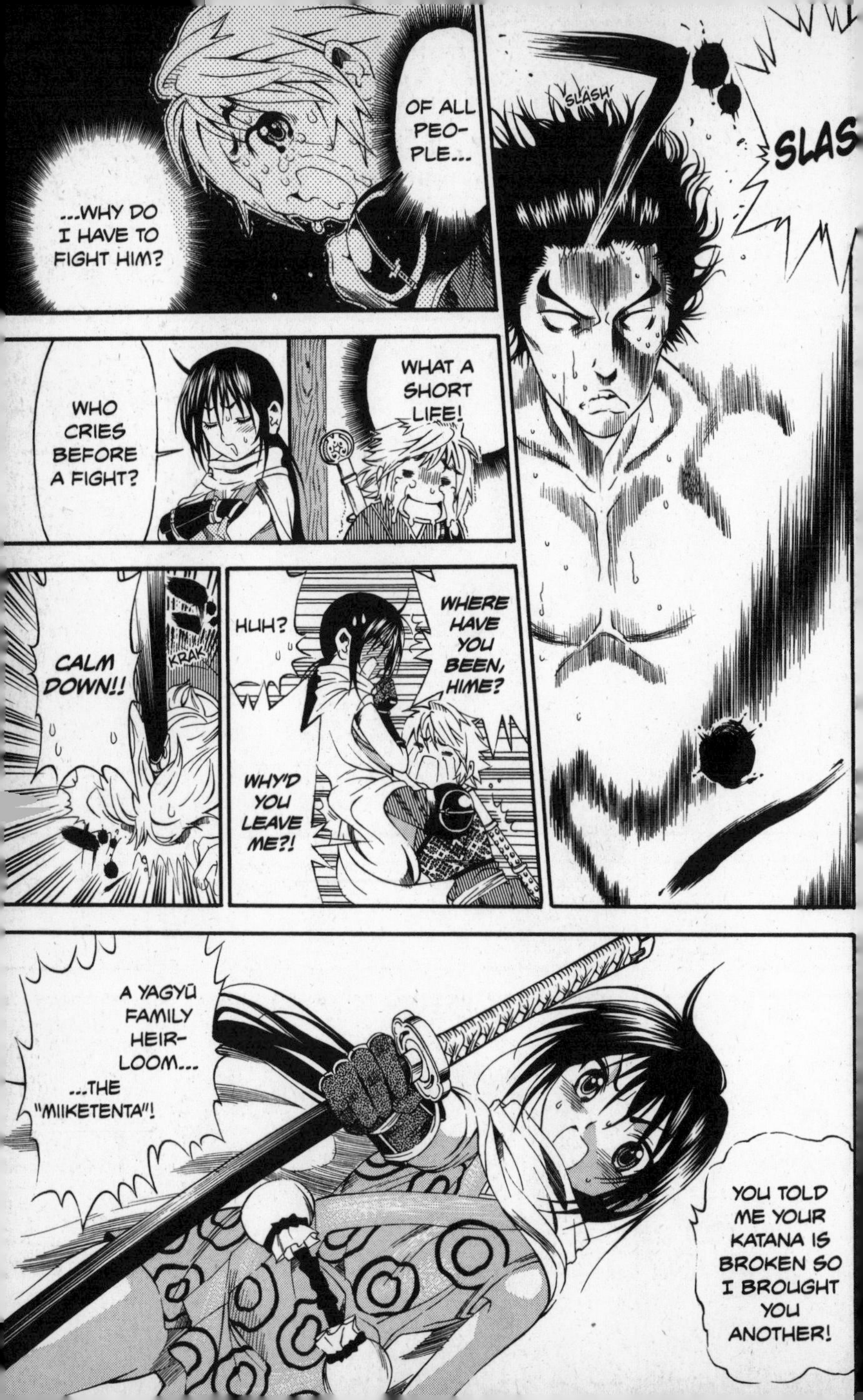
SLASH!
SLAS
OF ALL PEO-PLE...
...WHY DO I HAVE TO FIGHT HIM?
WHAT A SHORT LIFE!
WHO CRIES BEFORE A FIGHT?
WHERE HAVE YOU BEEN, HIME?
HUH?
WHY'D YOU LEAVE ME?!
KRAK
CALM DOWN!!
YOU TOLD ME YOUR KATANA IS BROKEN SO I BROUGHT YOU ANOTHER!
A YAGYŪ FAMILY HEIR-LOOM...
...THE "MIIKETENTA"!

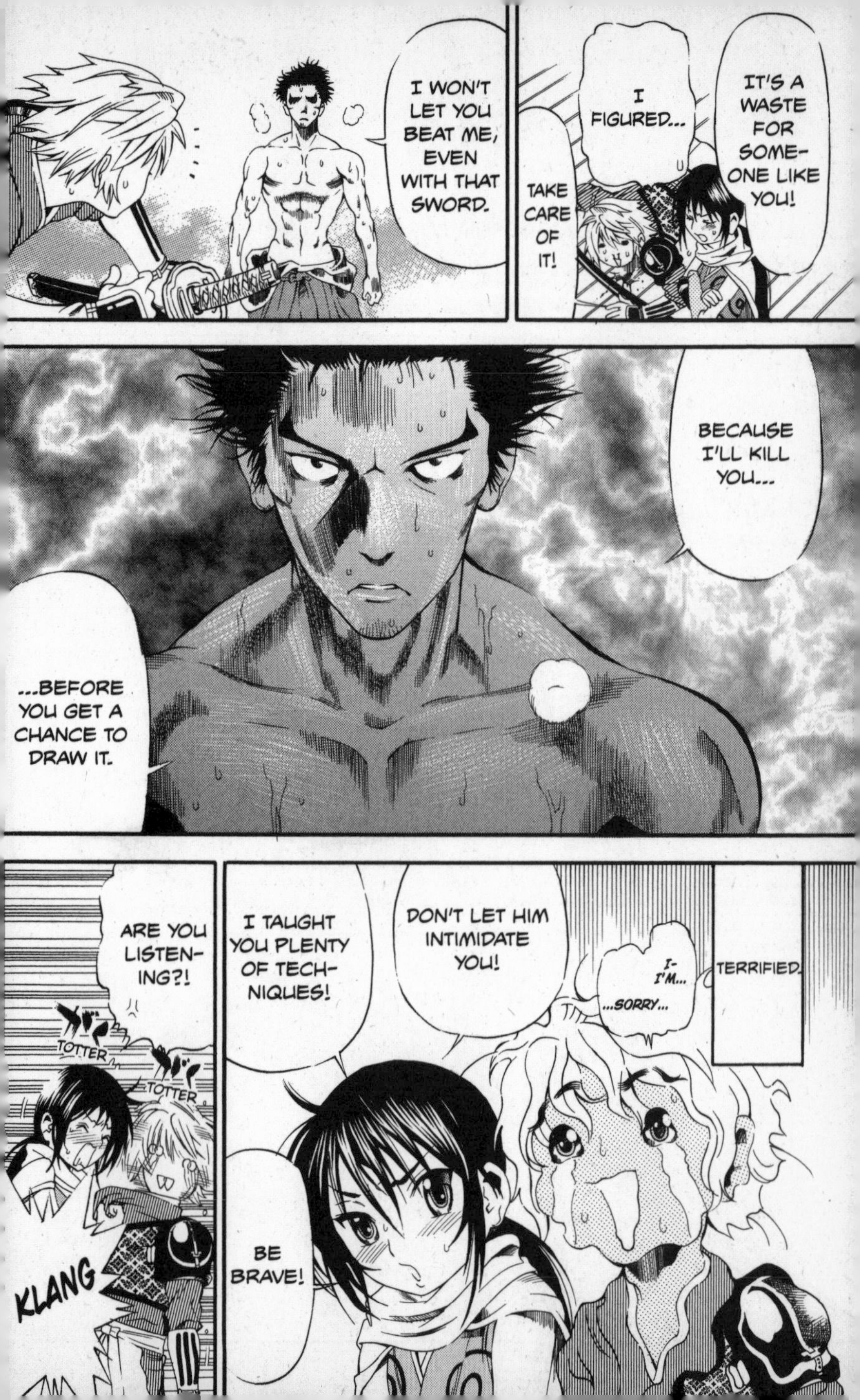
IT'S A WASTE FOR SOME-ONE LIKE YOU!
I FIGURED...
TAKE CARE OF IT!
I WON'T LET YOU BEAT ME, EVEN WITH THAT SWORD.
BECAUSE I'LL KILL YOU...
...BEFORE YOU GET A CHANCE TO DRAW IT.
TERRIFIED
I- I'M...
...SORRY...
DON'T LET HIM INTIMIDATE YOU!
I TAUGHT YOU PLENTY OF TECH-NIQUES!
BE BRAVE!
ARE YOU LISTEN-ING?!
TOTTER
TOTTER
KLANG

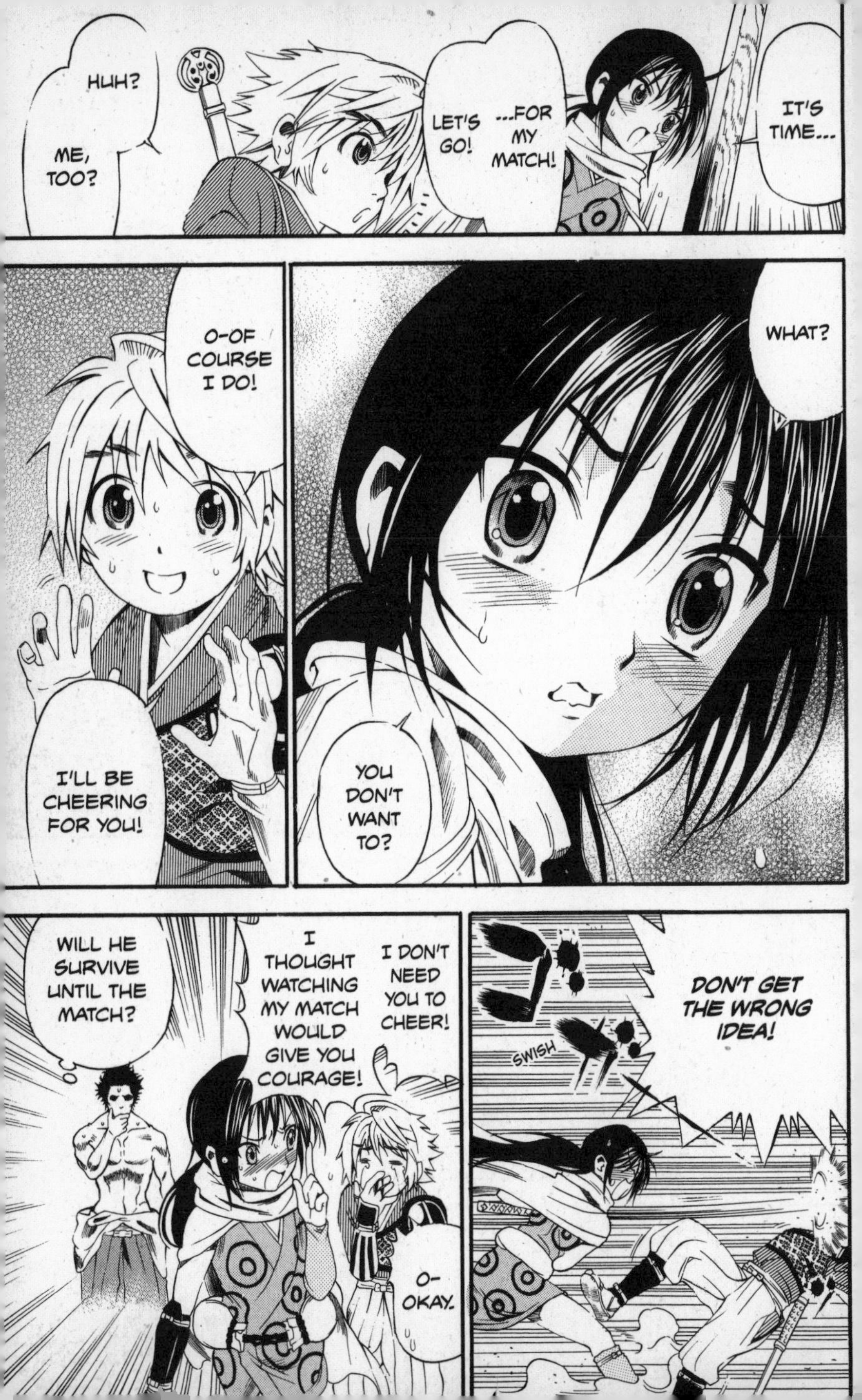
IT'S TIME...
...FOR MY MATCH!
LET'S GO!
HUH?
ME, TOO?
WHAT?
YOU DON'T WANT TO?
O-OF COURSE I DO!
I'LL BE CHEERING FOR YOU!
DON'T GET THE WRONG IDEA!
SWISH
I DON'T NEED YOU TO CHEER!
I THOUGHT WATCHING MY MATCH WOULD GIVE YOU COURAGE!
O-OKAY.
WILL HE SURVIVE UNTIL THE MATCH?

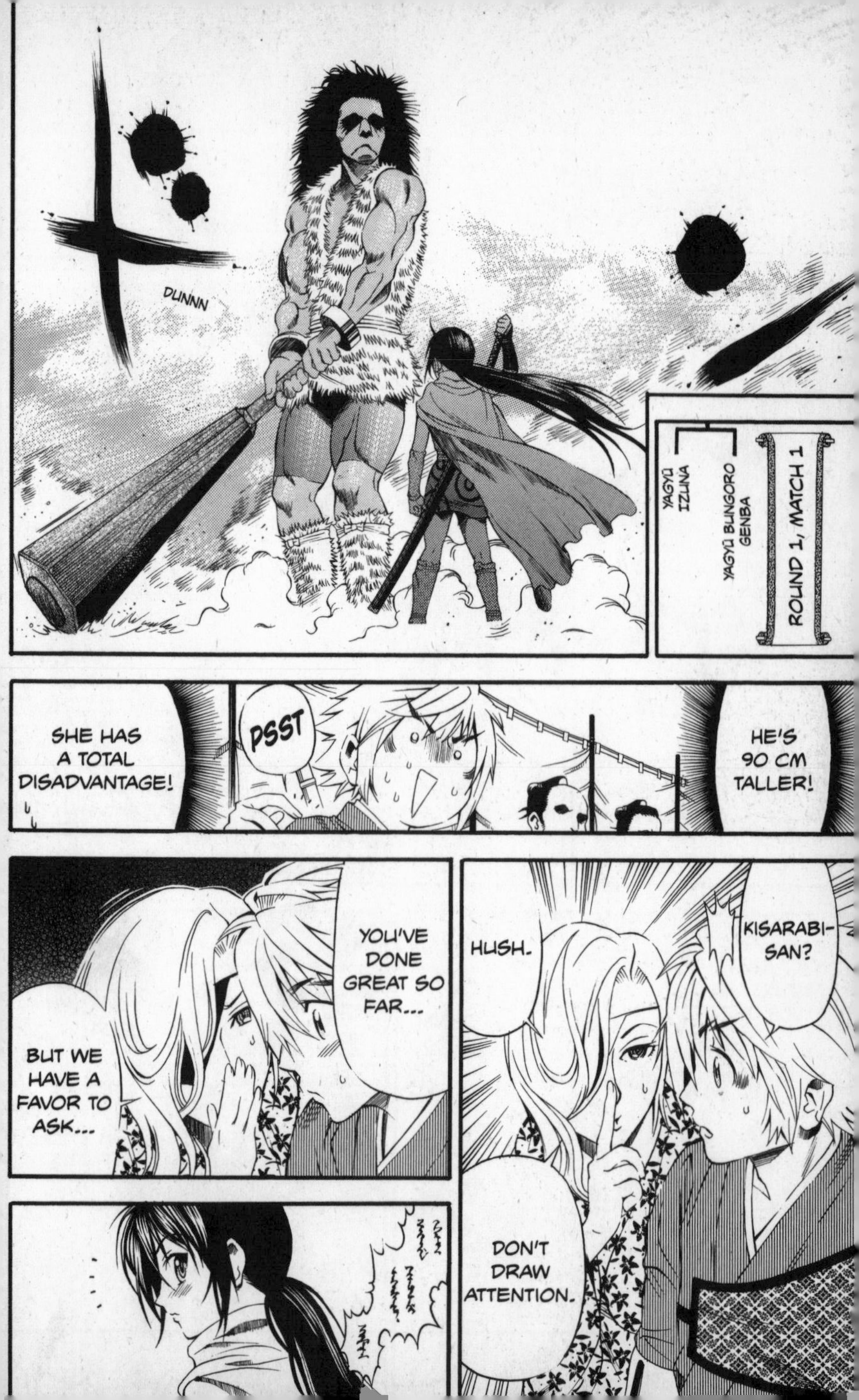
ROUND 1, MATCH 1
YAGYŪ BUNGORO GENBA
YAGYŪ IZUNA
DUNNN
HE'S 90 CM TALLER!
PSST
SHE HAS A TOTAL DISADVANTAGE!
KISARABI-SAN?
HUSH.
DON'T DRAW ATTENTION.
YOU'VE DONE GREAT SO FAR...
BUT WE HAVE A FAVOR TO ASK...
...

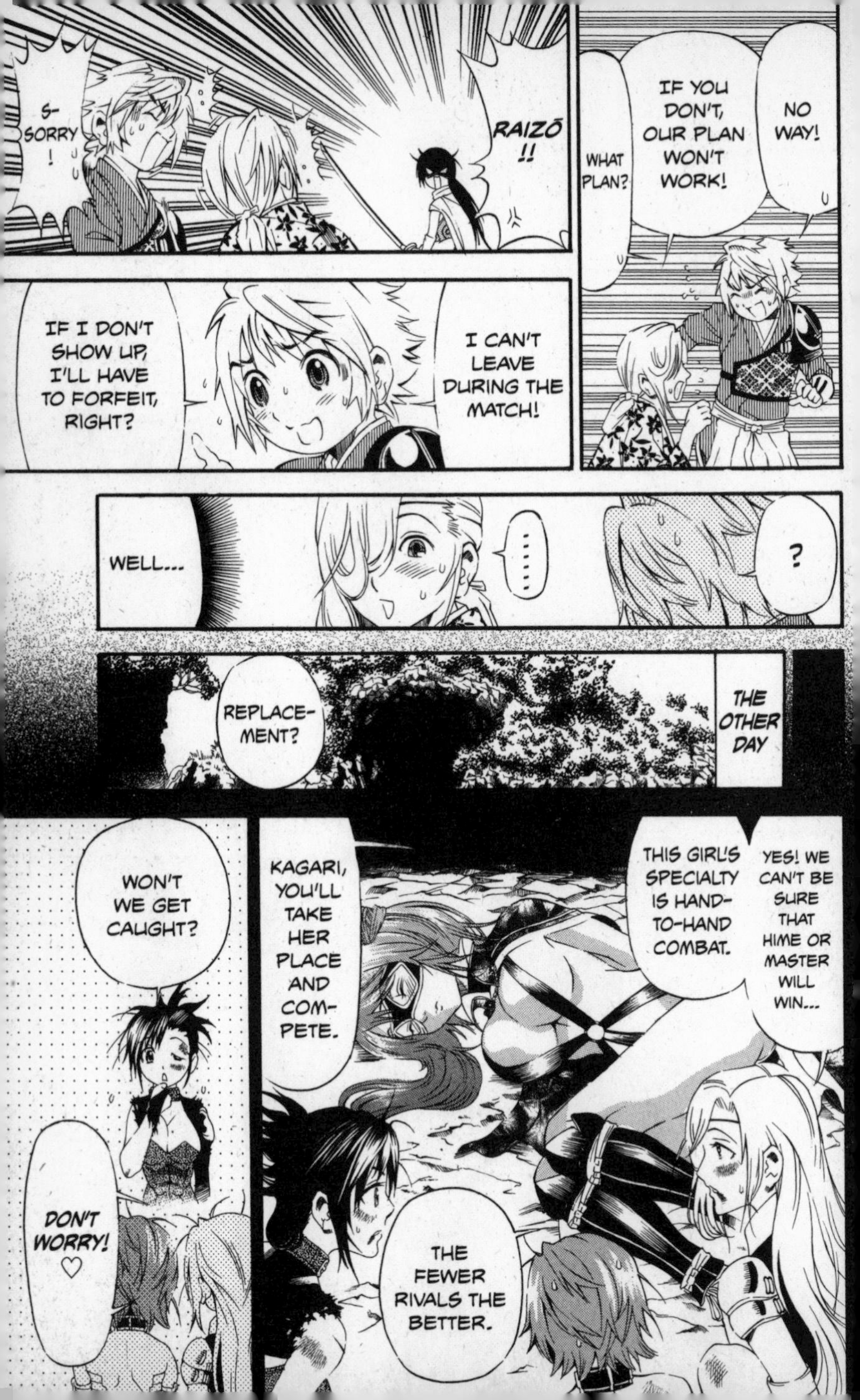
NO WAY!
IF YOU DON'T, OUR PLAN WON'T WORK!
WHAT PLAN?
RAIZŌ!!
S-SORRY!
I CAN'T LEAVE DURING THE MATCH!
IF I DON'T SHOW UP, I'LL HAVE TO FORFEIT, RIGHT?
?
......
WELL...
THE OTHER DAY
REPLACEMENT?
YES! WE CAN'T BE SURE THAT HIME OR MASTER WILL WIN...
THIS GIRL'S SPECIALTY IS HAND-TO-HAND COMBAT.
KAGARI, YOU'LL TAKE HER PLACE AND COMPETE.
THE FEWER RIVALS THE BETTER.
WON'T WE GET CAUGHT?
DON'T WORRY! ♡

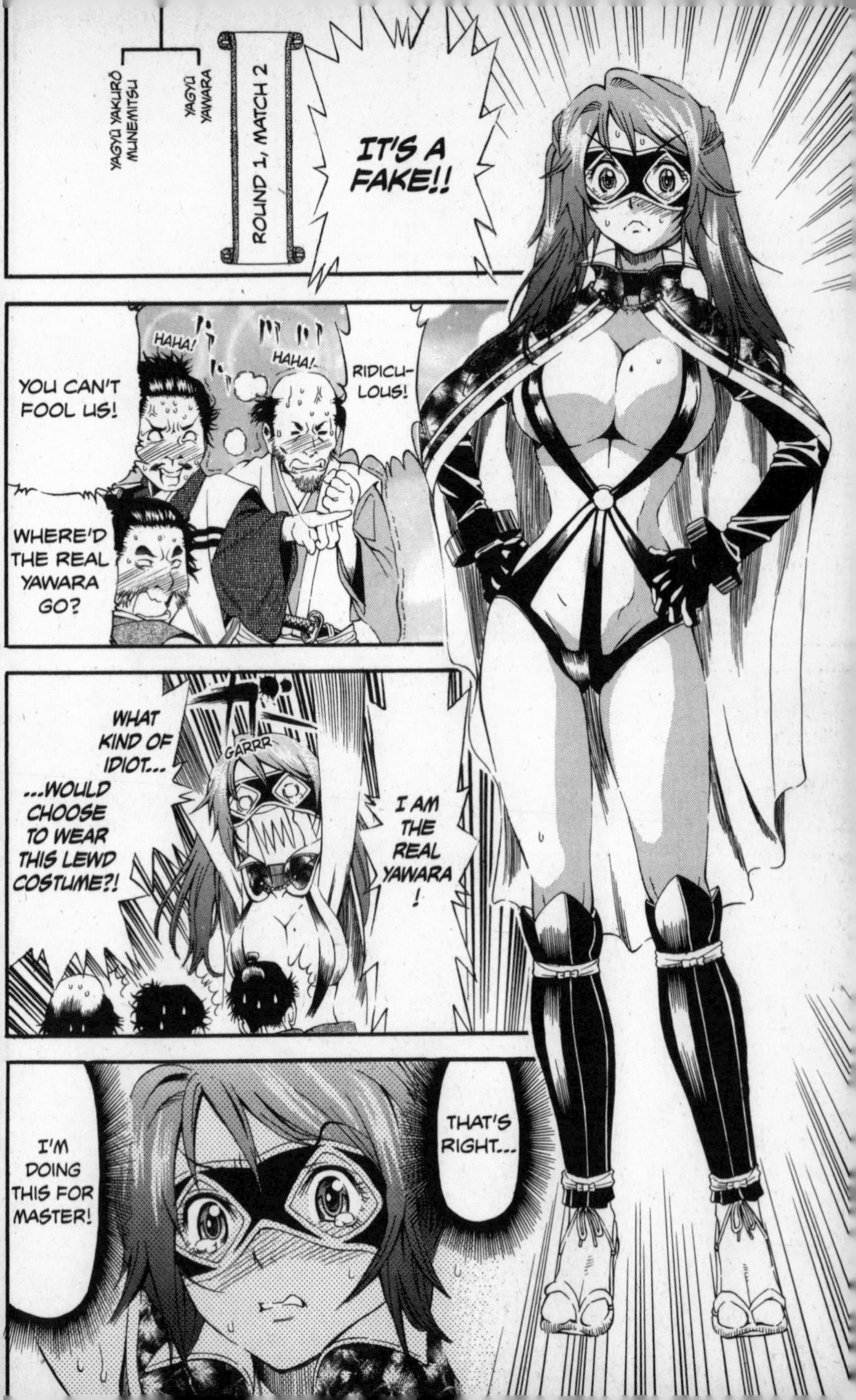
IT'S A FAKE!!
ROUND 1, MATCH 2
YAGYŪ YAWARA
YAGYŪ YAKURŌ MUNEMITSU
RIDICU-LOUS!
HAHA!
HAHA!
YOU CAN'T FOOL US!
WHERE'D THE REAL YAWARA GO?
I AM THE REAL YAWARA!
GARRR
WHAT KIND OF IDIOT...
...WOULD CHOOSE TO WEAR THIS LEWD COSTUME?!
THAT'S RIGHT...
I'M DOING THIS FOR MASTER!

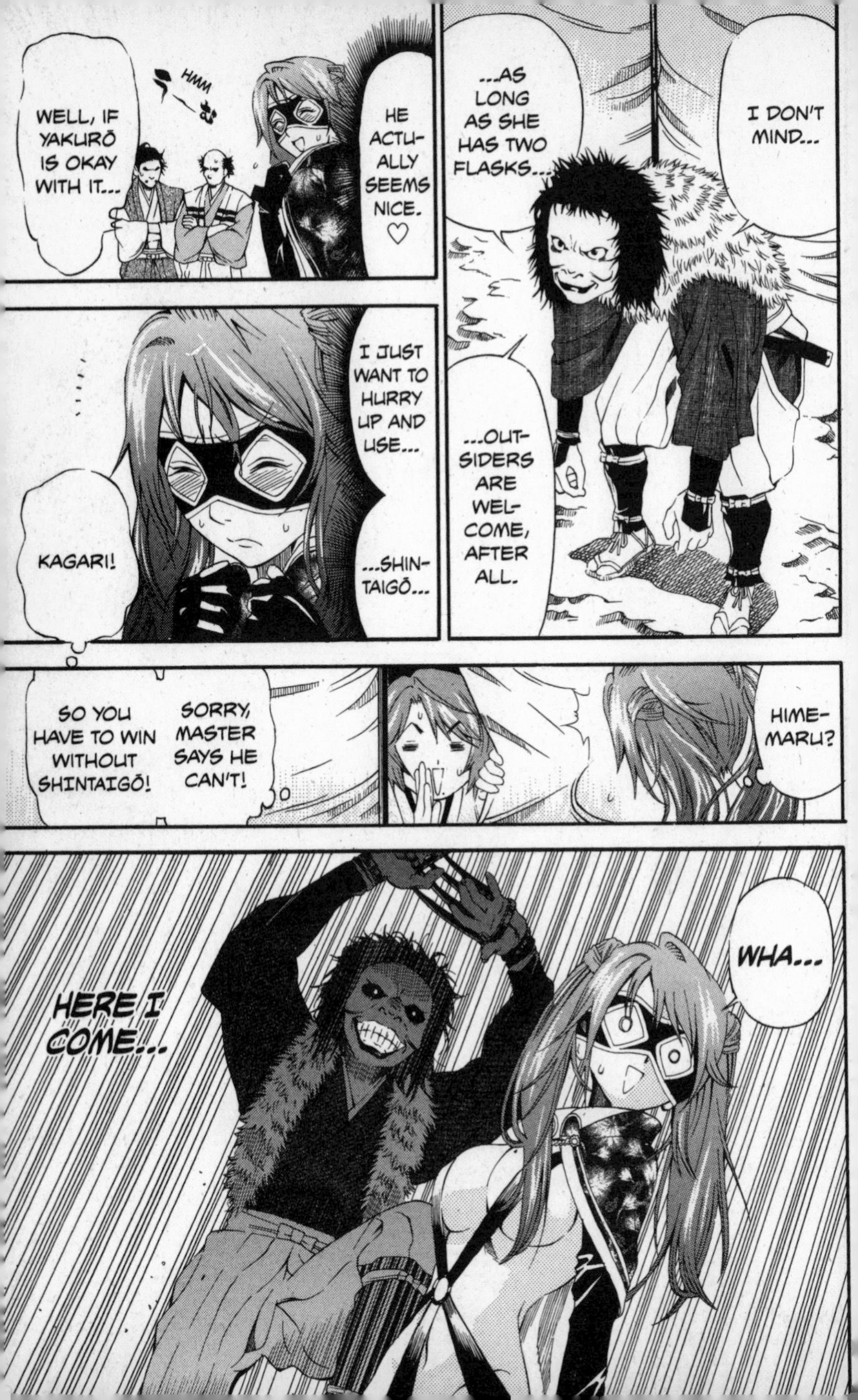
I DON'T MIND...
...AS LONG AS SHE HAS TWO FLASKS...
...OUTSIDERS ARE WELCOME, AFTER ALL.
HE ACTUALLY SEEMS NICE. ♡
HMM
WELL, IF YAKURŌ IS OKAY WITH IT...
I JUST WANT TO HURRY UP AND USE...
...SHINTAIGŌ...
......
KAGARI!
HIME-MARU?
SORRY, MASTER SAYS HE CAN'T!
SO YOU HAVE TO WIN WITHOUT SHINTAIGŌ!
WHA...
HERE I COME...

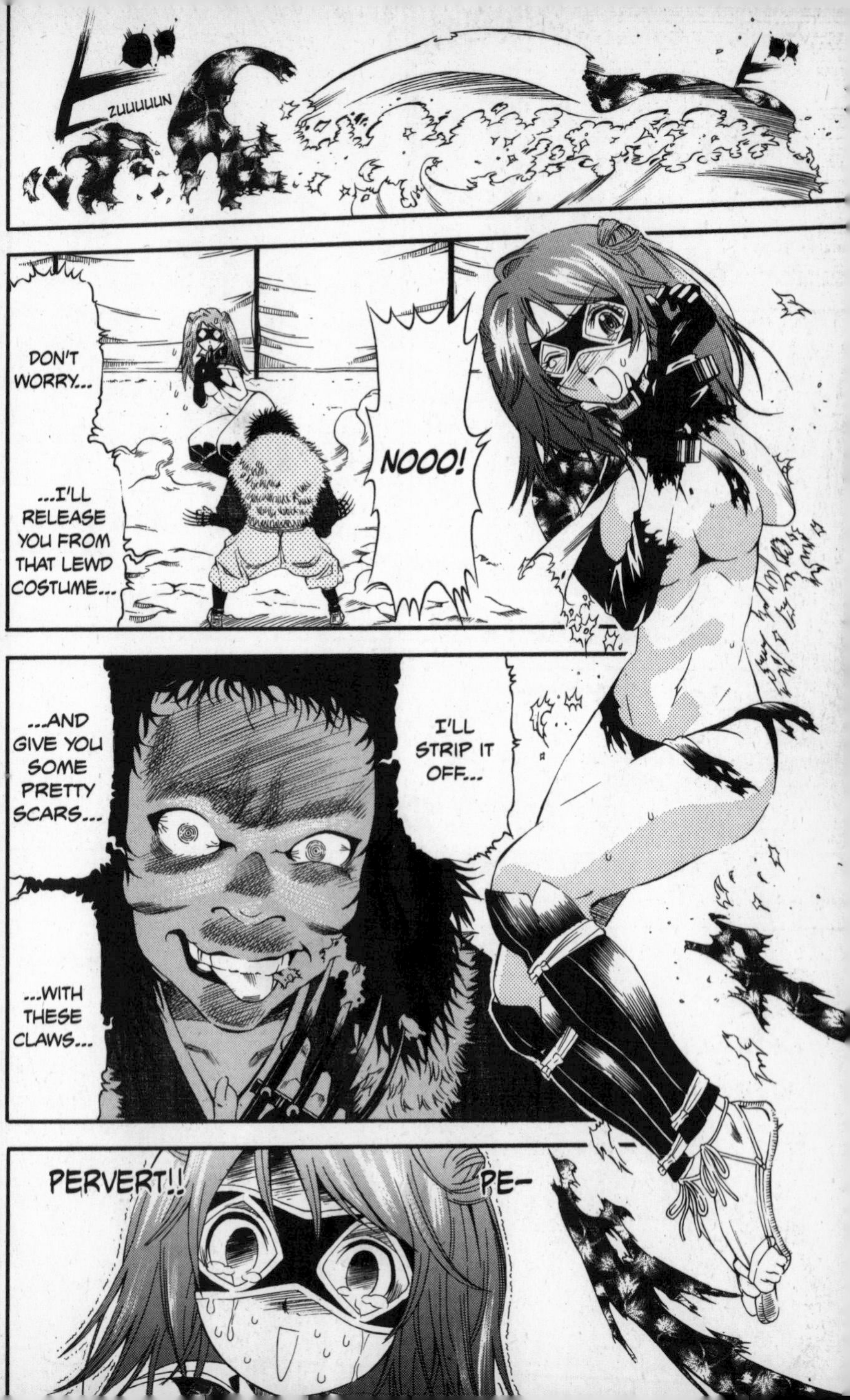
ZUUUUUN
NOOO!
DON'T WORRY...
...I'LL RELEASE YOU FROM THAT LEWD COSTUME...
I'LL STRIP IT OFF...
...AND GIVE YOU SOME PRETTY SCARS...
...WITH THESE CLAWS...
PE-
PERVERT!!

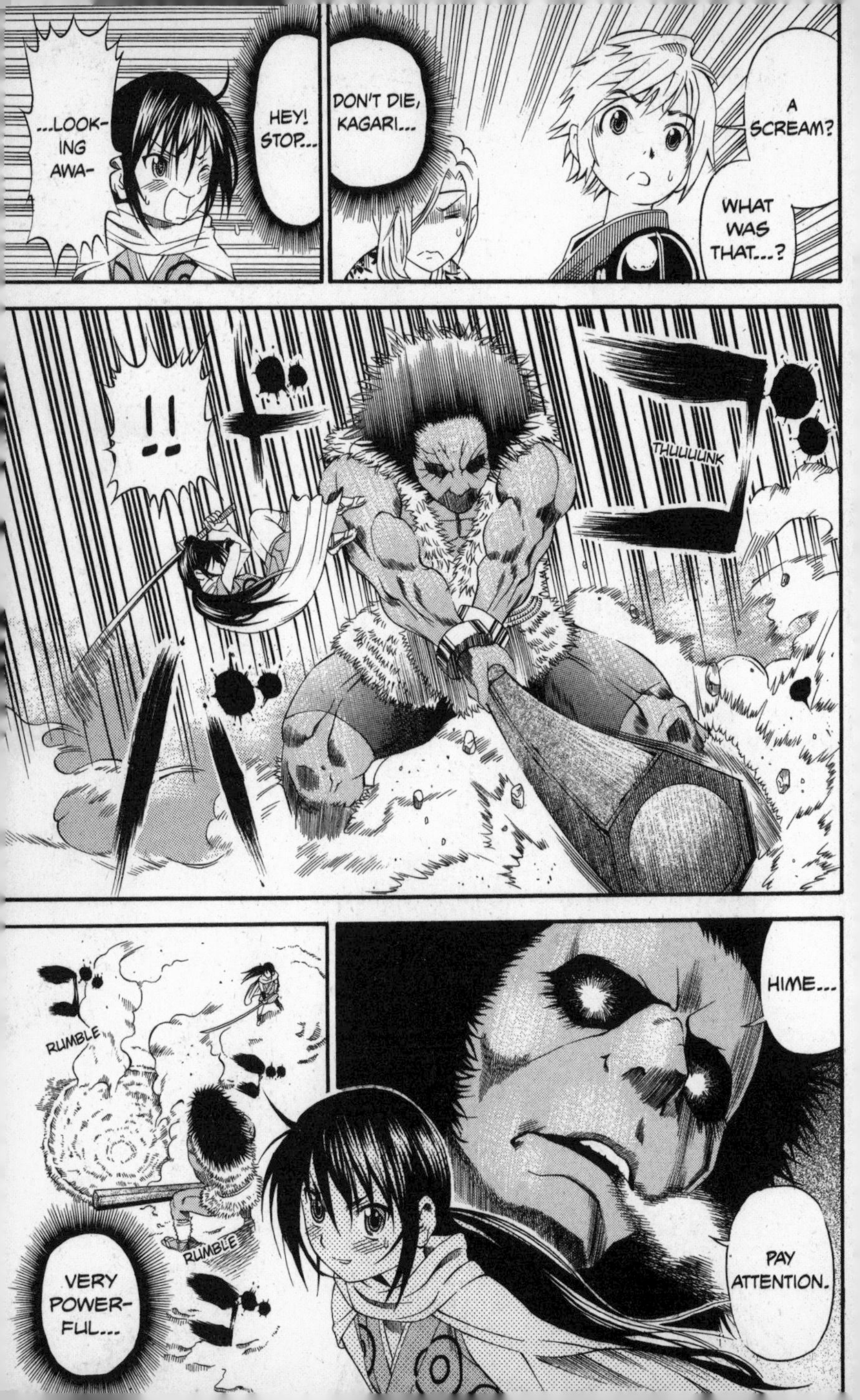
A SCREAM?
WHAT WAS THAT...?
DON'T DIE, KAGARI...
HEY! STOP...
...LOOKING AWA-
!!
THUUUUNK
HIME...
PAY ATTENTION.
RUMBLE
RUMBLE
VERY POWERFUL...

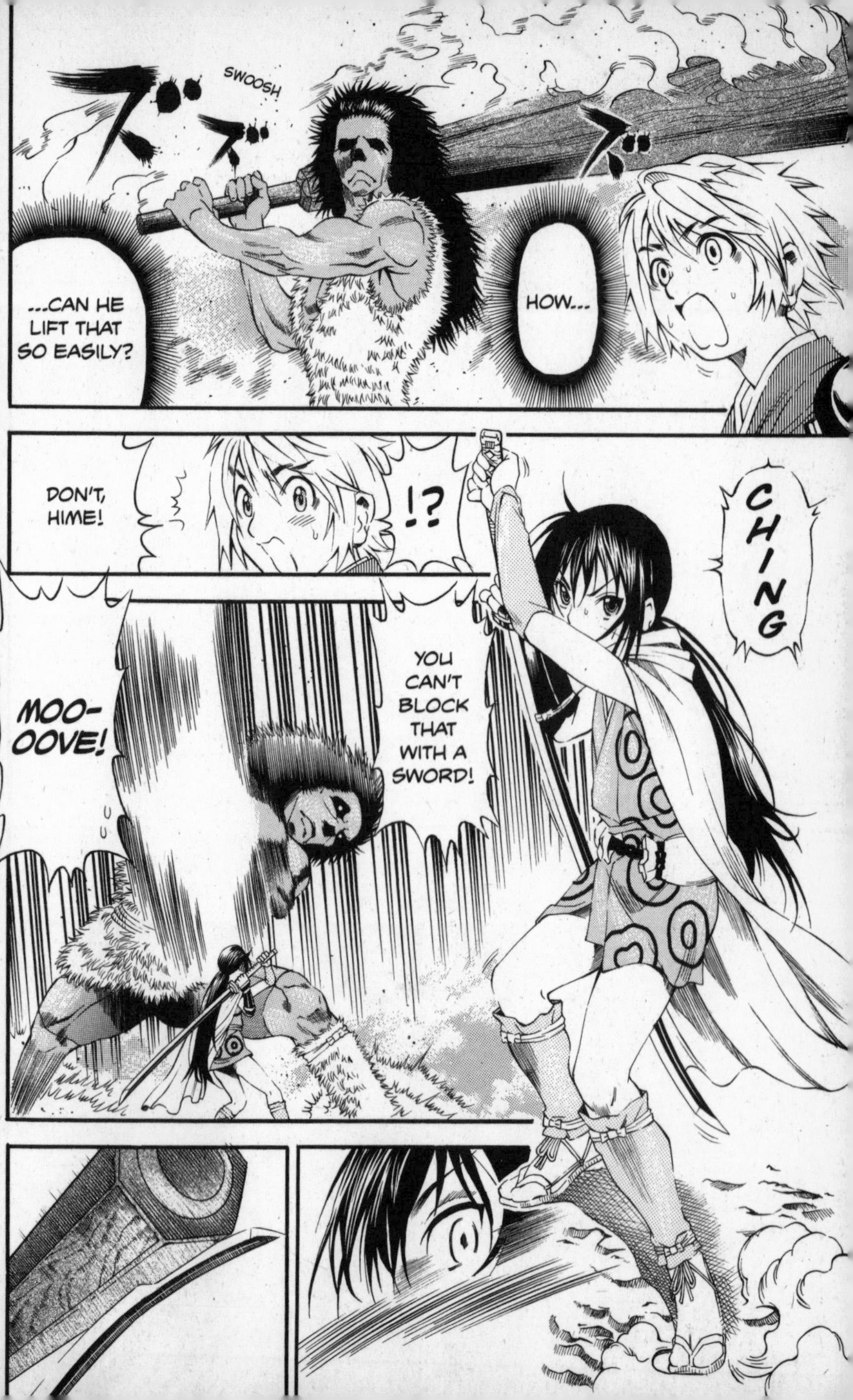
SWOOSH
HOW...
...CAN HE LIFT THAT SO EASILY?
CHING
!?
DON'T, HIME!
YOU CAN'T BLOCK THAT WITH A SWORD!
MOO-OOVE!

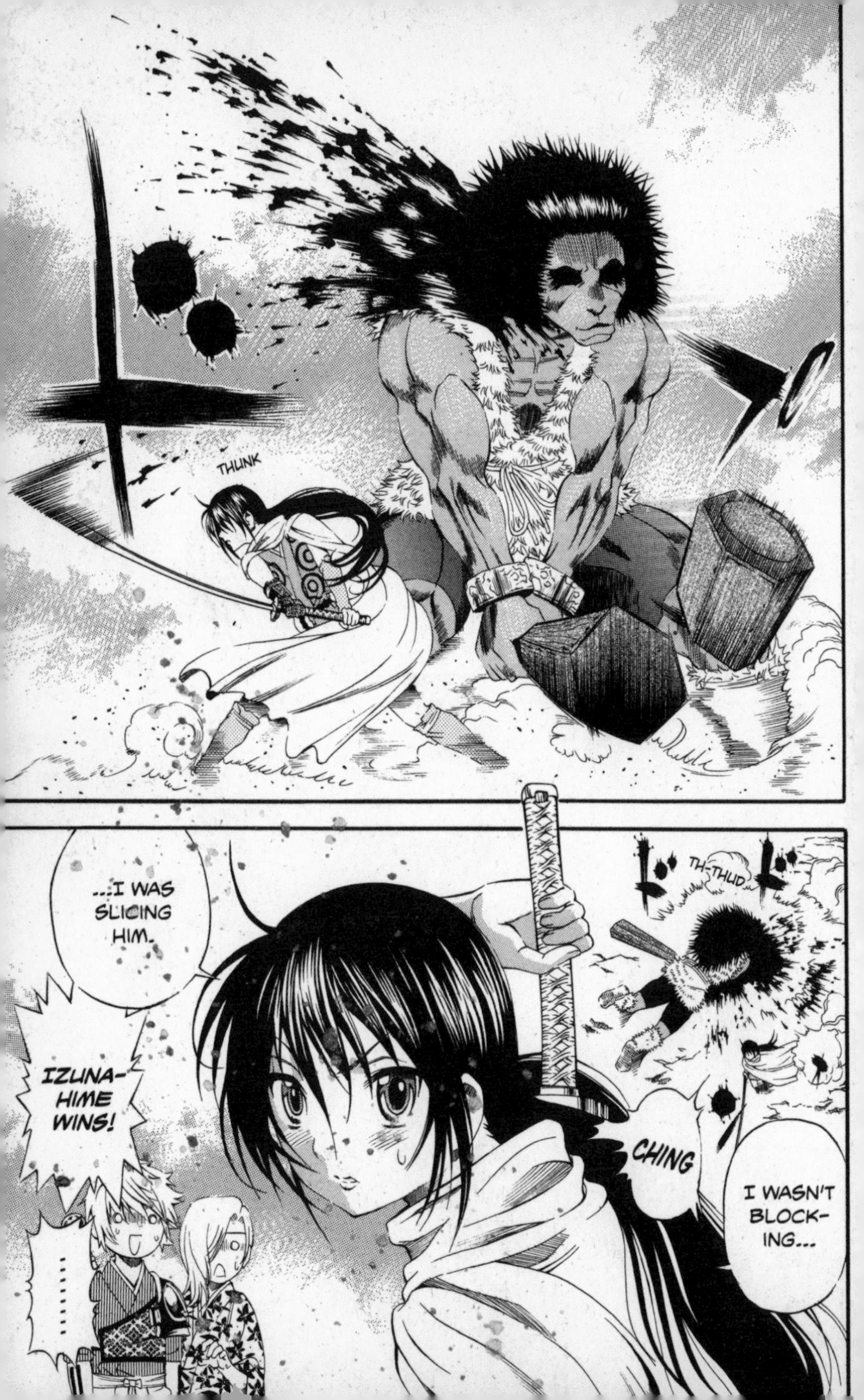
THUNK
TH-THUD
I WASN'T BLOCK-ING...
CHING
...I WAS SLICING HIM.
IZUNA-HIME WINS!
......

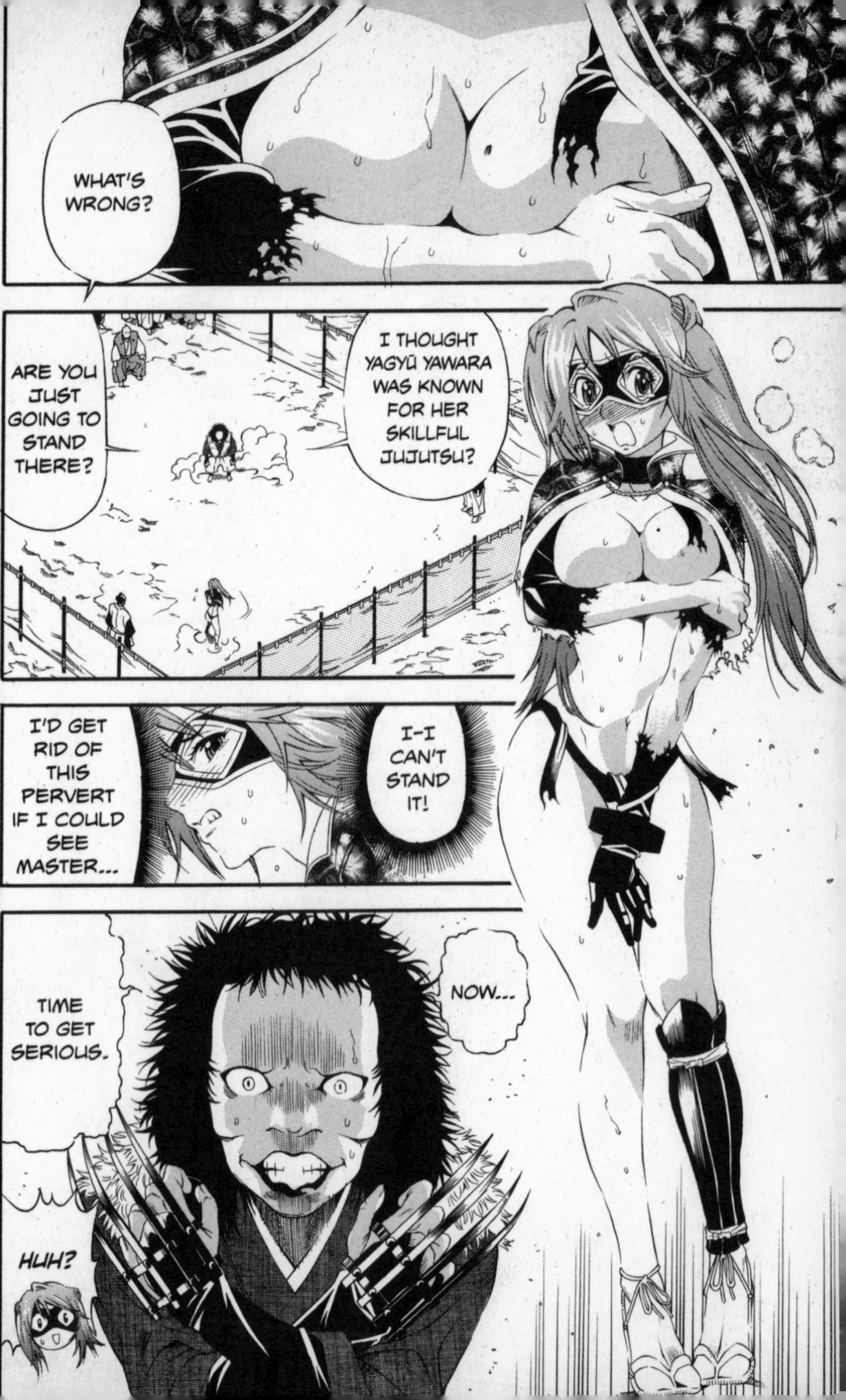
WHAT'S WRONG?
I THOUGHT YAGYŪ YAWARA WAS KNOWN FOR HER SKILLFUL JUJUTSU?
ARE YOU JUST GOING TO STAND THERE?
I-I CAN'T STAND IT!
I'D GET RID OF THIS PERVERT IF I COULD SEE MASTER...
NOW...
TIME TO GET SERIOUS.
HUH?

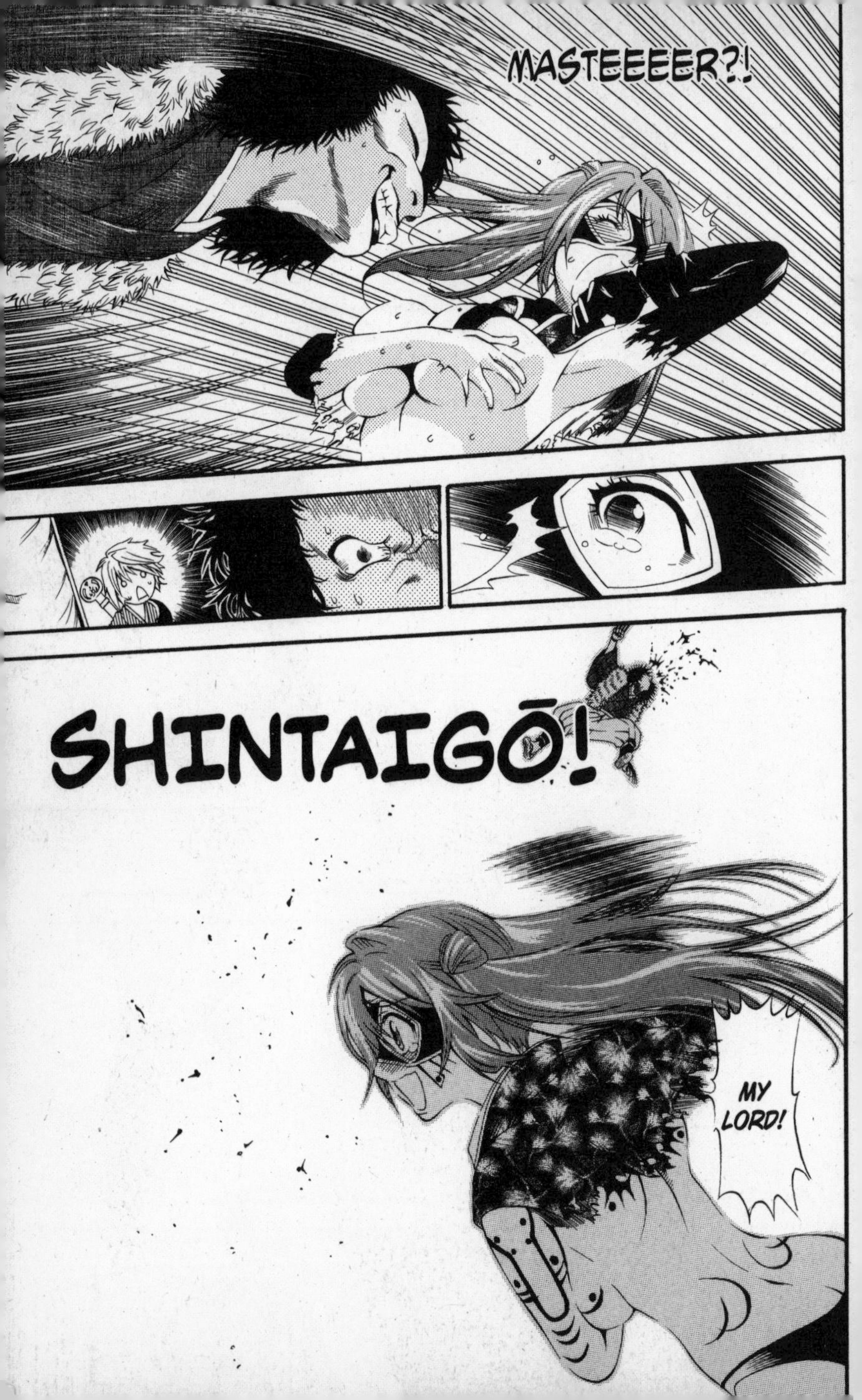
MASTEEEER?!
SHINTAIGŌ!
MY LORD!

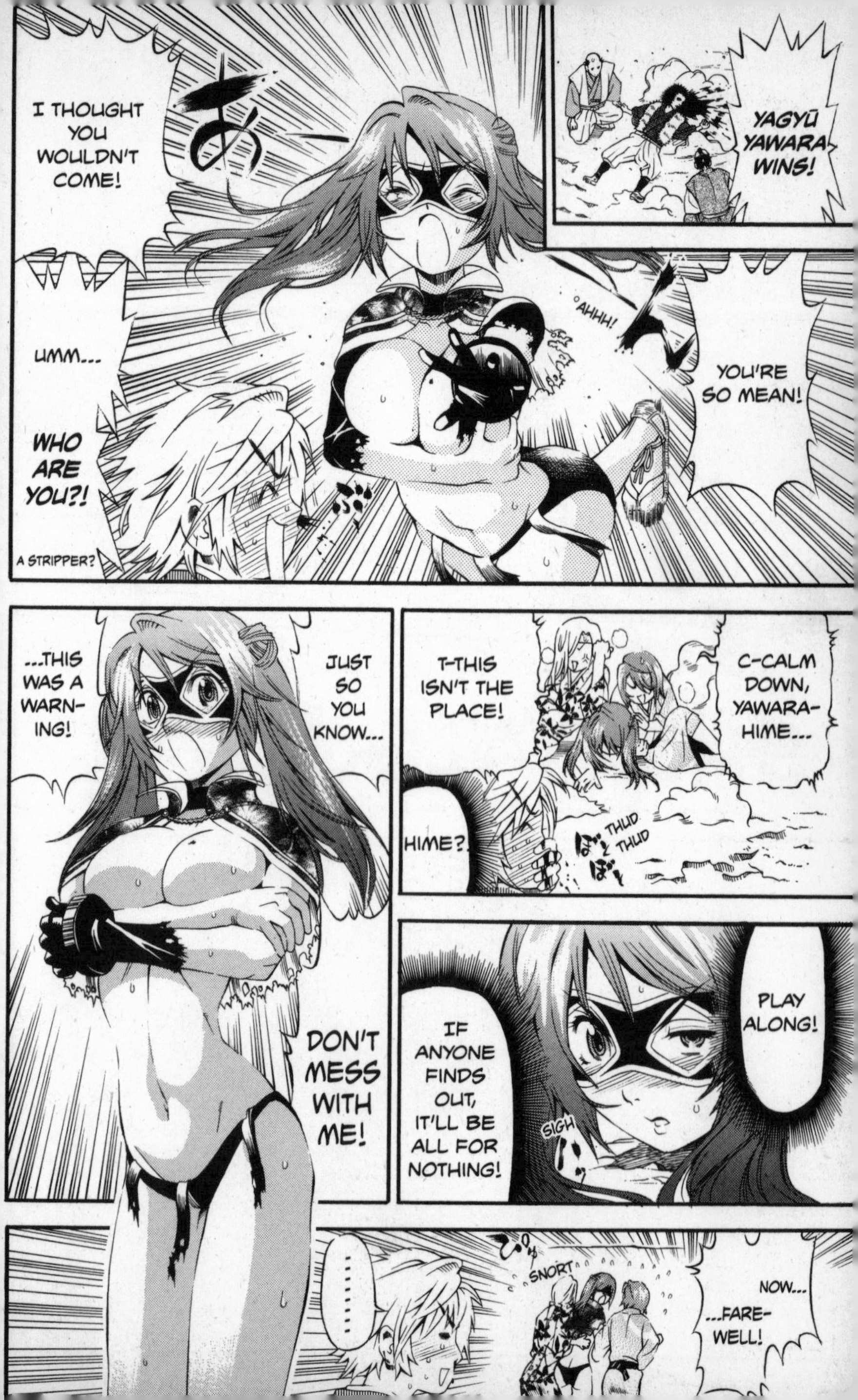
YAGYŪ YAWARA WINS!
AHHH!
YOU'RE SO MEAN!
I THOUGHT YOU WOULDN'T COME!
UMM...
WHO ARE YOU?!
A STRIPPER?
C-CALM DOWN, YAWARA-HIME...
T-THIS ISN'T THE PLACE!
THUD THUD
HIME?!
PLAY ALONG!
IF ANYONE FINDS OUT, IT'LL BE ALL FOR NOTHING!
SIGH
JUST SO YOU KNOW...
...THIS WAS A WARNING!
DON'T MESS WITH ME!
NOW...
...FARE-WELL!
SNORT
......

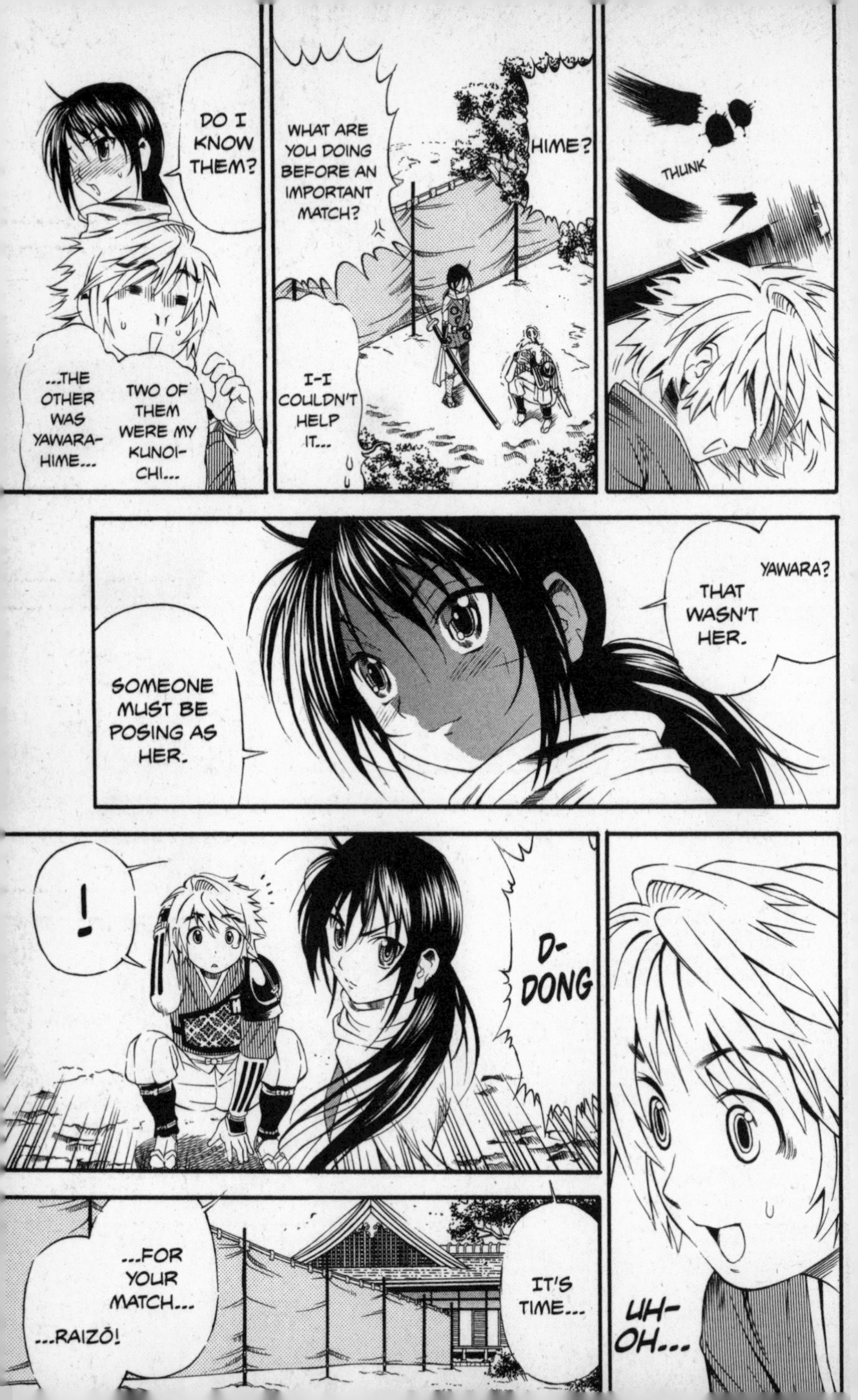
THUNK
HIME?
WHAT ARE YOU DOING BEFORE AN IMPORTANT MATCH?
I-I COULDN'T HELP IT...
DO I KNOW THEM?
TWO OF THEM WERE MY KUNOI-CHI...
...THE OTHER WAS YAWARA-HIME...
YAWARA? THAT WASN'T HER.
SOMEONE MUST BE POSING AS HER.
UH-OH...
D-DONG
!
IT'S TIME...
...FOR YOUR MATCH...
...RAIZŌ!

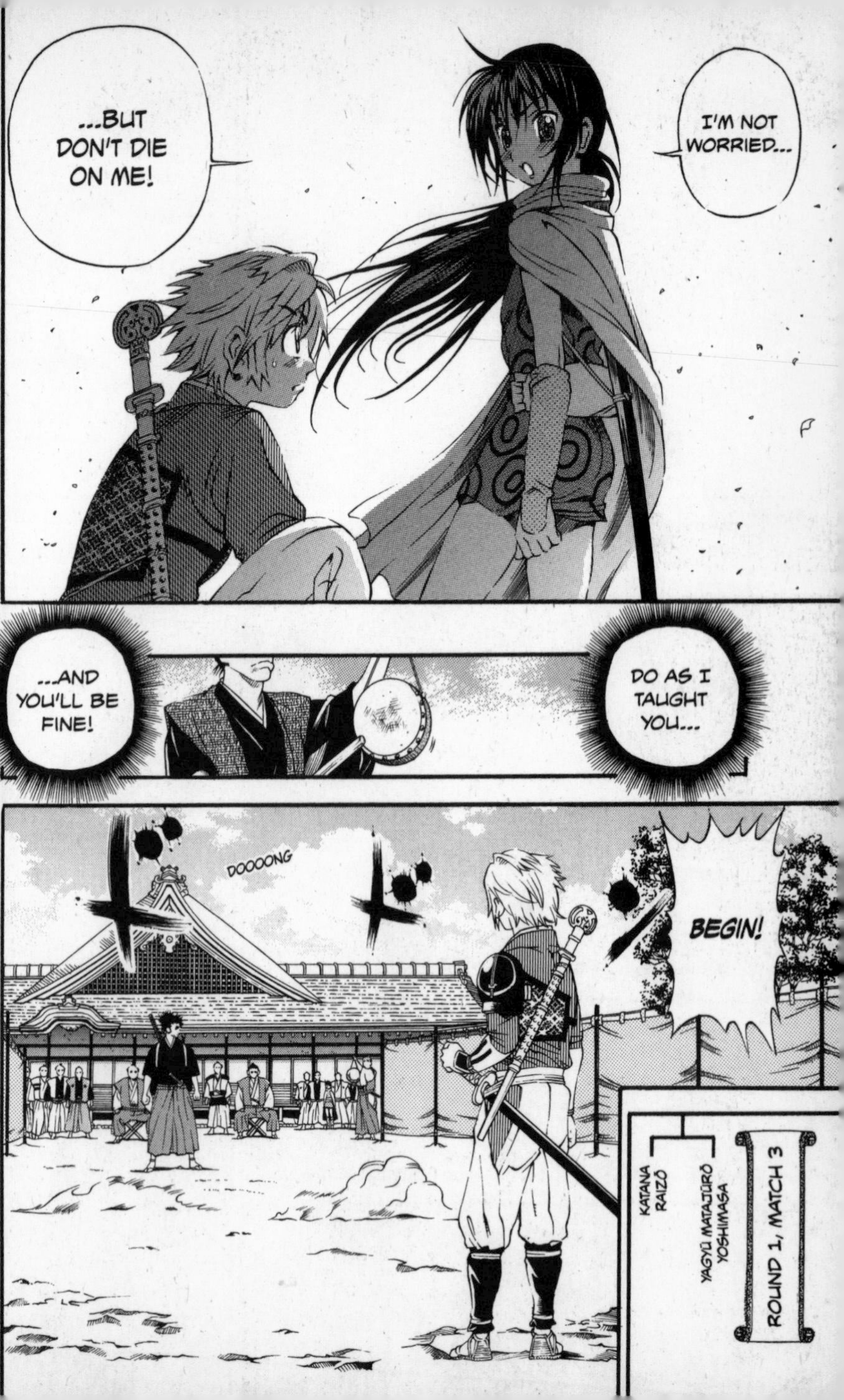
I'M NOT WORRIED...
...BUT DON'T DIE ON ME!
DO AS I TAUGHT YOU...
...AND YOU'LL BE FINE!
BEGIN!
DOOOONG
ROUND 1, MATCH 3
YAGYŪ MATAJŪRŌ YOSHIMASA
KATANA RAIZŌ

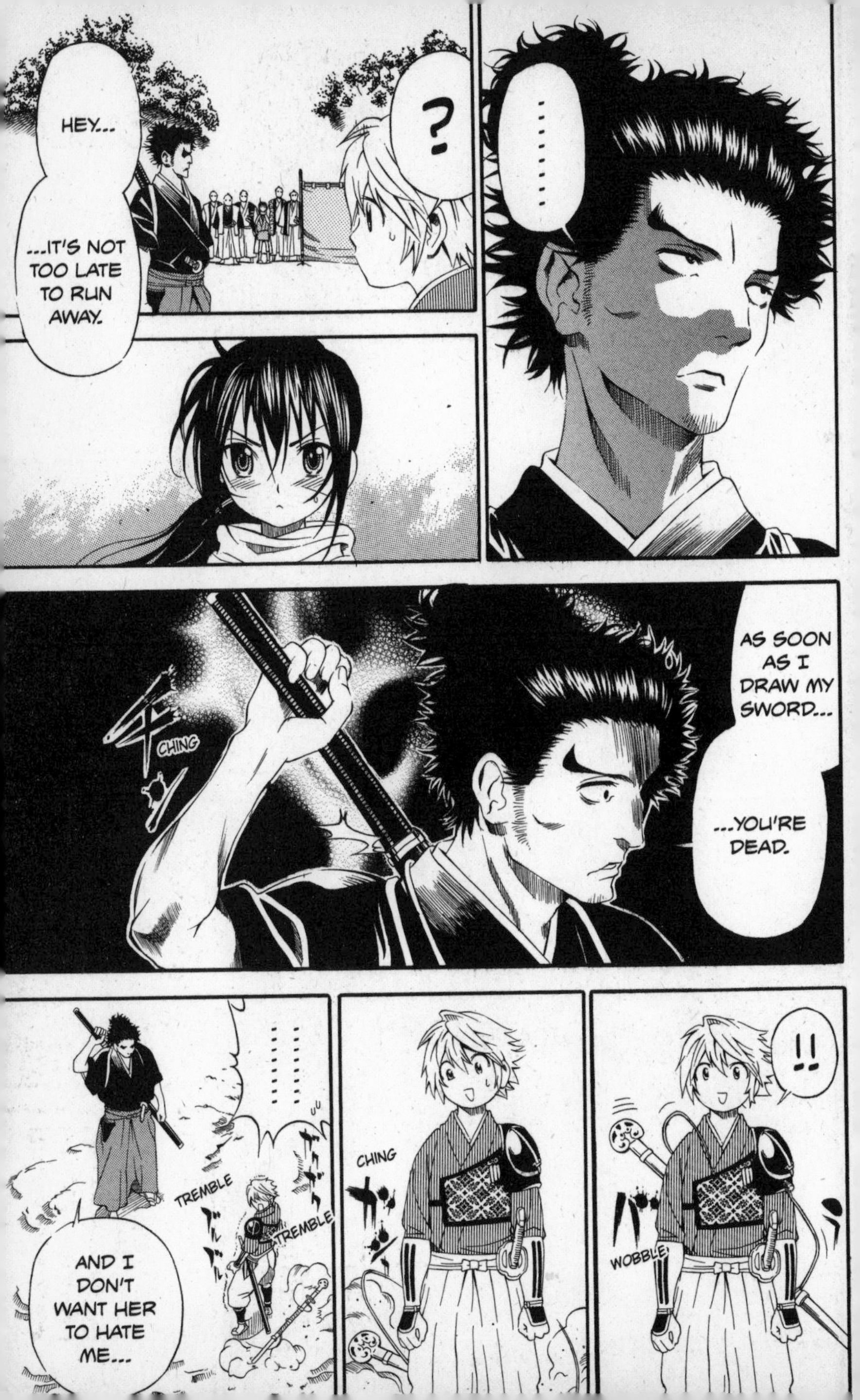
......
?
HEY...
...IT'S NOT TOO LATE TO RUN AWAY.
AS SOON AS I DRAW MY SWORD...
...YOU'RE DEAD.
CHING
!!
WOBBLE
CHING
......
TREMBLE
TREMBLE
AND I DON'T WANT HER TO HATE ME...

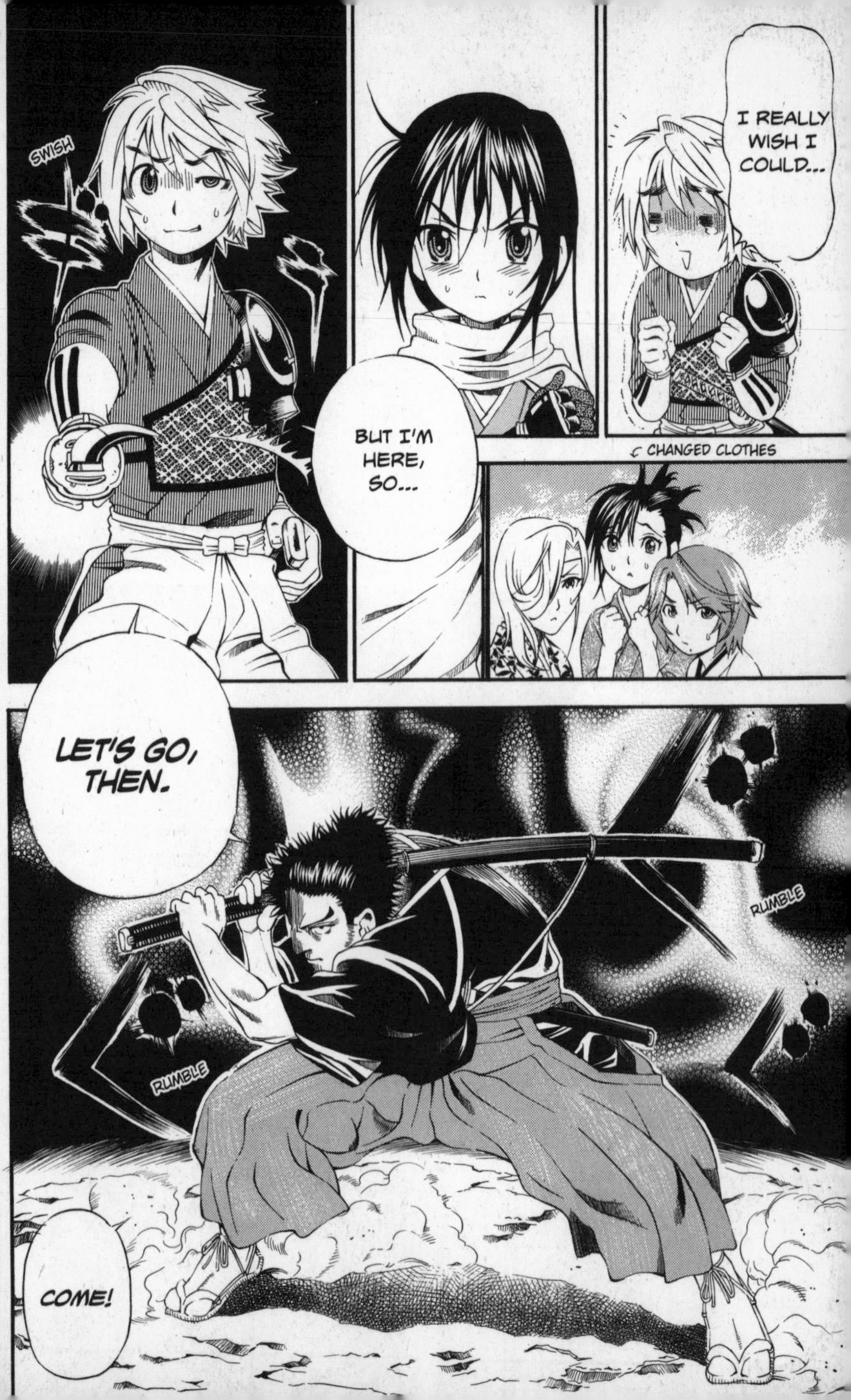
I REALLY WISH I COULD...
CHANGED CLOTHES
BUT I'M HERE, SO...
SWISH
LET'S GO, THEN.
RUMBLE
RUMBLE
COME!

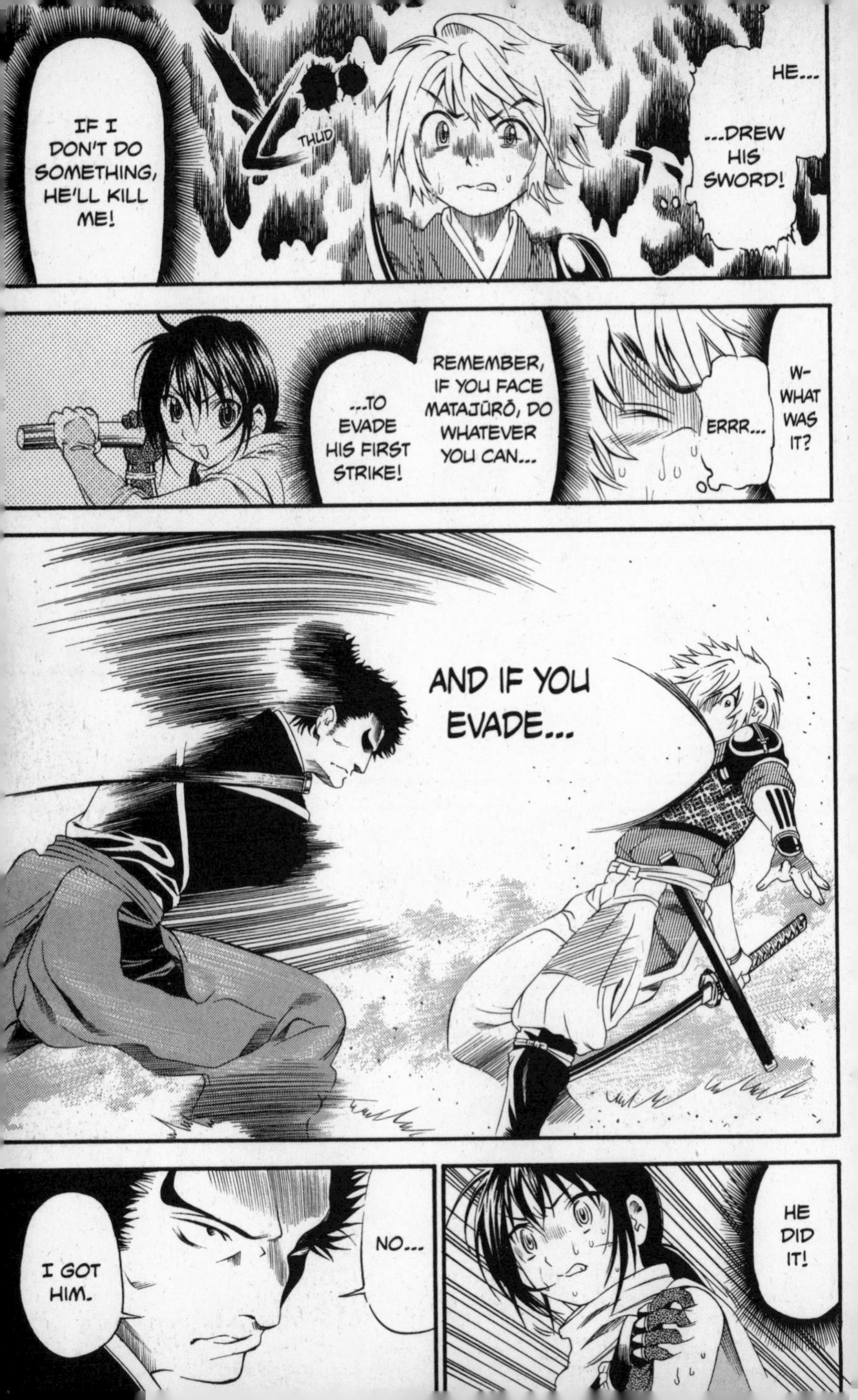
HE...
...DREW HIS SWORD!
THUD
IF I DON'T DO SOMETHING, HE'LL KILL ME!
W-WHAT WAS IT?
ERRR...
REMEMBER, IF YOU FACE MATAJŪRŌ, DO WHATEVER YOU CAN...
...TO EVADE HIS FIRST STRIKE!
AND IF YOU EVADE...
HE DID IT!
NO...
I GOT HIM.

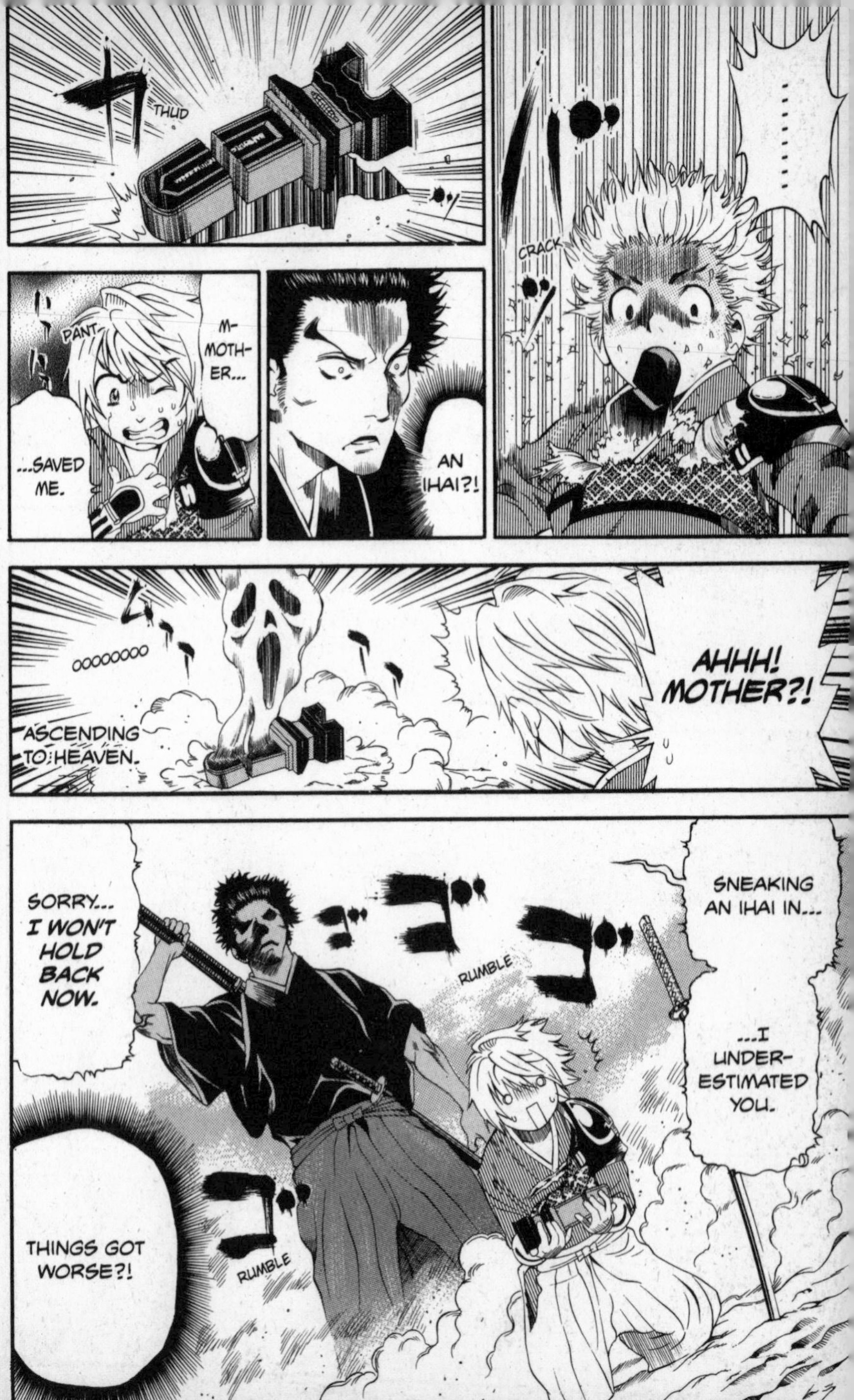
......
CRACK
THUD
AN IHAI?!
M-MOTHER...
...SAVED ME.
PANT
AHHH! MOTHER?!
OOOOOOOO
ASCENDING TO HEAVEN.
SNEAKING AN IHAI IN...
...I UNDERESTIMATED YOU.
RUMBLE
SORRY... I WON'T HOLD BACK NOW.
THINGS GOT WORSE?!
RUMBLE

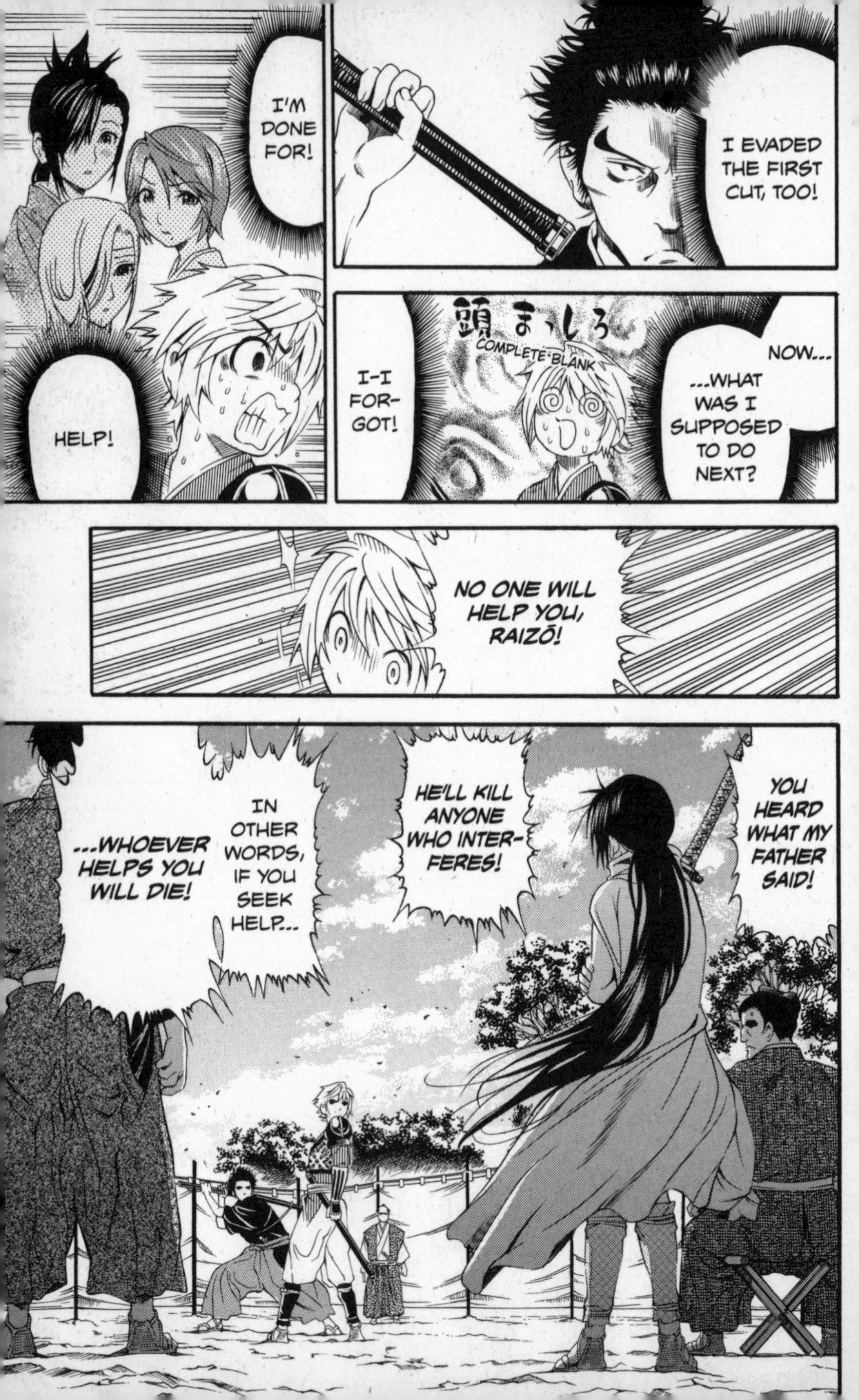
I EVADED THE FIRST CUT, TOO!
NOW...
...WHAT WAS I SUPPOSED TO DO NEXT?
頭まっしろ
COMPLETE BLANK
I-I FORGOT!
I'M DONE FOR!
HELP!
NO ONE WILL HELP YOU, RAIZŌ!
YOU HEARD WHAT MY FATHER SAID!
HE'LL KILL ANYONE WHO INTERFERES!
IN OTHER WORDS, IF YOU SEEK HELP...
...WHOEVER HELPS YOU WILL DIE!

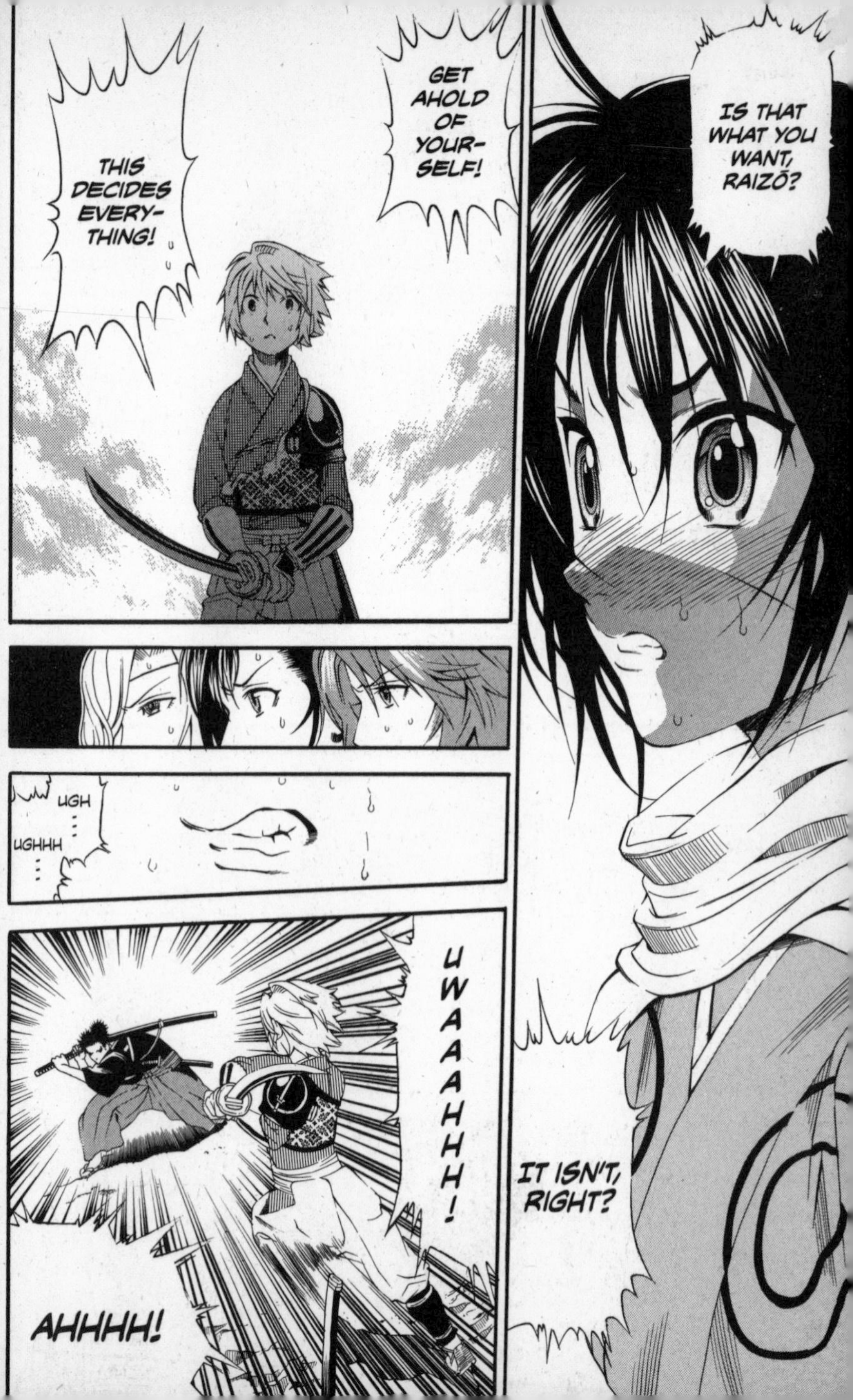
IS THAT WHAT YOU WANT, RAIZŌ?
IT ISN'T, RIGHT?
GET AHOLD OF YOURSELF!
THIS DECIDES EVERYTHING!
UGH... UGHHH...
UWAAAAHHHH!
AHHHH!

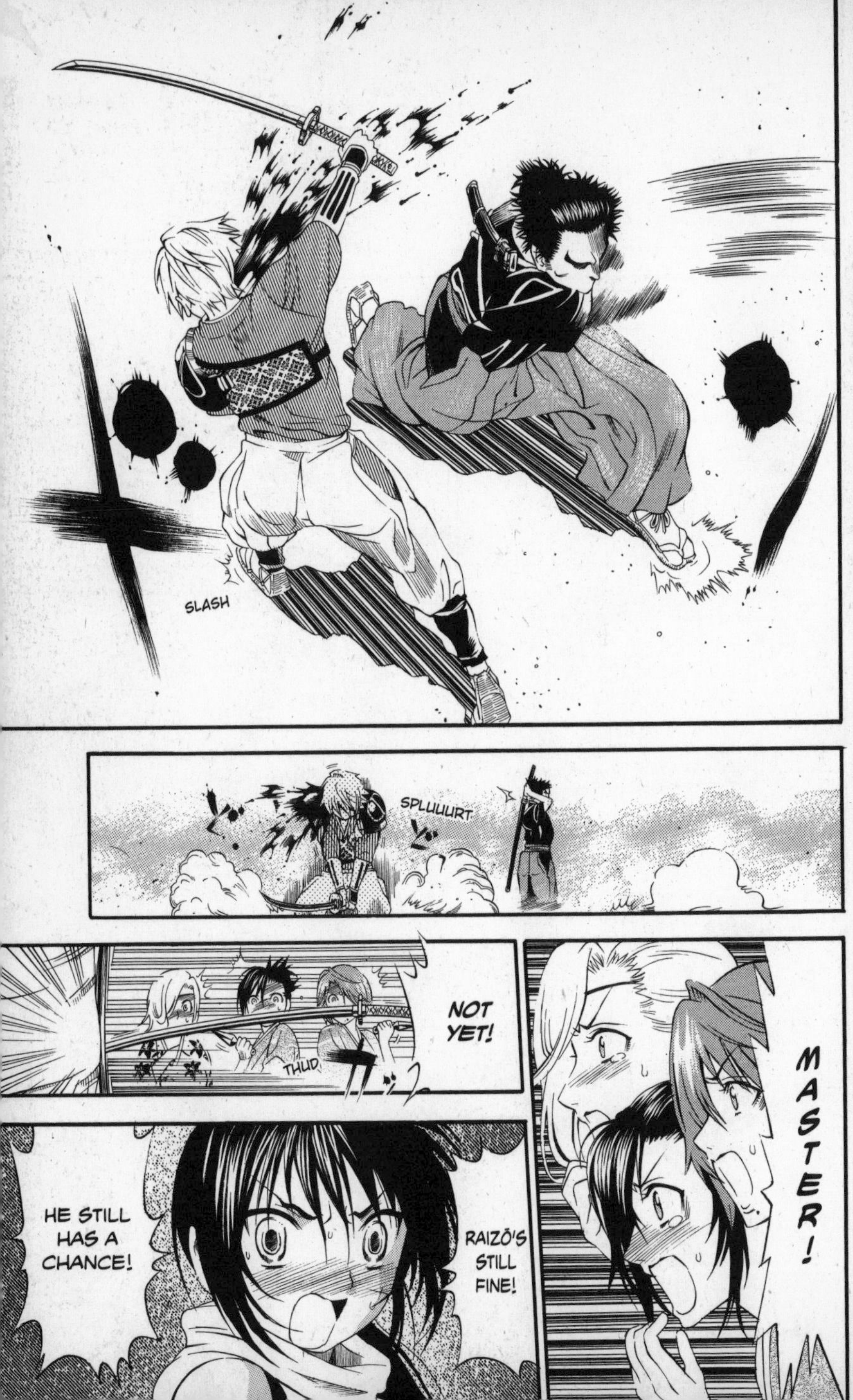
SLASH
SPLUUURT
MASTER!
NOT YET!
THUD
RAIZŌ'S STILL FINE!
HE STILL HAS A CHANCE!

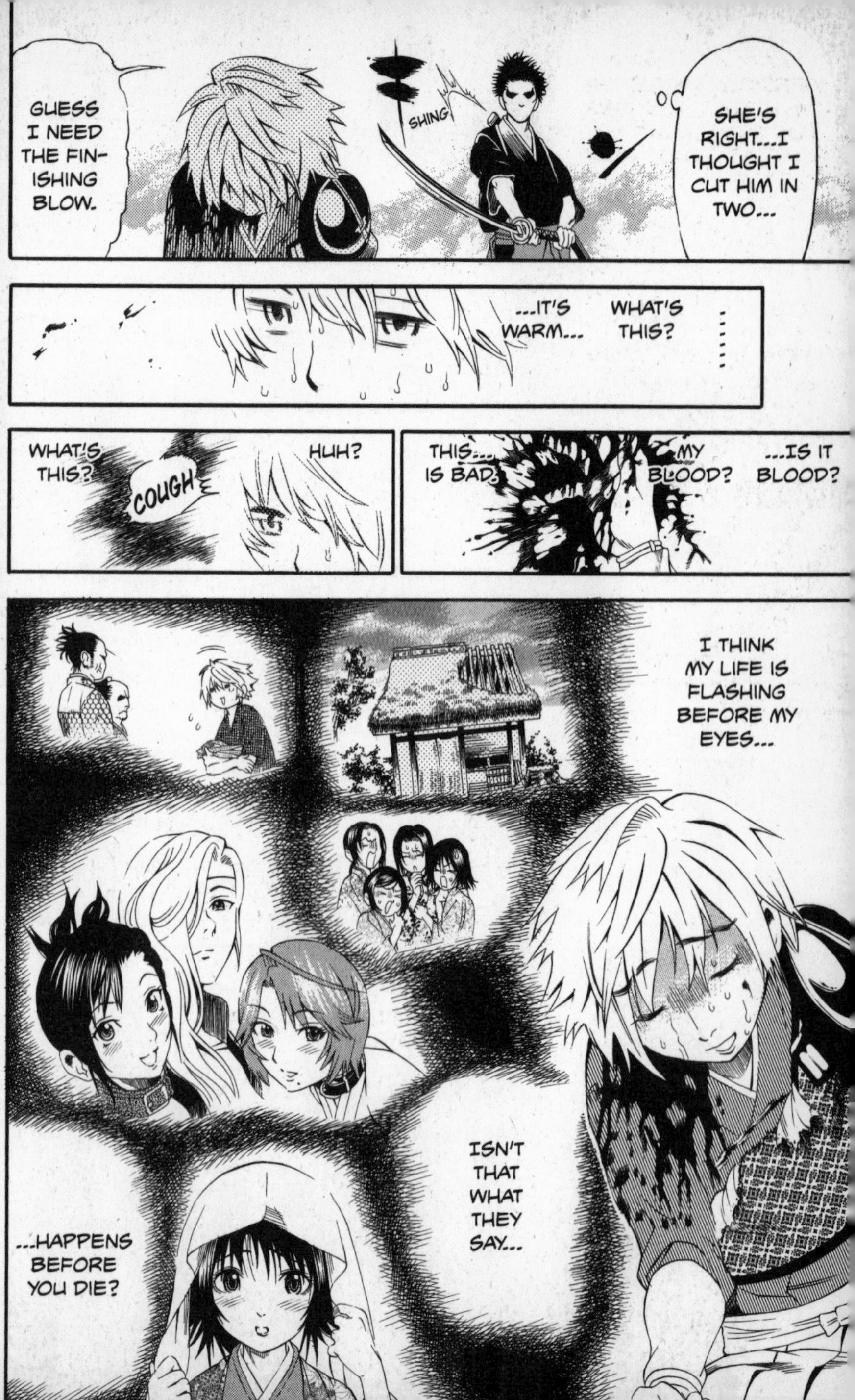
SHE'S RIGHT...I THOUGHT I CUT HIM IN TWO...
SHING
GUESS I NEED THE FIN-ISHING BLOW.
......
WHAT'S THIS?
...IT'S WARM...
...IS IT BLOOD?
MY BLOOD?
THIS... IS BAD.
HUH?
COUGH
WHAT'S THIS?
I THINK MY LIFE IS FLASHING BEFORE MY EYES...
ISN'T THAT WHAT THEY SAY...
...HAPPENS BEFORE YOU DIE?

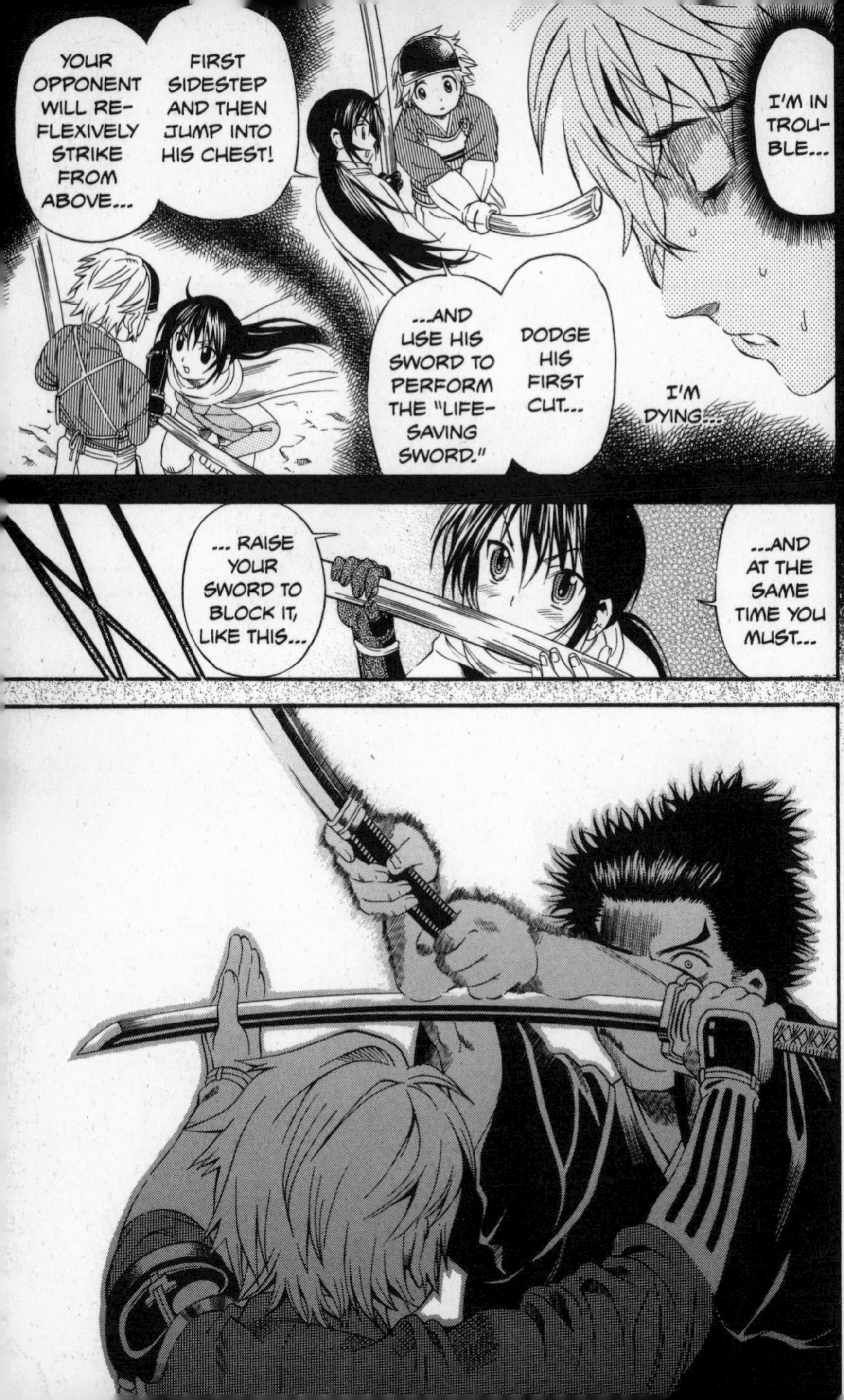
I'M IN TROUBLE...
I'M DYING...
DODGE HIS FIRST CUT...
...AND USE HIS SWORD TO PERFORM THE "LIFE-SAVING SWORD."
FIRST SIDESTEP AND THEN JUMP INTO HIS CHEST!
YOUR OPPONENT WILL REFLEXIVELY STRIKE FROM ABOVE...
...AND AT THE SAME TIME YOU MUST...
... RAISE YOUR SWORD TO BLOCK IT, LIKE THIS...

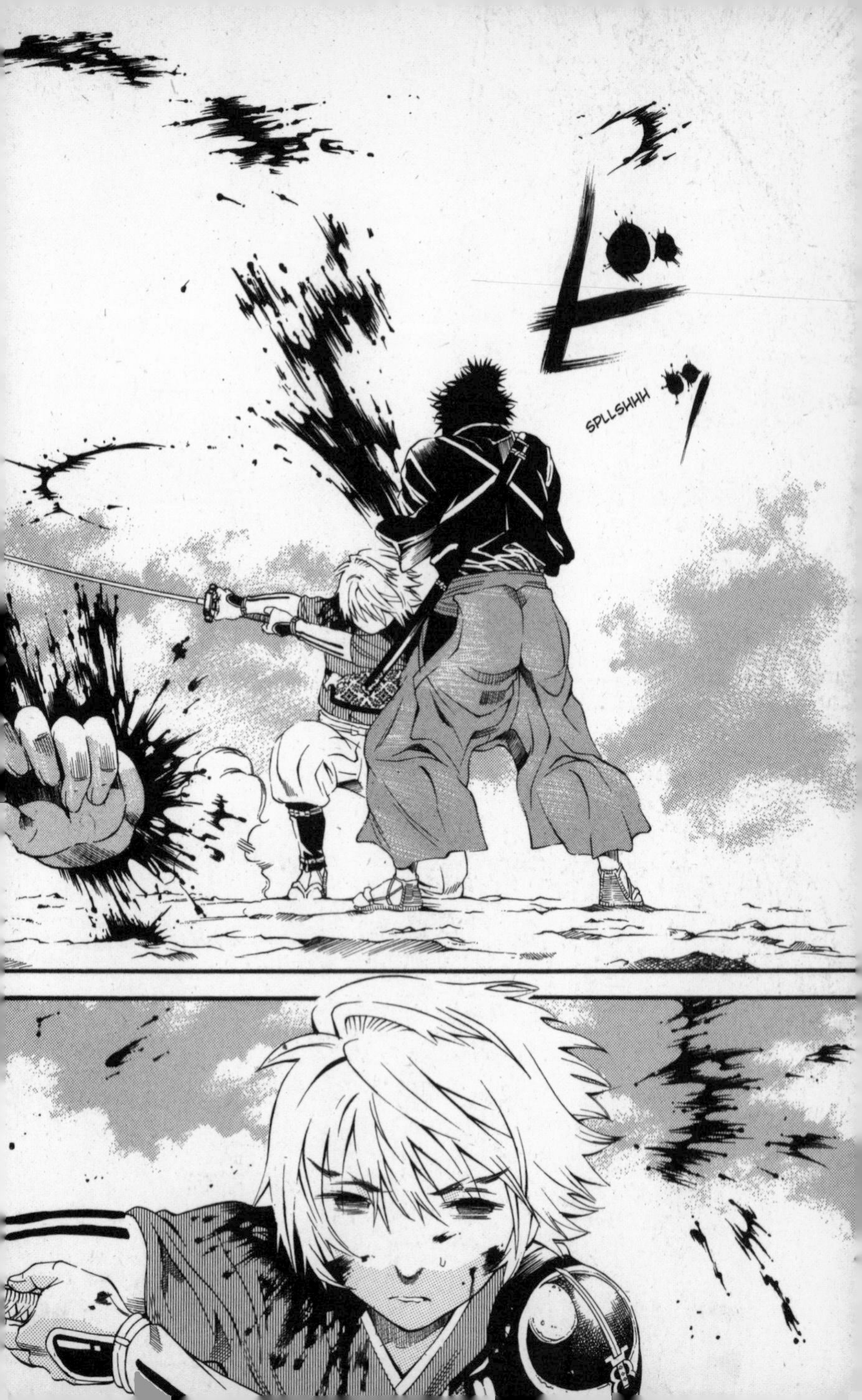
SPLLSHHH

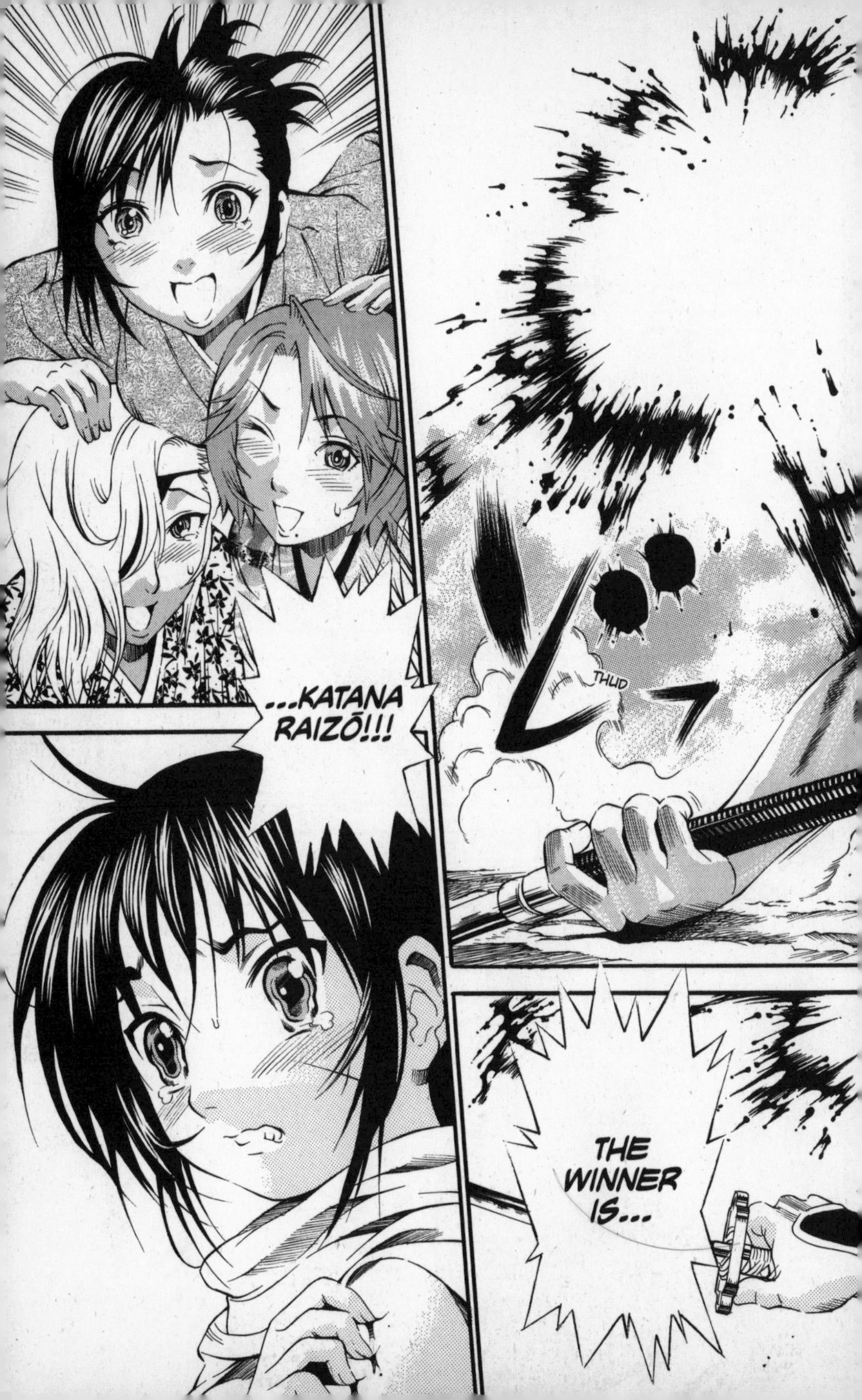
THUD
THE WINNER IS...
...KATANA RAIZŌ!!!

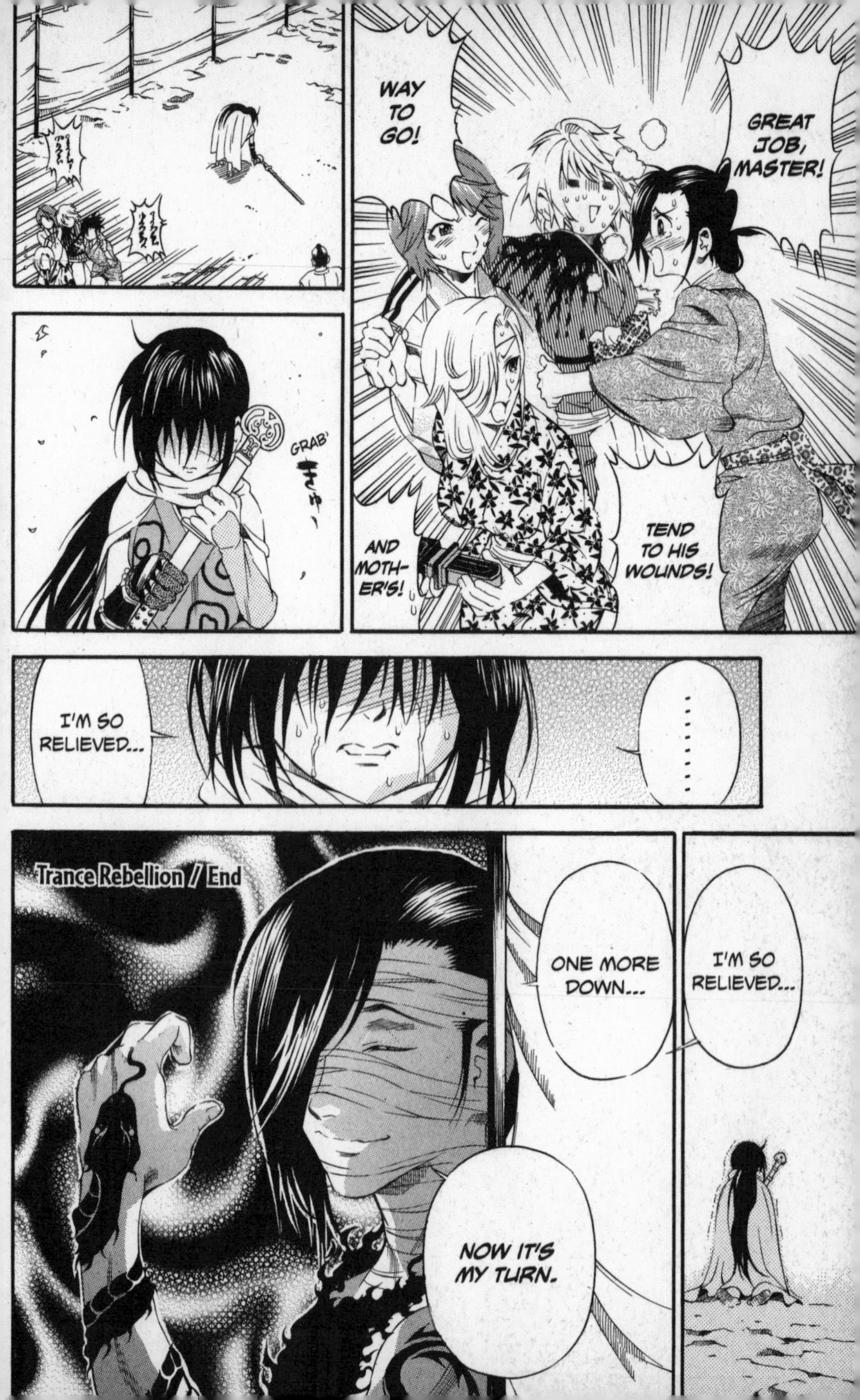
GREAT JOB, MASTER!
WAY TO GO!
TEND TO HIS WOUNDS!
AND MOTHER'S!
GRAB
......
I'M SO RELIEVED...
I'M SO RELIEVED...
ONE MORE DOWN...
NOW IT'S MY TURN.
Trance Rebellion / End

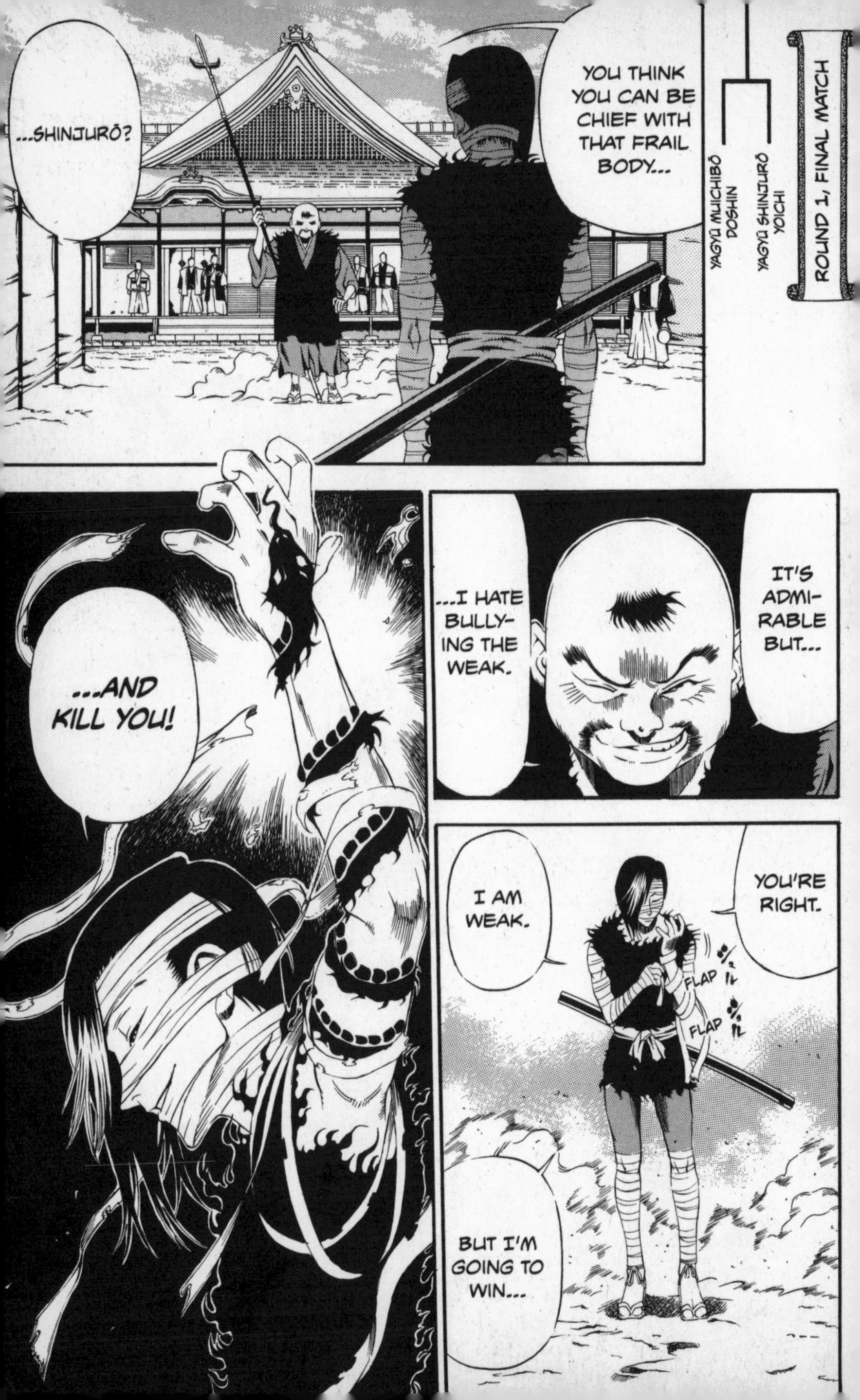
ROUND 1, FINAL MATCH
YAGYŪ SHINJURŌ YOICHI
YAGYŪ MUICHIBŌ DOSHIN
YOU THINK YOU CAN BE CHIEF WITH THAT FRAIL BODY...
...SHINJURŌ?
IT'S ADMIRABLE BUT...
...I HATE BULLYING THE WEAK.
YOU'RE RIGHT.
I AM WEAK.
FLAP
FLAP
BUT I'M GOING TO WIN...
...AND KILL YOU!

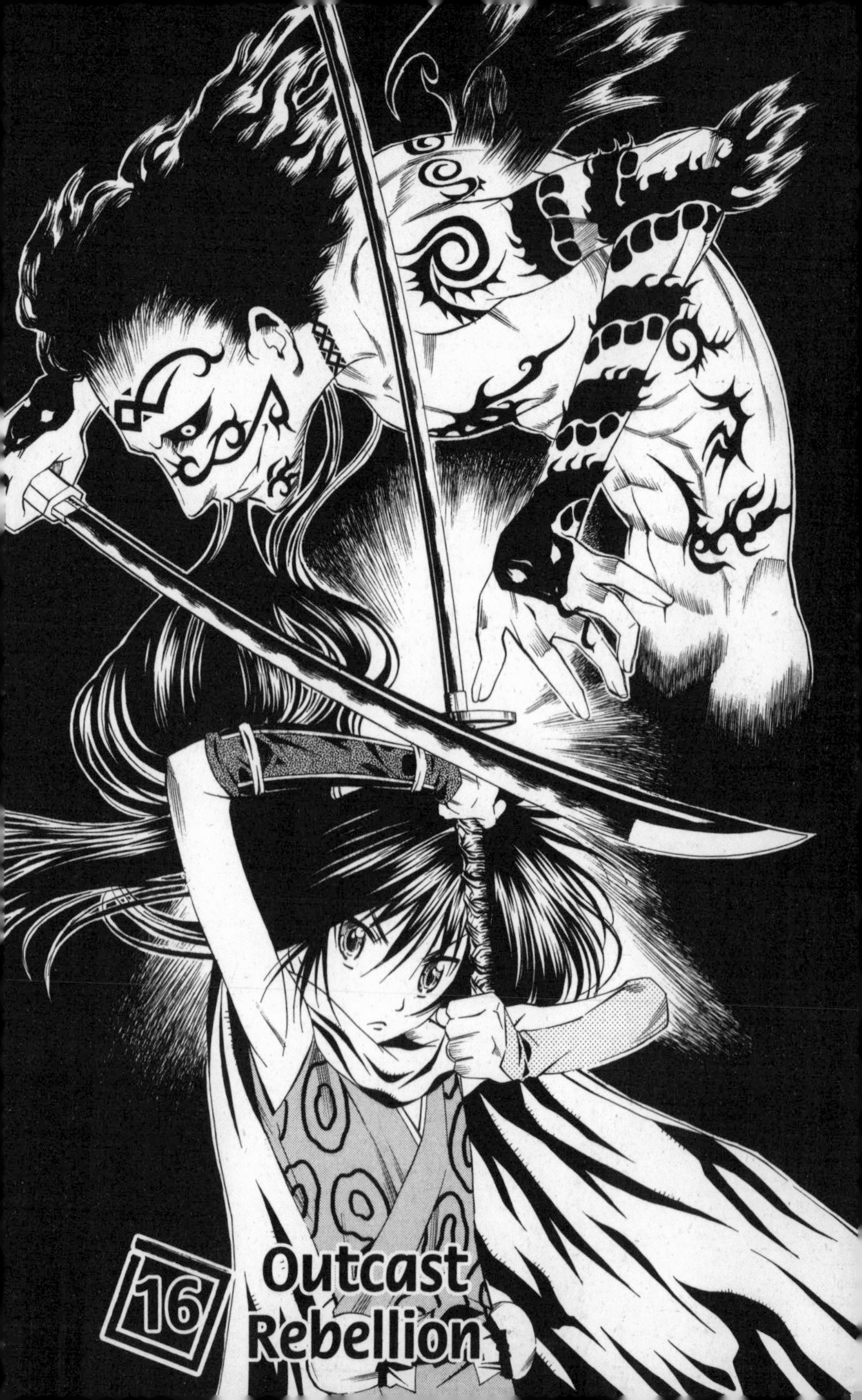
16
Outcast
Rebellion

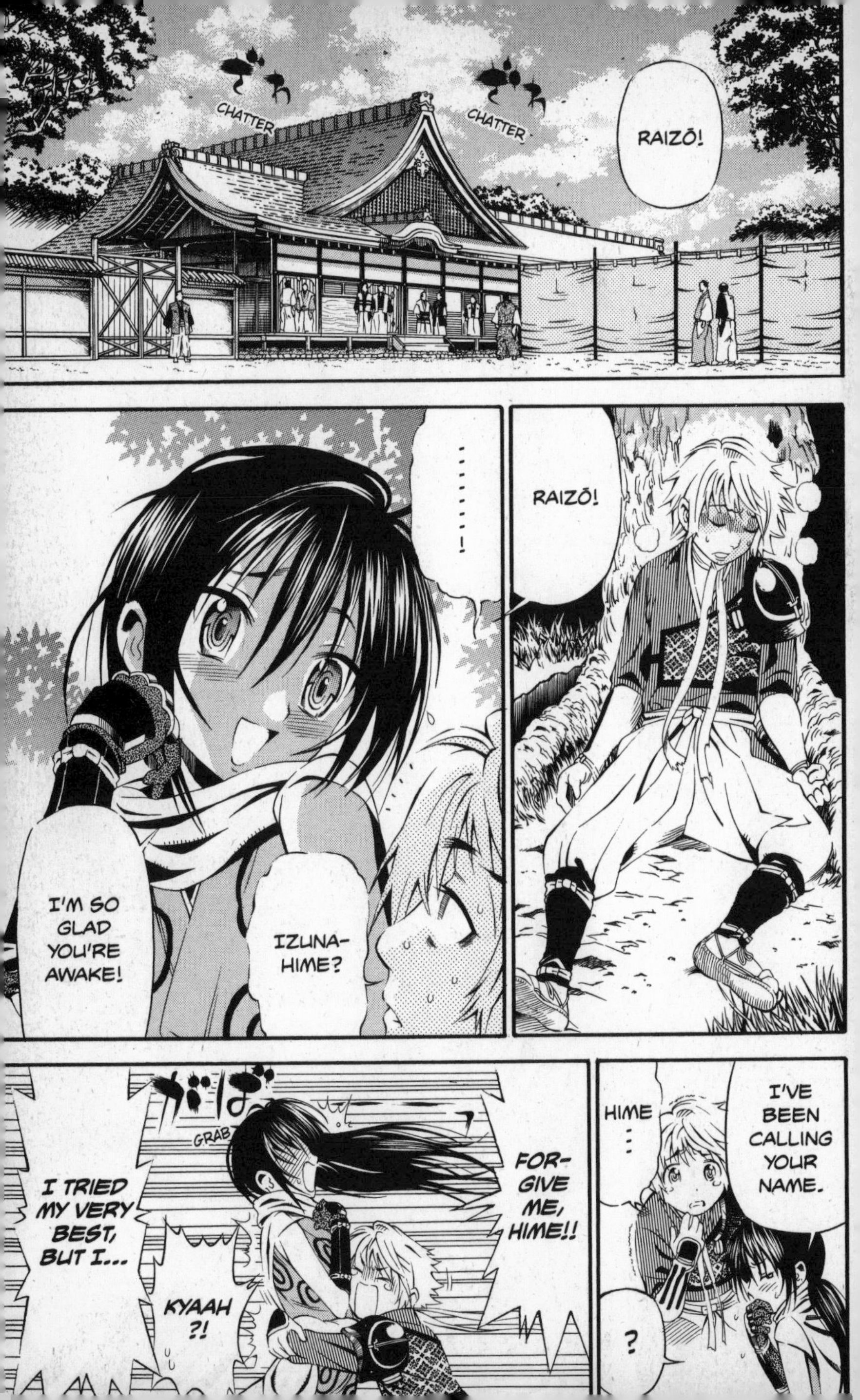
RAIZŌ!
CHATTER
CHATTER
RAIZŌ!
......!
IZUNA-HIME?
I'M SO GLAD YOU'RE AWAKE!
I'VE BEEN CALLING YOUR NAME.
HIME...
?
GRAB
FORGIVE ME, HIME!!
I TRIED MY VERY BEST, BUT I...
KYAAH?!

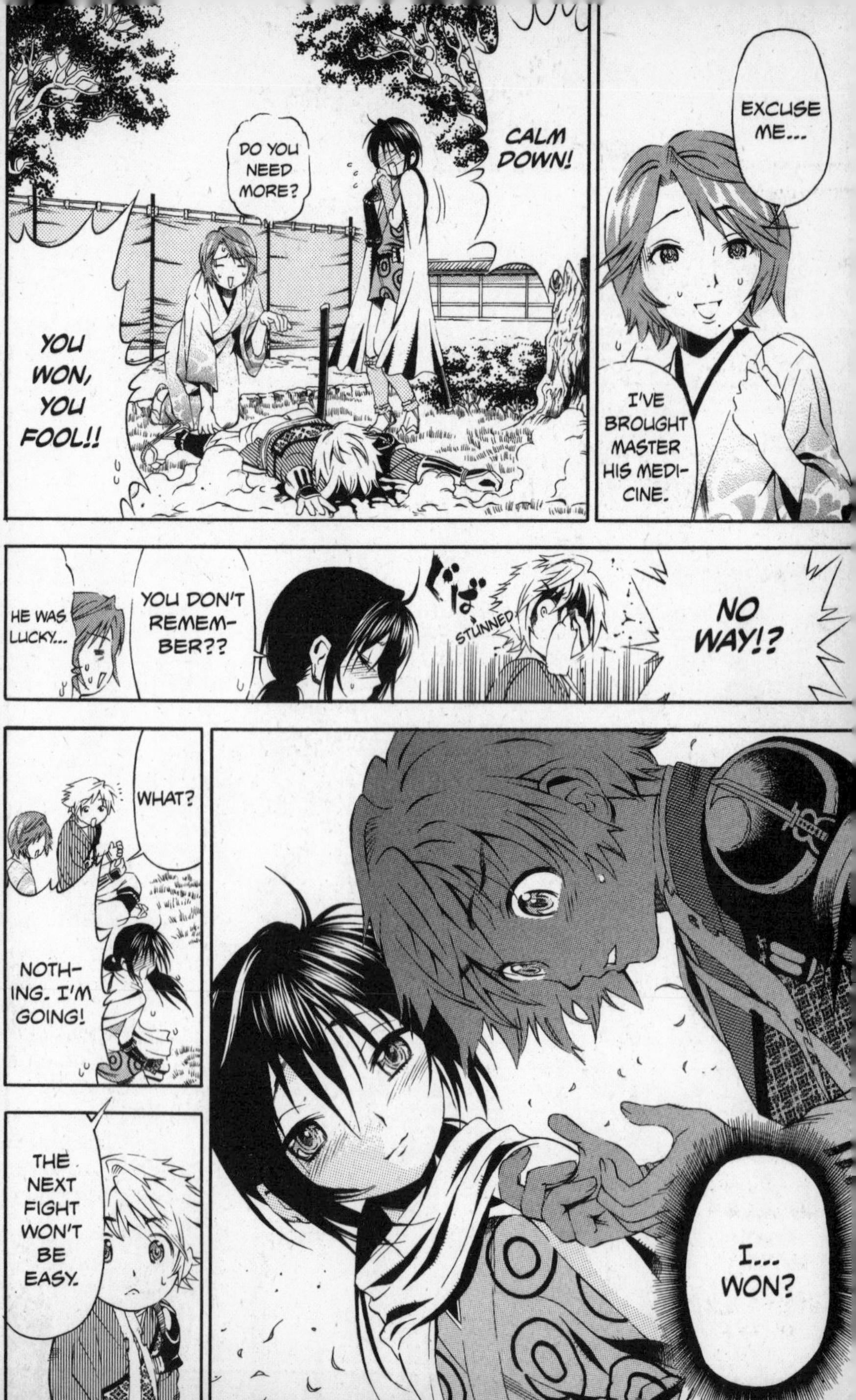
EXCUSE ME...
I'VE BROUGHT MASTER HIS MEDICINE.
CALM DOWN!
DO YOU NEED MORE?
YOU WON, YOU FOOL!!
NO WAY!?
STUNNED
YOU DON'T REMEMBER??
HE WAS LUCKY...
I... WON?
WHAT?
NOTHING. I'M GOING!
THE NEXT FIGHT WON'T BE EASY.

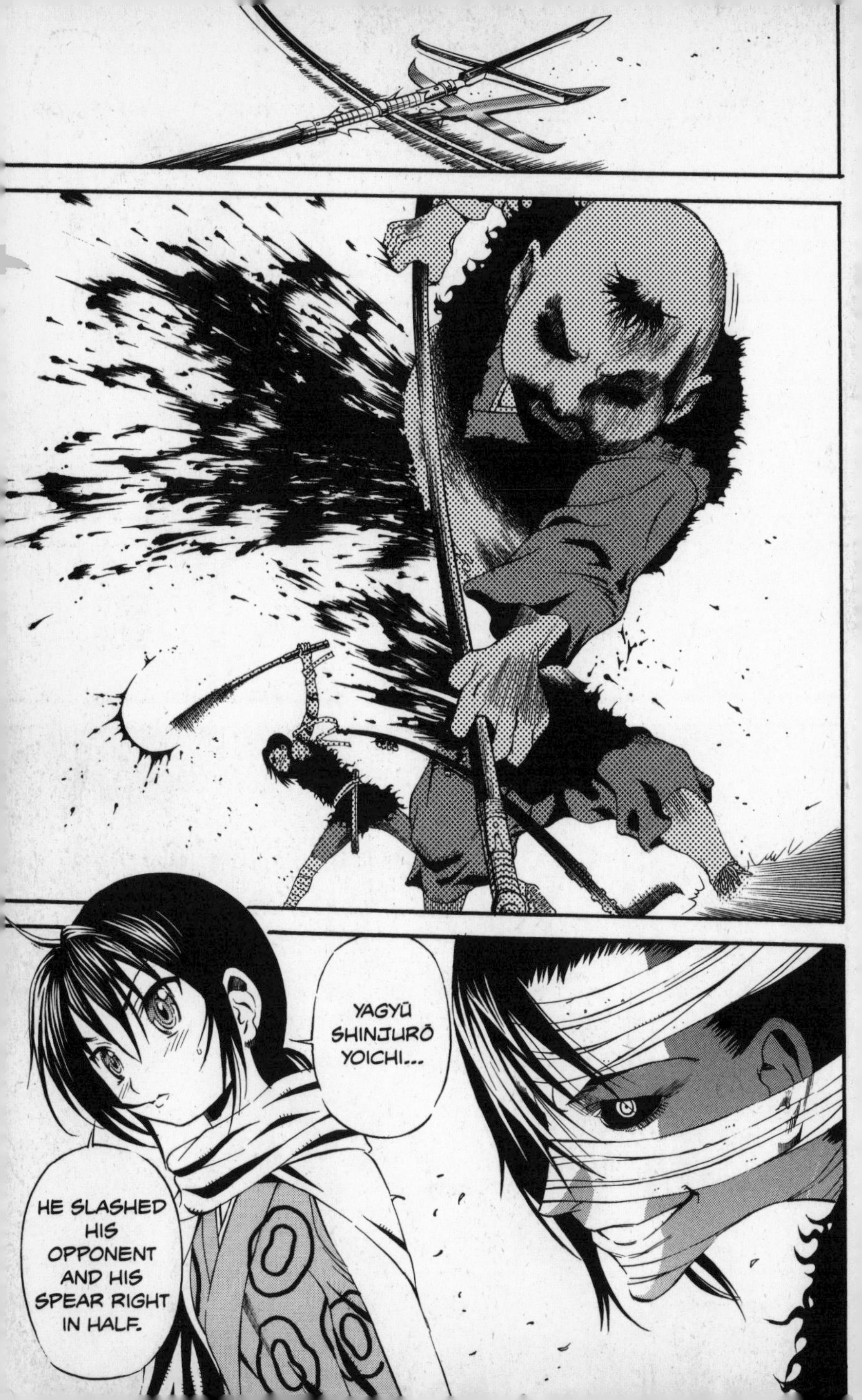
YAGYŪ SHINJURŌ YOICHI...
HE SLASHED HIS OPPONENT AND HIS SPEAR RIGHT IN HALF.

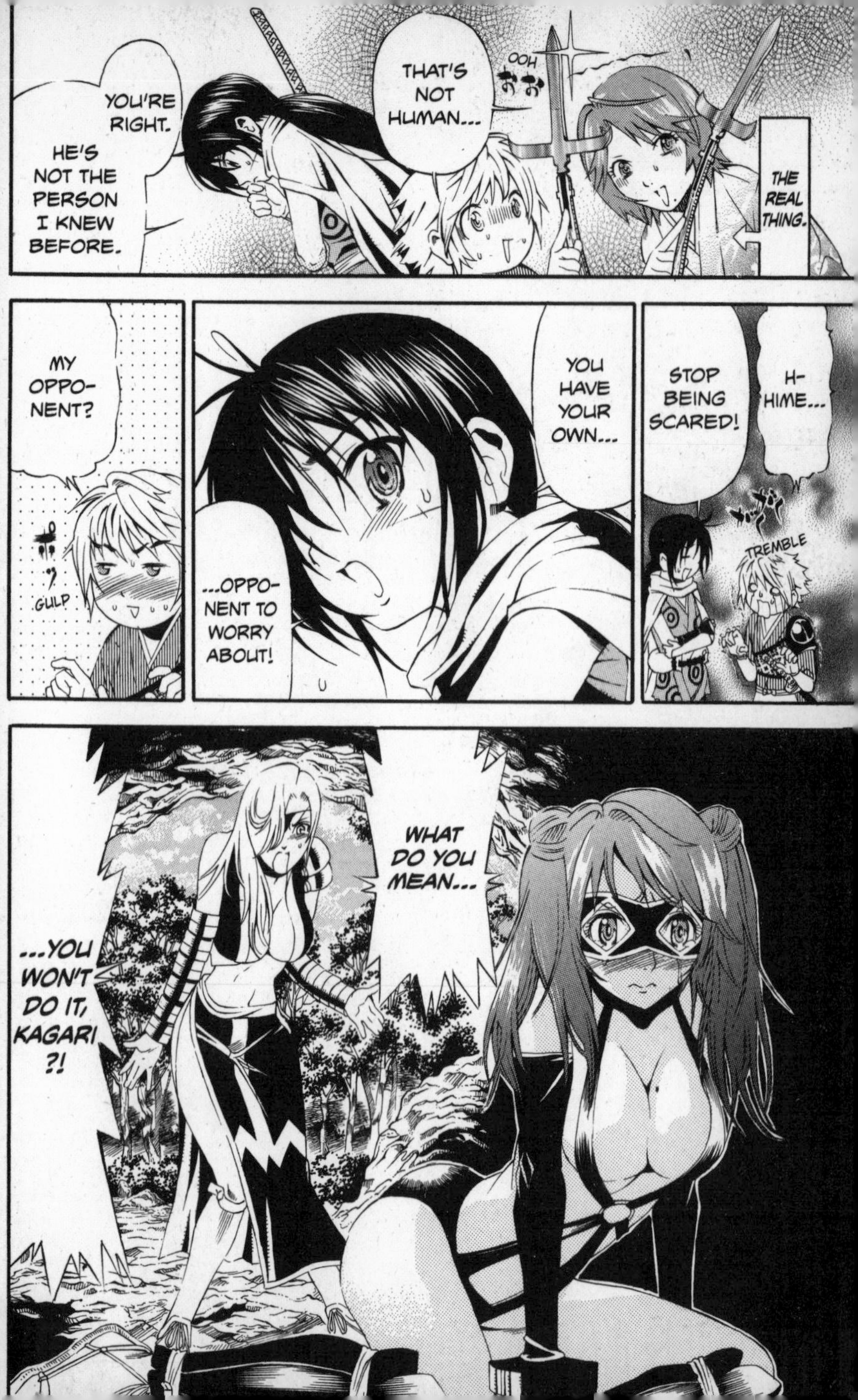
THE REAL THING.
OOH
THAT'S NOT HUMAN...
YOU'RE RIGHT.
HE'S NOT THE PERSON I KNEW BEFORE.
H-HIME...
STOP BEING SCARED!
TREMBLE
YOU HAVE YOUR OWN...
...OPPO-NENT TO WORRY ABOUT!
MY OPPO-NENT?
GULP
WHAT DO YOU MEAN...
...YOU WON'T DO IT, KAGARI ?!

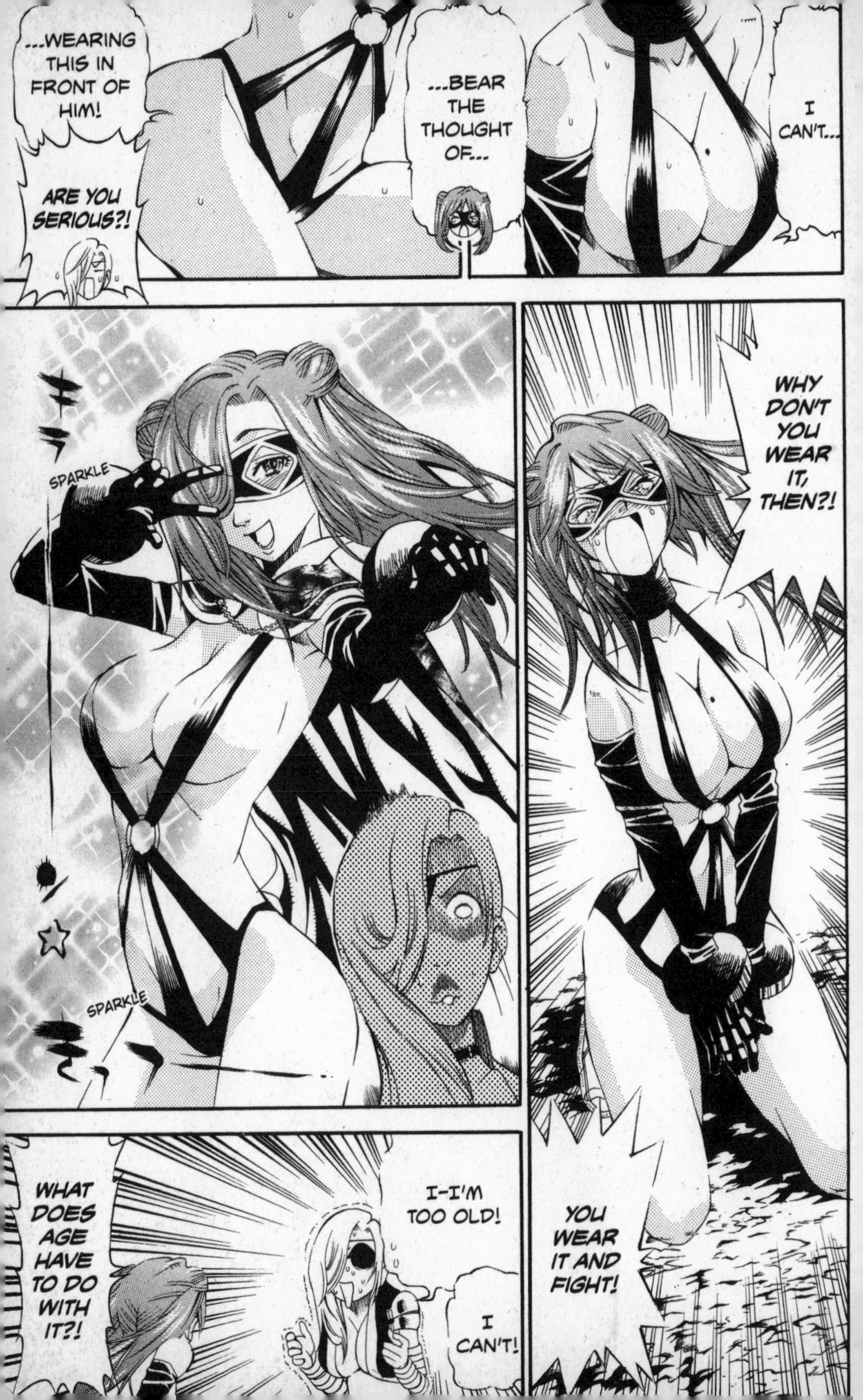
I CAN'T...
...BEAR THE THOUGHT OF...
...WEARING THIS IN FRONT OF HIM!
ARE YOU SERIOUS?!
WHY DON'T YOU WEAR IT, THEN?!
YOU WEAR IT AND FIGHT!
SPARKLE
SPARKLE
I-I'M TOO OLD!
I CAN'T!
WHAT DOES AGE HAVE TO DO WITH IT?!

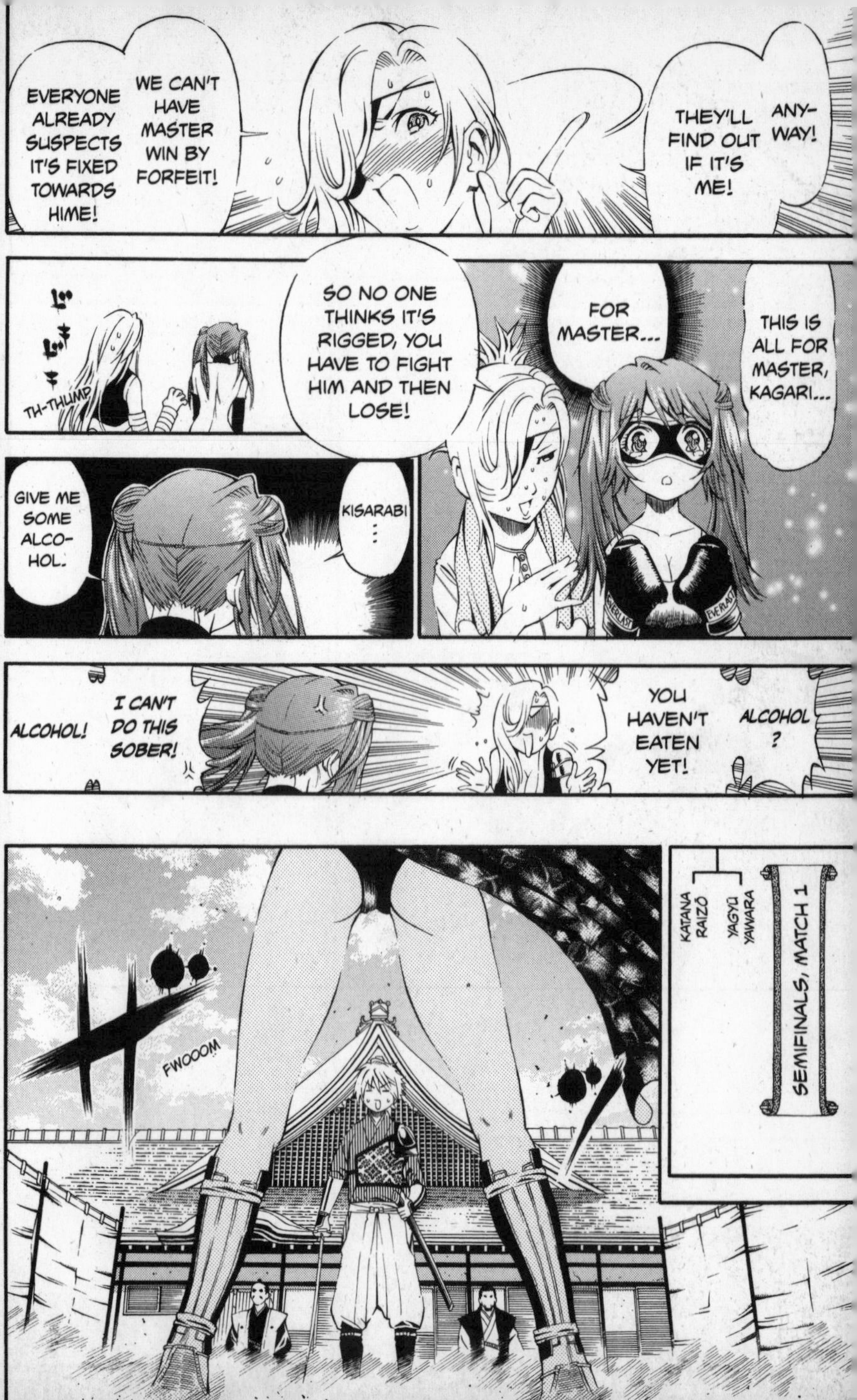
ANY-WAY!
THEY'LL FIND OUT IF IT'S ME!
WE CAN'T HAVE MASTER WIN BY FORFEIT!
EVERYONE ALREADY SUSPECTS IT'S FIXED TOWARDS HIME!
THIS IS ALL FOR MASTER, KAGARI...
FOR MASTER...
SO NO ONE THINKS IT'S RIGGED, YOU HAVE TO FIGHT HIM AND THEN LOSE!
TH-THUMP
KISARABI...
GIVE ME SOME ALCO-HOL.
ALCOHOL?
YOU HAVEN'T EATEN YET!
I CAN'T DO THIS SOBER!
ALCOHOL!
SEMIFINALS, MATCH 1
KATANA RAIZŌ
YAGYŪ YAWARA
FWOOOM

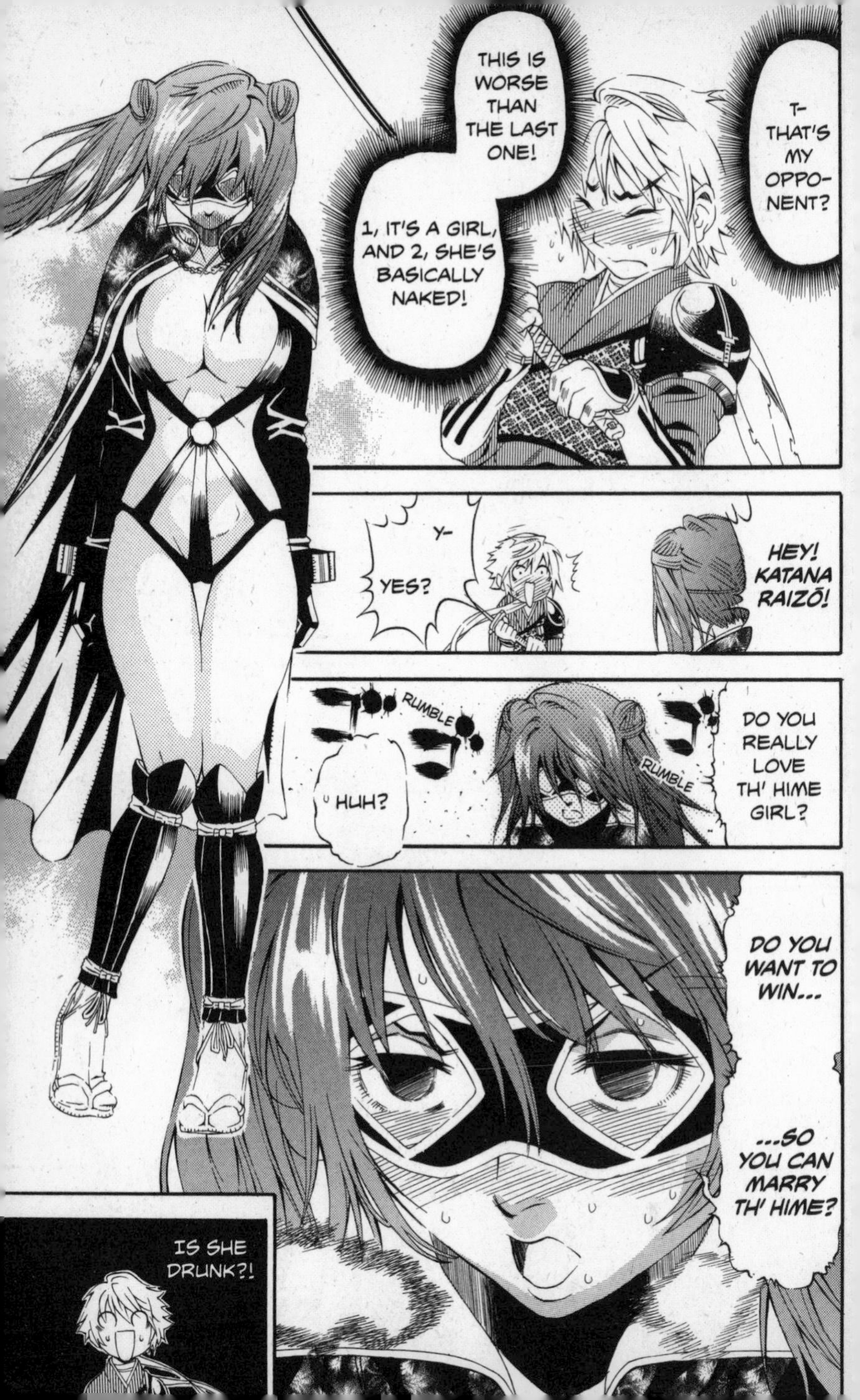
T-THAT'S MY OPPO-NENT?
THIS IS WORSE THAN THE LAST ONE!
1, IT'S A GIRL, AND 2, SHE'S BASICALLY NAKED!
HEY! KATANA RAIZŌ!
Y- YES?
DO YOU REALLY LOVE TH' HIME GIRL?
RUMBLE
RUMBLE
HUH?
DO YOU WANT TO WIN...
...SO YOU CAN MARRY TH' HIME?
IS SHE DRUNK?!

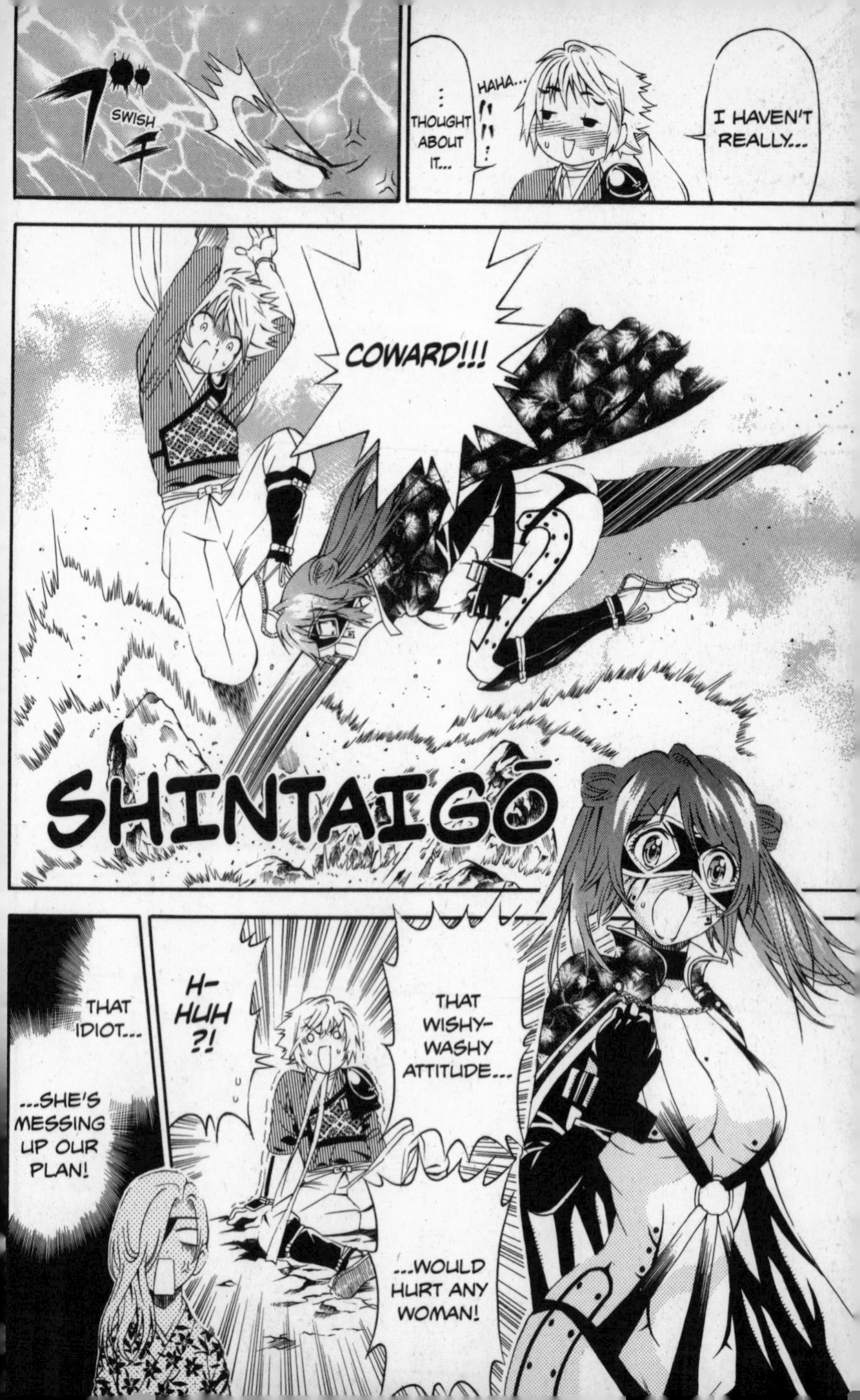
I HAVEN'T REALLY...
HAHA...
...THOUGHT ABOUT IT...
SWISH
COWARD!!!
SHINTAIGŌ
THAT WISHY-WASHY ATTITUDE...
...WOULD HURT ANY WOMAN!
H-HUH?!
THAT IDIOT...
...SHE'S MESSING UP OUR PLAN!

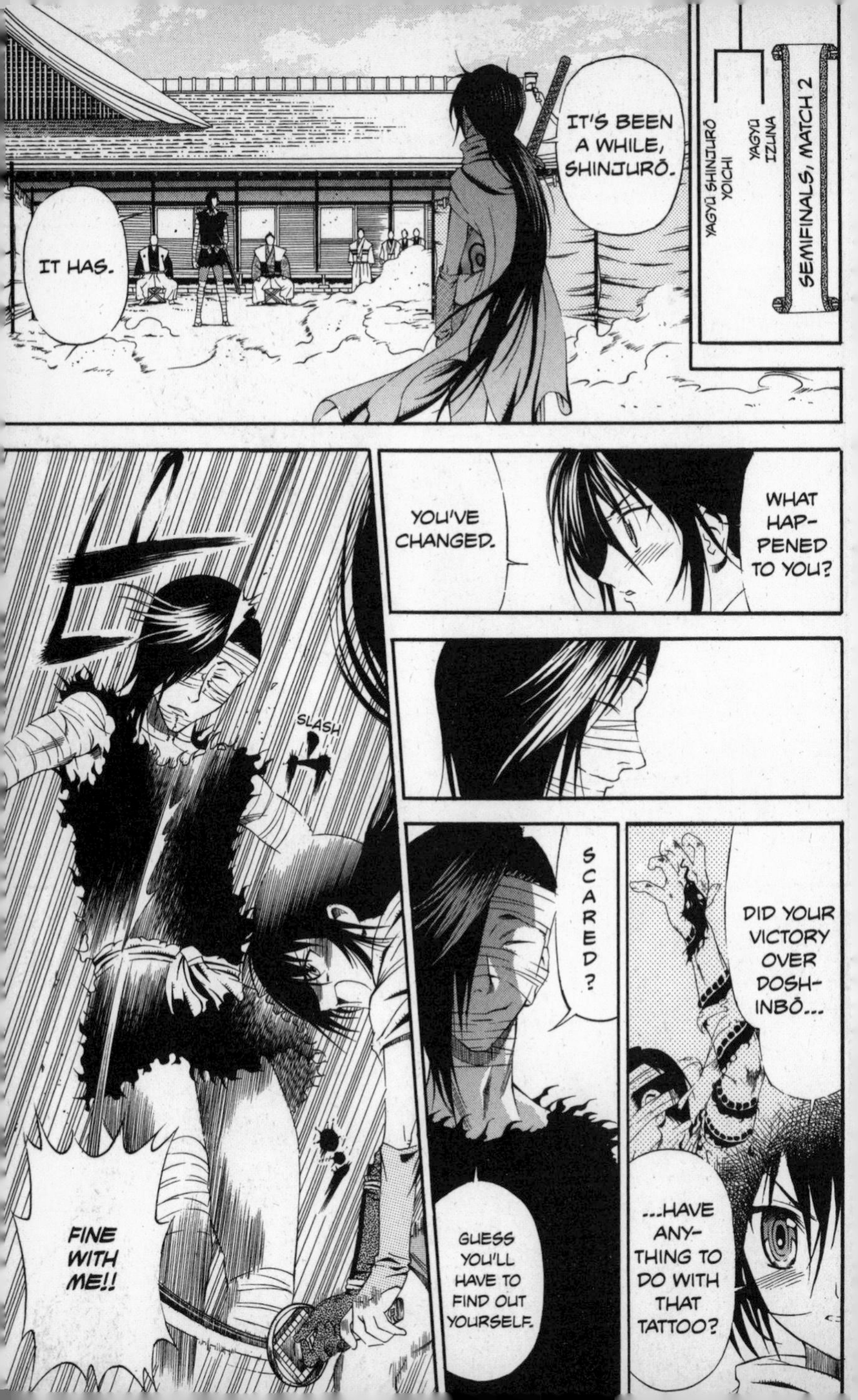
SEMIFINALS, MATCH 2
YAGYŪ IZUNA
YAGYŪ SHINJURŌ YOICHI
IT'S BEEN A WHILE, SHINJURŌ.
IT HAS.
WHAT HAPPENED TO YOU?
YOU'VE CHANGED.
DID YOUR VICTORY OVER DOSHINBŌ...
...HAVE ANYTHING TO DO WITH THAT TATTOO?
SCARED?
GUESS YOU'LL HAVE TO FIND OUT YOURSELF.
SLASH
FINE WITH ME!!

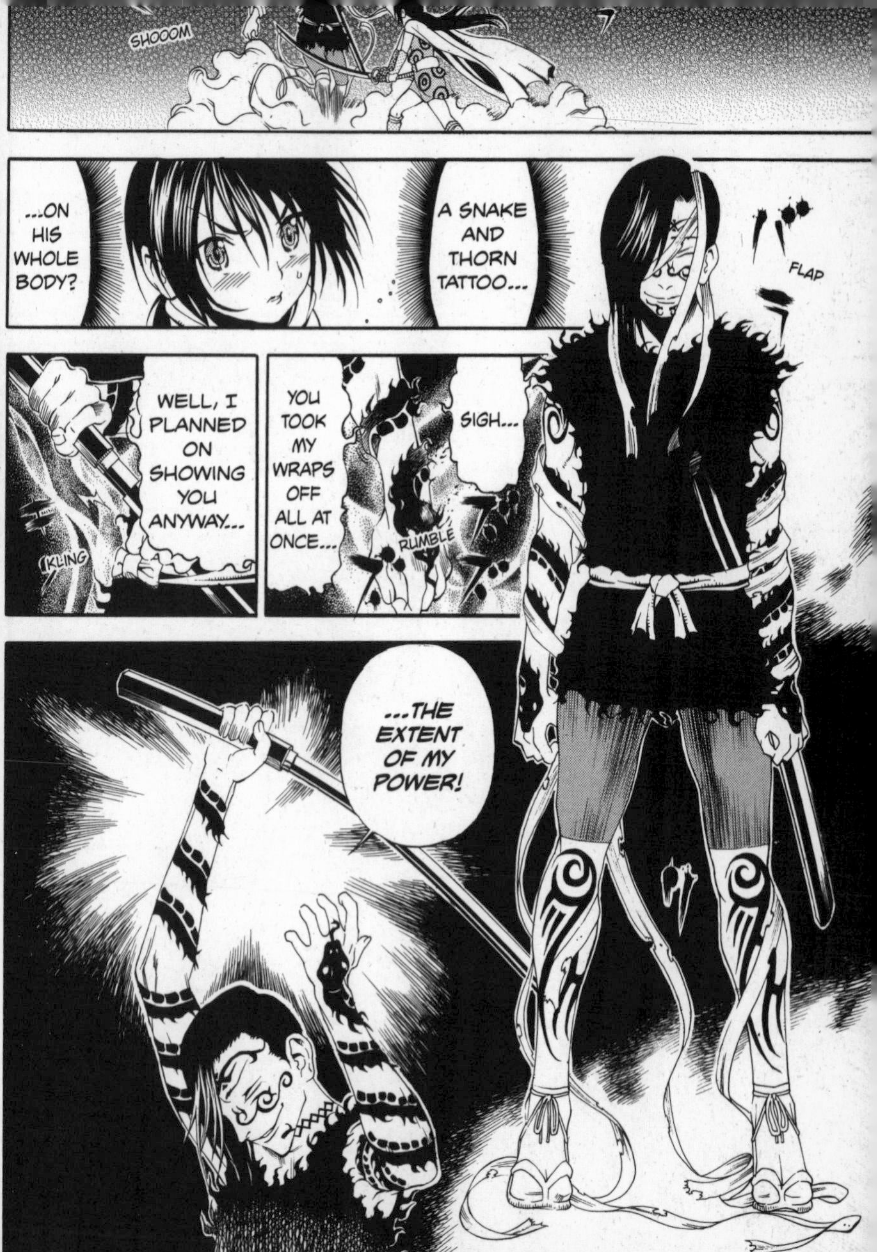
SHOOOM
FLAP
A SNAKE AND THORN TATTOO...
...ON HIS WHOLE BODY?
SIGH...
YOU TOOK MY WRAPS OFF ALL AT ONCE...
RUMBLE
WELL, I PLANNED ON SHOWING YOU ANYWAY...
KLING
...THE EXTENT OF MY POWER!

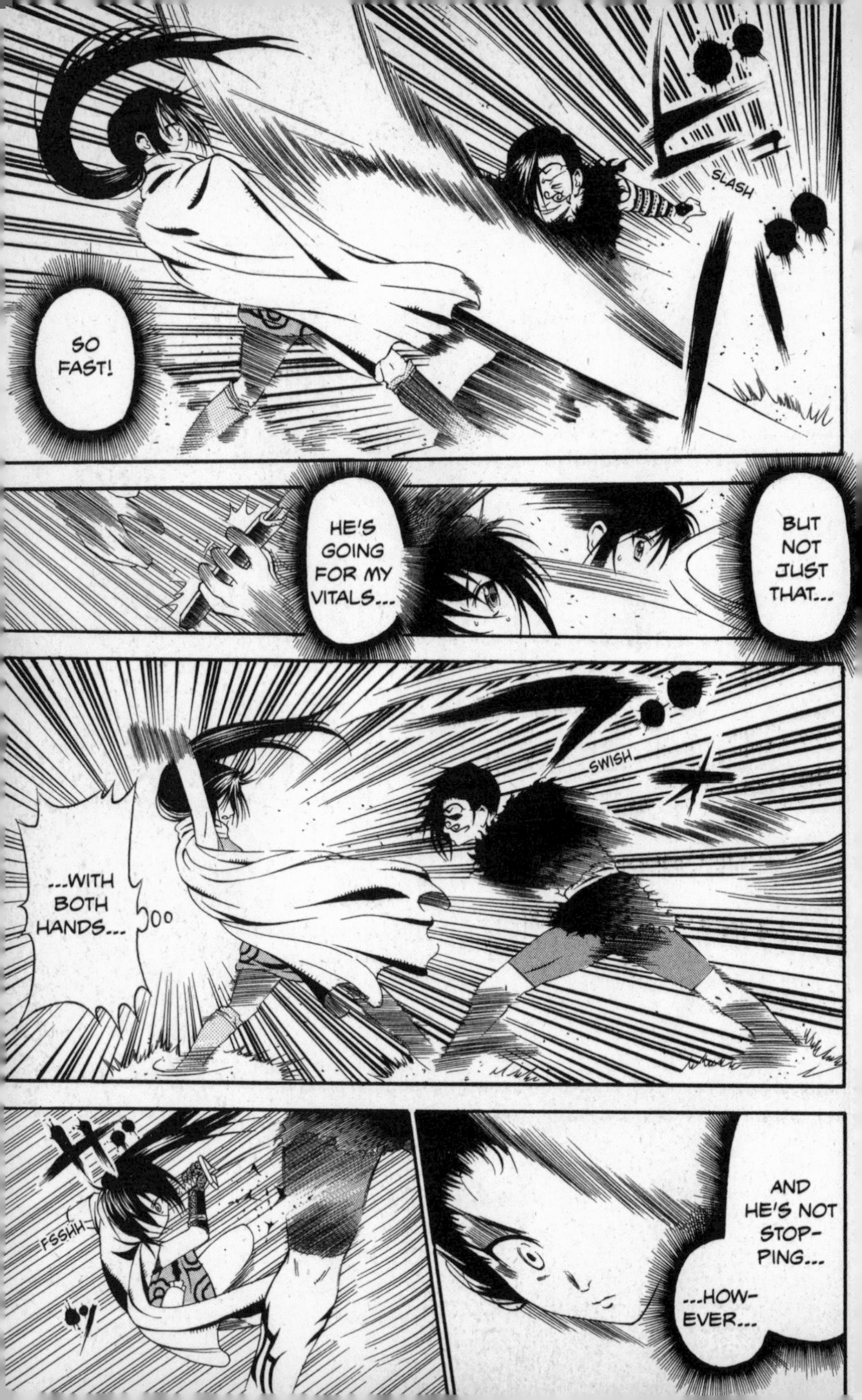
SLASH
SO FAST!
BUT NOT JUST THAT...
HE'S GOING FOR MY VITALS...
SWISH
...WITH BOTH HANDS...
AND HE'S NOT STOP-PING...
...HOW-EVER...
FSSHH

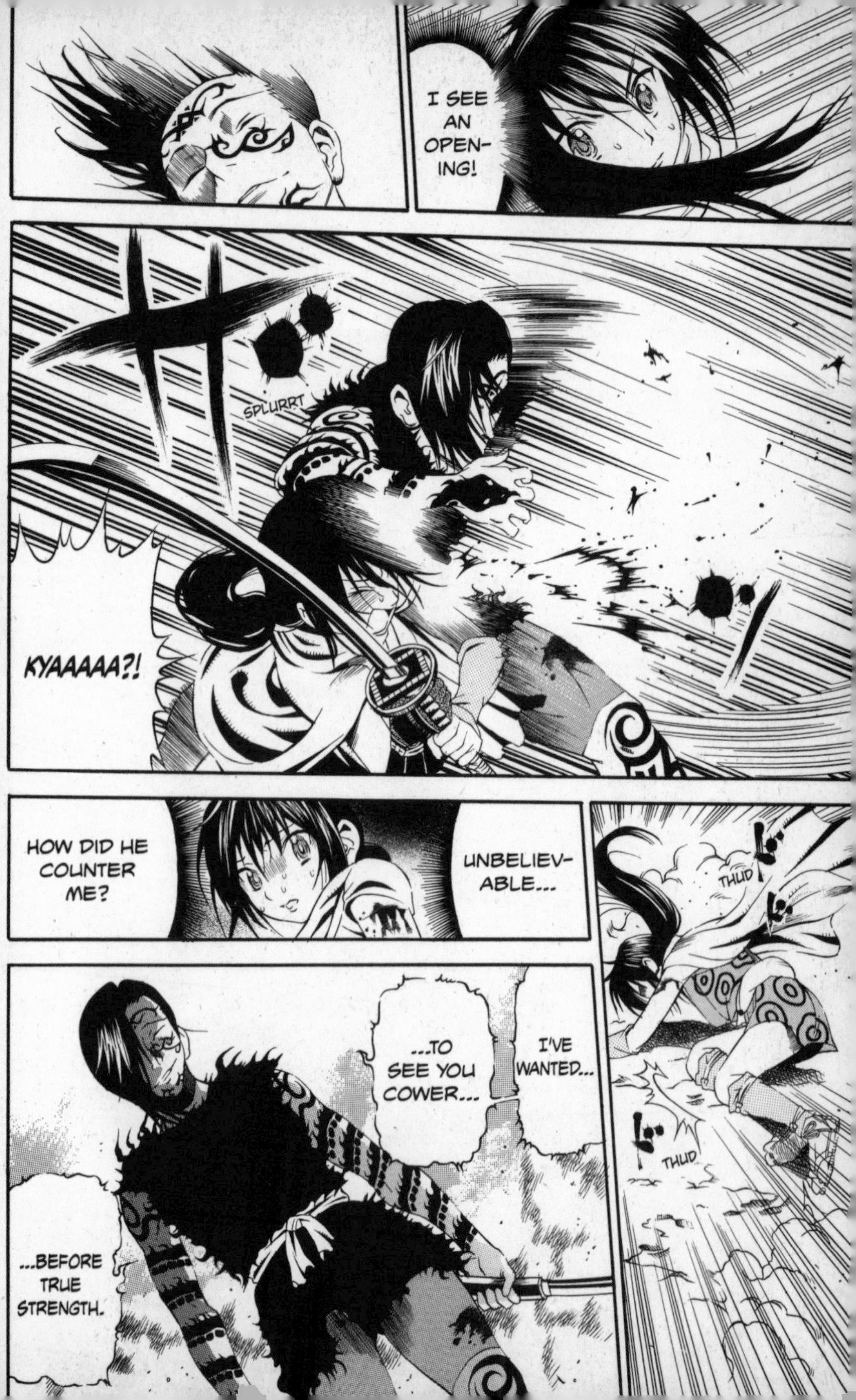
I SEE AN OPEN-ING!
SPLURRT
KYAAAAA?!
THUD
THUD
UNBELIEV-ABLE...
HOW DID HE COUNTER ME?
I'VE WANTED...
...TO SEE YOU COWER...
...BEFORE TRUE STRENGTH.

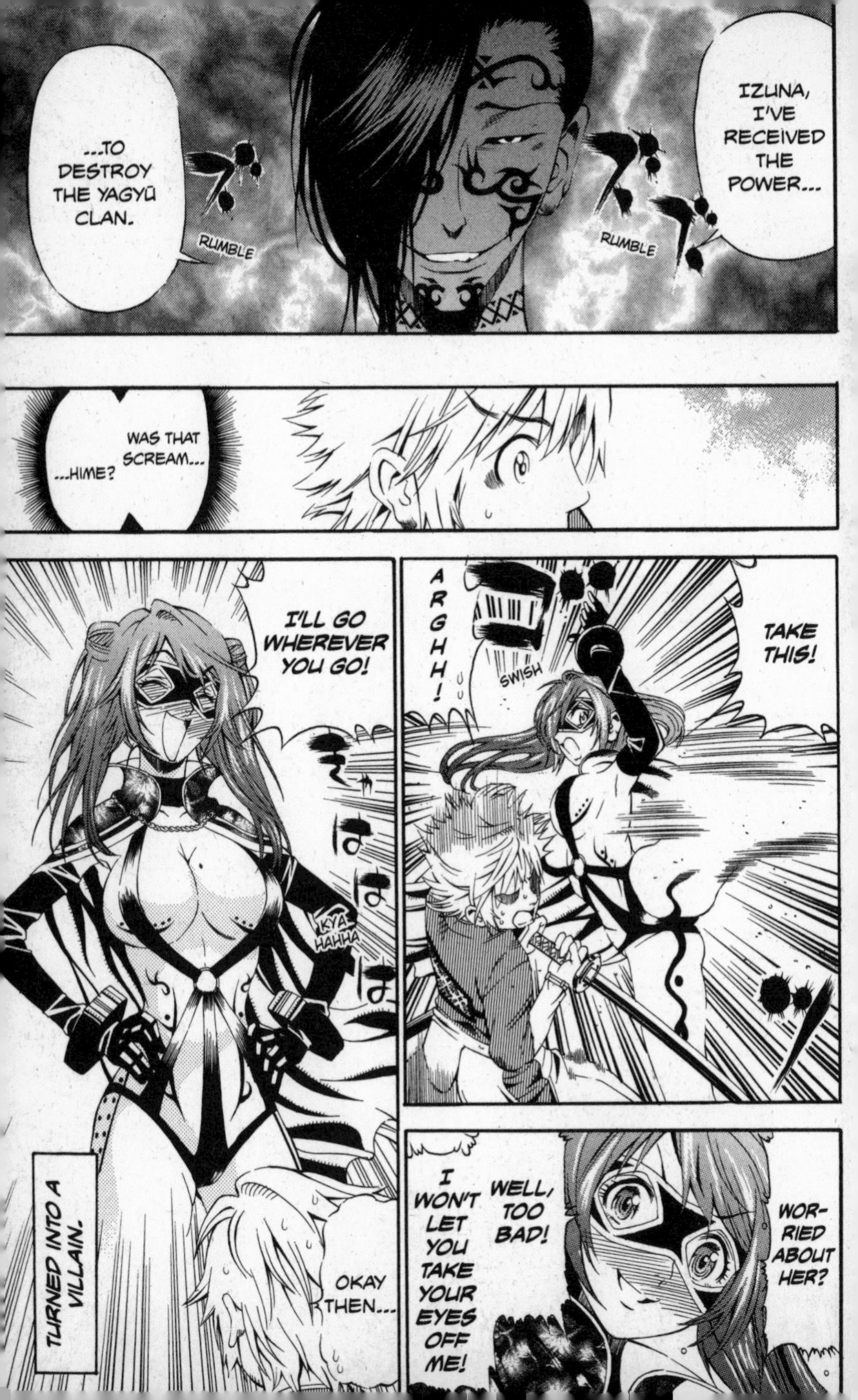
IZUNA, I'VE RECEIVED THE POWER...
RUMBLE
...TO DESTROY THE YAGYŪ CLAN.
RUMBLE
WAS THAT SCREAM...
...HIME?
TAKE THIS!
SWISH
ARGHH!
WOR-RIED ABOUT HER?
WELL, TOO BAD!
I WON'T LET YOU TAKE YOUR EYES OFF ME!
I'LL GO WHEREVER YOU GO!
KYA HAHHA
OKAY THEN...
TURNED INTO A VILLAIN.

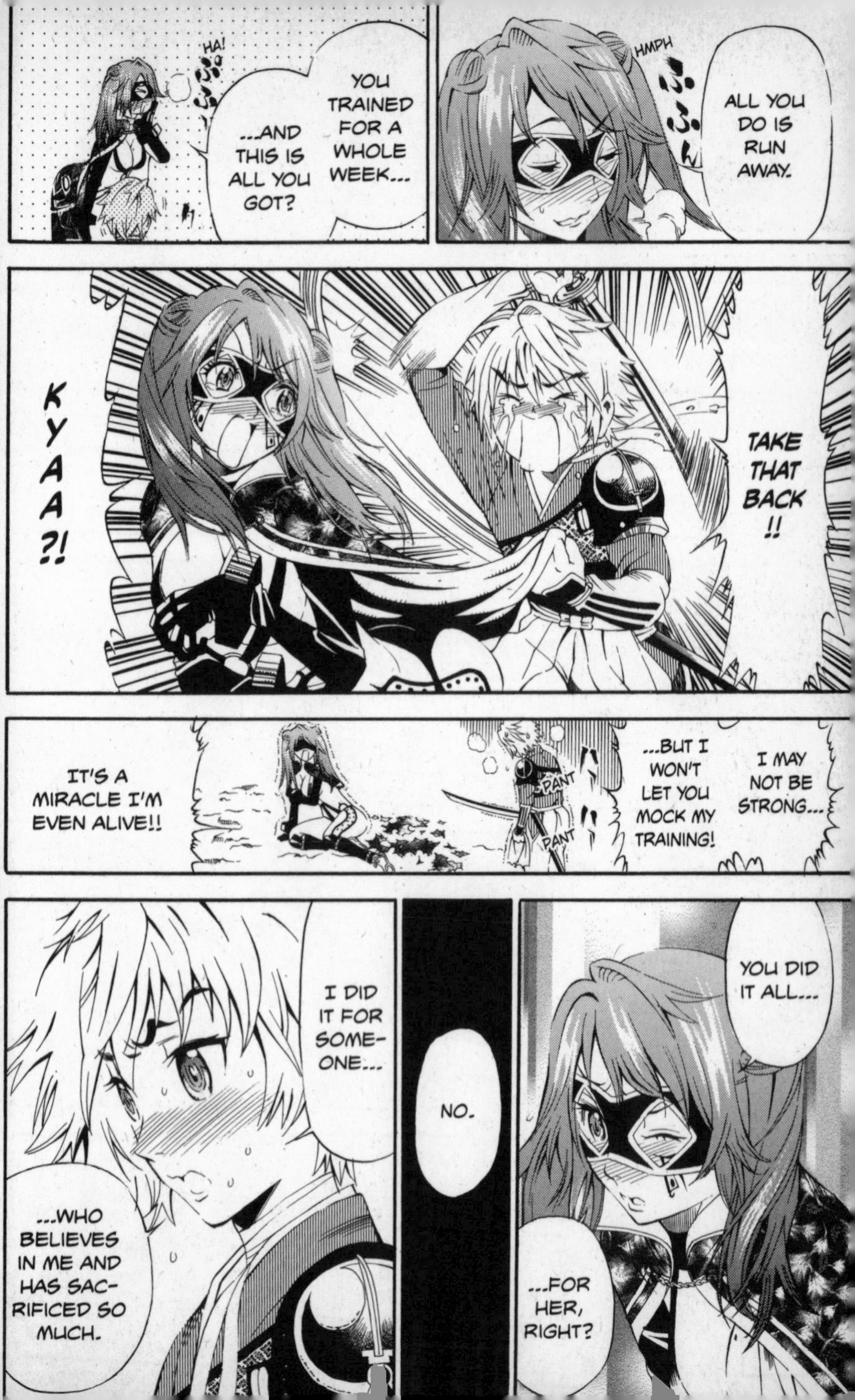
HMPH
ALL YOU DO IS RUN AWAY.
HA!
YOU TRAINED FOR A WHOLE WEEK...
...AND THIS IS ALL YOU GOT?
TAKE THAT BACK!!
KYAAA?!
I MAY NOT BE STRONG...
...BUT I WON'T LET YOU MOCK MY TRAINING!
PANT
PANT
IT'S A MIRACLE I'M EVEN ALIVE!!
YOU DID IT ALL...
...FOR HER, RIGHT?
NO.
I DID IT FOR SOMEONE...
...WHO BELIEVES IN ME AND HAS SACRIFICED SO MUCH.

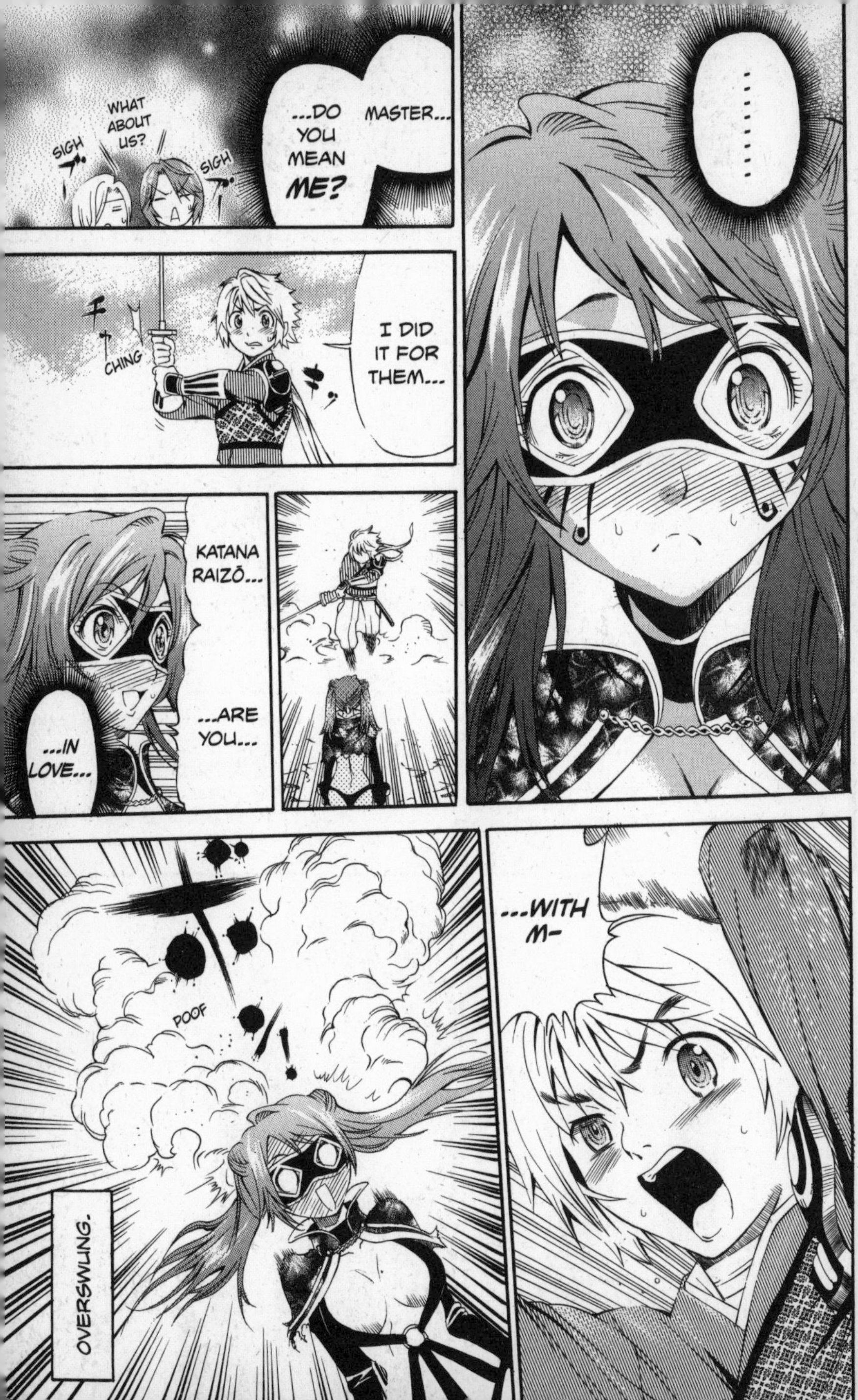
......
MASTER...
...DO YOU MEAN ME?
SIGH
WHAT ABOUT US?
SIGH
I DID IT FOR THEM...
CHING
KATANA RAIZŌ...
...ARE YOU...
...IN LOVE...
...WITH M-
POOF
!
OVERSWUNG.

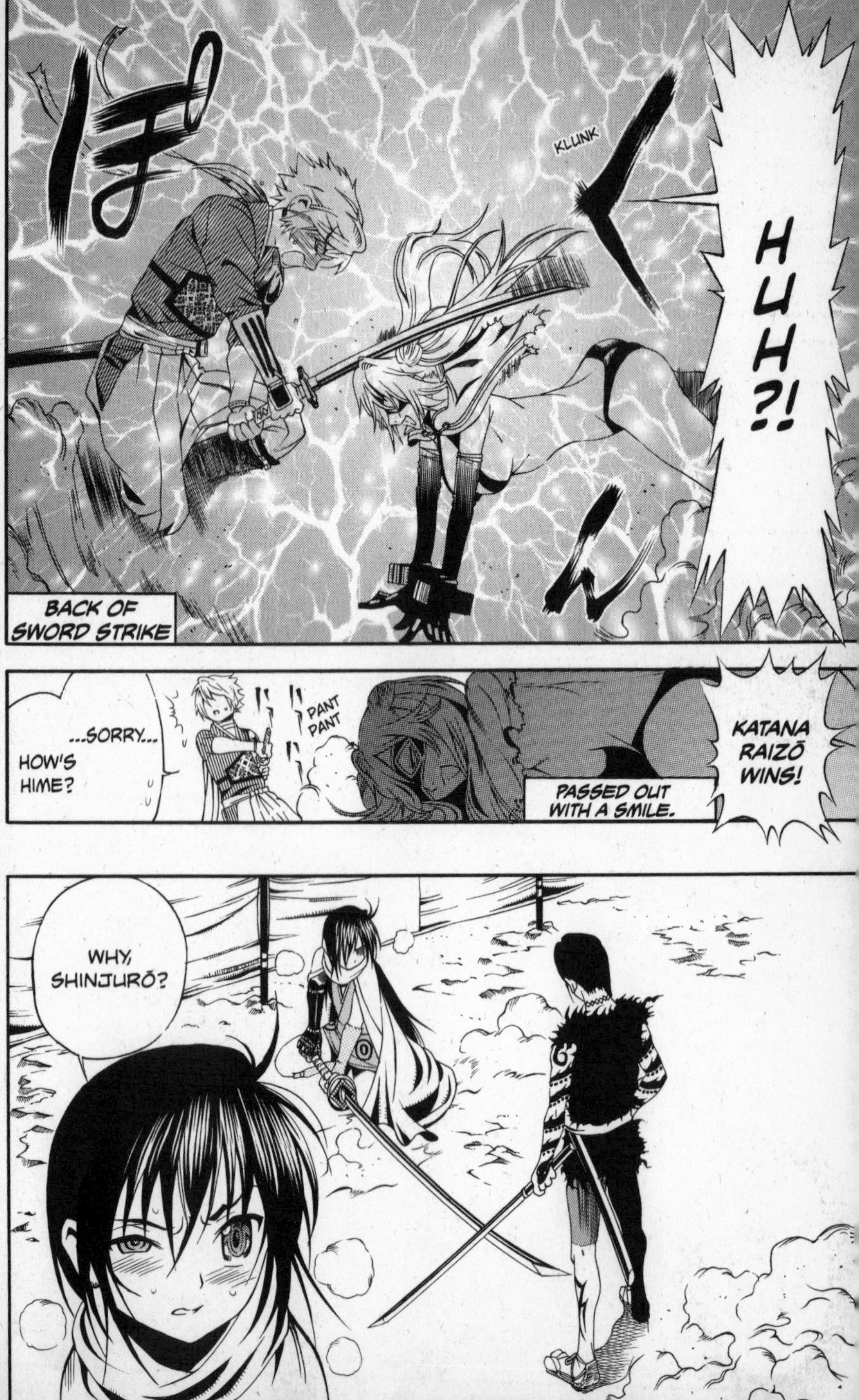
HUH?!
KLUNK
BACK OF SWORD STRIKE
KATANA RAIZŌ WINS!
PASSED OUT WITH A SMILE.
PANT PANT
...SORRY... HOW'S HIME?
WHY, SHINJURŌ?

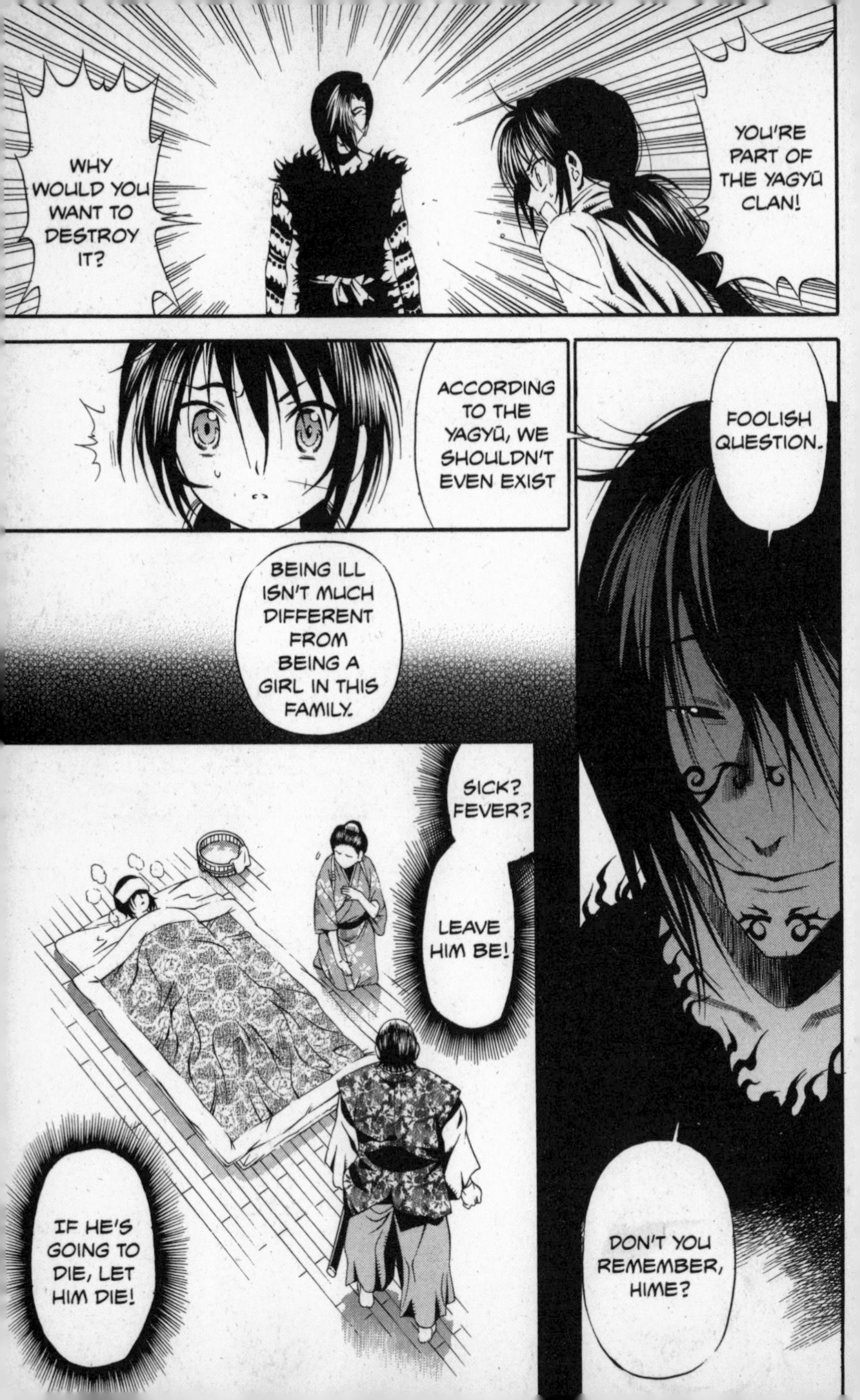
YOU'RE PART OF THE YAGYŪ CLAN!
WHY WOULD YOU WANT TO DESTROY IT?
FOOLISH QUESTION.
DON'T YOU REMEMBER, HIME?
ACCORDING TO THE YAGYŪ, WE SHOULDN'T EVEN EXIST
BEING ILL ISN'T MUCH DIFFERENT FROM BEING A GIRL IN THIS FAMILY.
SICK? FEVER?
LEAVE HIM BE!
IF HE'S GOING TO DIE, LET HIM DIE!

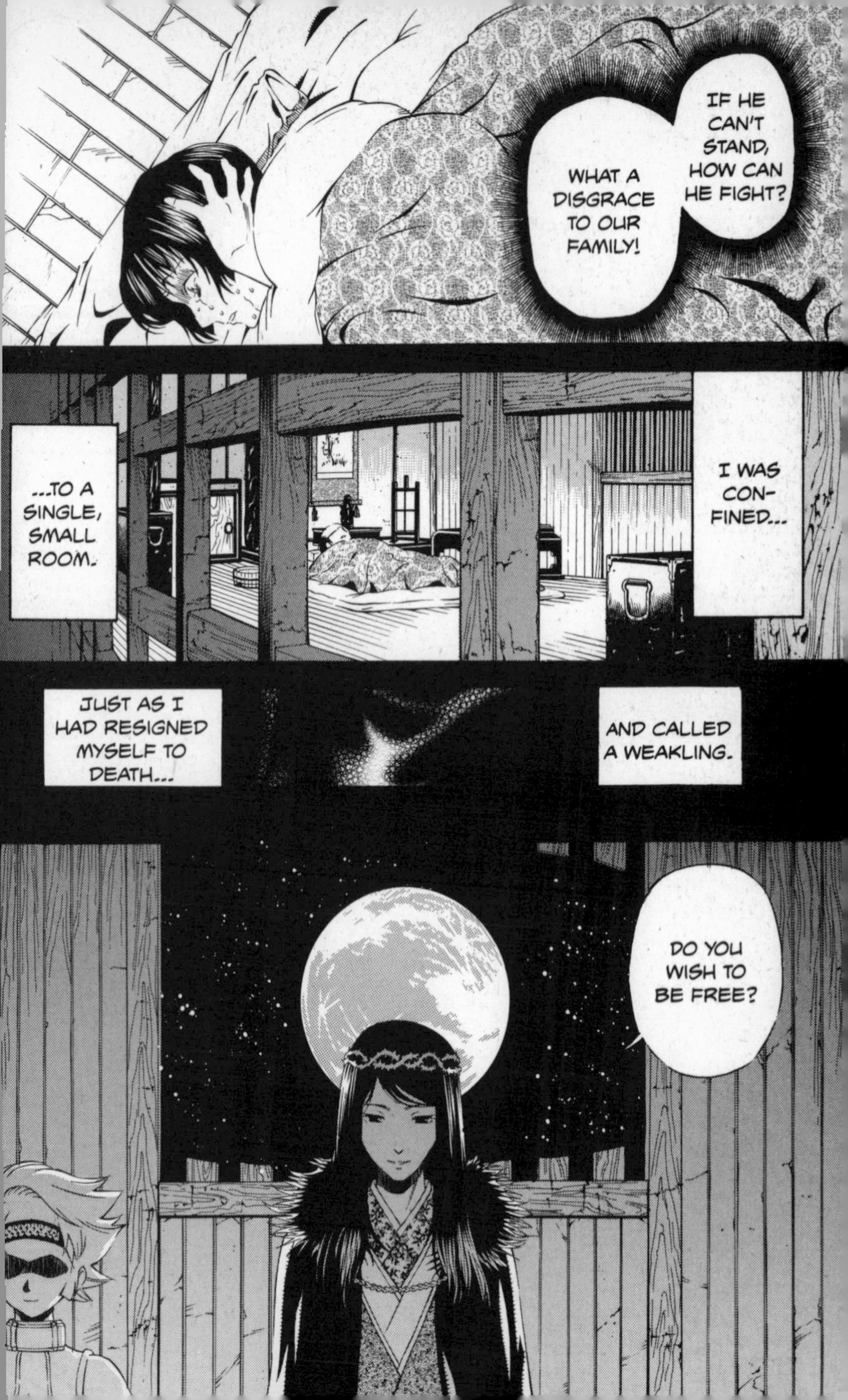
IF HE CAN'T STAND, HOW CAN HE FIGHT?
WHAT A DISGRACE TO OUR FAMILY!
I WAS CON-FINED...
...TO A SINGLE, SMALL ROOM.
AND CALLED A WEAKLING.
JUST AS I HAD RESIGNED MYSELF TO DEATH...
DO YOU WISH TO BE FREE?

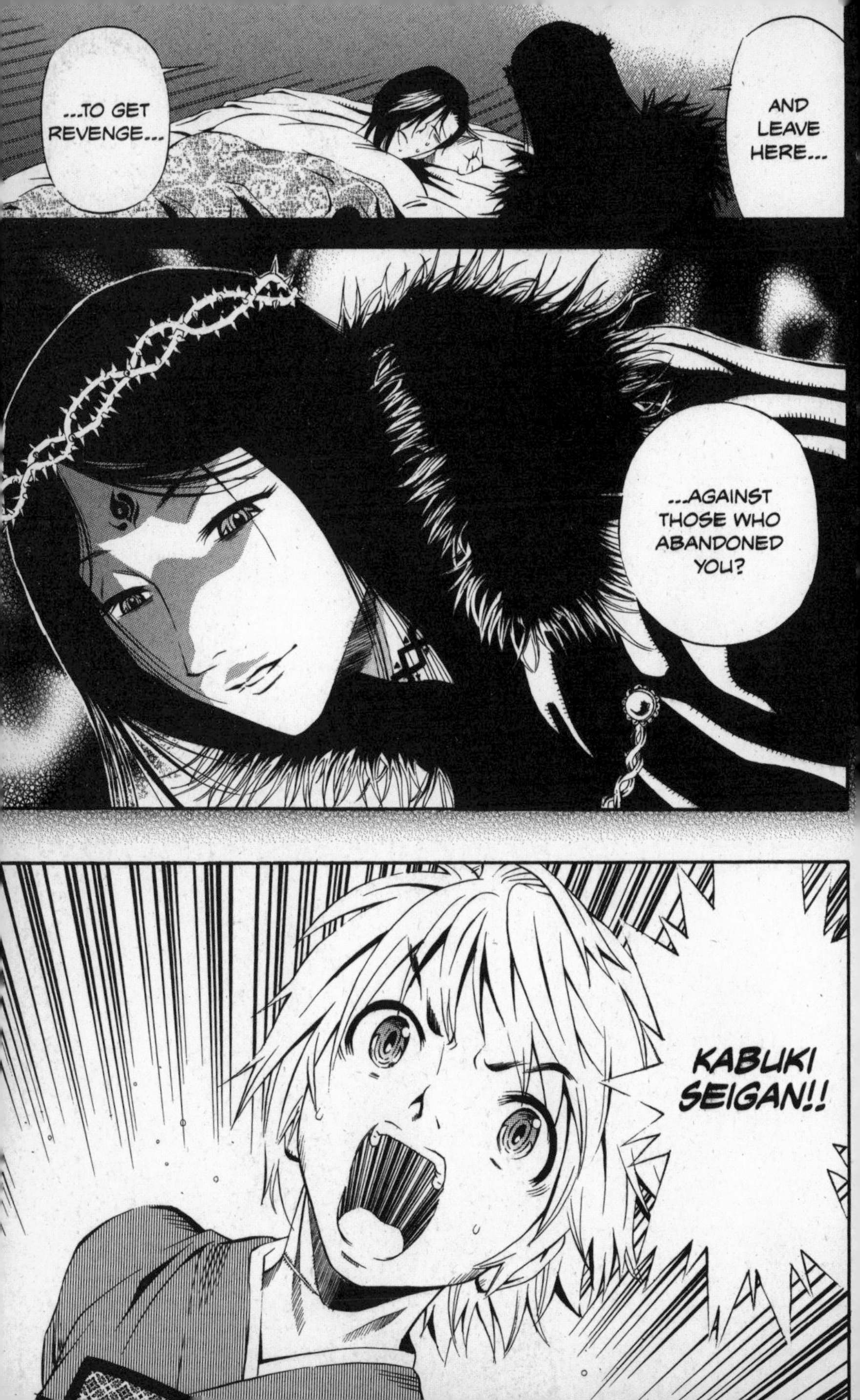
AND LEAVE HERE...
...TO GET REVENGE...
...AGAINST THOSE WHO ABANDONED YOU?
KABUKI SEIGAN!!

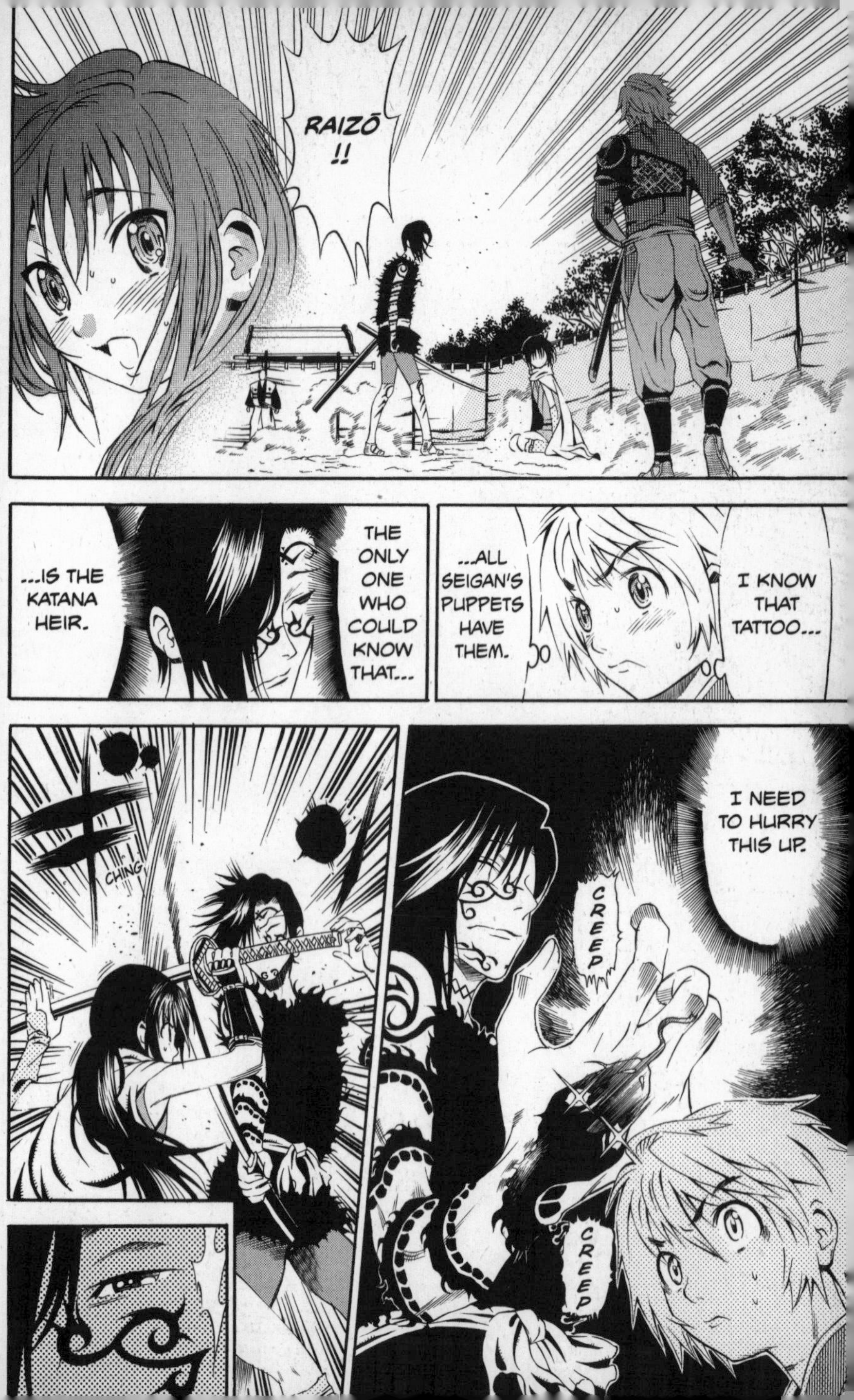
RAIZŌ !!
I KNOW THAT TATTOO...
...ALL SEIGAN'S PUPPETS HAVE THEM.
THE ONLY ONE WHO COULD KNOW THAT...
...IS THE KATANA HEIR.
I NEED TO HURRY THIS UP.
CREEP
CREEP
CHING

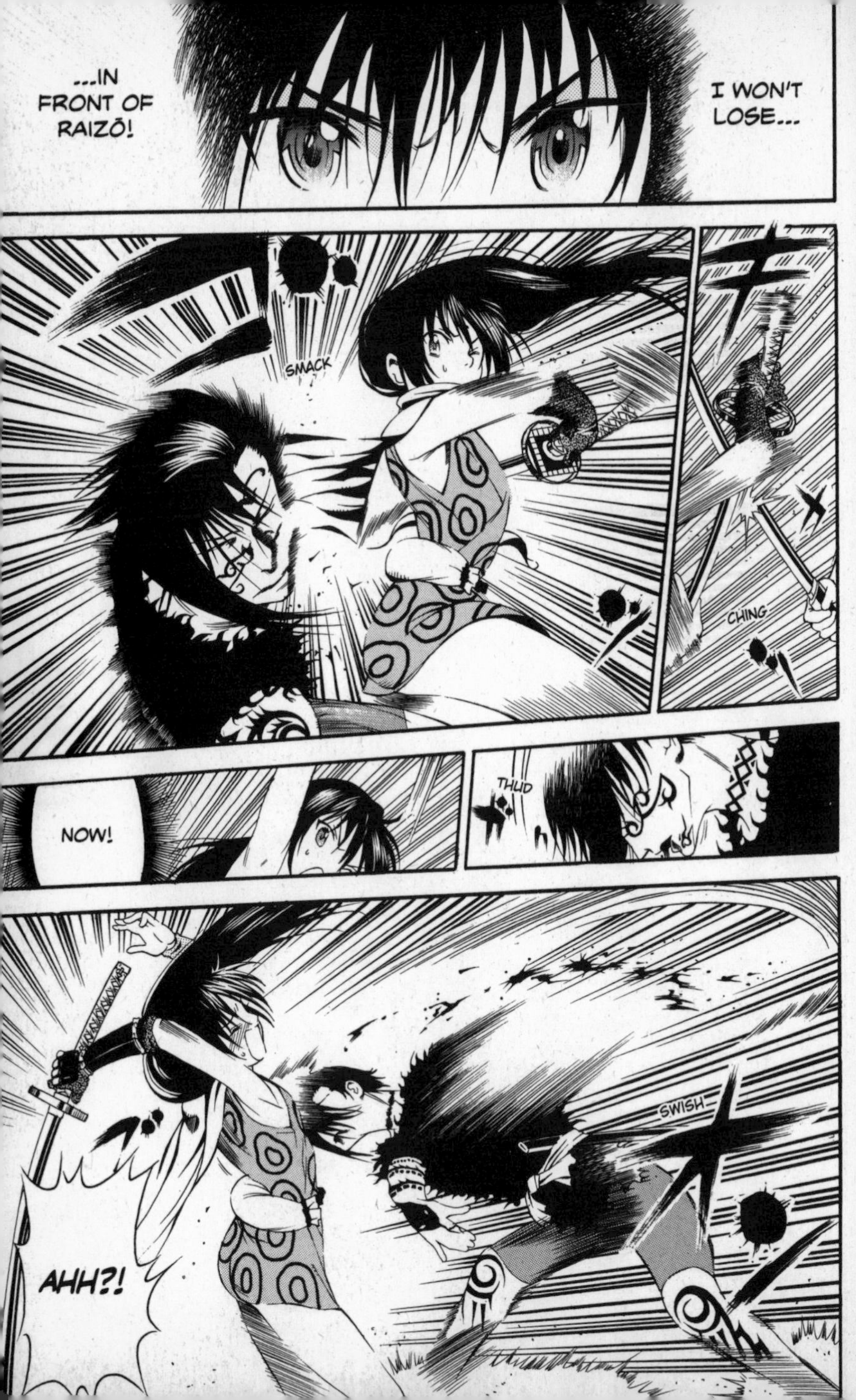
I WON'T LOSE...
...IN FRONT OF RAIZŌ!
CHING
SMACK
THUD
NOW!
SWISH
AHH?!

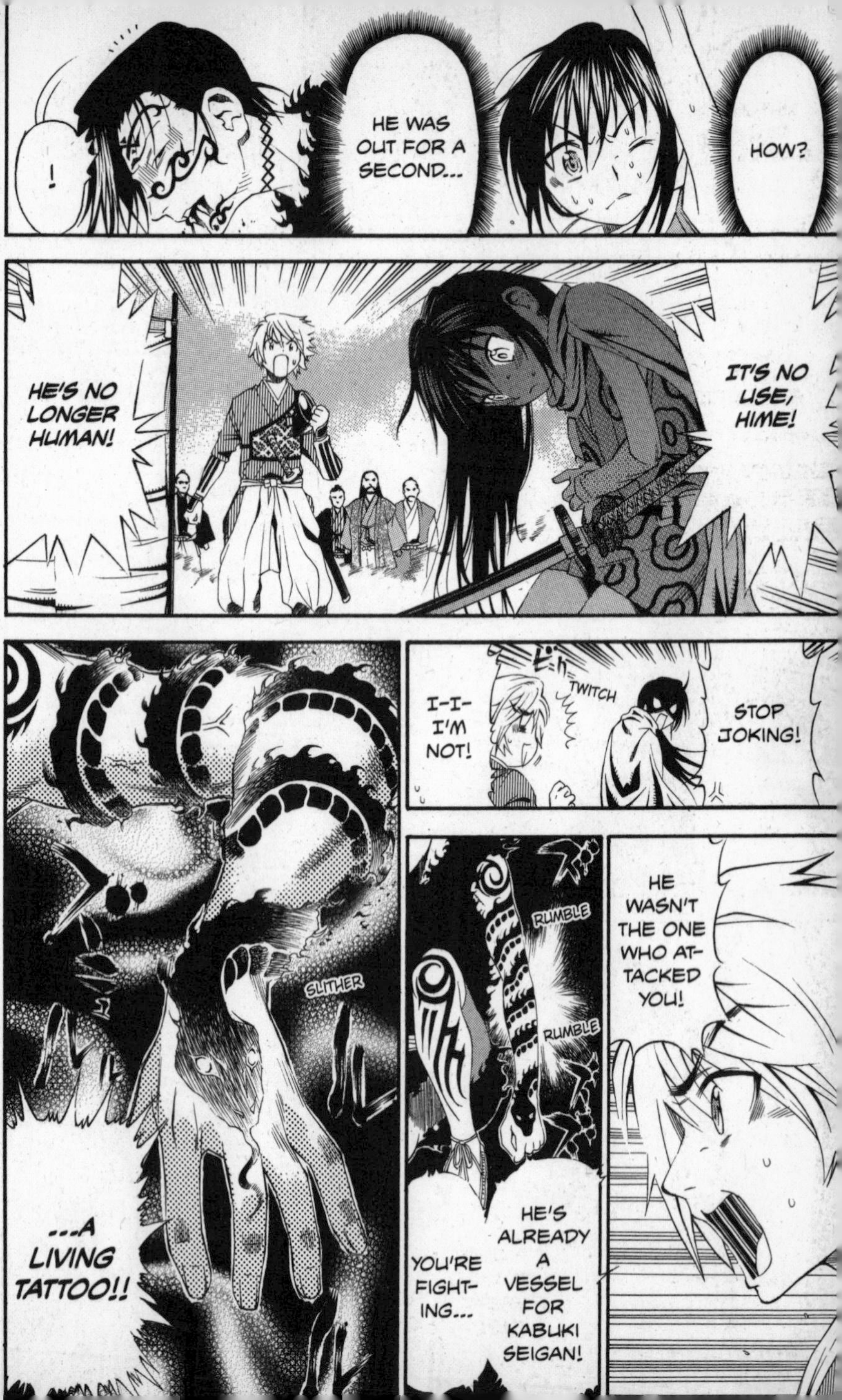
HOW?
HE WAS OUT FOR A SECOND...
!
IT'S NO USE, HIME!
HE'S NO LONGER HUMAN!
STOP JOKING!
TWITCH
I-I-I'M NOT!
HE WASN'T THE ONE WHO AT-TACKED YOU!
RUMBLE
RUMBLE
HE'S ALREADY A VESSEL FOR KABUKI SEIGAN!
YOU'RE FIGHT-ING...
SLITHER
...A LIVING TATTOO!!

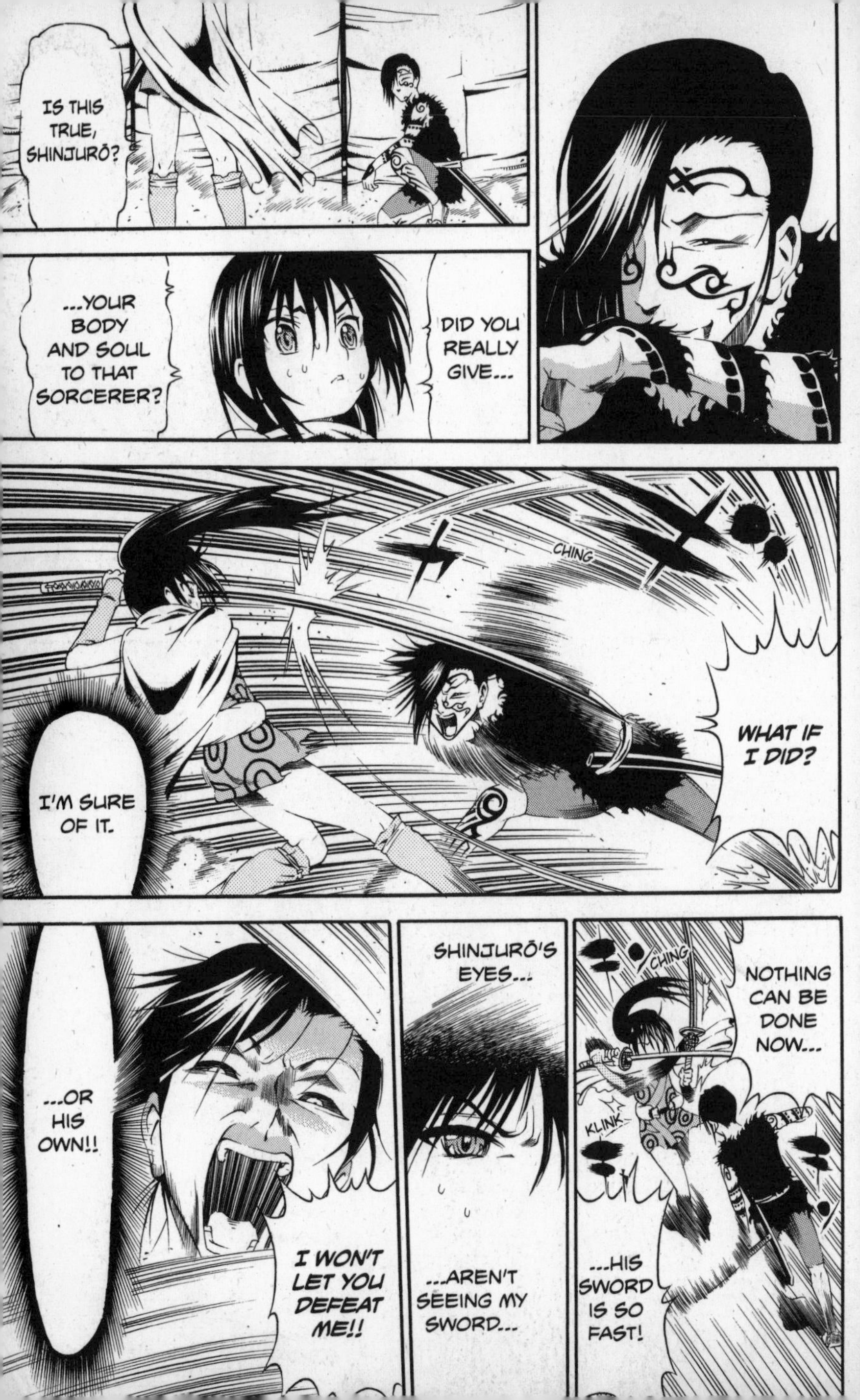
IS THIS TRUE, SHINJURŌ?
DID YOU REALLY GIVE...
...YOUR BODY AND SOUL TO THAT SORCERER?
CHING
WHAT IF I DID?
I'M SURE OF IT.
CHING
NOTHING CAN BE DONE NOW...
KLINK
...HIS SWORD IS SO FAST!
SHINJURŌ'S EYES...
...AREN'T SEEING MY SWORD...
...OR HIS OWN!!
I WON'T LET YOU DEFEAT ME!!

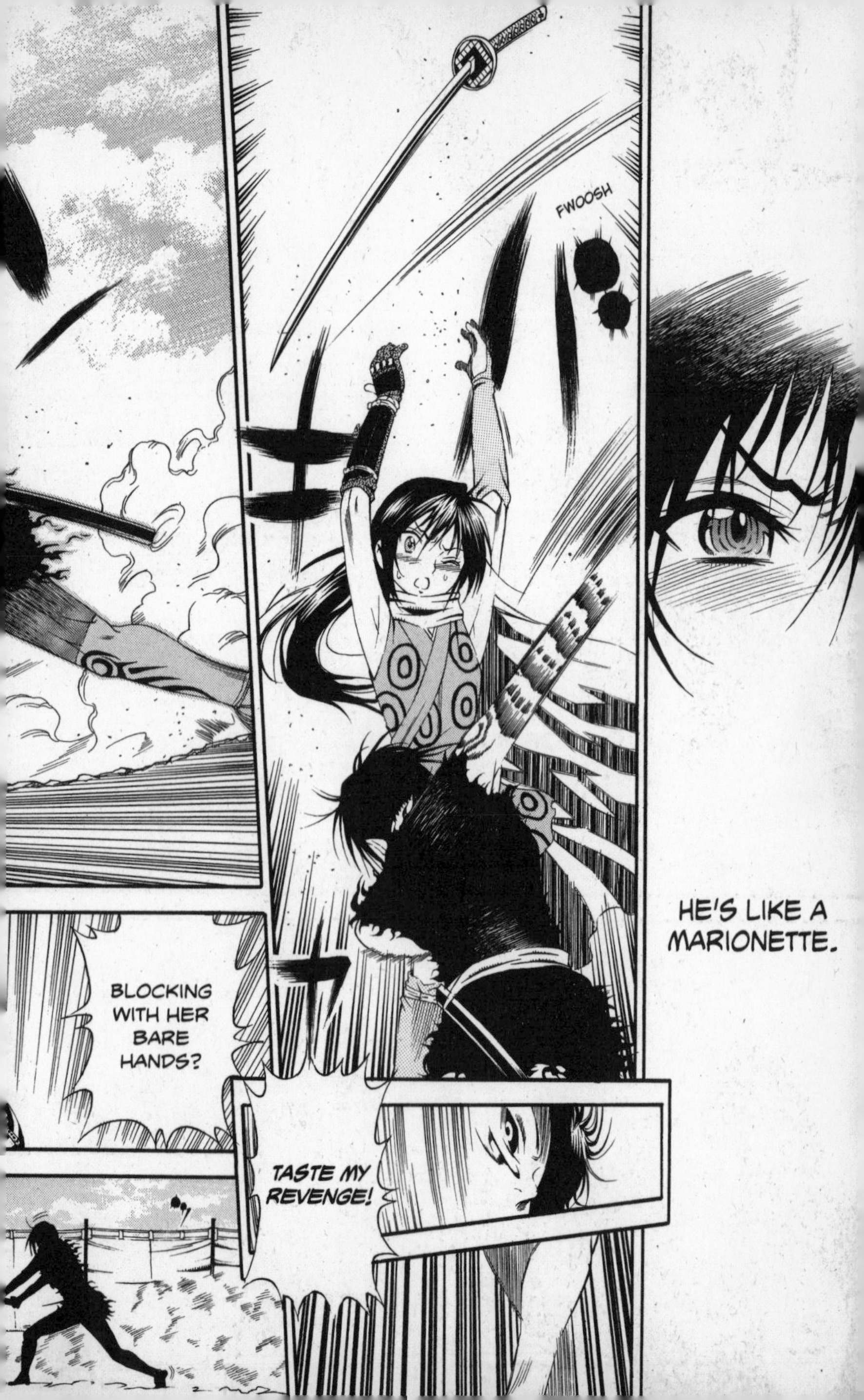
HE'S LIKE A MARIONETTE.
FWOOSH
BLOCKING WITH HER BARE HANDS?
TASTE MY REVENGE!

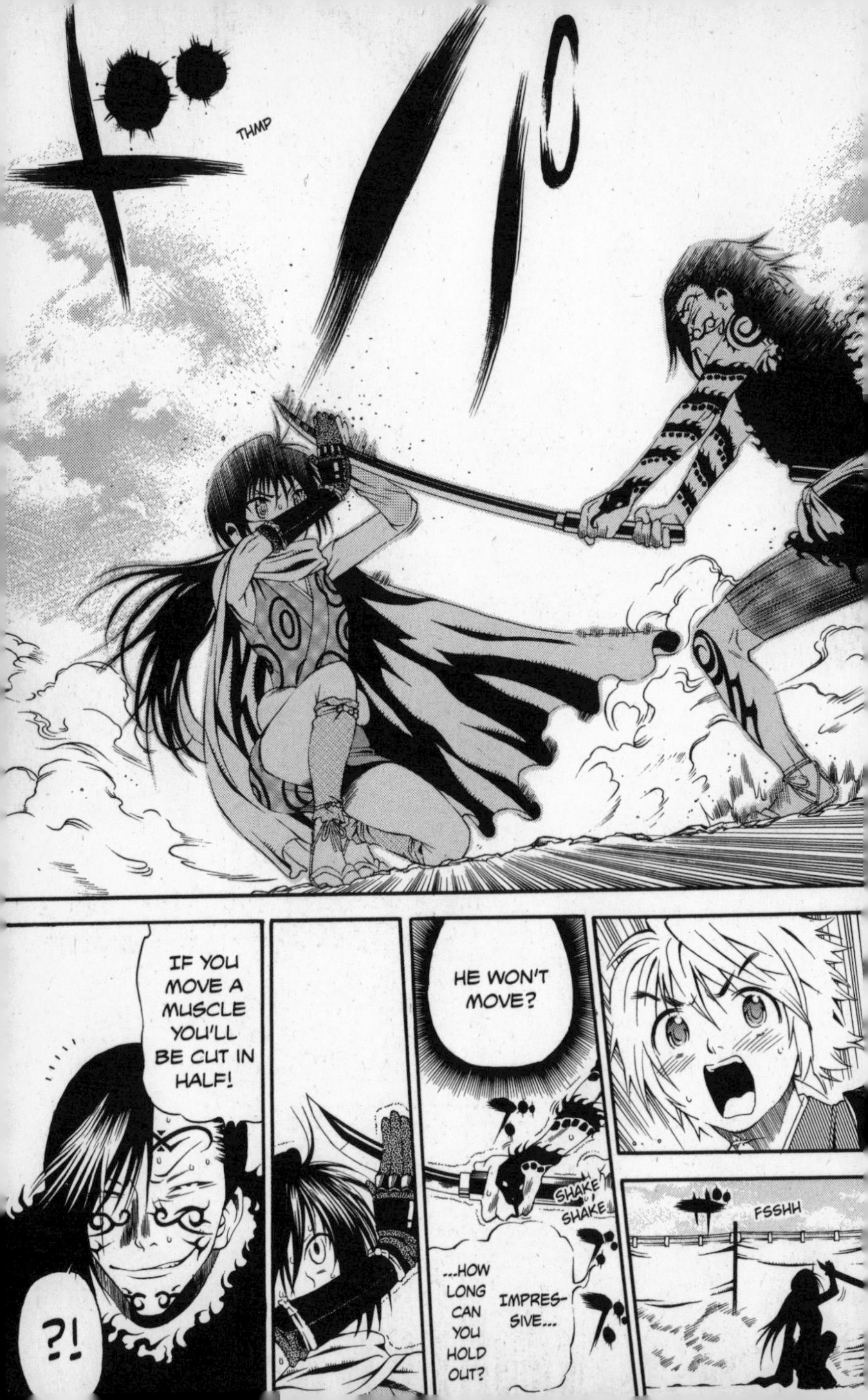
THMP
FSSHH
HE WON'T MOVE?
SHAKE SHAKE
IMPRES-SIVE...
...HOW LONG CAN YOU HOLD OUT?
IF YOU MOVE A MUSCLE YOU'LL BE CUT IN HALF!
?!

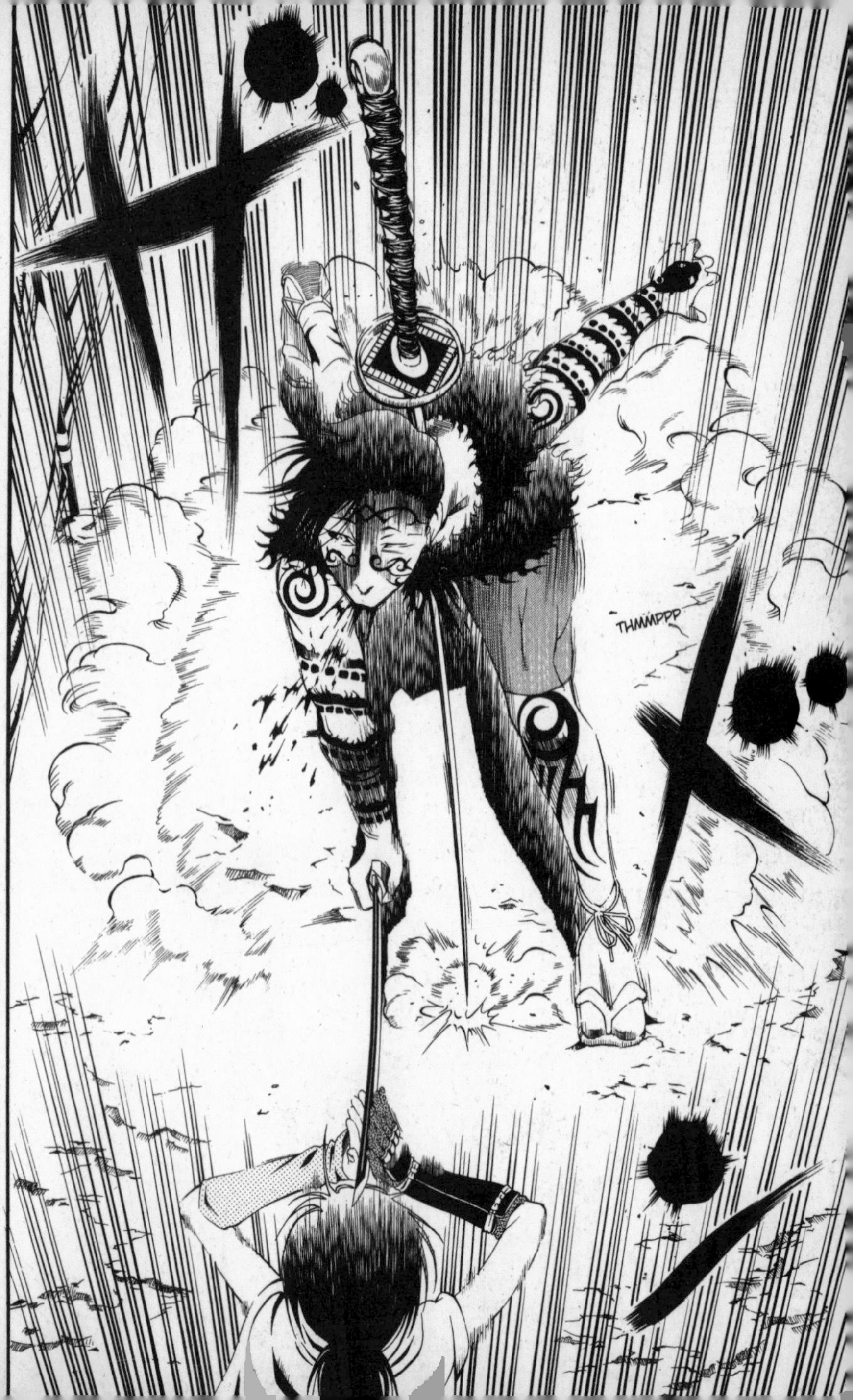
THMMPPP

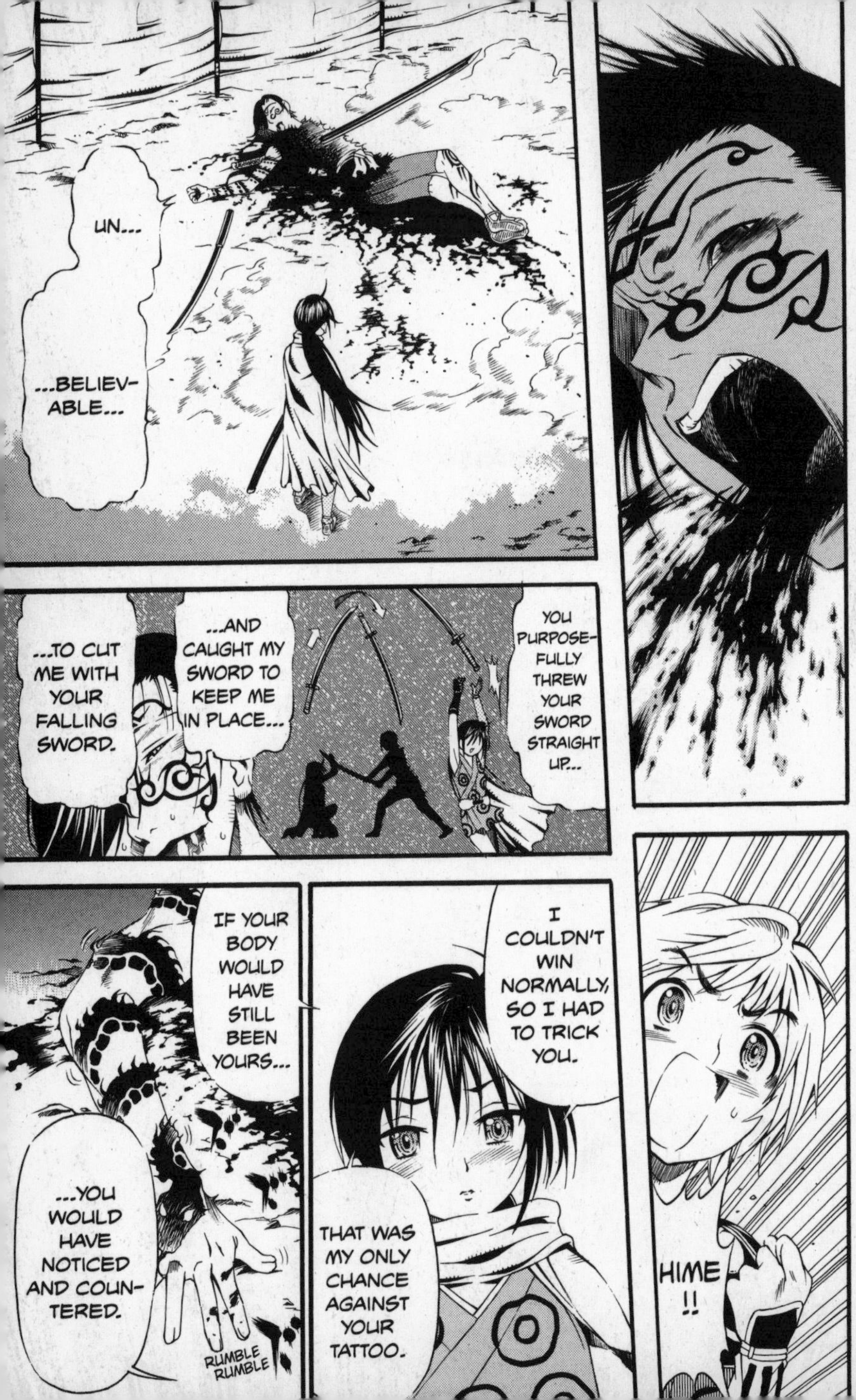
UN...
...BELIEV-ABLE...
YOU PURPOSE-FULLY THREW YOUR SWORD STRAIGHT UP...
...AND CAUGHT MY SWORD TO KEEP ME IN PLACE...
...TO CUT ME WITH YOUR FALLING SWORD.
HIME!!
I COULDN'T WIN NORMALLY, SO I HAD TO TRICK YOU.
THAT WAS MY ONLY CHANCE AGAINST YOUR TATTOO.
IF YOUR BODY WOULD HAVE STILL BEEN YOURS...
...YOU WOULD HAVE NOTICED AND COUN-TERED.
RUMBLE RUMBLE

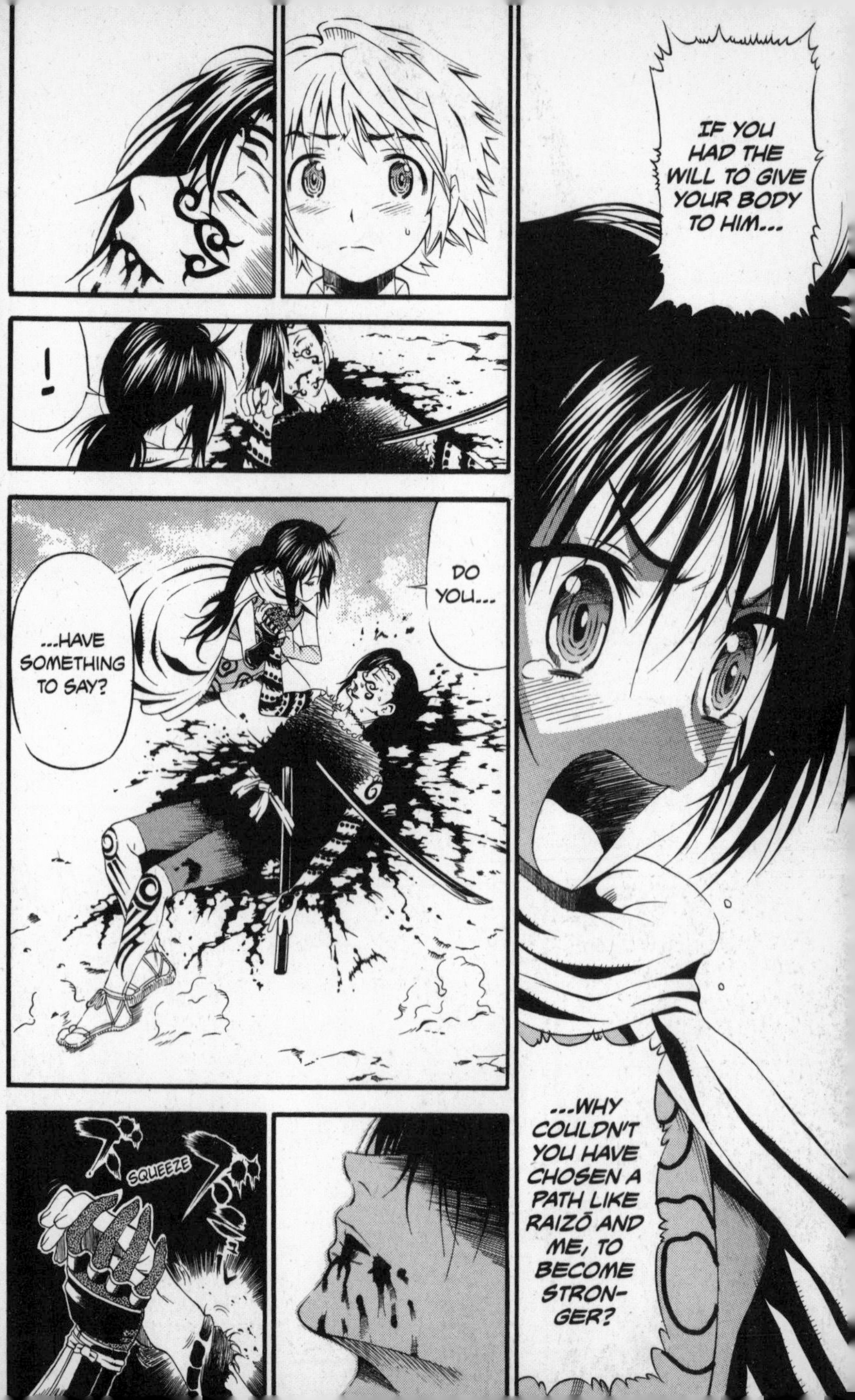
IF YOU HAD THE WILL TO GIVE YOUR BODY TO HIM...
...WHY COULDN'T YOU HAVE CHOSEN A PATH LIKE RAIZŌ AND ME, TO BECOME STRONGER?
!
DO YOU...
...HAVE SOMETHING TO SAY?
SQUEEZE

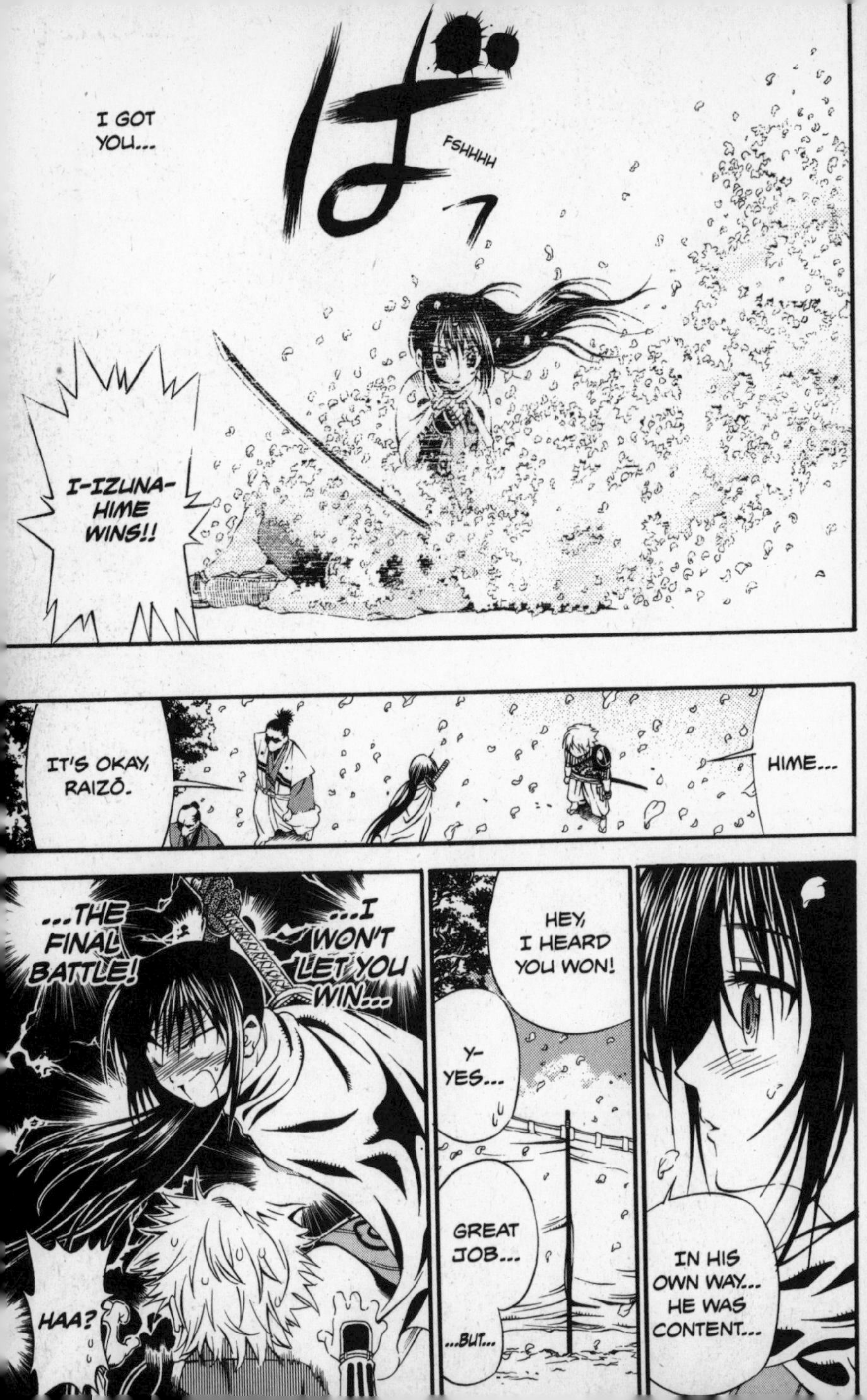
ぱっ
FSHHHH
I GOT YOU...
I-IZUNA-HIME WINS!!
HIME...
IT'S OKAY, RAIZŌ.
IN HIS OWN WAY... HE WAS CONTENT...
HEY, I HEARD YOU WON!
Y-YES...
GREAT JOB...
...BUT...
...I WON'T LET YOU WIN...
...THE FINAL BATTLE!
HAA?

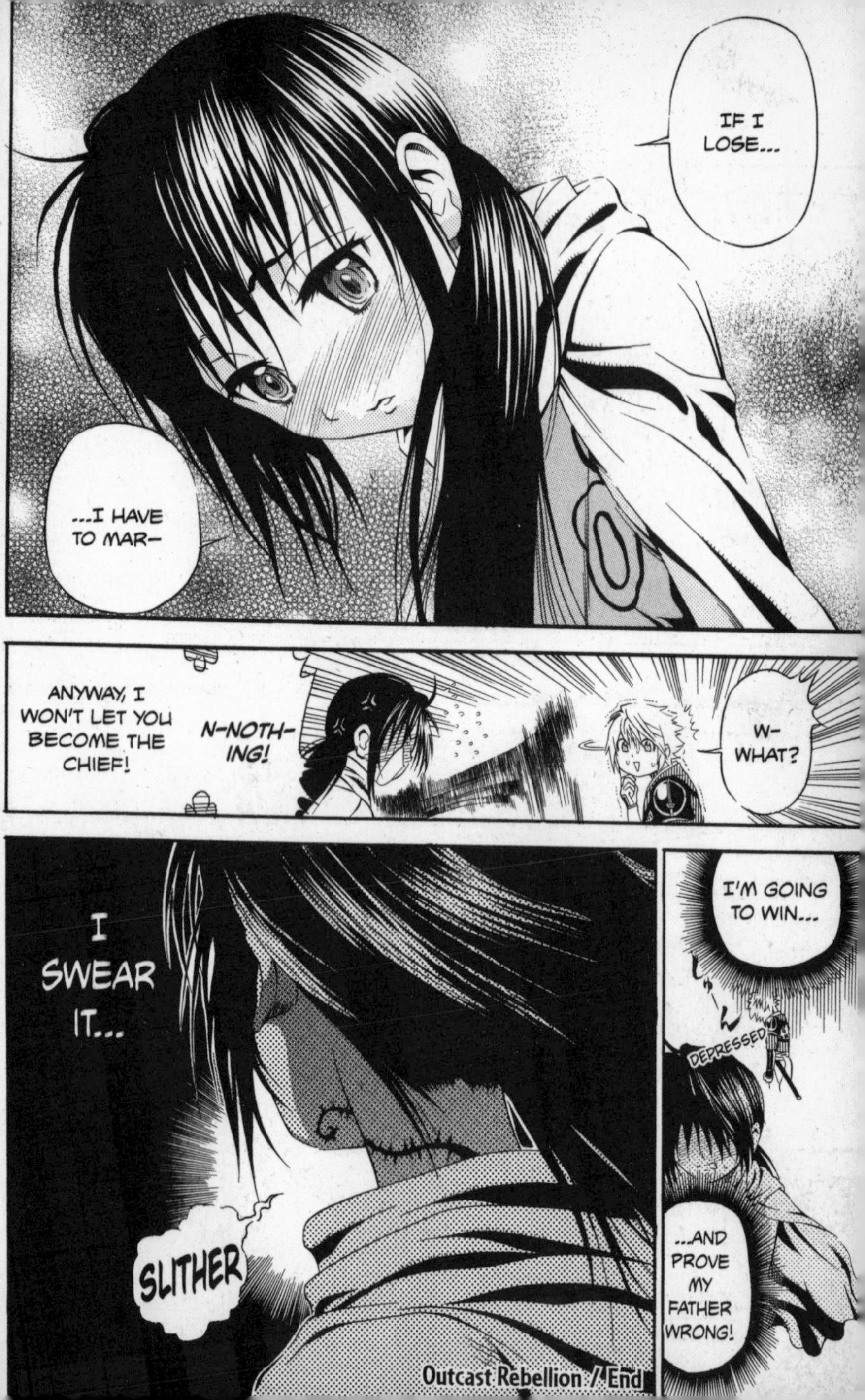
IF I LOSE...
...I HAVE TO MAR—
W-WHAT?
N-NOTHING!
ANYWAY, I WON'T LET YOU BECOME THE CHIEF!
I'M GOING TO WIN...
じゅ〜ん
DEPRESSED
...AND PROVE MY FATHER WRONG!
I SWEAR IT...
SLITHER
Outcast Rebellion / End

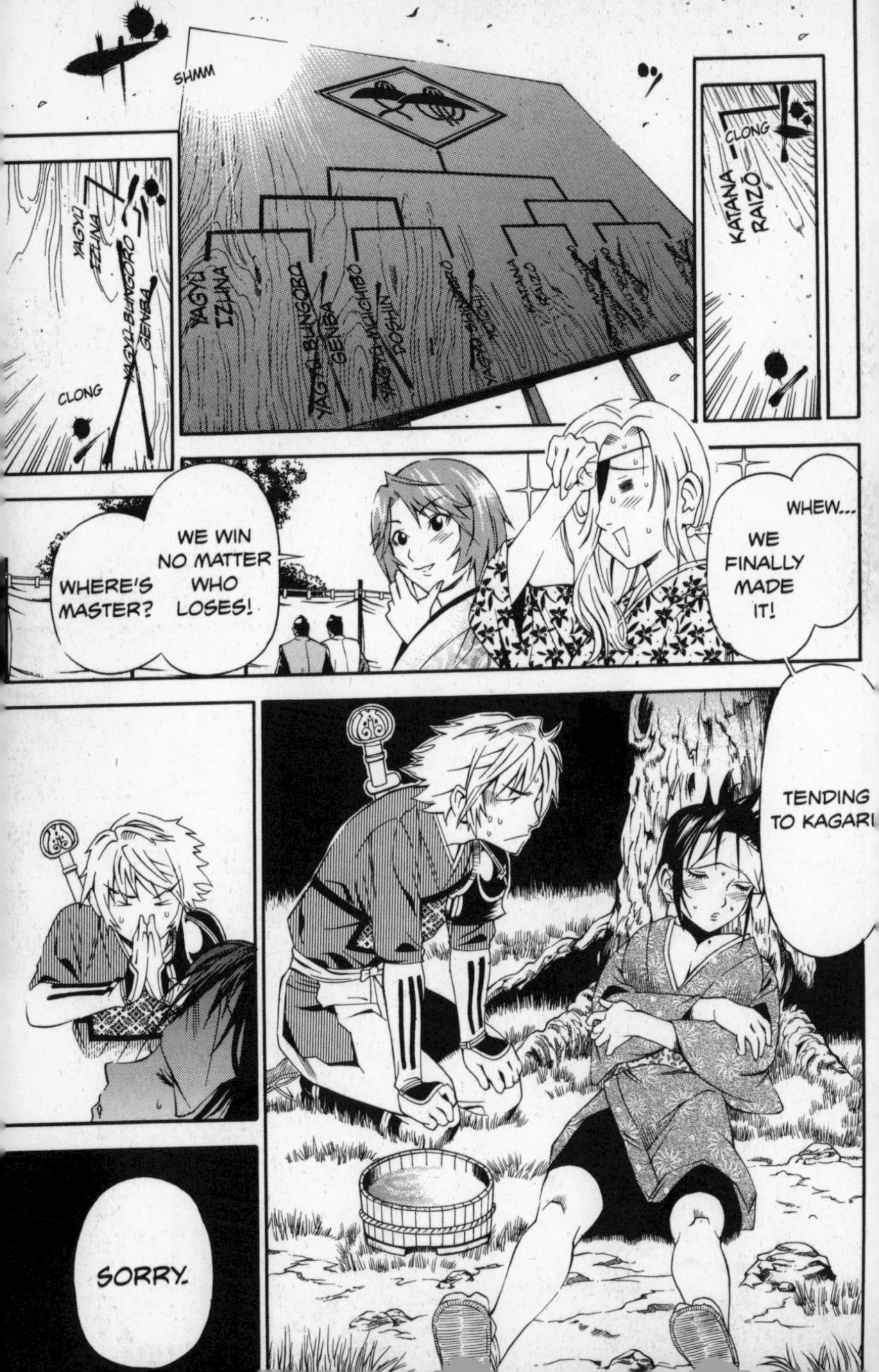
CLONG
KATANA RAIZŌ
SHMM
YAGYŪ IZUNA
YAGYŪ BUNGORO GENBA
CLONG
WHEW... WE FINALLY MADE IT!
WE WIN NO MATTER WHO LOSES!
WHERE'S MASTER?
TENDING TO KAGARI
SORRY.

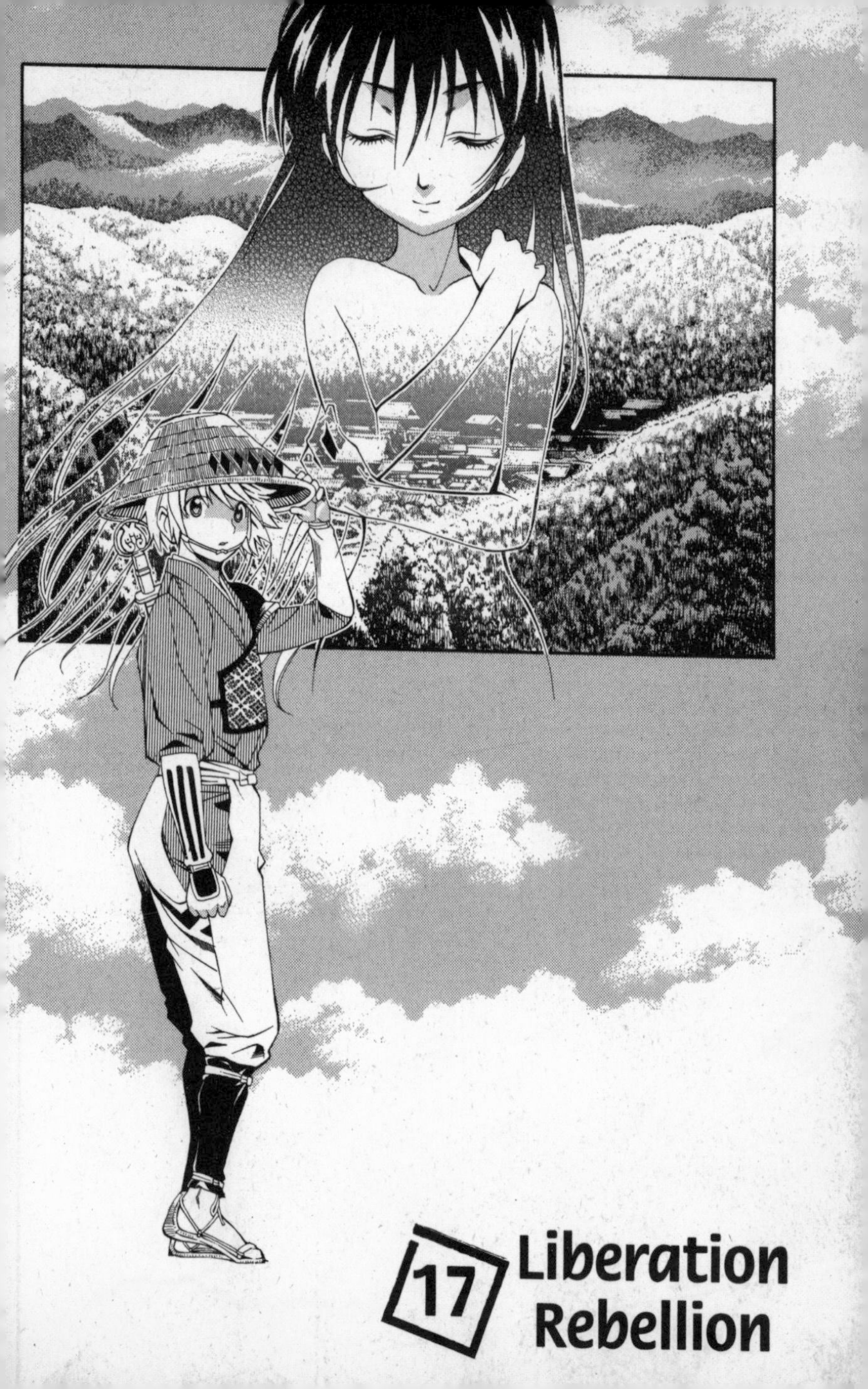
17
Liberation Rebellion

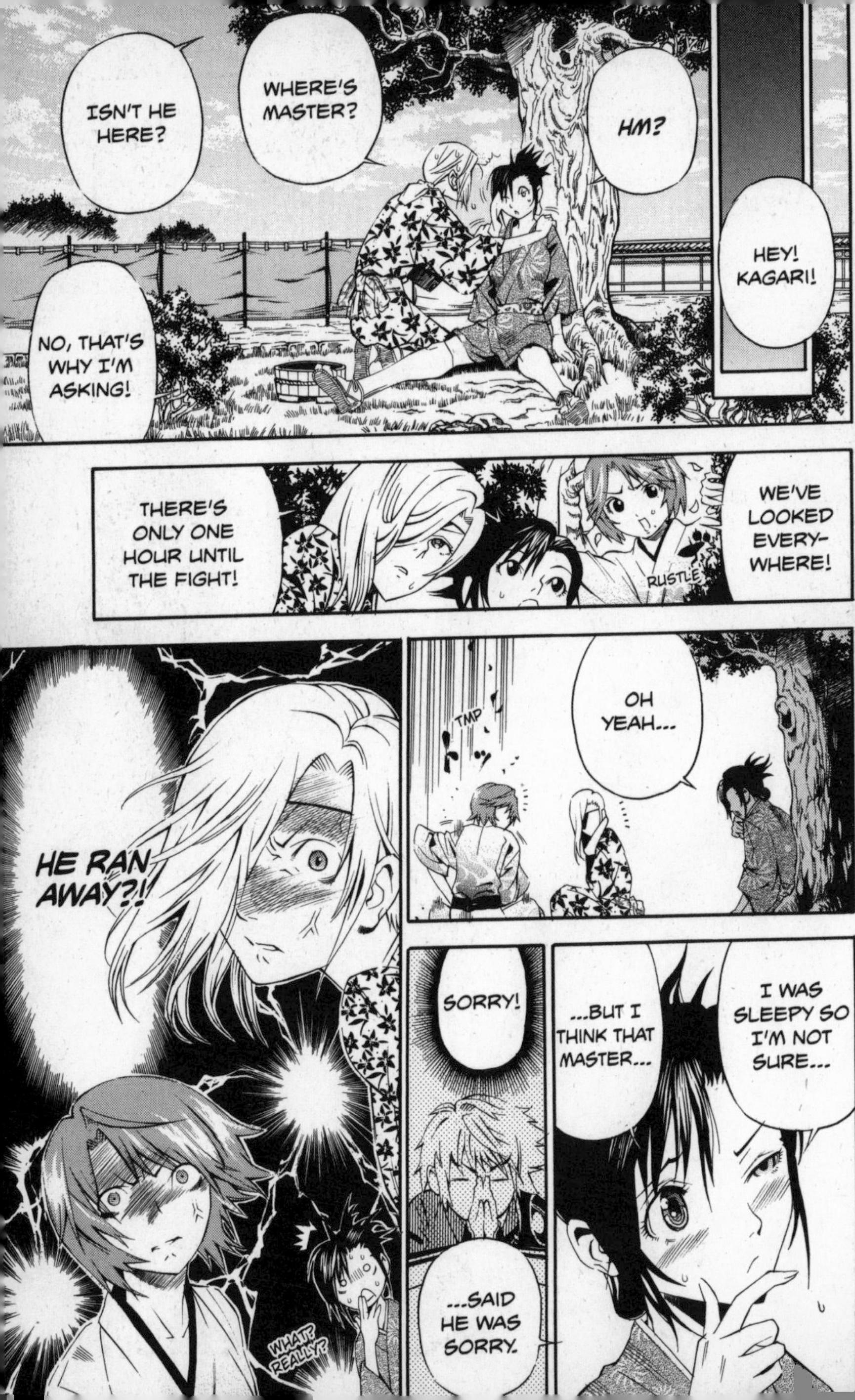
HEY! KAGARI!
HM?
WHERE'S MASTER?
ISN'T HE HERE?
NO, THAT'S WHY I'M ASKING!
WE'VE LOOKED EVERYWHERE!
RUSTLE
THERE'S ONLY ONE HOUR UNTIL THE FIGHT!
TMP
OH YEAH...
I WAS SLEEPY SO I'M NOT SURE...
...BUT I THINK THAT MASTER...
SORRY!
...SAID HE WAS SORRY.
HE RAN AWAY?!
WHAT? REALLY?

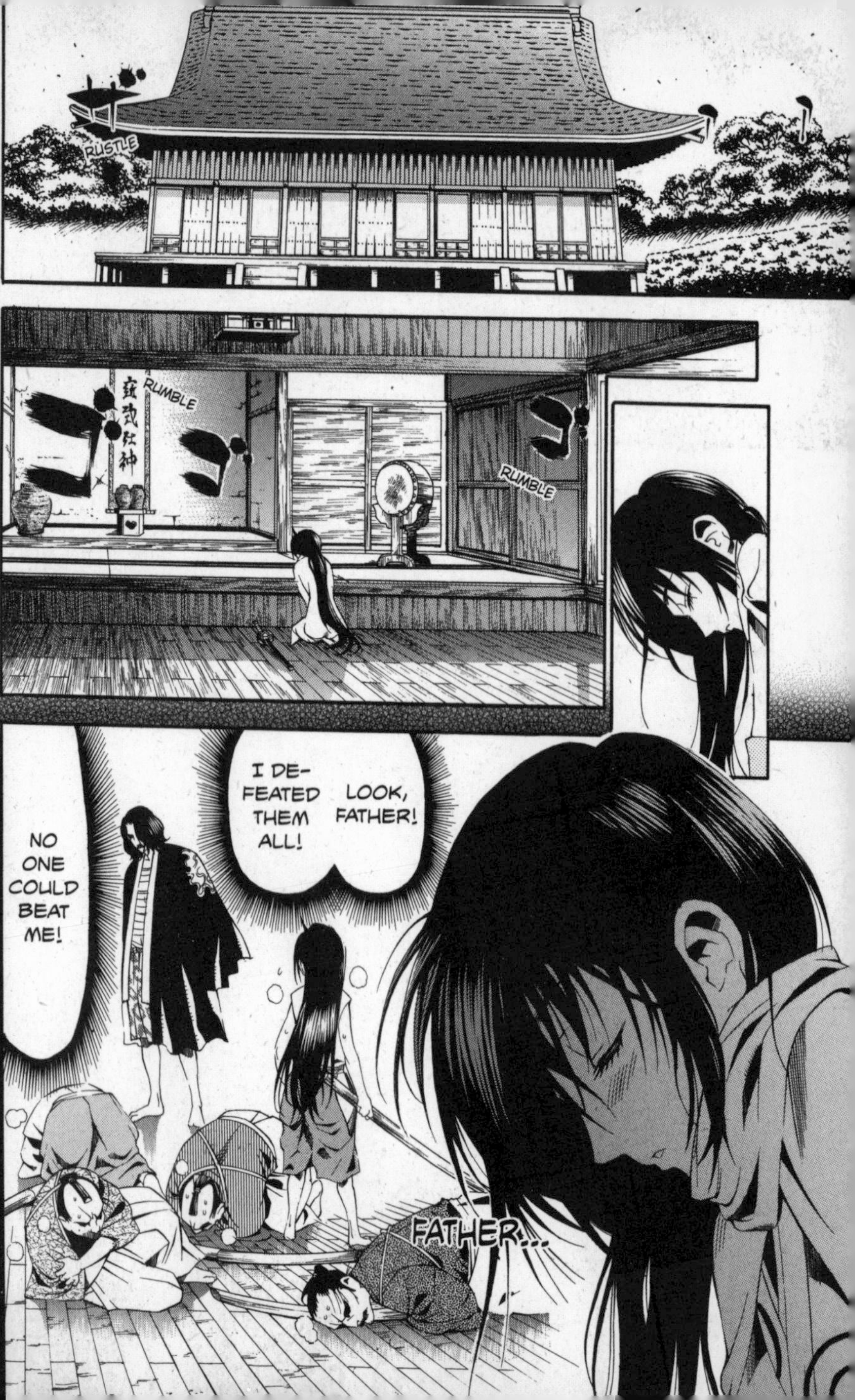
RUSTLE
RUMBLE
RUMBLE
LOOK, FATHER!
I DE-FEATED THEM ALL!
NO ONE COULD BEAT ME!
FATHER...

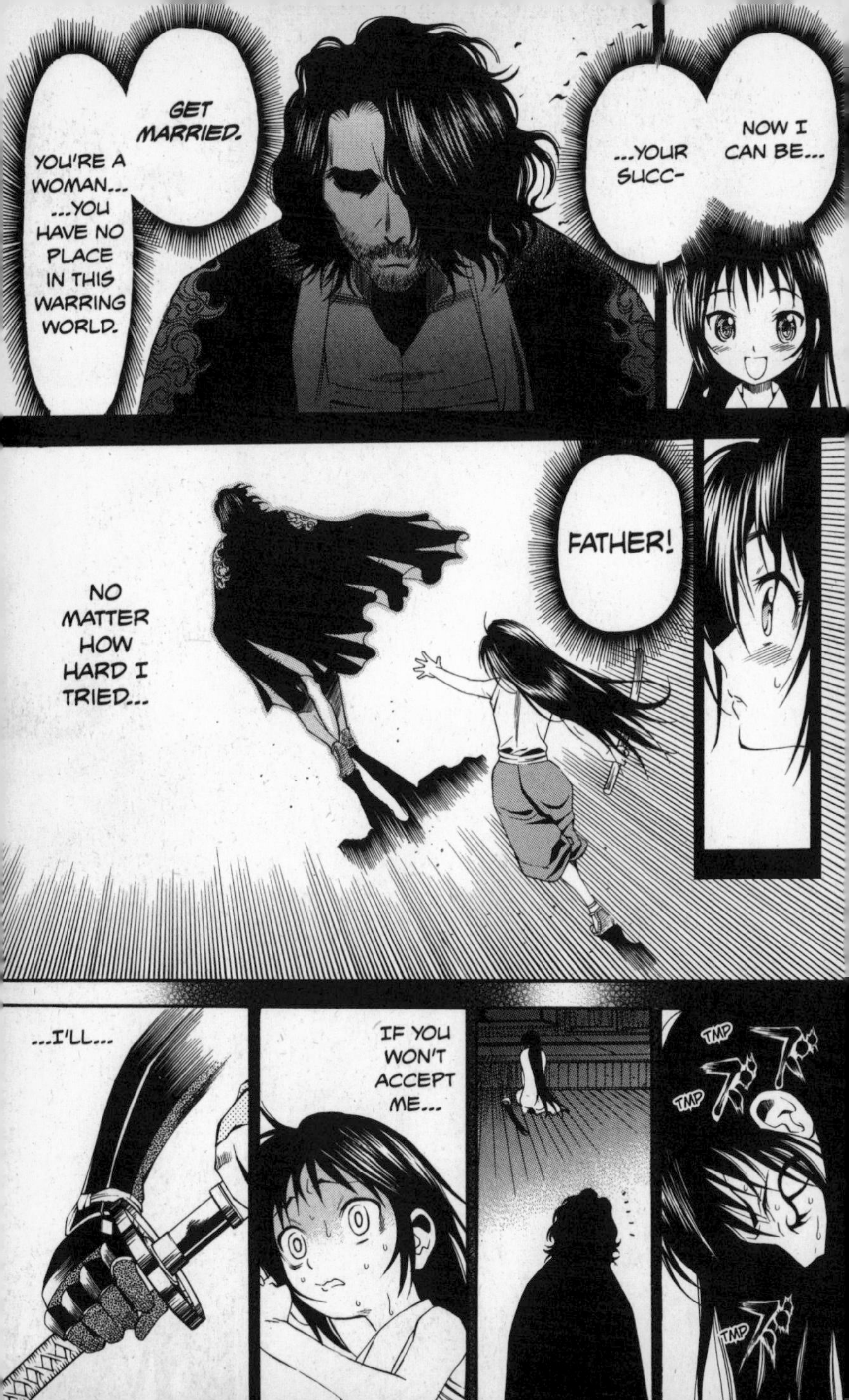
NOW I CAN BE...
...YOUR SUCC-
GET MARRIED.
YOU'RE A WOMAN...
...YOU HAVE NO PLACE IN THIS WARRING WORLD.
FATHER!
NO MATTER HOW HARD I TRIED...
TMP
TMP
TMP
IF YOU WON'T ACCEPT ME...
...I'LL...

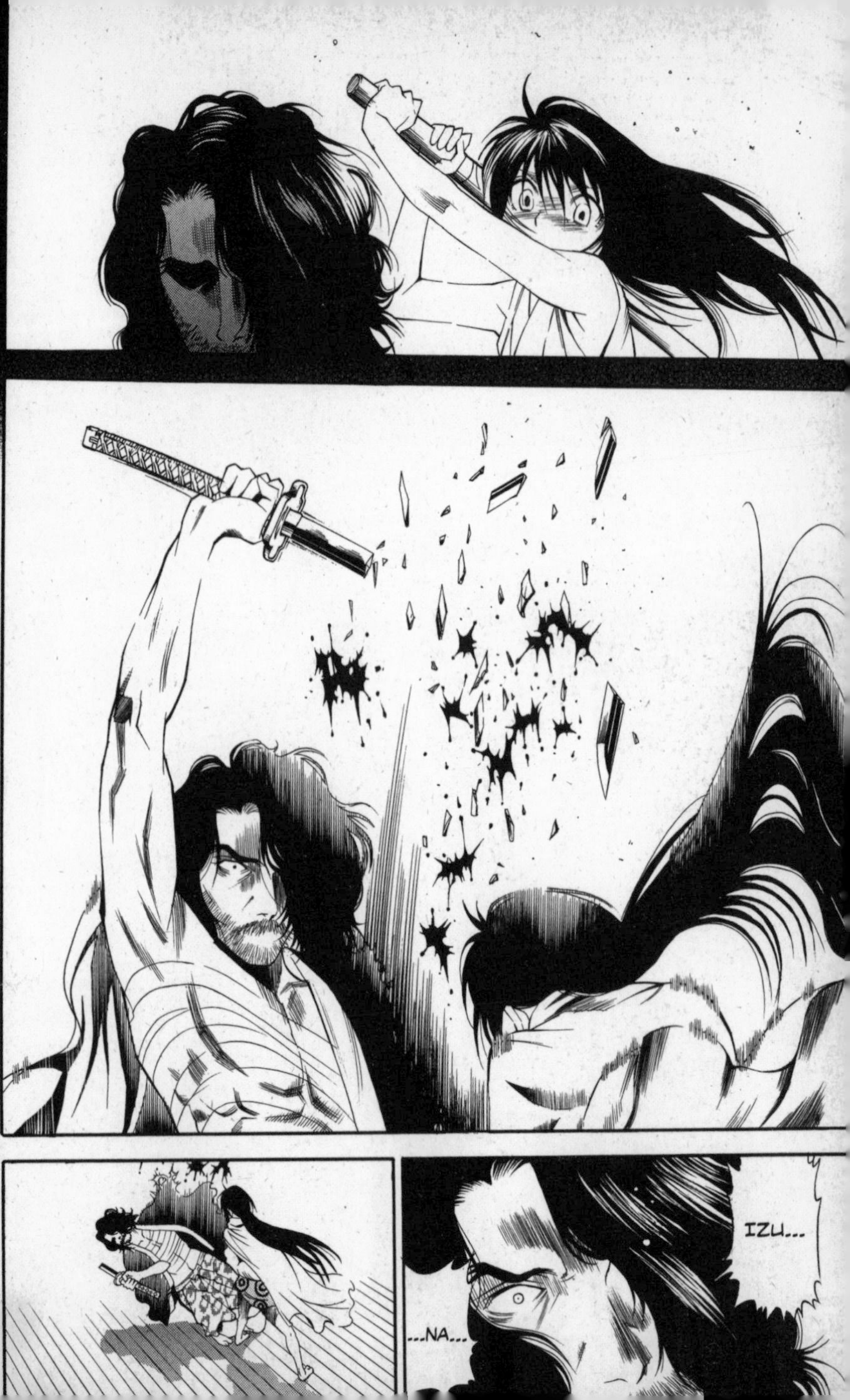
IZU...
...NA...

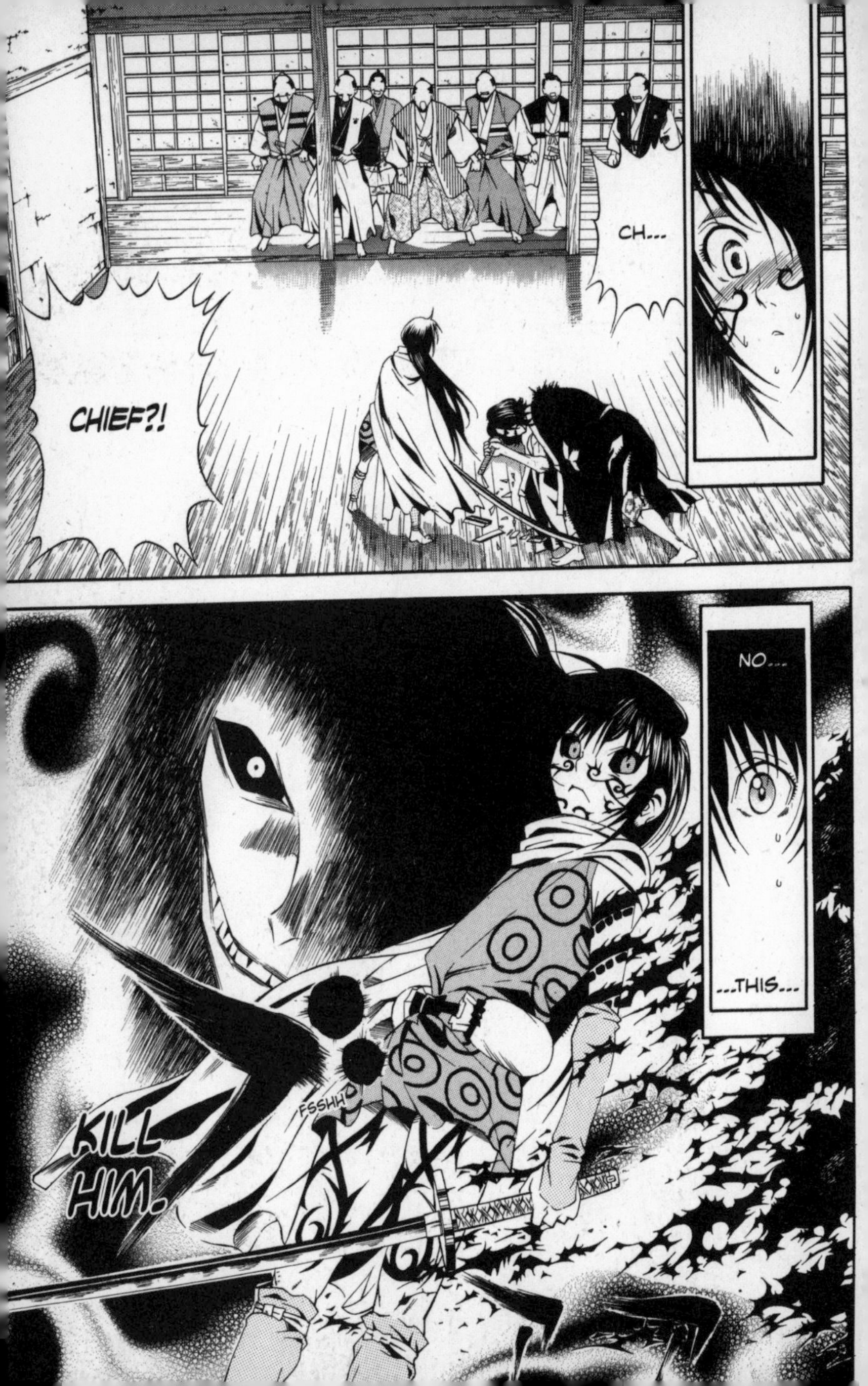
CH...
CHIEF?!
NO...
...THIS...
FSSHH
KILL HIM.

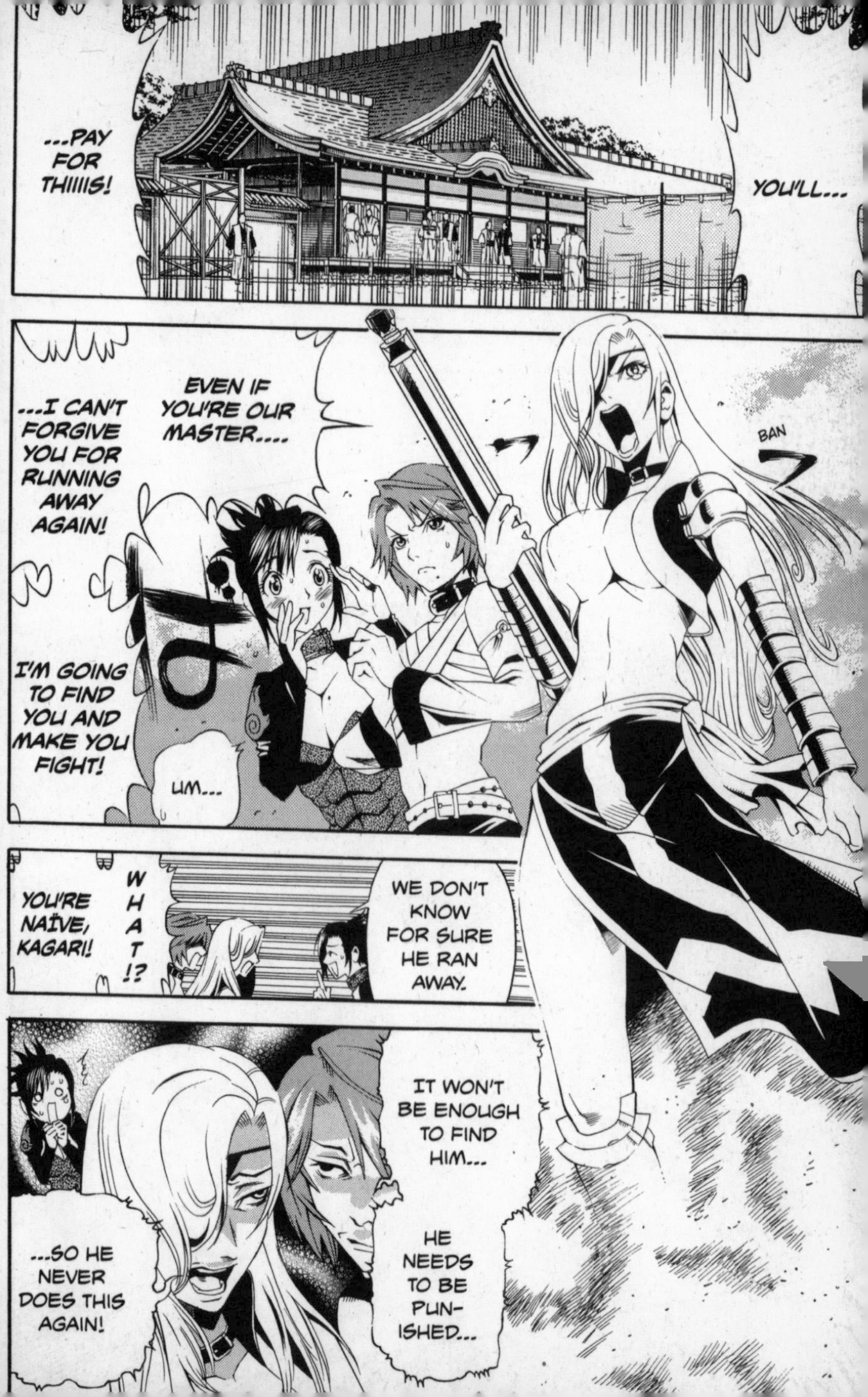
YOU'LL...
...PAY FOR THIIIIS!
BAN
EVEN IF YOU'RE OUR MASTER....
...I CAN'T FORGIVE YOU FOR RUNNING AWAY AGAIN!
I'M GOING TO FIND YOU AND MAKE YOU FIGHT!
UM...
WE DON'T KNOW FOR SURE HE RAN AWAY.
WHAT!?
YOU'RE NAÏVE, KAGARI!
IT WON'T BE ENOUGH TO FIND HIM...
HE NEEDS TO BE PUN-ISHED...
...SO HE NEVER DOES THIS AGAIN!

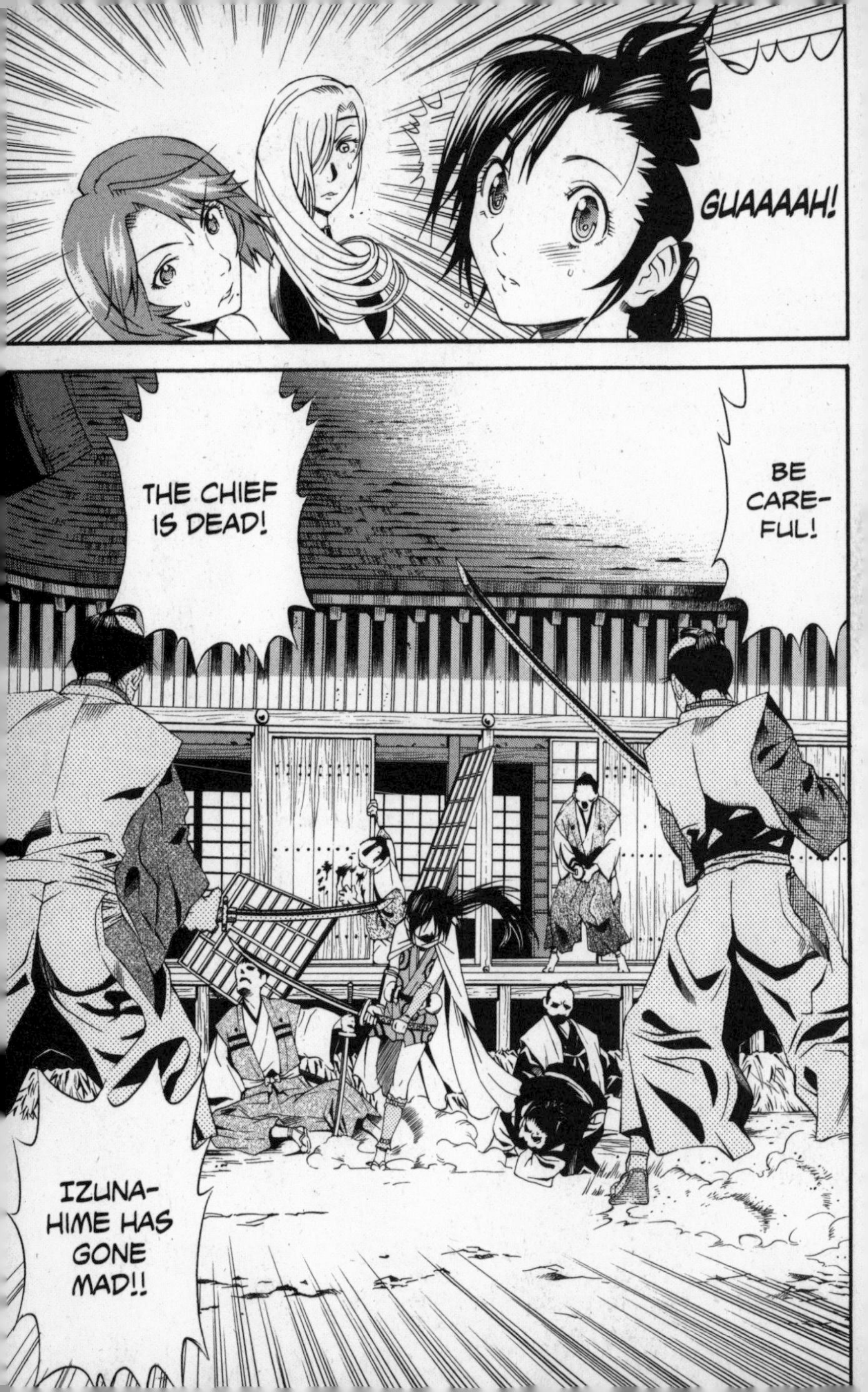
GUAAAAH!
BE CARE-FUL!
THE CHIEF IS DEAD!
IZUNA-HIME HAS GONE MAD!!

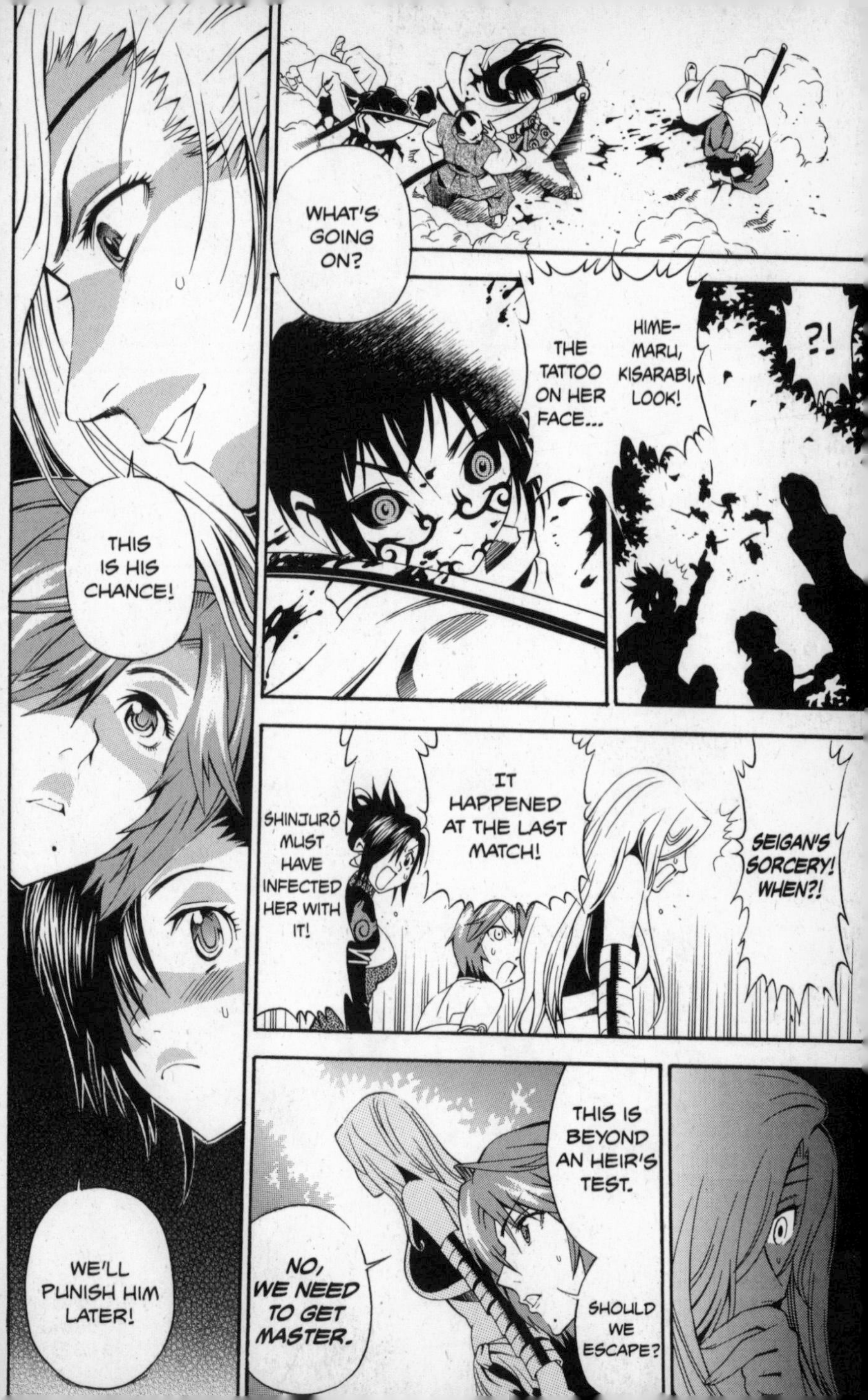
WHAT'S GOING ON?
?!
HIME-MARU, KISARABI, LOOK!
THE TATTOO ON HER FACE...
SEIGAN'S SORCERY! WHEN?!
IT HAPPENED AT THE LAST MATCH!
SHINJURŌ MUST HAVE INFECTED HER WITH IT!
THIS IS BEYOND AN HEIR'S TEST.
SHOULD WE ESCAPE?
NO, WE NEED TO GET MASTER.
THIS IS HIS CHANCE!
WE'LL PUNISH HIM LATER!

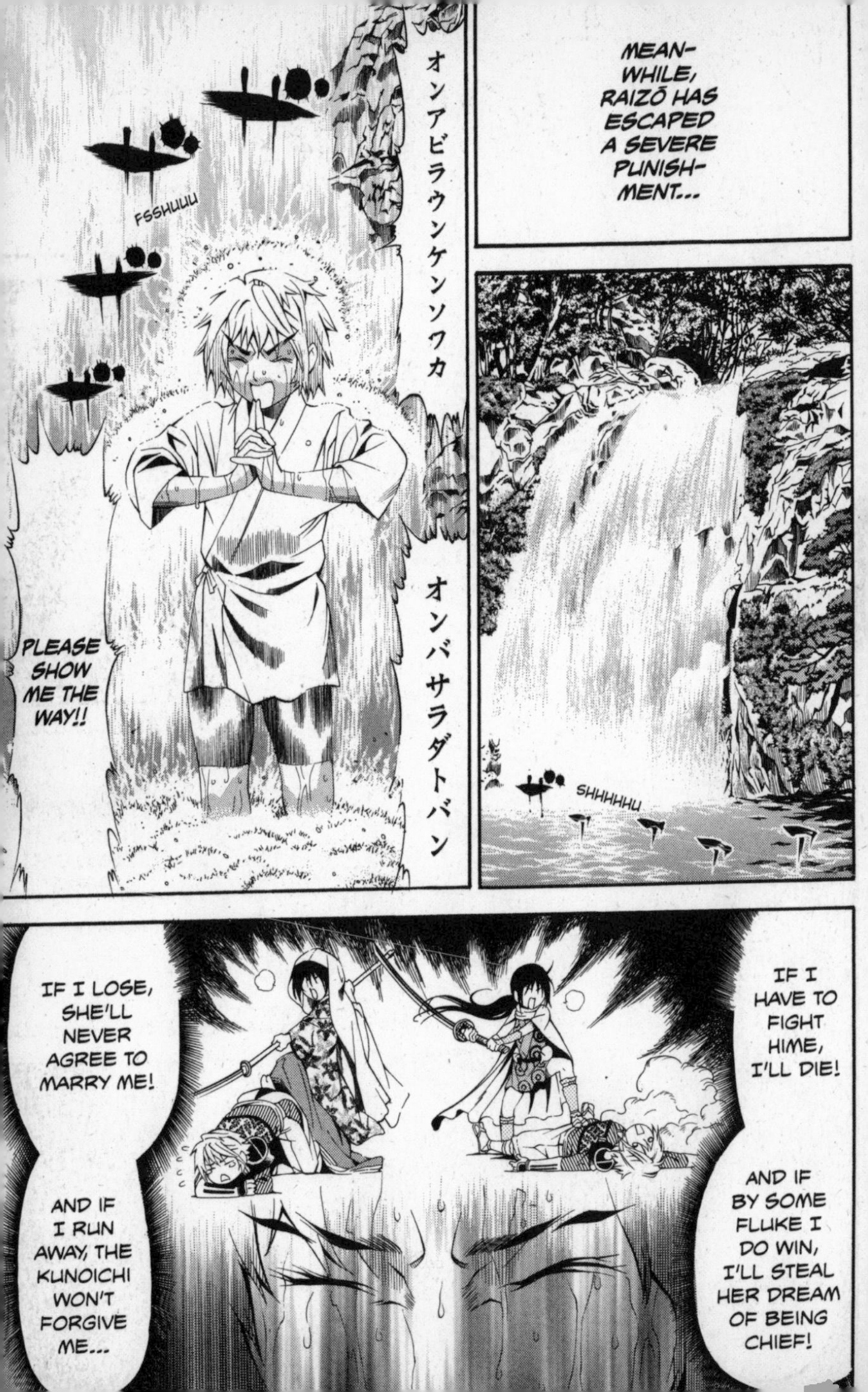
MEAN-WHILE, RAIZŌ HAS ESCAPED A SEVERE PUNISHMENT...
SHHHHHU
オンアビラウンケンソワカ
オンバサラダトバン
FSSHUUU
PLEASE SHOW ME THE WAY!!
IF I HAVE TO FIGHT HIME, I'LL DIE!
IF I LOSE, SHE'LL NEVER AGREE TO MARRY ME!
AND IF BY SOME FLUKE I DO WIN, I'LL STEAL HER DREAM OF BEING CHIEF!
AND IF I RUN AWAY, THE KUNOICHI WON'T FORGIVE ME...

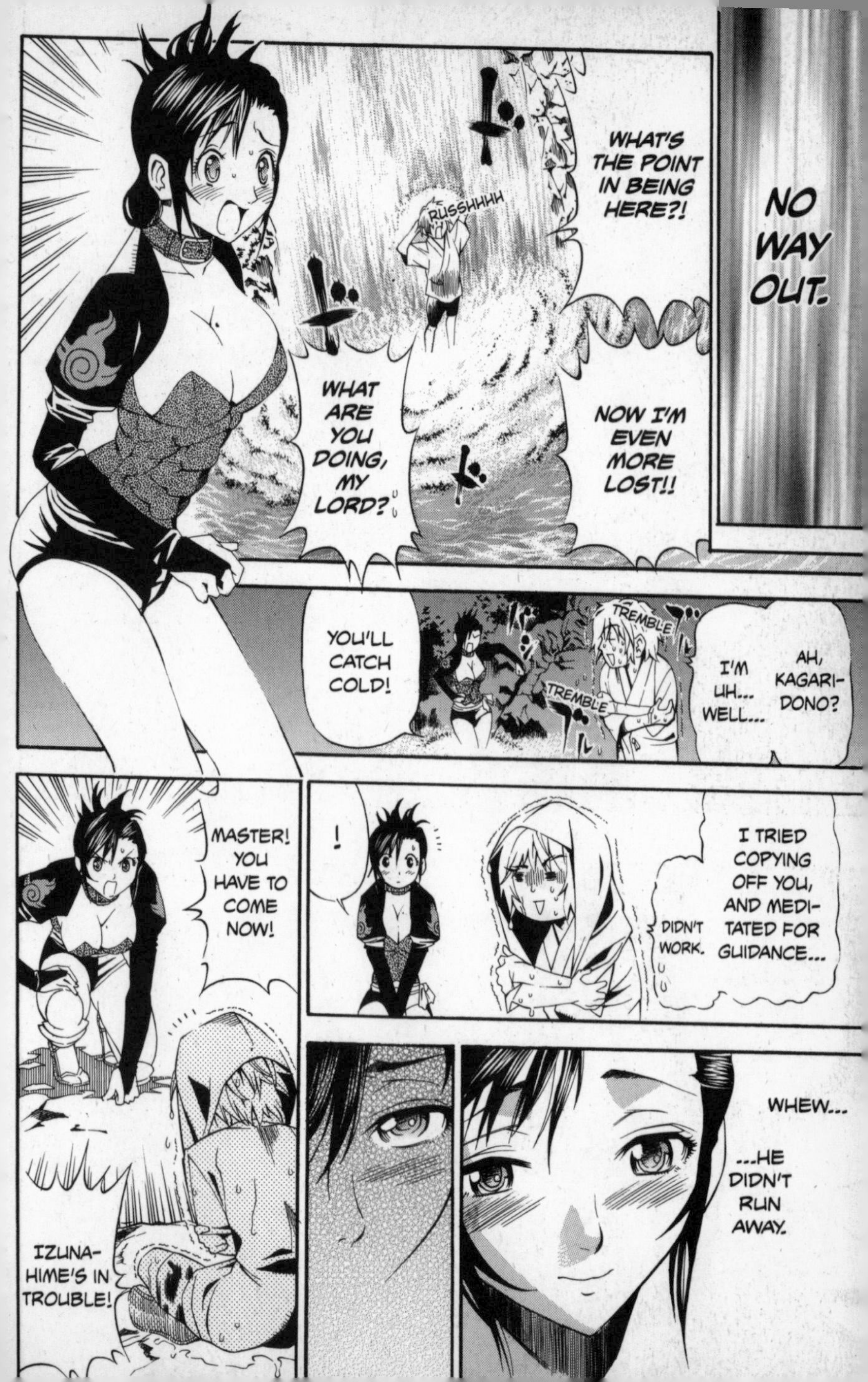
NO WAY OUT.
WHAT'S THE POINT IN BEING HERE?!
RUSSHHHH
NOW I'M EVEN MORE LOST!!
WHAT ARE YOU DOING, MY LORD?
AH, KAGARI-DONO?
I'M UH... WELL...
TREMBLE
TREMBLE
YOU'LL CATCH COLD!
I TRIED COPYING OFF YOU, AND MEDITATED FOR GUIDANCE...
DIDN'T WORK.
!
WHEW...
...HE DIDN'T RUN AWAY.
MASTER! YOU HAVE TO COME NOW!
IZUNA-HIME'S IN TROUBLE!

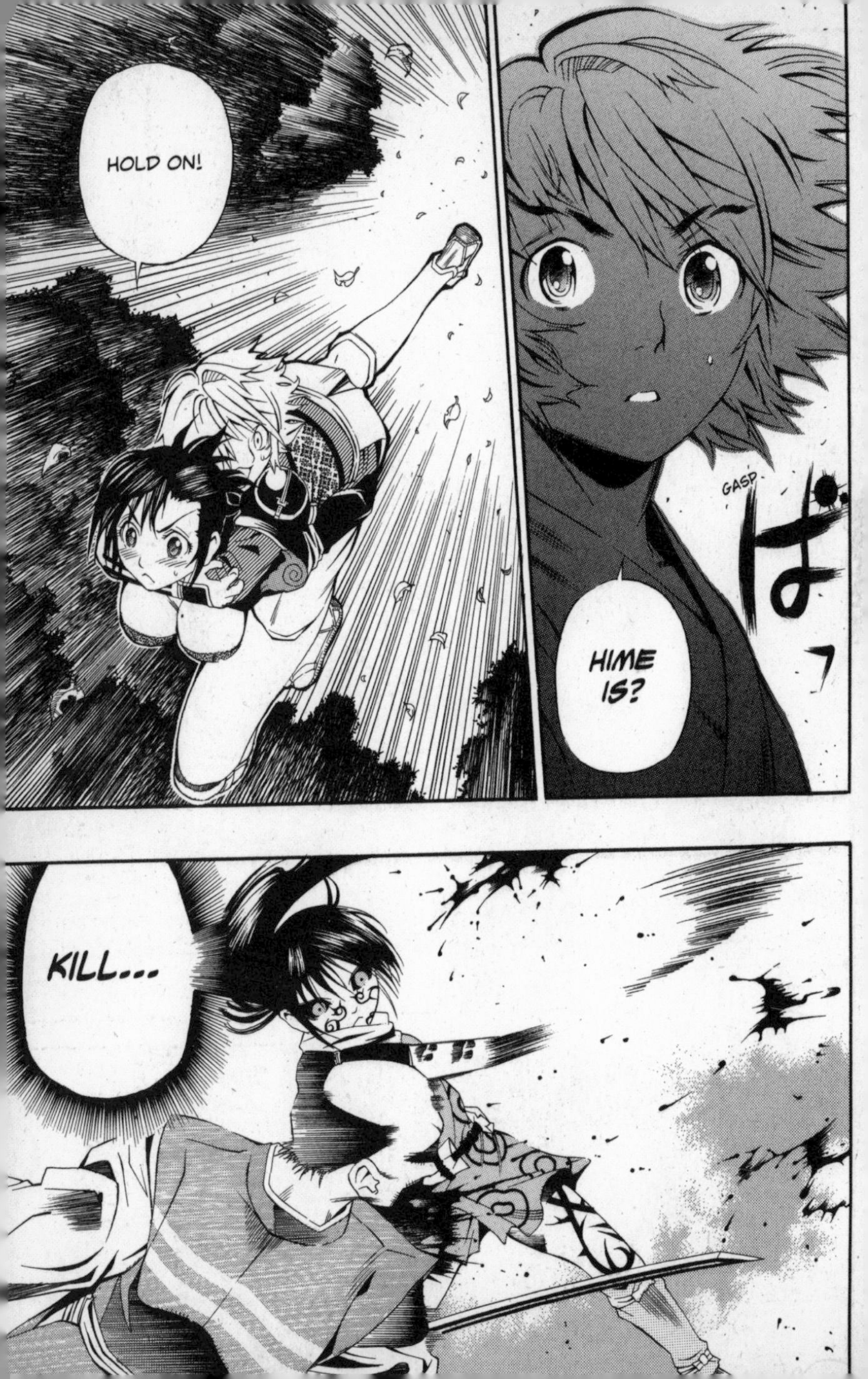
GASP
ぱっ
HIME IS?
HOLD ON!
KILL...

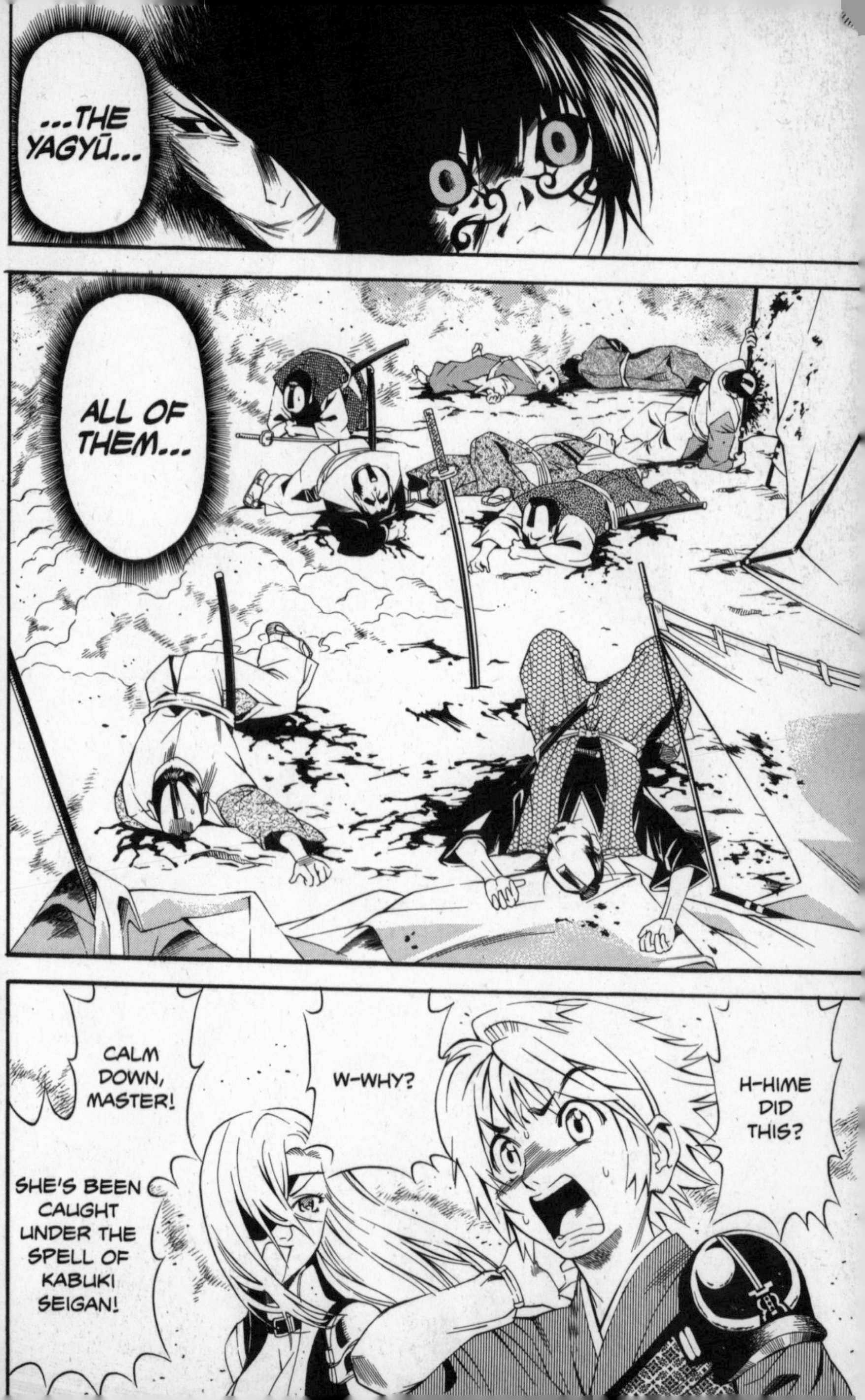
...THE YAGYŪ...
ALL OF THEM...
H-HIME DID THIS?
W-WHY?
CALM DOWN, MASTER!
SHE'S BEEN CAUGHT UNDER THE SPELL OF KABUKI SEIGAN!

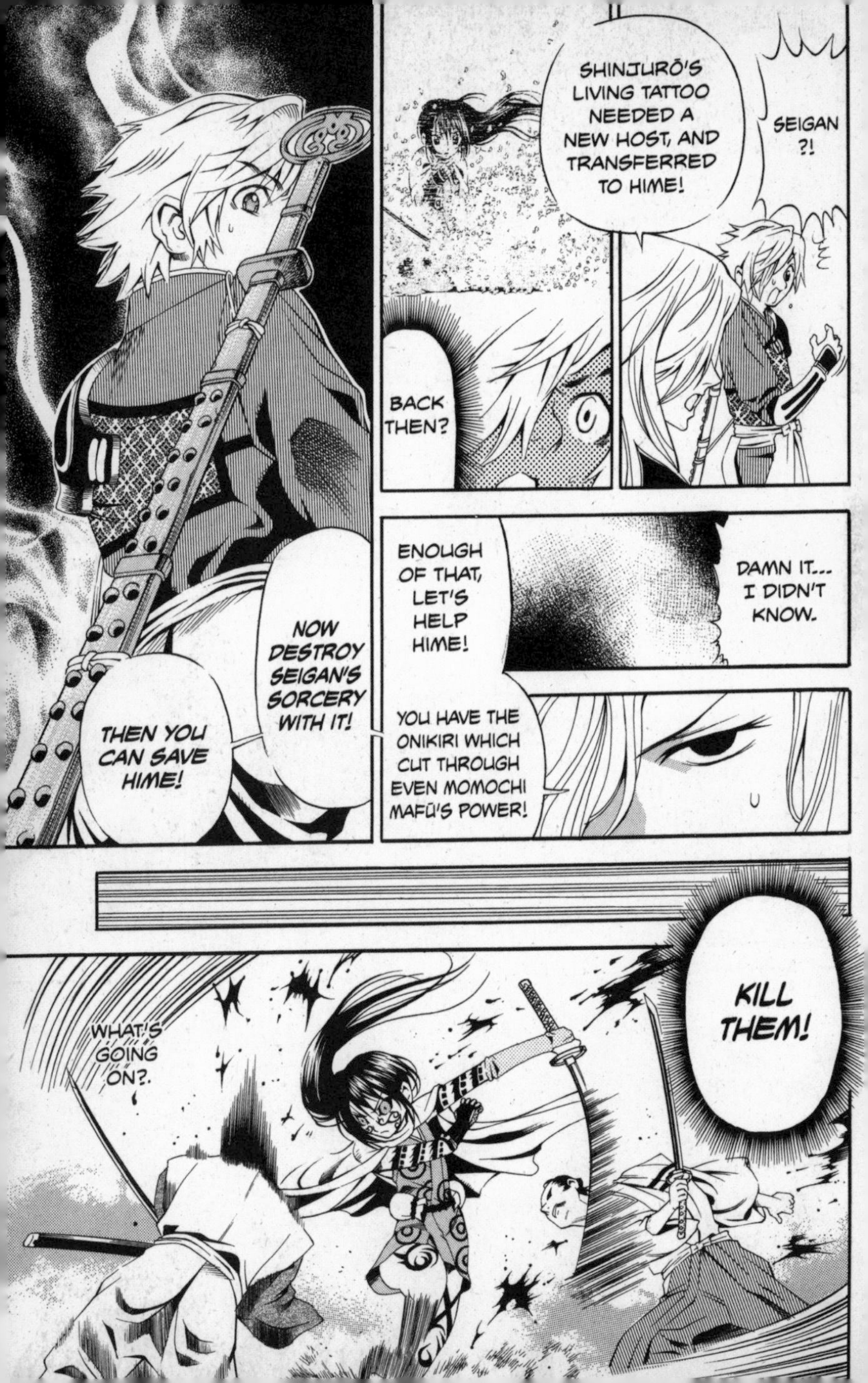
SEIGAN ?!
SHINJURŌ'S LIVING TATTOO NEEDED A NEW HOST, AND TRANSFERRED TO HIME!
BACK THEN?
DAMN IT... I DIDN'T KNOW.
ENOUGH OF THAT, LET'S HELP HIME!
YOU HAVE THE ONIKIRI WHICH CUT THROUGH EVEN MOMOCHI MAFŪ'S POWER!
NOW DESTROY SEIGAN'S SORCERY WITH IT!
THEN YOU CAN SAVE HIME!
KILL THEM!
WHAT'S GOING ON?.

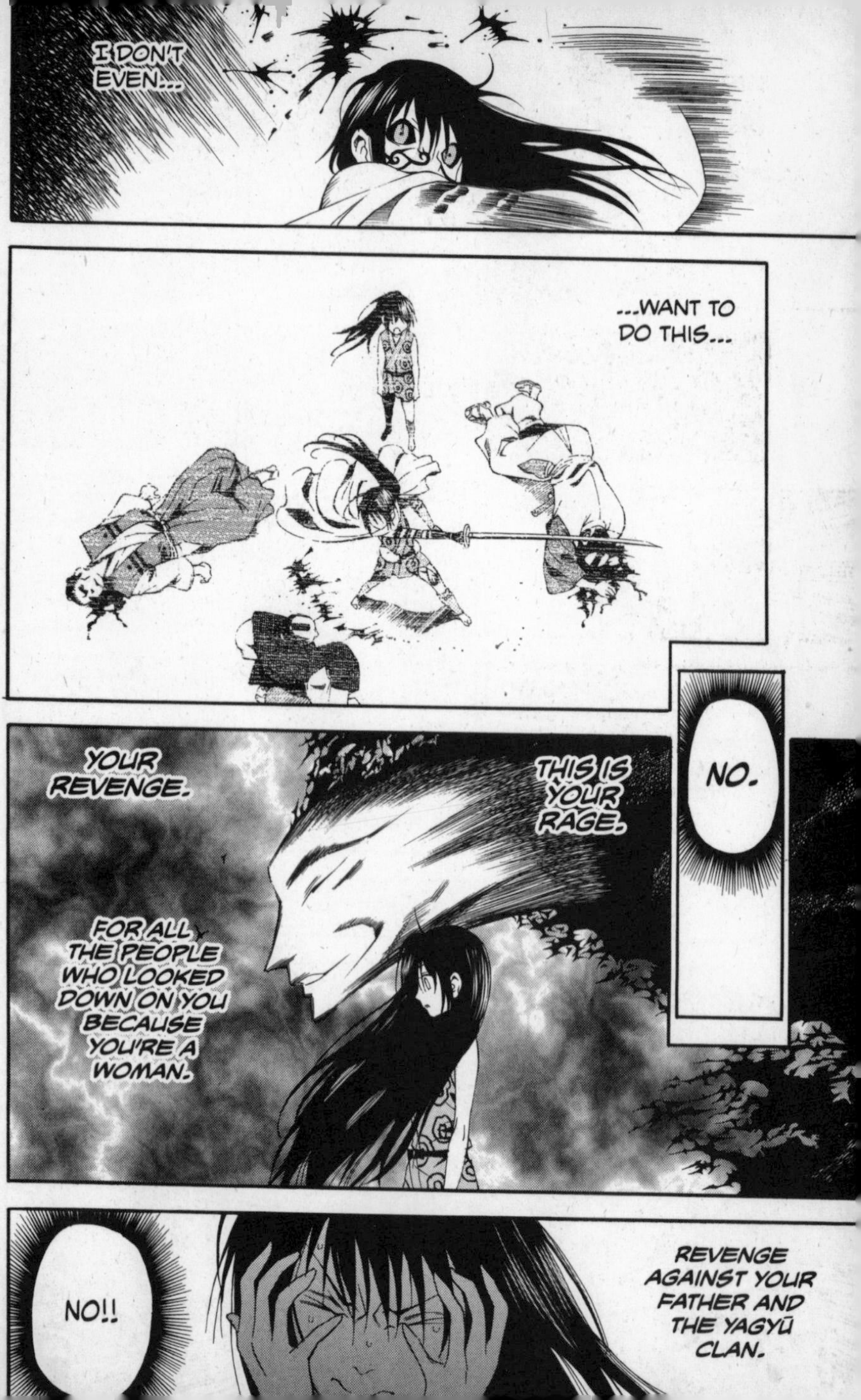
I DON'T EVEN...
...WANT TO DO THIS...
NO.
THIS IS YOUR RAGE.
YOUR REVENGE.
FOR ALL THE PEOPLE WHO LOOKED DOWN ON YOU BECAUSE YOU'RE A WOMAN.
REVENGE AGAINST YOUR FATHER AND THE YAGYŪ CLAN.
NO!!

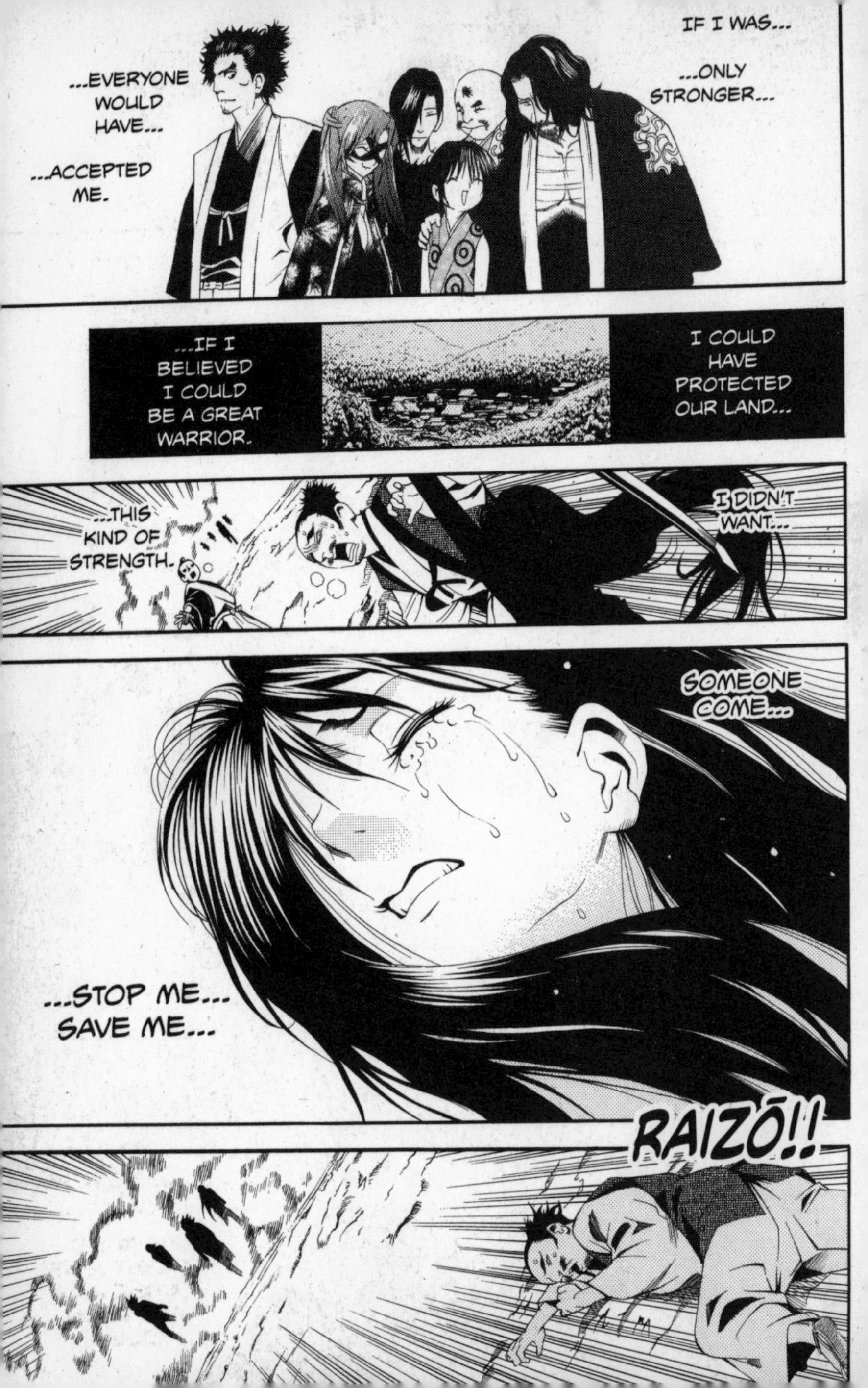
IF I WAS...
...ONLY STRONGER...
...EVERYONE WOULD HAVE...
...ACCEPTED ME.
I COULD HAVE PROTECTED OUR LAND...
...IF I BELIEVED I COULD BE A GREAT WARRIOR.
I DIDN'T WANT...
...THIS KIND OF STRENGTH.
SOMEONE COME...
...STOP ME... SAVE ME...
RAIZŌ!!

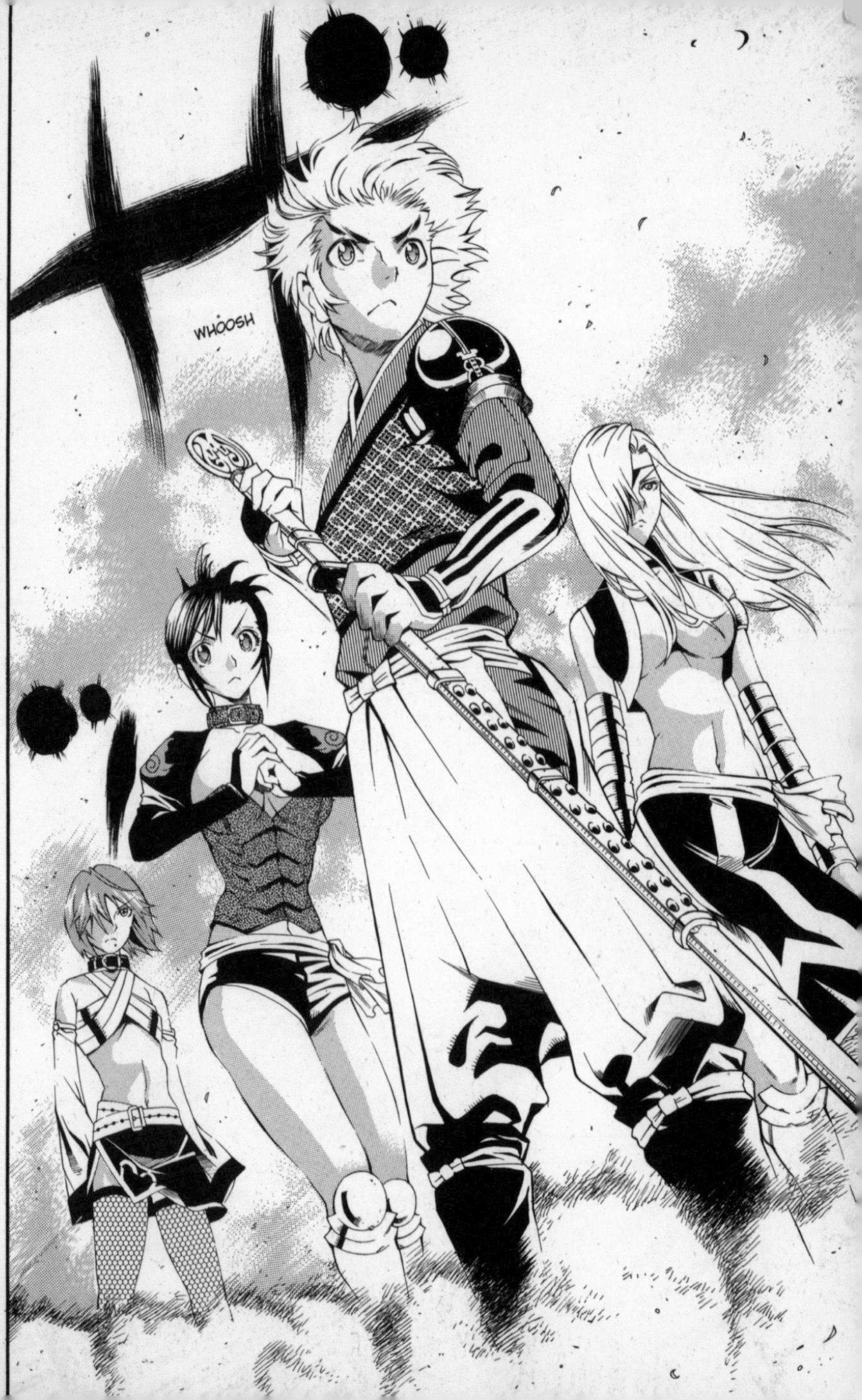
WHOOSH

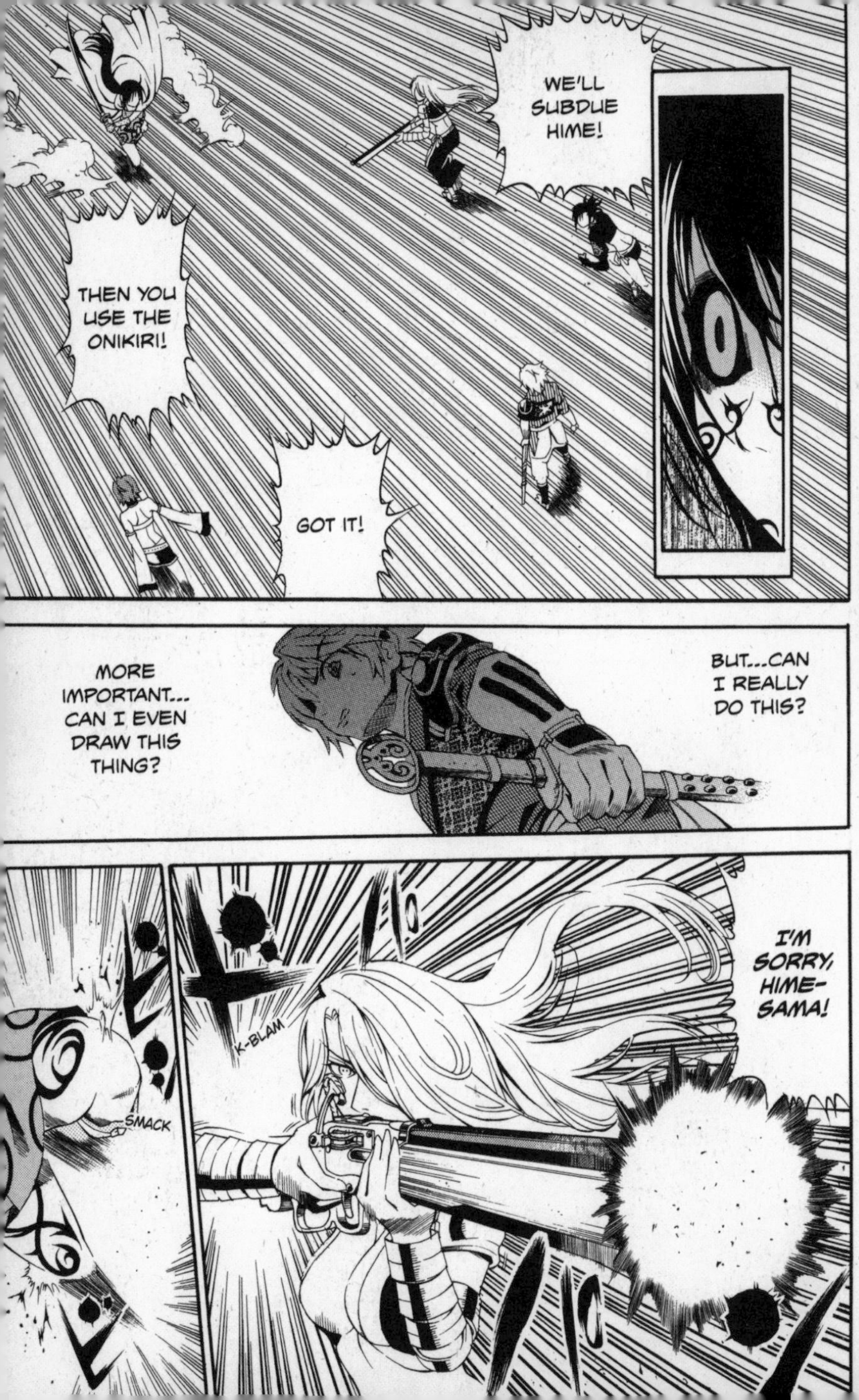
WE'LL SUBDUE HIME!
THEN YOU USE THE ONIKIRI!
GOT IT!
BUT...CAN I REALLY DO THIS?
MORE IMPORTANT... CAN I EVEN DRAW THIS THING?
I'M SORRY, HIME-SAMA!
K-BLAM
SMACK

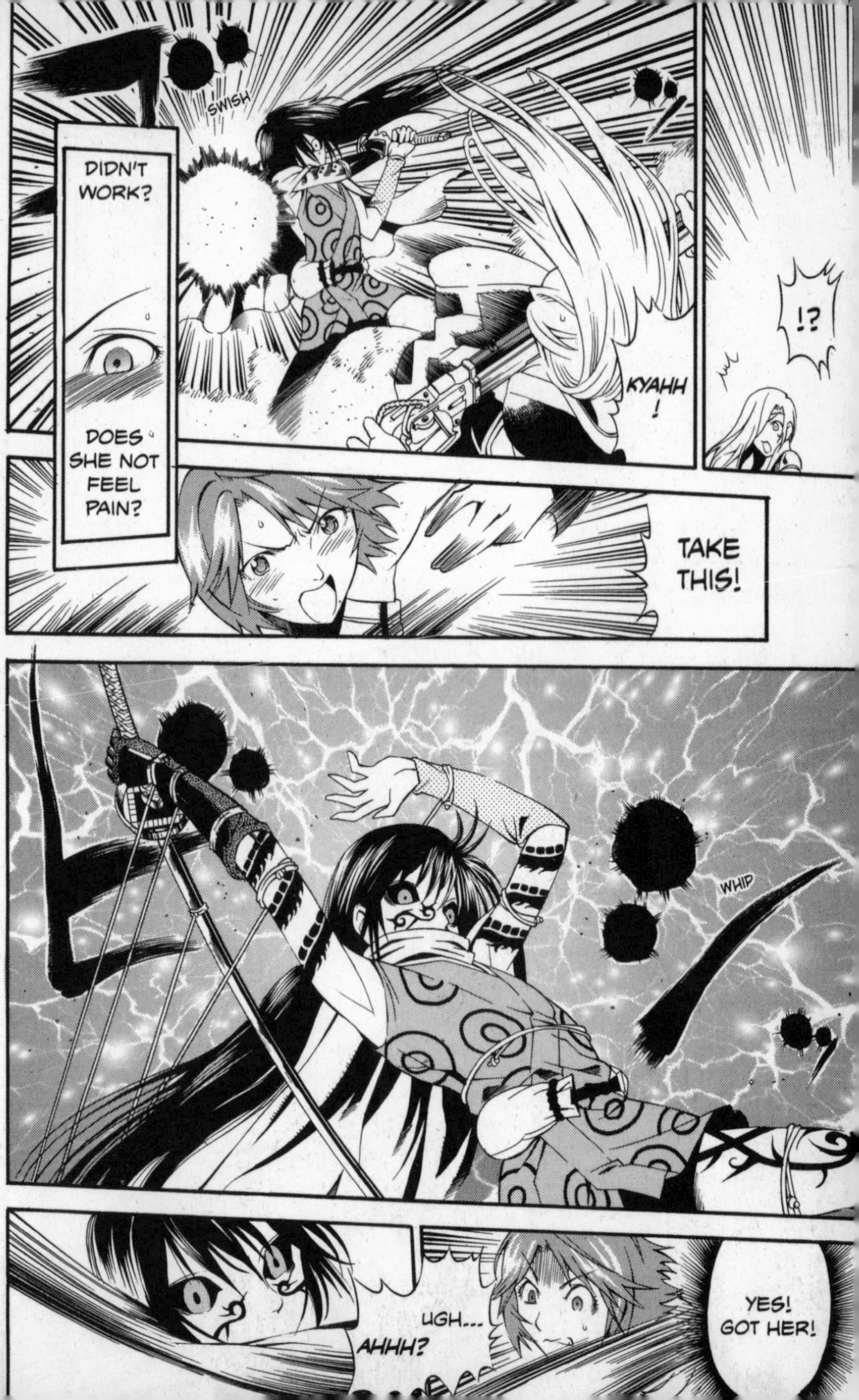
!?
SWISH
KYAHH!
DIDN'T WORK?
DOES SHE NOT FEEL PAIN?
TAKE THIS!
WHIP
YES! GOT HER!
UGH...
AHHH?

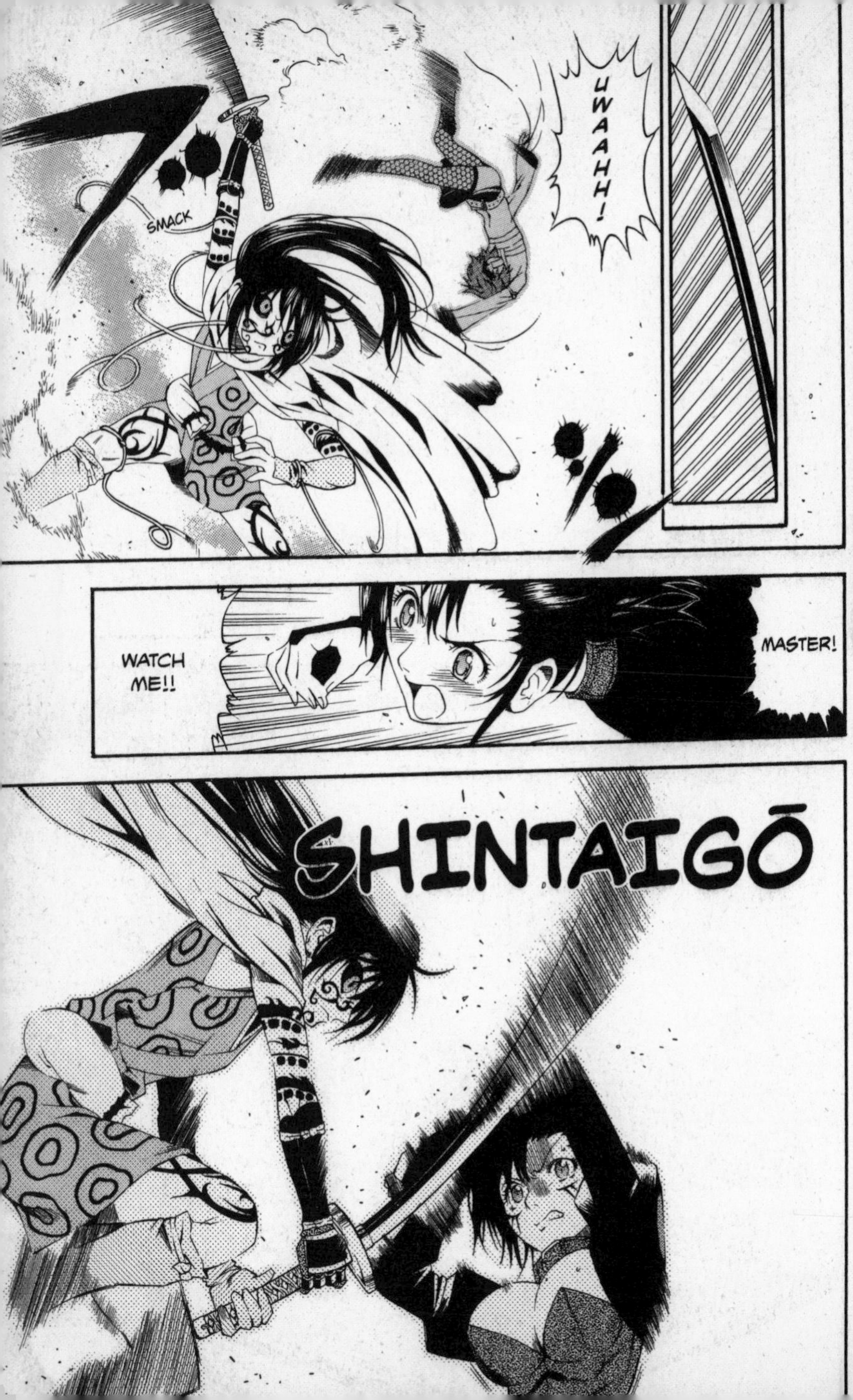
UWAAAHH!
SMACK
MASTER!
WATCH ME!!
SHINTAIGŌ

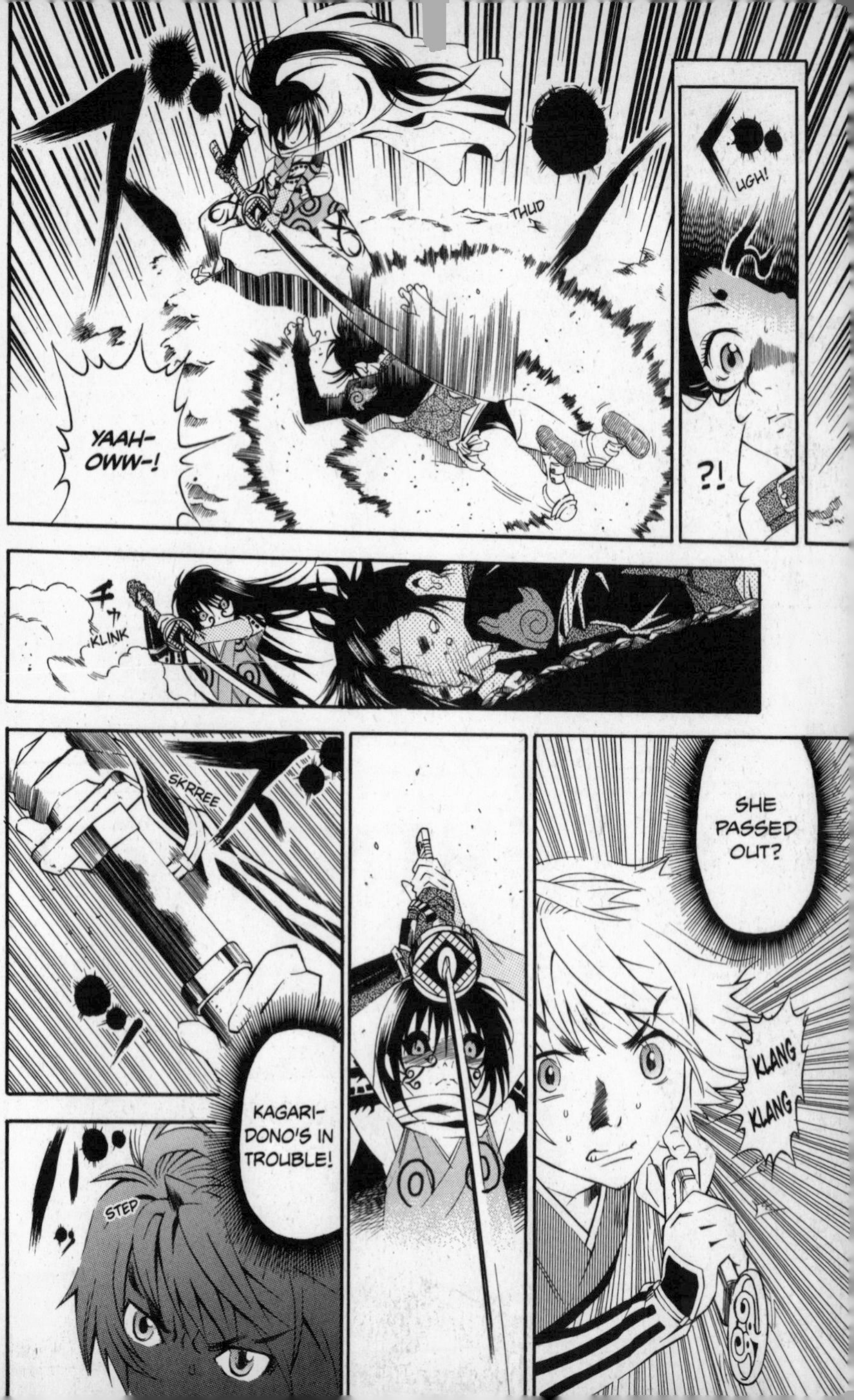
UGH!
?!
THUD
YAAH-OWW-!
KLINK
SHE PASSED OUT?
KLANG KLANG
KAGARI-DONO'S IN TROUBLE!
SKRREE
STEP

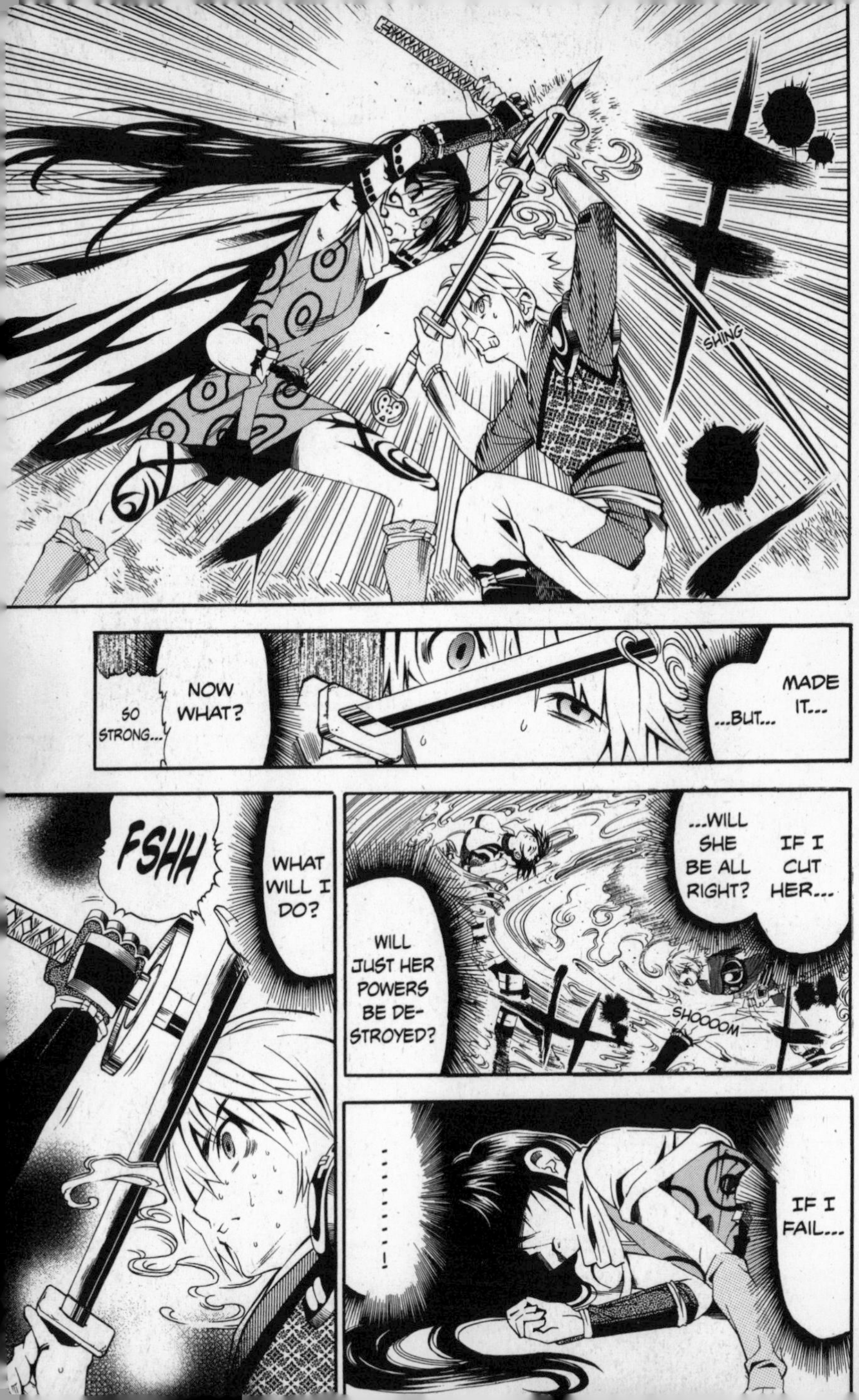
SHING
MADE IT...
...BUT...
NOW WHAT?
SO STRONG...
IF I CUT HER...
...WILL SHE BE ALL RIGHT?
WILL JUST HER POWERS BE DE-STROYED?
SHOOOOM
IF I FAIL...
......!
FSHH
WHAT WILL I DO?

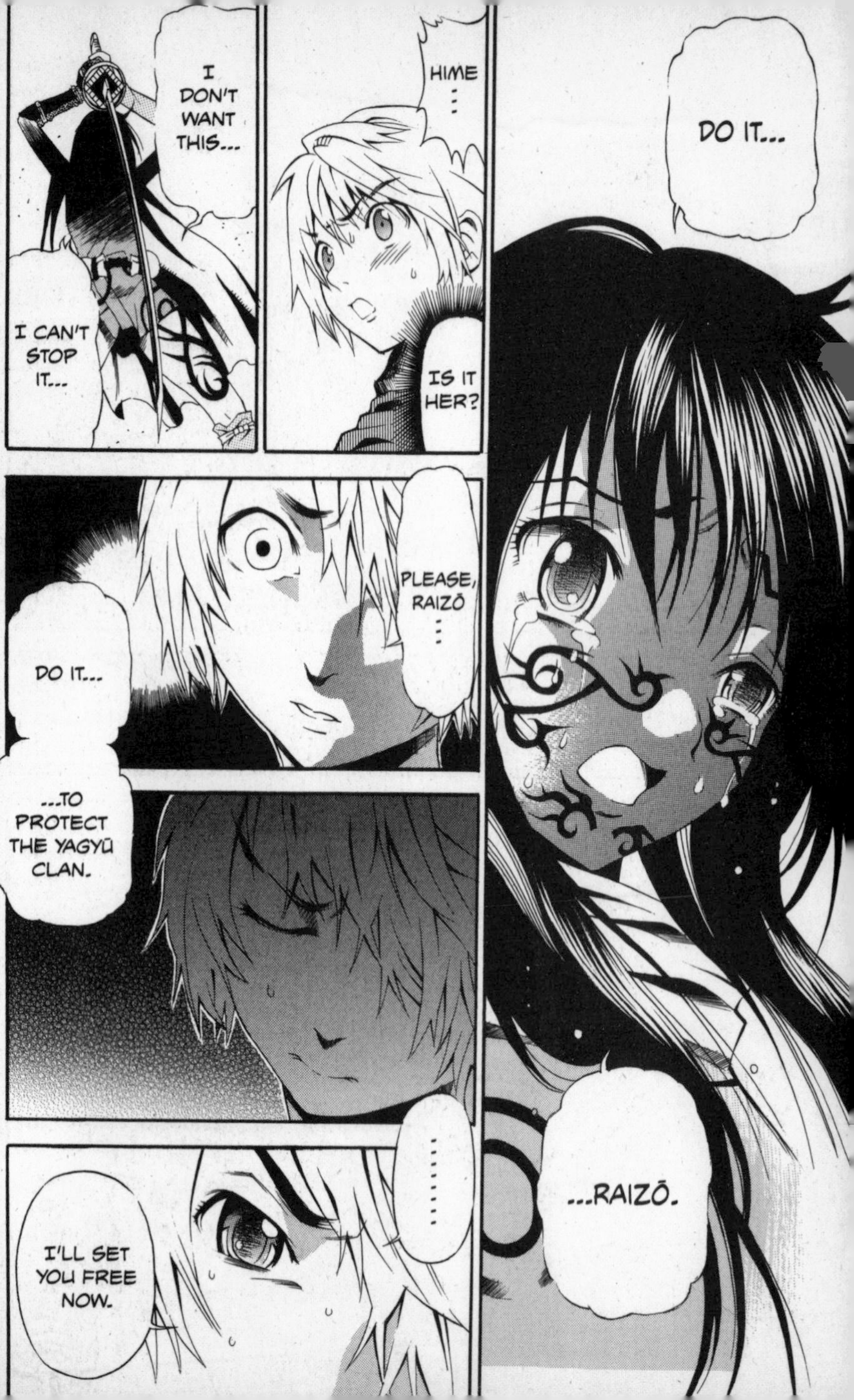
DO IT...
...RAIZŌ.
HIME...
IS IT HER?
I DON'T WANT THIS...
I CAN'T STOP IT...
PLEASE, RAIZŌ...
DO IT...
...TO PROTECT THE YAGYŪ CLAN.
......
I'LL SET YOU FREE NOW.

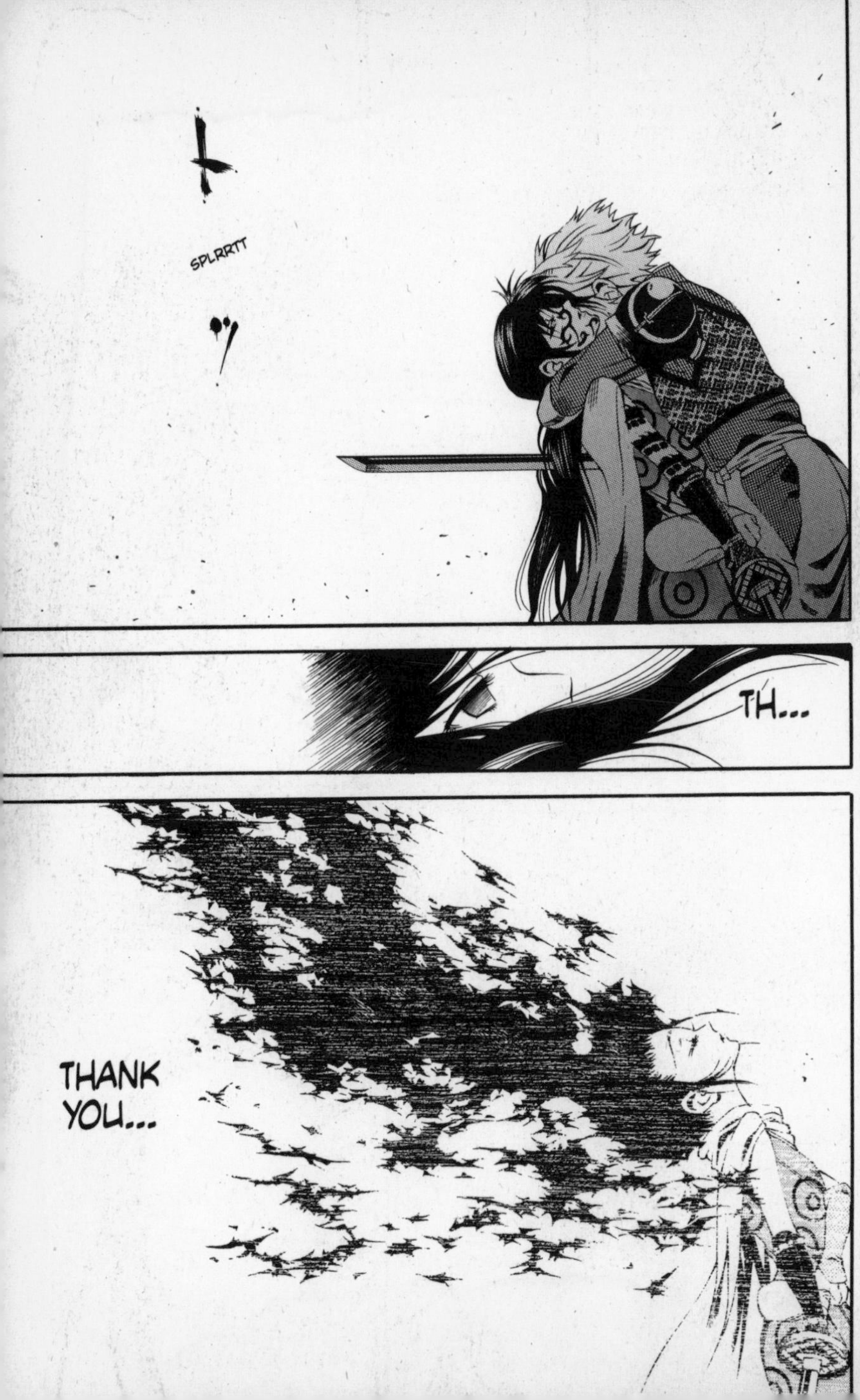
SPLRRTT
TH...
THANK YOU...

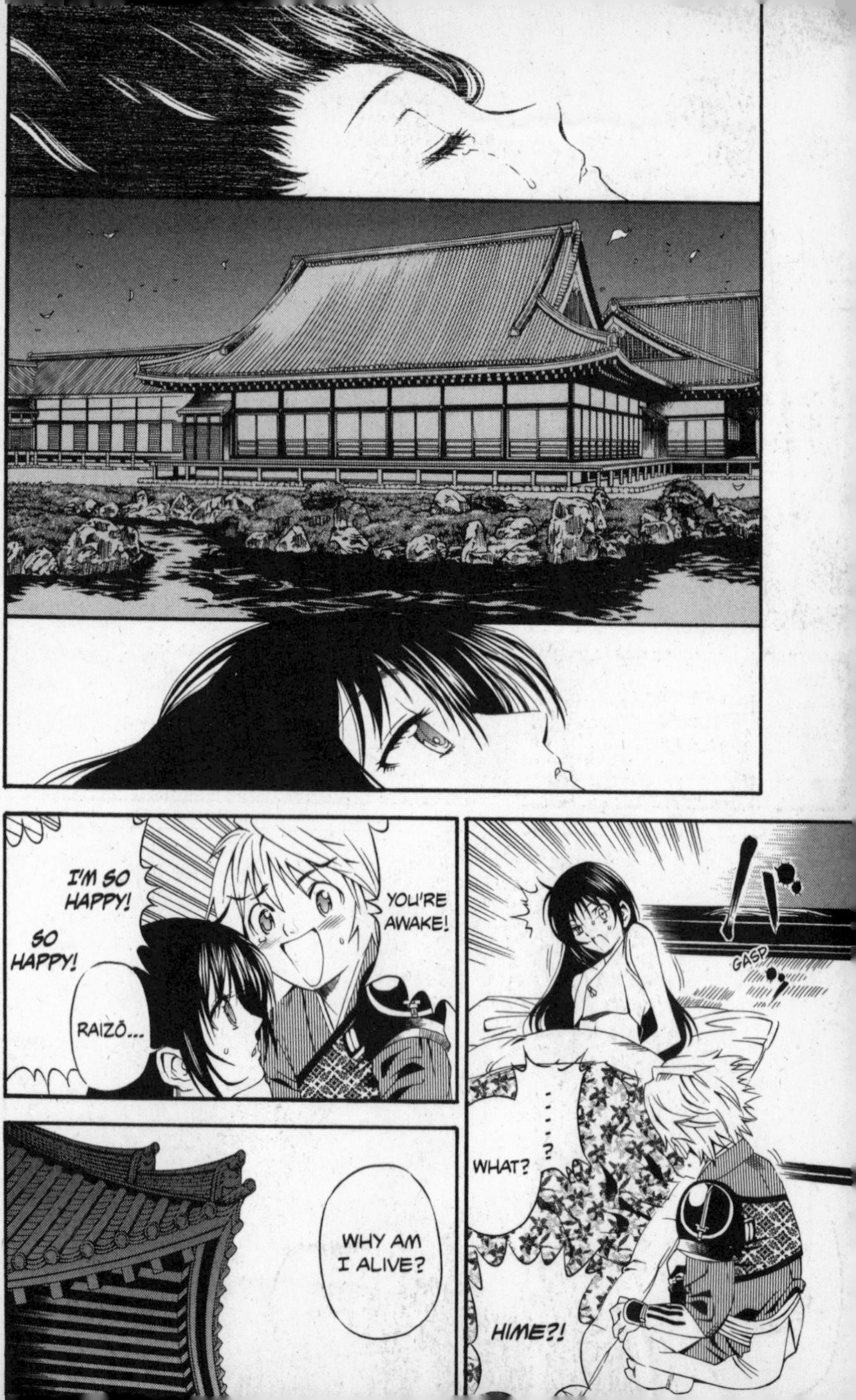
GASP
.....?
WHAT?
HIME?!
YOU'RE AWAKE!
I'M SO HAPPY!
SO HAPPY!
RAIZŌ...
WHY AM I ALIVE?

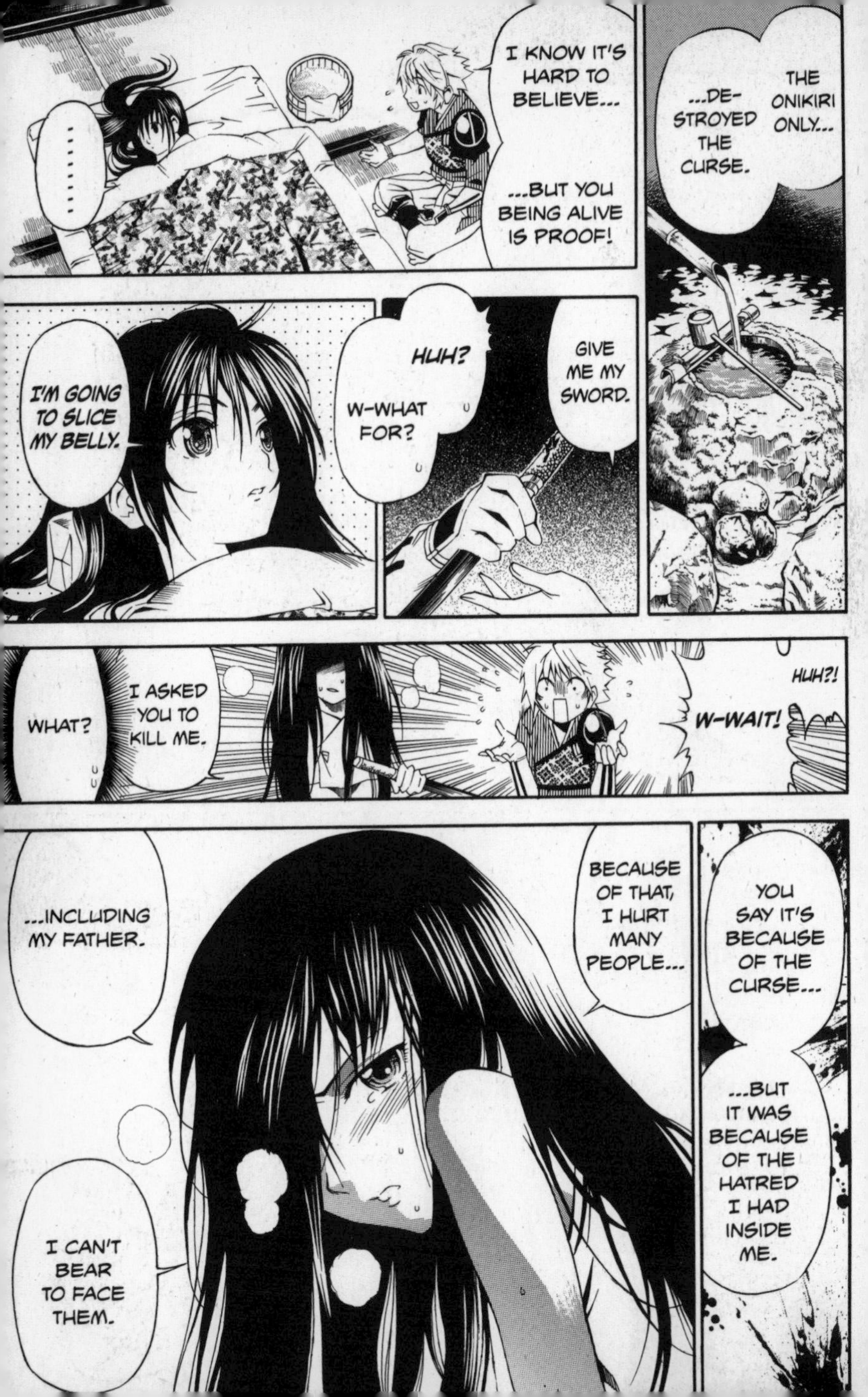
THE ONIKIRI ONLY...
...DE-STROYED THE CURSE.
I KNOW IT'S HARD TO BELIEVE...
...BUT YOU BEING ALIVE IS PROOF!
......
GIVE ME MY SWORD.
HUH?
W-WHAT FOR?
I'M GOING TO SLICE MY BELLY.
HUH?!
W-WAIT!
I ASKED YOU TO KILL ME.
WHAT?
YOU SAY IT'S BECAUSE OF THE CURSE...
...BUT IT WAS BECAUSE OF THE HATRED I HAD INSIDE ME.
BECAUSE OF THAT, I HURT MANY PEOPLE...
...INCLUDING MY FATHER.
I CAN'T BEAR TO FACE THEM.

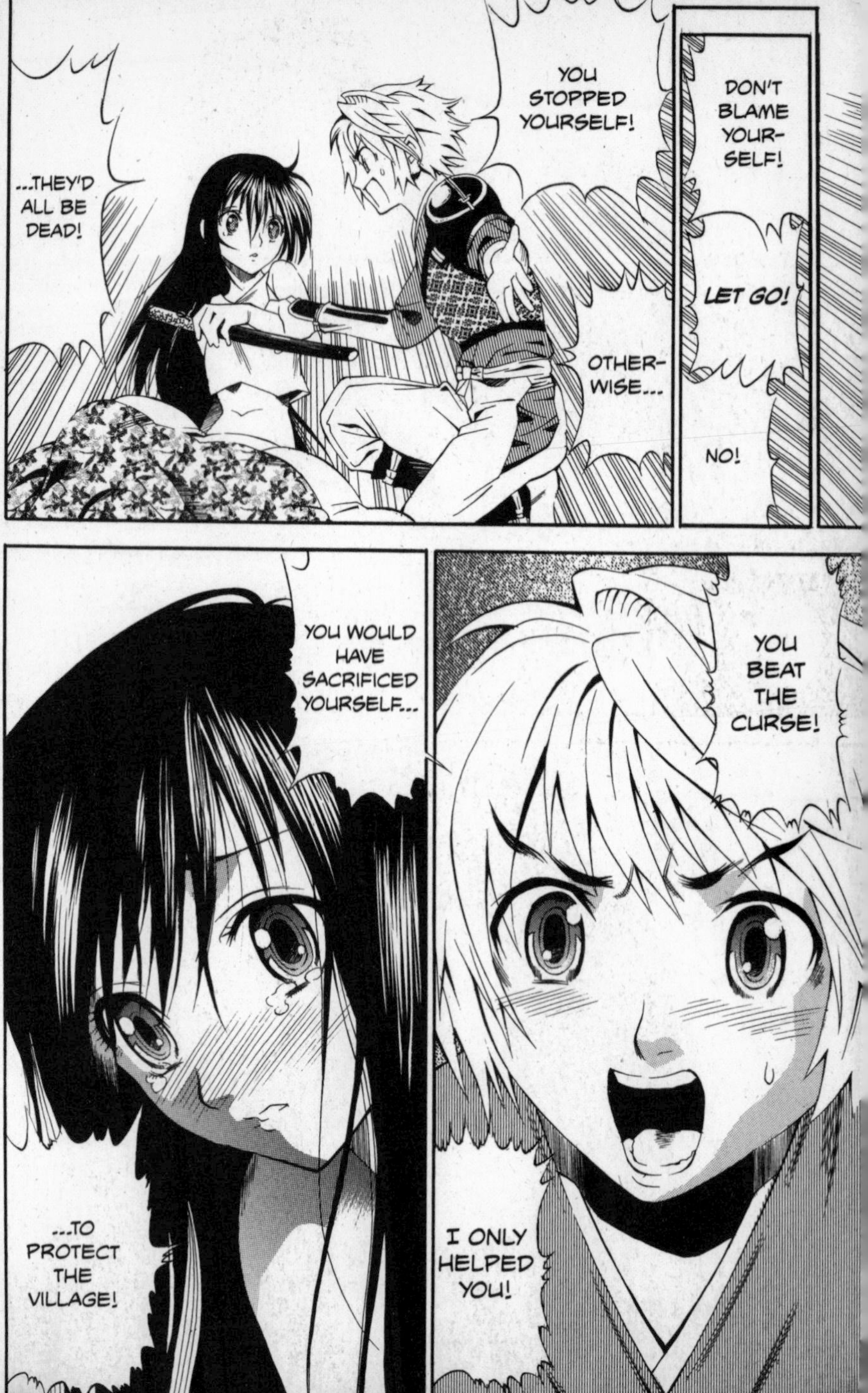
DON'T BLAME YOUR-SELF!
LET GO!
NO!
YOU STOPPED YOURSELF!
OTHER-WISE...
...THEY'D ALL BE DEAD!
YOU BEAT THE CURSE!
I ONLY HELPED YOU!
YOU WOULD HAVE SACRIFICED YOURSELF...
...TO PROTECT THE VILLAGE!

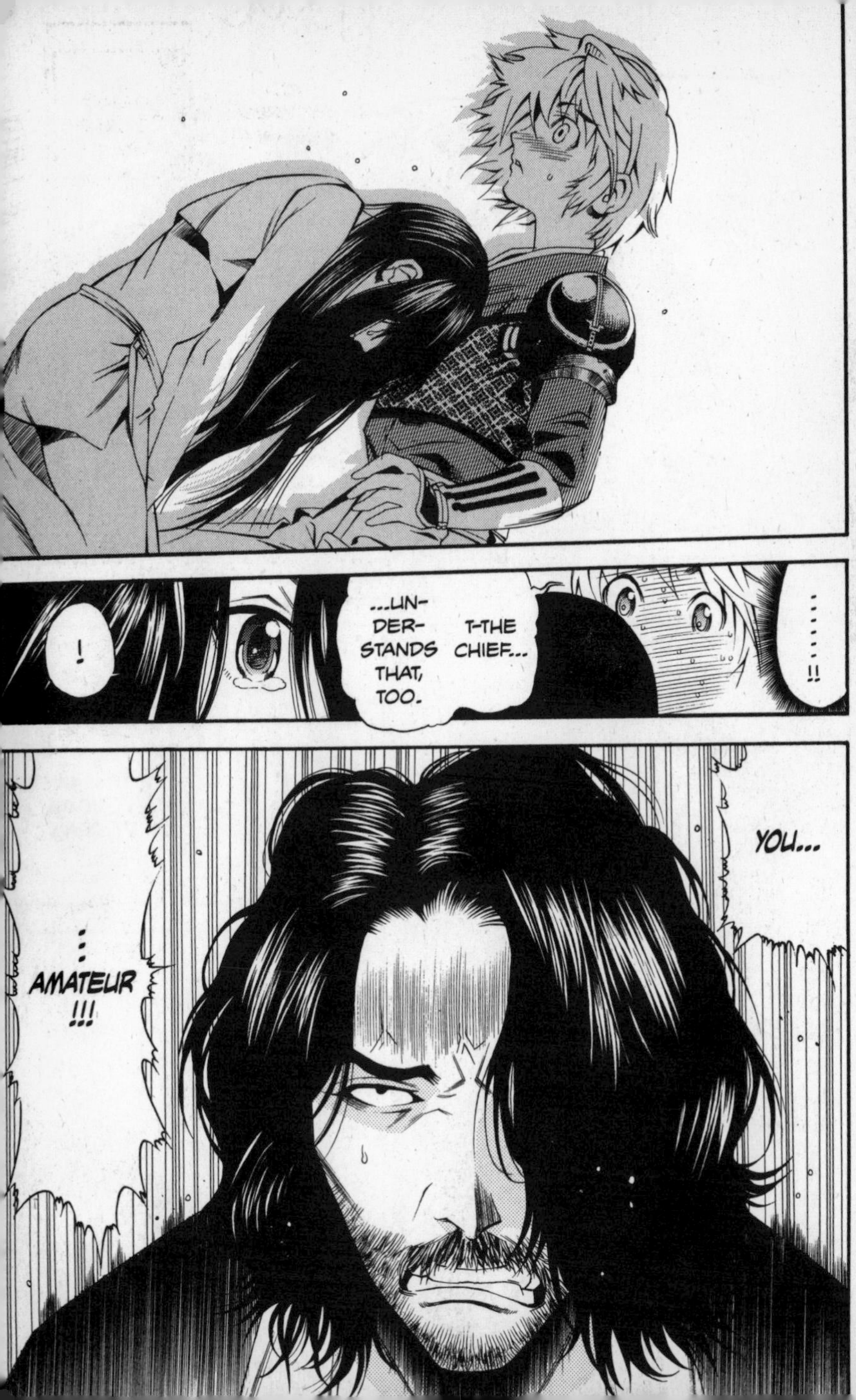
......!!
T-THE CHIEF...
...UN-DER-STANDS THAT, TOO.
!
YOU...
...AMATEUR!!!

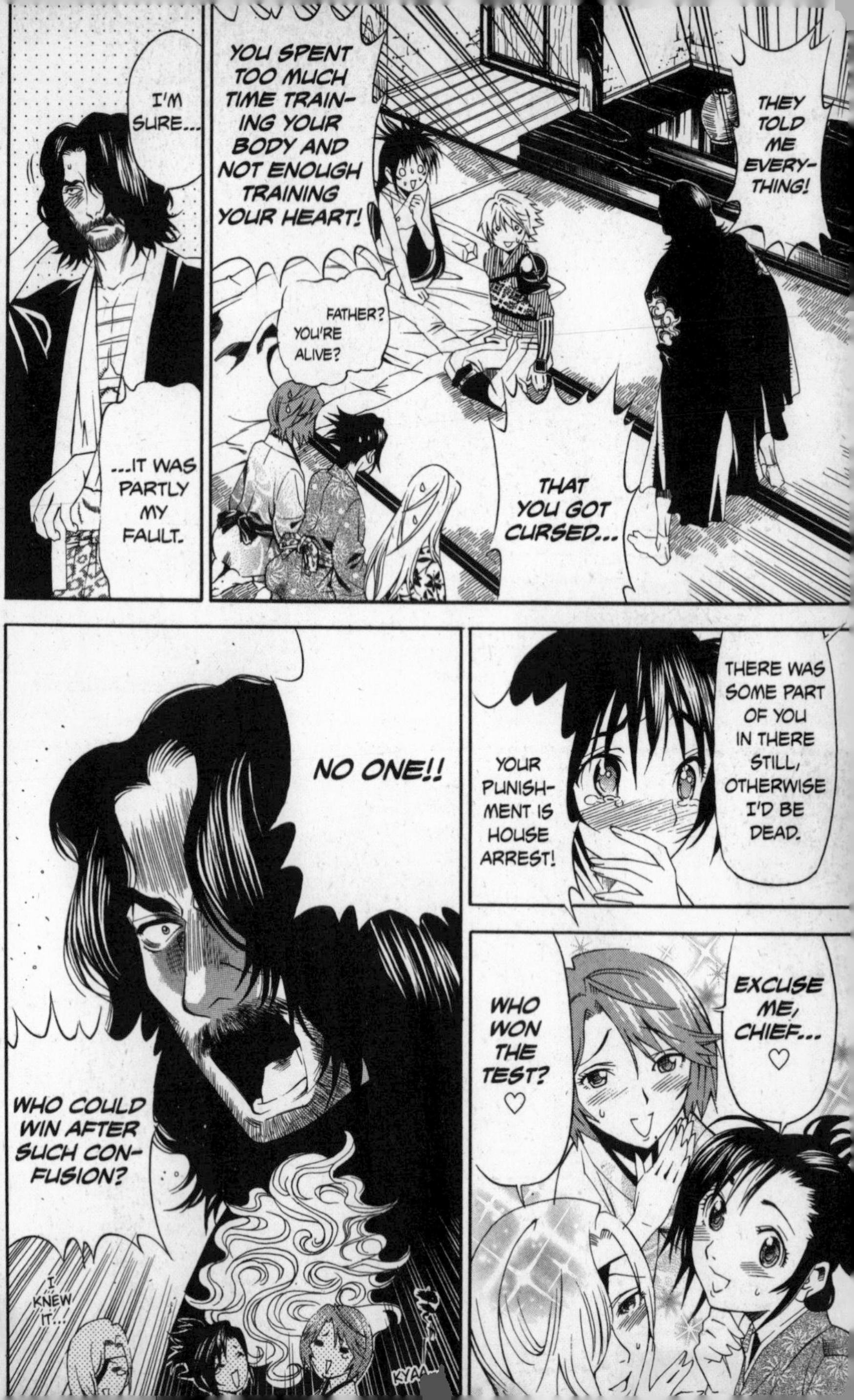
THEY TOLD ME EVERYTHING!
THAT YOU GOT CURSED...
YOU SPENT TOO MUCH TIME TRAINING YOUR BODY AND NOT ENOUGH TRAINING YOUR HEART!
FATHER? YOU'RE ALIVE?
I'M SURE...
...IT WAS PARTLY MY FAULT.
THERE WAS SOME PART OF YOU IN THERE STILL, OTHERWISE I'D BE DEAD.
YOUR PUNISHMENT IS HOUSE ARREST!
EXCUSE ME, CHIEF... ♡
WHO WON THE TEST? ♡
NO ONE!!
WHO COULD WIN AFTER SUCH CONFUSION?
I... KNEW IT...
KYAA

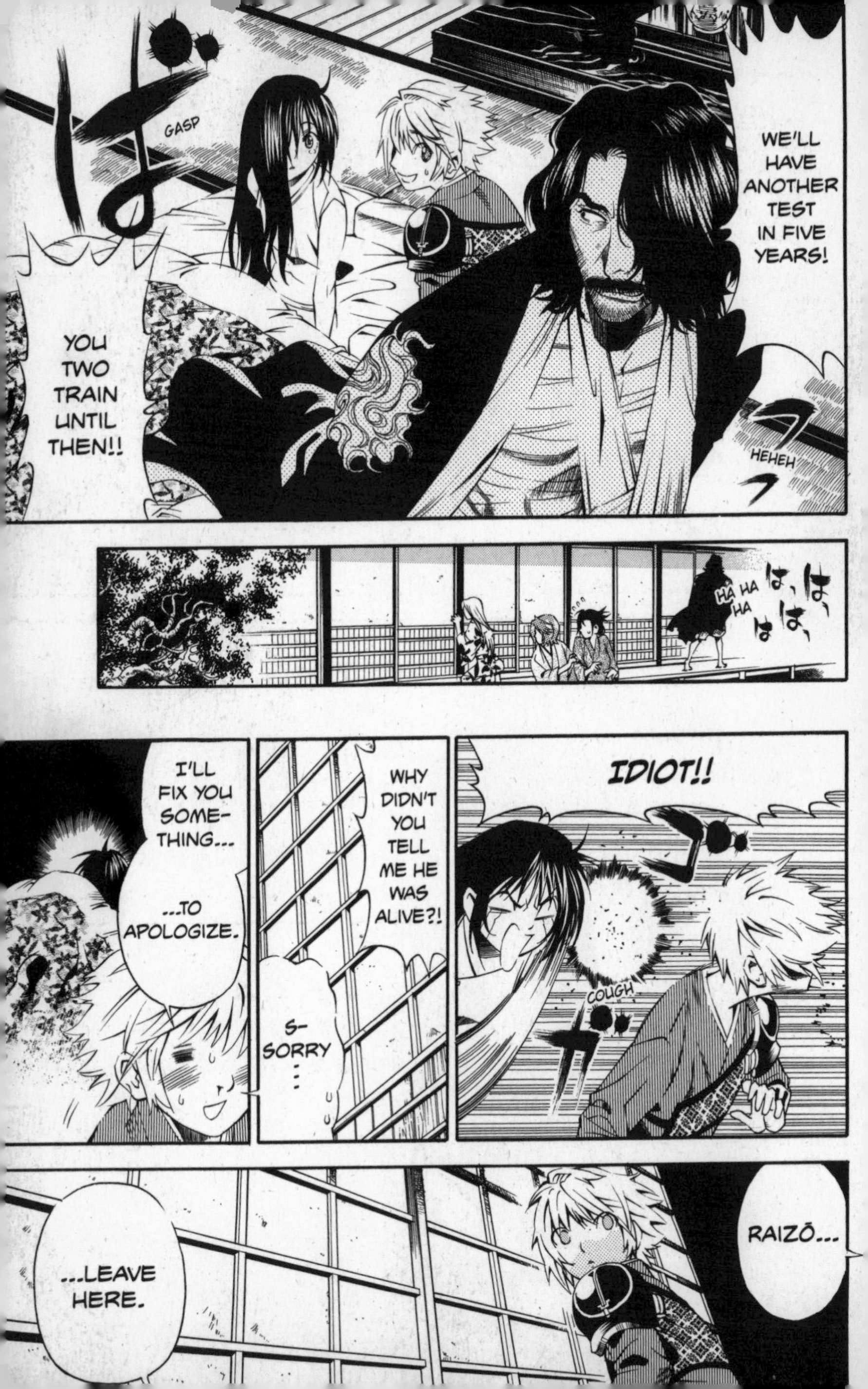
WE'LL HAVE ANOTHER TEST IN FIVE YEARS!
HEHEH
GASP
YOU TWO TRAIN UNTIL THEN!!
HA HA HA
IDIOT!!
COUGH
WHY DIDN'T YOU TELL ME HE WAS ALIVE?!
S-SORRY...
I'LL FIX YOU SOME-THING...
...TO APOLOGIZE.
RAIZŌ...
...LEAVE HERE.

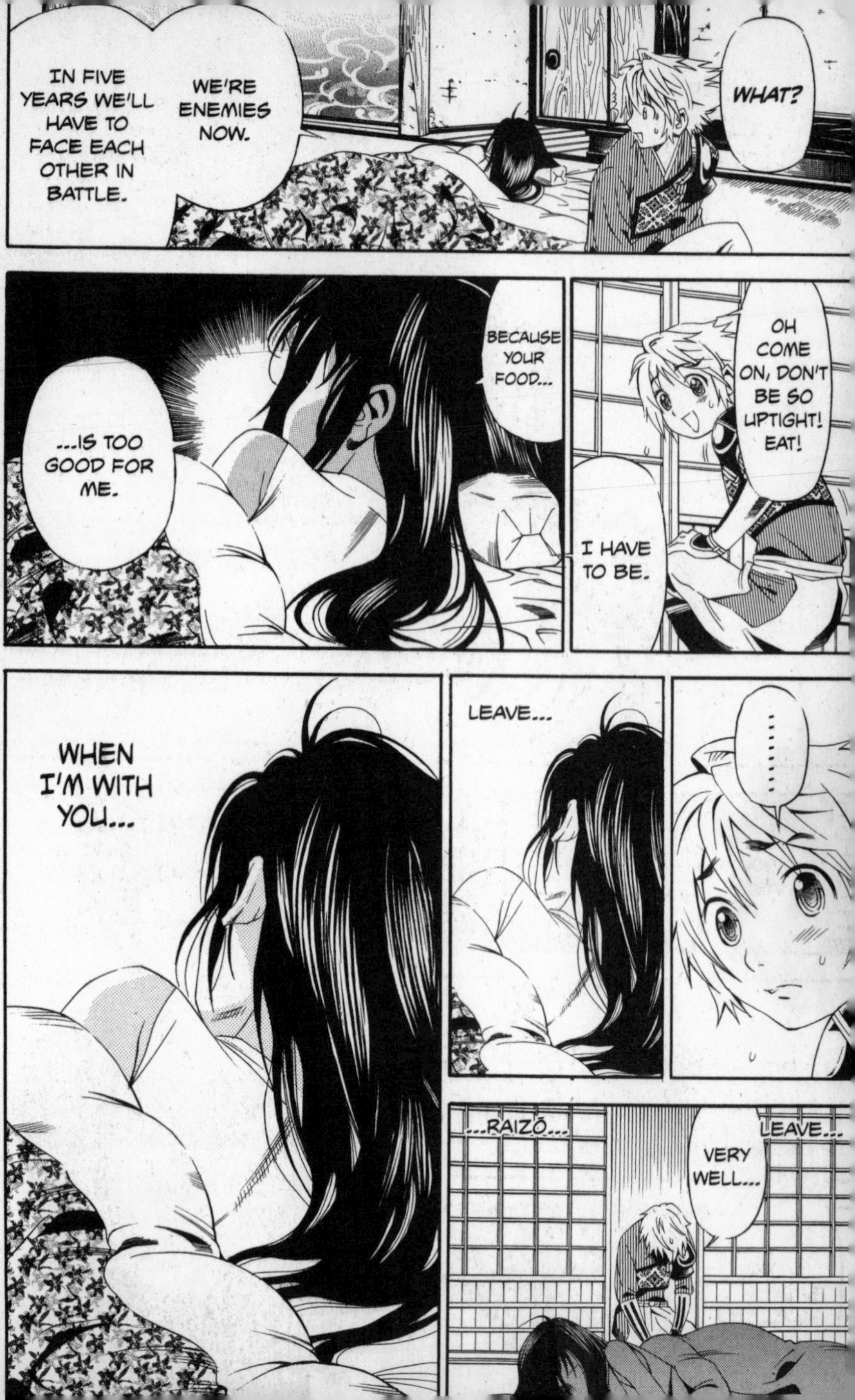
WHAT?
WE'RE ENEMIES NOW.
IN FIVE YEARS WE'LL HAVE TO FACE EACH OTHER IN BATTLE.
OH COME ON, DON'T BE SO UPTIGHT! EAT!
I HAVE TO BE.
BECAUSE YOUR FOOD...
...IS TOO GOOD FOR ME.
......
LEAVE...
LEAVE...
VERY WELL...
...RAIZŌ...
WHEN I'M WITH YOU...

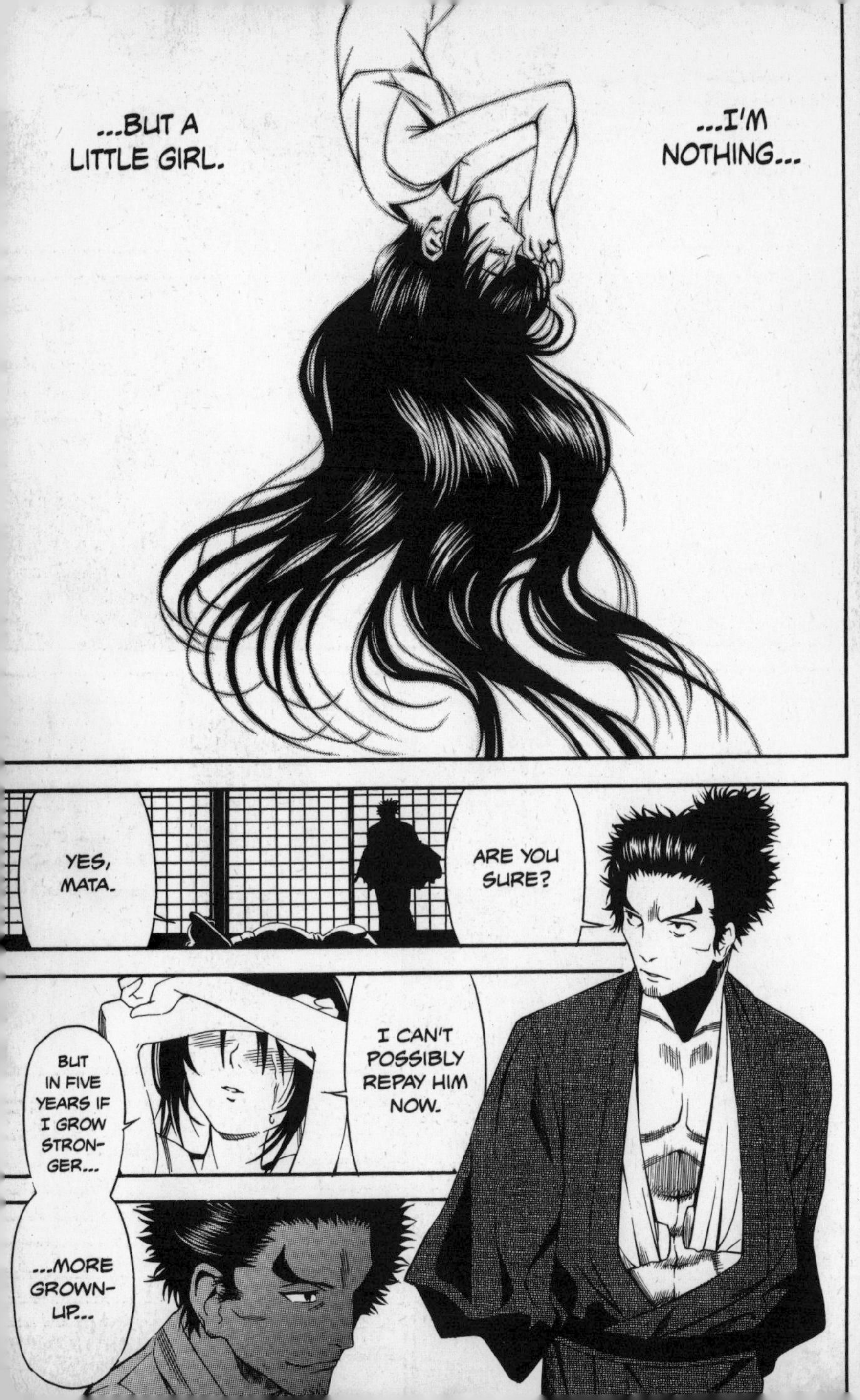
...I'M NOTHING...
...BUT A LITTLE GIRL.
ARE YOU SURE?
YES, MATA.
I CAN'T POSSIBLY REPAY HIM NOW.
BUT IN FIVE YEARS IF I GROW STRONGER...
...MORE GROWN-UP...

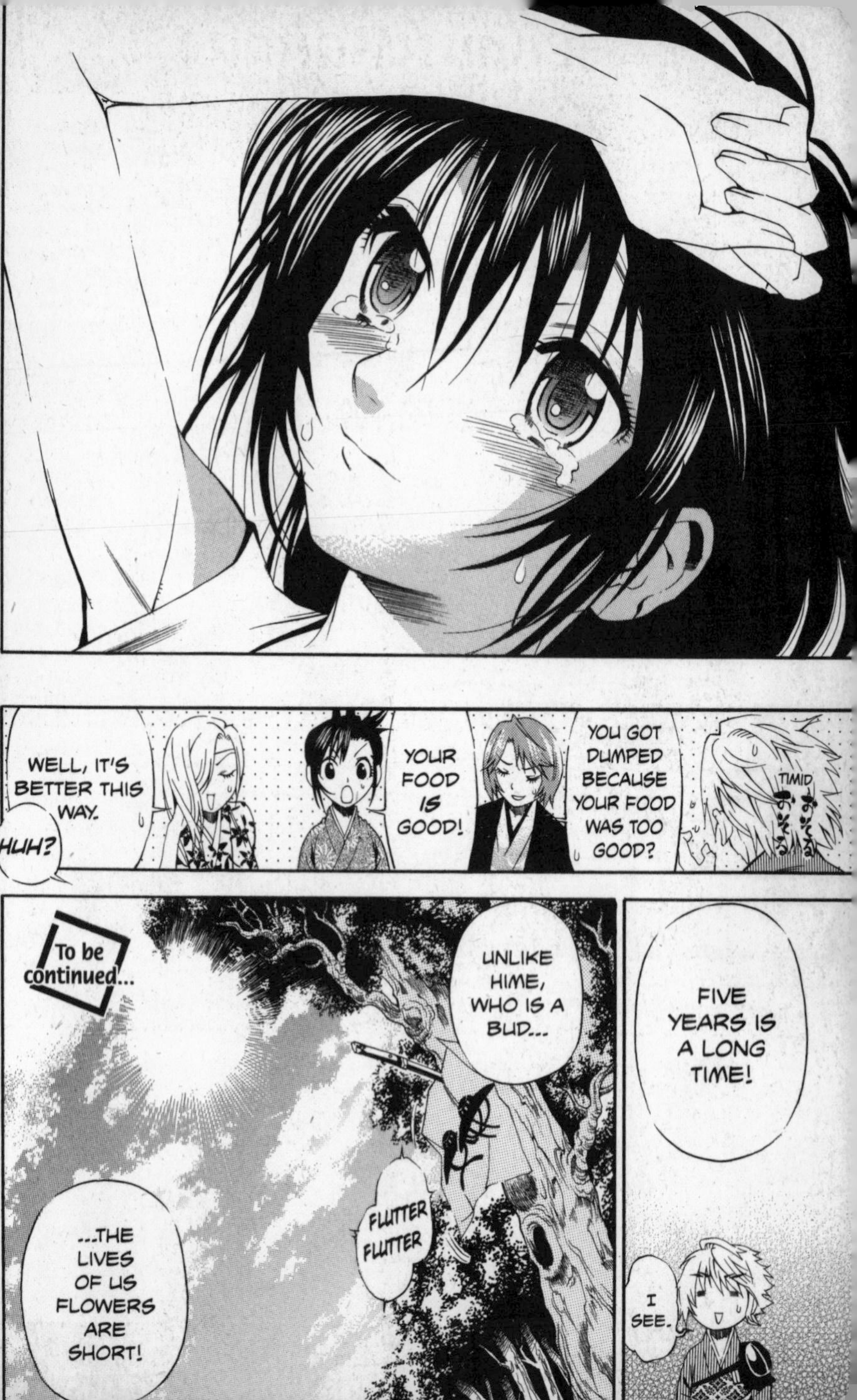
TIMID
YOU GOT DUMPED BECAUSE YOUR FOOD WAS TOO GOOD?
YOUR FOOD IS GOOD!
WELL, IT'S BETTER THIS WAY.
HUH?
FIVE YEARS IS A LONG TIME!
I SEE.
UNLIKE HIME, WHO IS A BUD...
FLUTTER FLUTTER
...THE LIVES OF US FLOWERS ARE SHORT!
To be continued...

Bonus Manga

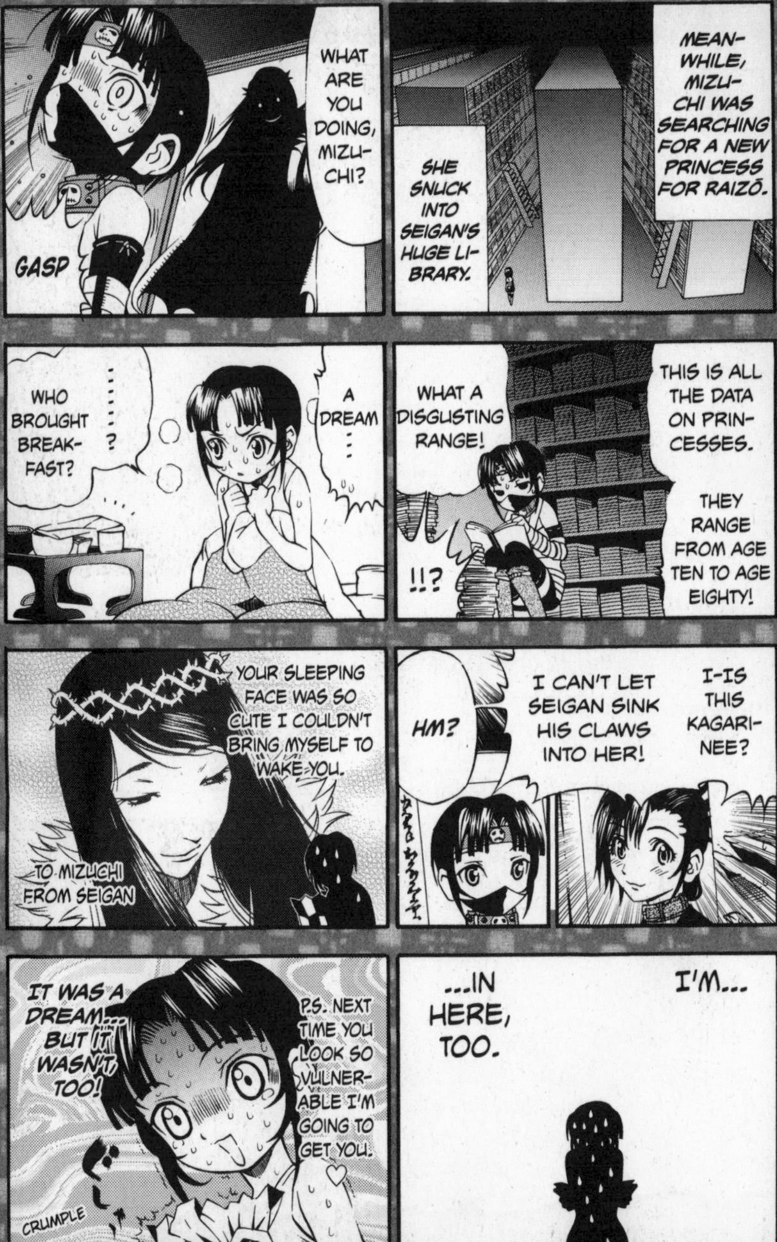
MEAN-WHILE, MIZU-CHI WAS SEARCHING FOR A NEW PRINCESS FOR RAIZŌ.
SHE SNUCK INTO SEIGAN'S HUGE LI-BRARY.
THIS IS ALL THE DATA ON PRIN-CESSES.
THEY RANGE FROM AGE TEN TO AGE EIGHTY!
WHAT A DISGUSTING RANGE!
!!?
I-IS THIS KAGARI-NEE?
I CAN'T LET SEIGAN SINK HIS CLAWS INTO HER!
HM?
I'M...
...IN HERE, TOO.
WHAT ARE YOU DOING, MIZU-CHI?
GASP
A DREAM
......?
WHO BROUGHT BREAK-FAST?
YOUR SLEEPING FACE WAS SO CUTE I COULDN'T BRING MYSELF TO WAKE YOU.
TO MIZUCHI FROM SEIGAN
P.S. NEXT TIME YOU LOOK SO VULNER-ABLE I'M GOING TO GET YOU. ♡
IT WAS A DREAM... BUT IT WASN'T, TOO!
CRUMPLE

TRANSLATION NOTES

Japanese is a tricky language for most Westerners, and translation is often more art than science. For your edification and reading pleasure, here are notes on some of the places where we could have gone in a different direction in our translation of the work, or where a Japanese cultural reference is used.

Kunoichi

A *kunoichi* is a female ninja. It is written くノ一, which symbolizes the strokes necessary to write 女, "woman."

Sengoku era

Sengoku jidai (Warring States Era) lasted from the mid–fifteenth century to the beginning of the seventeenth century. As its name suggests, it was a time of civil war in Japan, with regional lords (*daimyo*) taking control because of a weak central government. The most famous *daimyo* were Oda Nobunaga, known for his military prowess, and Tokugawa Ieyasu, who went on to become the first shogun of Japan's final shogunate.

Shinobi

Another word for ninja. *Shinobi* was the more commonly used term for ninja until its usage declined in popularity post–World War II.

Hime

Hime means "princess."

DEAR OSHI-SAMA ...
THIS IS KISARABI, A KATANA SHINOBI WHO IS WORKING TOWARD THE RESTORATION OF THE FAMILY...

Oshi-sama, page 3

A respectful form of address towards one's master, teacher, or mentor.

YOU'RE NOT THE ONLY ONE WHO CAN DO RASENGAN.
YOU FAILED BECAUSE YOU TOOK THE SHOT WHEN THE WIND WAS MOVING UPWARD.
I READ YOUR INTENTIONS IN ONE MOMENT.

Rasengan, page 20

Kisarabi's special *ninpo* attack. It's written with the characters meaning "wizard" and "eye."

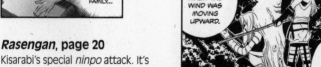

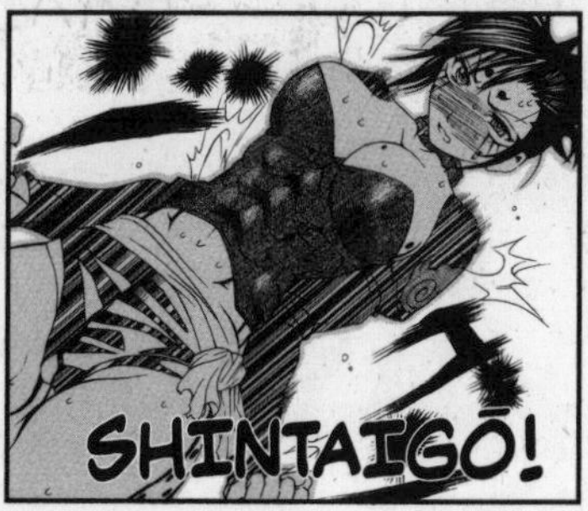
SHINTAIGŌ!

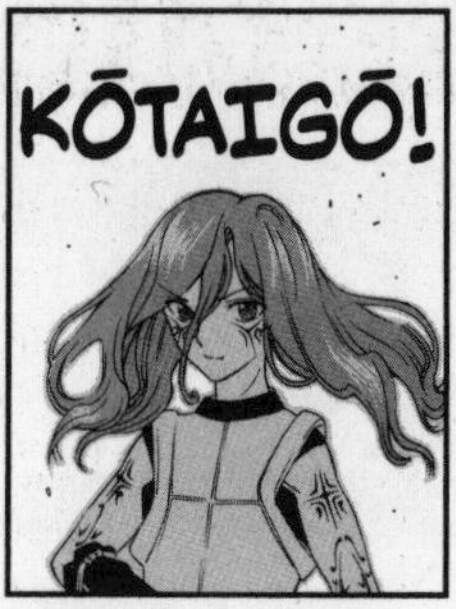
KŌTAIGŌ!

***Shintaigō*, page 24**
Kagari's special *ninpo* attack. It's written with the characters "god," "body," and "conjunction."

***Kōtaigō*, page 25**
One of Mafu's special *ninpo* attacks. It's written with the characters meaning "steel," "body," and "conjunction."

***Sangakuen-no-tachi*, page 81**
A special move of the Yagyū style of swordsmanship, which is still practiced today.

***Ihai*, page 124**
An *ihai* is a mortuary tablet that's often placed on a Buddhist altar to honor a deceased loved one. It's usually a wood or stone tablet that's engraved with the deceased person's posthumous name, which is given to them by the Buddhist priest who performed their funerary rites.

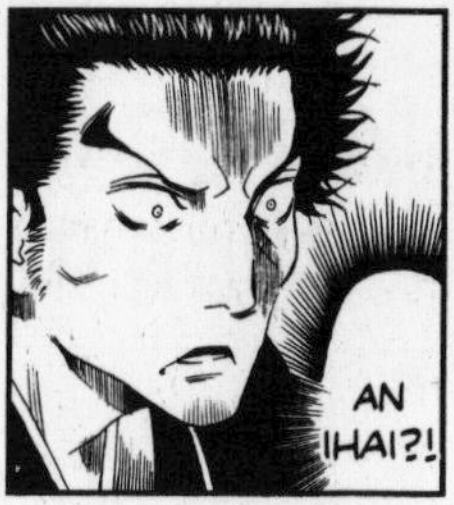
AN IHAI?!

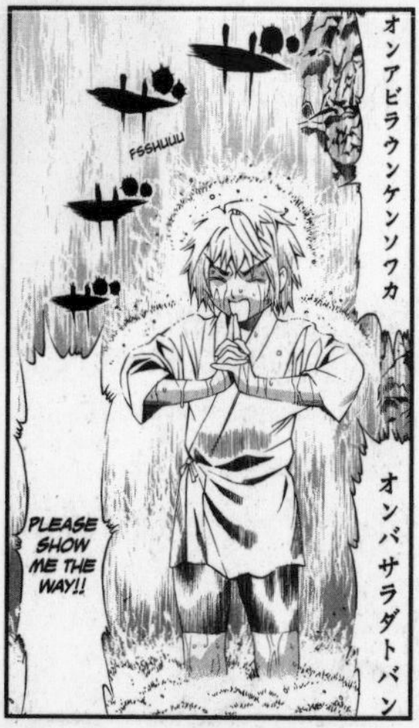
オンアビラウンケンソワカ
オンバサラダトバン
FSSHUUU
PLEASE SHOW ME THE WAY!!

Please show me the way, page 175
Just as Kagari once did on a previous occasion, Raizō is attempting to meditate under a waterfall, a very traditional thing to do. Raizō is chanting the Mahavairocana Mantra, a Buddhist mantra. For your convenience, here are both the romanization and translation.

Raizō: *Om a vi ra hum kham...*
Oh, All-Pervading One...
Om vajra-dhatu vam...
Imperishable One...

TOMARE!

[STOP!]

You are going the wrong way!

Manga is a completely different type of reading experience.

To start at the *beginning*, go to the *end*!

That's right! Authentic manga is read the traditional Japanese way—from right to left, exactly the *opposite* of how American books are read. It's easy to follow: Just go to the other end of the book, and read each page—and each panel—from the right side to the left side, starting at the top right. Now you're experiencing manga as it was meant to be.

AUG 2010